# THE PIRATES OWN BOOK

# THE PIRATES OWN BOOK

Ellms, Charles

www.General-Books.net

***Publication Data:***

Title: The Pirates Own Book
Author: Ellms, Charles
Reprinted: 2010, General Books, Memphis, Tennessee, USA

*How We Made This Book for You*
We made this book exclusively for you using patented Print on Demand technology.
First we scanned the original rare book using a robot which automatically flipped and photographed each page.
We automated the typing, proof reading and design of this book using Optical Character Recognition (OCR) software on the scanned copy. That let us keep your cost as low as possible.
If a book is very old, worn and the type is faded, this can result in numerous typos or missing text. This is also why our books don't have illustrations; the OCR software can't distinguish between an illustration and a smudge.
We understand how annoying typos, missing text or illustrations, foot notes in the text or an index that doesn't work, can be. That's why we provide a free digital copy of most books exactly as they were originally published. You can also use this PDF edition to read the book on the go. Simply go to our website (www.general-books.net) to check availability. And we provide a free trial membership in our book club so you can get free copies of other editions or related books.
OCR is not a perfect solution but we feel it's more important to make books available for a low price than not at all. So we warn readers on our website and in the descriptions we provide to book sellers that our books don't have illustrations and may have numerous typos or missing text. We also provide excerpts from books to book sellers and on our website so you can preview the quality of the book before buying it.
If you would prefer that we manually type, proof read and design your book so that it's perfect, simply contact us for the cost. Since many of our books only sell one or two copies a year, unlike mass market books we have to split the production costs between those one or two buyers.

# 1

# THE PIRATES OWN BOOK

**THE PIRATES OWN BOOK**
**Authentic Narratives of the Most Celebrated Sea Robbers.**
**by**
**Charles Ellms**
**Originally published 1837**

Page 4 Illustration

**PREFACE**

In the mind of the mariner, there is a superstitious horror connected with the name of Pirate; and there are few subjects that interest and excite the curiosity of mankind generally, more than the desperate exploits, foul doings, and diabolical career of these monsters in human form. A piratical crew is generally formed of the desperadoes and runagates of every clime and nation. The pirate, from the perilous nature of his occupation, when not cruising on the ocean, the great highway of nations, selects the most lonely isles of the sea for his retreat, or secretes himself near the shores of rivers, bays and lagoons of thickly wooded and uninhabited countries, so that if pursued he can escape to the woods and mountain glens of the interior. The islands of the Indian Ocean, and the east and west coasts of Africa, as well as the West Indies, have been their haunts for centuries; and vessels navigating the Atlantic and Indian Oceans, are often captured by them, the passengers and crew murdered, the money and most valuable part of the cargo plundered, the vessel destroyed, thus obliterating all trace of their unhappy fate, and leaving friends and relatives to mourn their loss from the inclemencies of the elements, when they were butchered in cold blood by their fellow men, who by practically adopting the maxim that "dead men tell no tales," enable themselves to pursue their diabolical career with impunity. The pirate is truly fond of women and wine, and when not engaged in robbing, keeps maddened with intoxicating liquors, and passes his time in debauchery, singing old songs with chorusses like

"Drain, drain the bowl, each fearless soul,
Let the world wag as it will:
Let the heavens growl, let the devil howl,
Drain, drain the deep bowl and fill."

Thus his hours of relaxation are passed in wild and extravagant frolics amongst the lofty forests of palms and spicy groves of the Torrid Zone, and amidst the aromatic and beautiful flowering vegetable productions of that region. He has fruits delicious to taste, and as companions, the unsophisticated daughters of Africa and the Indies. It would be supposed that his wild career would be one of delight.

But the apprehension and foreboding of the mind, when under the influence of remorse, are powerful, and every man, whether civilized or savage, has interwoven in his constitution a moral sense, which secretly condemns him when he has committed an atrocious action, even when he is placed in situations which raise him above the fear of human punishment, for

"Conscience, the torturer of the soul, unseen.
Does fiercely brandish a sharp scourge within;
Severe decrees may keep our tongues in awe,
But to our minds what edicts can give law?
Even you yourself to your own breast shall tell
Your crimes, and your own conscience be your hell."

With the name of pirate is also associated ideas of rich plunder, caskets of buried jewels, chests of gold ingots, bags of outlandish coins, secreted in lonely, out of the way places, or buried about the wild shores of rivers, and unexplored sea coasts, near rocks and trees bearing mysterious marks, indicating where the treasure was hid. And as it is his invariable practice to secrete and bury his booty, and from the perilous life he leads, being often killed or captured, he can never re-visit the spot again; immense sums remain buried in those places, and are irrecoverably lost. Search is often made by persons who labor in anticipation of throwing up with their spade and pickaxe, gold bars, diamond crosses sparkling amongst the dirt, bags of golden doubloons, and chests, wedged close with moidores, ducats and pearls; but although great treasures lie hid in this way, it seldom happens that any is so recovered.

Page 10 Illustration

## INTRODUCTION

By the universal law of nations, robbery or forcible depredation upon the "high seas," *animo furandi*, is piracy. The meaning of the phrase "high seas," embraces not only the waters of the ocean, which are out of sight of land, but the waters on the sea coast below low water mark, whether within the territorial boundaries of a foreign nation, or of a domestic state. Blackstone says that the main sea or high sea begins at low water mark. But between the high water mark and low water mark, where the tide ebbs and flows, the common law and the Admiralty have *divisum imperium*, an alternate jurisdiction, one upon the water when it is full sea; the other upon the land when it is ebb. He doubtless here refers to the waters of the ocean on the sea coast, and not in creeks and inlets. Lord Hale says that the sea is either that which lies within the body of a country or without. That which lies without the body of a country is called the main sea or ocean. So far then as regards the states of the American union, "high seas," may be taken to mean that part of the ocean which washes the sea coast, and is without the body of any country, according to the common law; and so far as regards foreign nations, any waters on their sea coasts, below low water mark.

Piracy is an offence against the universal law of society, a pirate being according to Sir Edward Coke, *hostis humani generis*. As, therefore, he has renounced all the benefits of society and government, and has reduced himself to the savage state of nature, by declaring war against all mankind, all mankind must declare war against him; so that every community has a right by the rule of self-defense, to inflict that punishment upon him which every individual would in a state of nature otherwise have been entitled to do, for any invasion of his person or personal property. By various statutes in England and the United States, other offences are made piracy. Thus, if a subject of either of these nations commit any act of hostility against a fellow subject on the high seas, under color of a commission from any foreign power, this act is piracy. So if any captain of any vessel, or mariner, run away with the vessel, or the goods, or yield them up to a pirate voluntarily, or if any seaman lay violent hands on his commander, to hinder him from fighting in defence of the ship or goods committed to his charge, or make a revolt in the ship, these offences are acts of piracy, by the laws of the United States and England. In England by the statute of 8 George I, c. 24, the trading or corresponding with known pirates, or the forcibly boarding any merchant vessel, (though without seizing her or carrying her off,) and destroying any of the goods on board, are declared to be acts of piracy; and by the statute 18 George II. c. 30, any natural born subject or denizen who in time of war, shall commit any hostilities at sea, against any of his fellow subjects, or shall assist an enemy, on that element, is liable to be punished as a pirate. By statute of George II. c. 25, the ransoming of any neutral vessel, which has been taken by the captain of a private ship of war, is declared piracy. By the act of congress, April 30, 1790, if any person upon the high seas, or in any river, haven, or bay, out of the jurisdiction of any particular state, commit murder or robbery, or any other offence which if committed within the body of a county, would by the laws of the United States, be punishable by death, such offender is to be deemed a pirate. By the act of congress, 1820, c. 113, if any citizen of the United States, being of the crew of any foreign vessel, or any person being of the crew of any vessel owned in whole or part by any citizen of the United States, shall be engaged in the foreign slave trade, he shall be adjudged a pirate. Notwithstanding the expression used in this statute, the question, says Chancellor Kent, remains to be settled, whether the act of being concerned in the slave trade would be adjudged piracy, within the code of international law. In England by the act of parliament passed March

31, 1824, the slave trade is also declared to be piracy. An attempt has been made to effect a convention between the United States and Great Britain, by which it should be agreed that both nations should consider the slave trade as piratical; but this attempt has hitherto been unsuccessful. In the time of Richard III, by the laws of Oberon, all infidels were regarded as pirates, and their property liable to seizure wherever found. By the law of nations, the taking of goods by piracy does not divest the actual owner of them. By the civil institutions of Spain and Venice, ships taken from pirates became the property of those who retake them. Piracy is every where pursued and punished with death, and pirates can gain no rights by conquest. It is of no importance, for the purpose of giving jurisdiction in cases of piracy, on whom or where a piratical offence is committed. A pirate who is one by the law of nations, may be tried and punished in any country where he may be found; for he is reputed to be out of the protection of all laws. But if the statute of any government declares an offence, committed on board one of their own vessels, to be piracy; such an offence will be punished exclusively by the nation which passes the statute. In England the offence was formerly cognizable only by the Admiralty courts, which proceeded without a jury in a method founded on the civil law. But by the statute of Henry VIII. c. 15, it was enacted that piracy should be tried by commissioners nominated by the lord chancellor, the indictment being first found by a grand jury, of twelve men, and afterwards tried by another jury, as at common law. Among the commissioners, there are always some of the common law judges. In the United States, pirates are tried before the circuit court of the United States. Piracy has been known from the remotest antiquity; for in the early ages every small maritime state was addicted to piracy, and navigation was perilous. This habit was so general, that it was regarded with indifference, and, whether merchant, traveller, or pirate, the stranger was received with the rights of hospitality. Thus Nestor, having given Mentor and Telemachus a plenteous repast, remarks, that the banquet being finished, it was time to ask his guests to their business. "Are you," demands the aged prince, "merchants destined to any port, or are you merely adventurers and pirates, who roam the seas without any place of destination, and live by rapine and ruin."

Page 14 Illustration

## THE DANISH AND NORMAN PIRATES

The Saxons, a people supposed to be derived from the Cimbri, uniting the occupations of fishing and piracy, commenced at an early period their ravages in the German Ocean; and the shores of Gaul and Britain were for ages open to their depredations. About the middle of the fifth century, the unwarlike Vortigern, then king of Britain, embraced the fatal resolution of requesting these hardy warriors to deliver him from the harassing inroads of the Picts and Scots; and the expedition of Hengist and Horsa was the consequence. Our mention of this memorable epoch is not for its political importance, great as that is, but for its effects on piracy; for the success attending such enterprises seems to have turned the whole of the northern nations towards sea warfare. The Danes, Norwegians, and Swedes, from their superior knowledge of navigation, gave into it most; and on whatever coast the winds carried them, they made free with all that came in their way. Canute the Fourth endeavored in vain to repress these lawless disorders among his subjects; but they felt so galled by his restrictions, that they assassinated him. On the king of Sweden being taken by the Danes, permission was given to such of his subjects as chose, to arm themselves against the enemy, pillage his possessions, and sell their prizes at Ribnitz and Golnitz. This proved a fertile nursery of pirates, who became so formidable under the name of "Victalien Broders," that several princes were obliged to arm against them, and hang some of their chiefs.

Even the females of the North caught the epidemic spirit, and proudly betook themselves to the dangers of sea-life. Saxo-Grammaticus relates an interesting story of one of them. Alwilda, the daughter of Synardus, a Gothic king, to deliver herself from the violence imposed on her inclination, by a marriage with Alf, the son of Sygarus, king of Denmark, embraced the life of a rover; and attired as a man, she embarked in a vessel of which the crew was composed of other young women of tried courage, dressed in the same manner. Among the first of her cruises, she landed at a place where a company of pirates were bewailing the loss of their commander; and the strangers were so captivated with the air and agreeable manners of Alwilda, that they unanimously chose her for their leader. By this reinforcement she became so formidable, that Prince Alf was despatched to engage her. She sustained his attacks with great courage and talent; but during a severe action in the gulf of Finland, Alf boarded her vessel, and having killed the greatest part of her crew, seized the captain, namely herself; whom nevertheless he knew not, because she had a casque which covered her visage. The prince was agreeably surprised, on removing the helmet, to recognize his beloved Alwilda; and it seems that his valor had now recommended him to the fair princess, for he persuaded her to accept his hand, married her on board, and then led her to partake of his wealth, and share his throne.

Charlemagne, though represented as naturally generous and humane, had been induced, in his extravagant zeal for the propagation of those tenets which he had himself adopted, to enforce them throughout Germany at the point of the sword; and his murders and decimations on that account disgrace humanity. The more warlike of the Pagans flying into Jutland, from whence the Saxons had issued forth, were received with kindness, and furnished with the means of punishing their persecutor, by harassing his coasts. The maritime towns of France were especially ravaged by those pirates called "Normands," or men of the North; and it was owing to their being joined by many malcontents, in the provinces since called Normandy, that that district acquired its name. Charlemagne, roused by this effrontery, besides fortifying the mouths of the great rivers, determined on building himself a fleet, which he did, consisting of 400 of the largest galleys then known, some having five or six benches of oars. His people were, however, extremely ignorant of maritime affairs, and in the progress of having them taught, he was suddenly called to the south, by the invasion of the Saracens.

Awilda, the Female Pirate

***Awilda, the Female Pirate.***

Another division of Normans, some years afterwards, in the same spirit of emigration, and thirsting, perhaps, to avenge their injured ancestors, burst into the provinces of France, which the degeneracy of Charlemagne's posterity, and the dissensions which prevailed there, rendered an affair of no great difficulty. Louis le Debonnaire had taken every means of keeping on good terms with them; annually persuading some to become Christians, and then sending them home so loaded with presents, that it was discovered they came to be baptized over and over again, merely for the sake of the gifts, as Du Chesne tells us. But on the subsequent division of the empire among the undutiful sons of Louis, the pirates did not fail to take advantage of the general confusion; braving the sea almost every summer in their light coracles, sailing up the Seine, the Somme, or the Loire, and devastating the best parts of France, almost without resistance. In 845, they went up to Paris, pillaged it, and were on the point of attacking the royal camp at St. Dennis; but receiving a large sum of money from Charles the Bald, they retreated from thence, and with the new means thus supplied them, ravaged Bordeaux, and were there joined by Pepin, king of Aquitaine. A few years afterwards, they returned in great numbers. Paris was again sacked, and the magnificent abbey of St. Germain des Prés burnt. In 861, Wailand, a famous Norman pirate, returning from England, took up his winter quarters on the banks of the Loire, devastated the country as high as Tourraine, shared the women and girls among his crews, and even carried off the male children, to be brought up in his own profession. Charles the Bald, not having the power to expel him, engaged the freebooter, for 500 pounds of silver, to dislodge his countrymen, who were harassing the vicinity of Paris. In consequence of this subsidy, Wailand, with a fleet of 260 sail, went up the Seine, and attacked the Normans in the isle of Oiselle: after a long and obstinate resistance, they were obliged to capitulate; and having paid 6000 pounds of gold and silver, by way of ransom, had leave to join their victors. The riches thus acquired rendered a predatory life so popular, that the pirates were continually increasing in number, so that under a "sea-king" called Eric, they made a descent in the Elbe and the Weser, pillaged Hamburg, penetrated far into Germany, and after gaining two battles, retreated with immense booty. The pirates, thus reinforced on all sides, long continued to devastate Germany, France, and England; some penetrated into Andalusia and Hetruria, where they destroyed the flourishing town of Luni; whilst others, descending the Dnieper, penetrated even into Russia.

A Priest thrown from the Ramparts of an Abbey.

**A Priest thrown from the Ramparts of an Abbey.**

Meanwhile the Danes had been making several attempts to effect a *lodgment* in England; and allured by its fertility, were induced to try their fortune in various expeditions, which were occasionally completely successful, and at other times most fatally disastrous. At length, after a struggle of several years, their success was so decided, that king Alfred was obliged for a time to abandon his kingdom, as we all know, to their ravages. They immediately passed over to Ireland, and divided it into three sovereignties; that of Dublin fell to the share of Olauf; that of Waterford to Sitrih; and that of Limerick to Yivar. These arrangements dispersed the forces of the enemy, and watching his opportunity, Alfred issued from his retreat, fell on them like a thunderbolt, and made a great carnage of them. This prince, too wise to exterminate the pirates after he had conquered them, sent them to settle Northumberland, which had been wasted by their countrymen, and by this humane policy gained their attachment and services. He then retook London, embellished it, equipped fleets, restrained the Danes in England, and prevented others from landing. In the twelve years of peace which followed his fifty-six battles, this great man composed his body of laws; divided England into counties, hundreds, and tithings, and founded the University of Oxford. But after Alfred's death, fresh swarms of pirates visited the shores, among the most formidable of whom were the Danes, who spread desolation and misery along the banks of the Thames, the Medway, the Severn, the Tamar, and the Avon, for more than a century, though repeatedly tempted to desist by weighty bribes, raised by an oppressive and humiliating tax called *Danegelt*, from its object; and which, like most others, were continued long after it had answered its intent.

About the end of the 9th century, one of the sons of Rognwald, count of the Orcades, named Horolf, or Rollo, having infested the coasts of Norway with piratical descents, was at length defeated and banished by Harold, king of Denmark. He fled for safety to the Scandinavian island of Soderoe, where finding many outlaws and discontented fugitives, he addressed their passions, and succeeded in placing himself at their head. Instead of measuring his sword with his sovereign again, he adopted the wiser policy of imitating his countrymen, in making his fortune by plundering the more opulent places of southern Europe. The first attempt of this powerful gang was upon England, where, finding Alfred too powerful to be coped with, he stood over to the mouth of the Seine, and availed himself of the state to which France was reduced. Horolf, however, did not limit his ambition to the acquisition of booty; he wished permanently to enjoy some of the fine countries he was ravaging, and after many treaties made and broken, received the dutchy of Normandy from the lands of Charles the Simple, as a fief, together with Gisla, the daughter of the French monarch, in marriage. Thus did a mere pirate found the family which in a few years gave sovereigns to England, Naples, and Sicily, and spread the fame of their talents and prowess throughout the world.

Nor was Europe open to the depredations of the northern pirates only. Some Asiatic moslems, having seized on Syria, immediately invaded Africa, and their subsequent conquests in Spain facilitated their irruption into France, where they pillaged the devoted country, with but few substantial checks. Masters of all the islands in the Mediterranean, their corsairs insulted the coasts of Italy, and even threatened the destruction of the Eastern empire. While Alexis was occupied in a war with Patzinaces, on the banks of the Danube, Zachas, a Saracen pirate, scoured the Archipelago, having, with the assistance of an able Smyrniote, constructed a flotilla of forty brigantines, and some light fast-rowing boats, manned by adventurers like himself. After taking several of the surrounding islands, he established himself sovereign of Smyrna, that place being about the centre of his newly-acquired dominions. Here his fortunes prospered for a time, and Soliman, sultan of Nicea, son of the grand Soliman, sought his alliance, and married his daughter, about AD. 1093. But in the following year, young Soliman being persuaded that his father-in-law had an eye to his possessions, with his own hand stabbed Zachas to the heart. The success of this freebooter shows that the Eastern emperors could no longer protect, or even assist, their islands.

Maritime pursuits had now revived, the improvement of nautical science was progressing rapidly, and the advantages of predatory expeditions, especially when assisted and masked by commerce, led people of family and acquirements to embrace the profession. The foremost of these were the Venetians and Genoese, among whom the private adventurers, stimulated by an enterprising spirit, fitted out armaments, and volunteered themselves into the service of those nations who thought proper to retain them; or they engaged in such schemes of plunder as were likely to repay their pains and expense. About the same time, the Roxolani or Russians, became known in history, making their debut in the character of pirates, ravenous for booty, and hungry for the pillage of Constantinople–a longing which 900 years have not yet satisfied. Pouring hundreds of boats down the Borysthenes, the Russian marauders made four desperate attempts to plunder the city of the Caesars, in less than two centuries, and appear only to have been repulsed by the dreadful effects of the celebrated Greek fire.

England, in the mean time, had little to do with piracy; nor had she any thing worthy the name of a navy; yet Coeur de Lion had given maritime laws to Europe; her seamen, in point of skill, were esteemed superior to their contemporaries; and King John enacted that those foreign ships which refused to lower their flags to that of Britain should, if taken, be deemed lawful prizes. Under Henry III., though Hugh de Burgh, the governor of Dover Castle, had defeated a French fleet by casting lime into the eyes of his antagonists, the naval force was impaired to such a degree that the Normans and Bretons were too powerful for the Cinque Ports, and compelled them to seek relief from the other ports of the kingdom. The taste for depredation had become so general and contagious, that privateers were now allowed to be fitted out, which equipments quickly degenerated to the most cruel of pirates. Nay more: on the disputes which took place between Henry and his Barons, in 1244, the Cinque Ports, who had shown much indifference to the royal requisitions, openly espoused the cause of the revolted nobles; and, under the orders of Simon de Montfort, burnt Portsmouth. From this, forgetful of their motives for arming, they proceeded to commit various acts of piracy, and considering nothing but their private interests, extended their violence not only against the shipping of all countries unfortunate enough to fall in their way, but even to perpetrate the most unwarrantable ravages on the property of their own countrymen. Nor was this confined to the Cinque Port vessels only; the example and the profits were too stimulating to the restless; and one daring association on the coast of Lincolnshire seized the Isle of Ely, and made it their receptacle for the plunder of all the adjacent countries. One William Marshall fortified the little island of Lundy, in the mouth of the Severn, and did so much mischief by his piracies, that at length it became necessary to fit out a squadron to reduce him, which was accordingly done, and he was executed in London; yet the example did not deter other persons from similar practices. The sovereign, however, did not possess sufficient naval means to suppress the enormities of the great predatory squadrons, and their ravages continued to disgrace the English name for upwards of twenty years, when the valor and conciliation of the gallant Prince Edward brought them to that submission which his royal parent had failed in procuring.

Those "harum-scarum" expeditions, the Crusades, were perhaps influential in checking piracy, although the rabble that composed the majority of them had as little principle as the worst of the freebooters. From the time that Peter the Hermit set Europe in a blaze, all ranks, and all nations, streamed to the East, so that few vessels were otherwise employed than in conveying the motly groups who sought the shores of Palestine; some from religious zeal; some from frantic fanaticism; some from desire of distinction; some for the numberless privileges which the crusaders acquired; and the rest and greater portion, for the spoil and plunder of which they had a prospect. The armaments, fitted in no fewer than nine successive efforts, were mostly equipped with such haste and ignorance, and with so little choice, that ruinous delays, shipwrecks, and final discomfiture, were naturally to be expected. Still, the effect of such incredible numbers of people betaking themselves to foreign countries, advanced civilization, although vast means of forwarding its cause were buried in the East; and those who assert that no benefit actually resulted, cannot deny that at least some evils were thereby removed. Montesquieu says, that Europe then required a general shock, to teach her, but the sight of contrasts, the theorems of public economy most conducive to happiness. And it is evident, that notwithstanding these follies wasted the population of Europe, squandered its treasures, and infected us with new vices and diseases, still the crusades diminished the bondage of the feudal system, by augmenting the power of the King, and the strength of the Commons; while they also occasioned a very increased activity in commerce: thus taming the ferocity of men's spirits, increasing agriculture in value from the safety it enjoyed, and establishing a base for permanent prosperity.

Page 26 Illustration

**ADVENTURES AND EXPLOITS OF CAPTAIN AVERY**

Containing an Account of his capturing one of the great Mogul's ship's laden with treasure: and an interesting history of a Colony of Pirates on the Island of Madagascar.

During his own time the adventures of Captain Avery were the subject of general conversation in Europe. It was reported that he had married the Great Mogul's daughter, who was taken in an Indian ship that fell into his hands, and that he was about to be the founder of a new monarchy–that he gave commissions in his own name to the captains of his ships, and the commanders of his forces, and was acknowledged by them as their prince. In consequence of these reports, it was at one time resolved to fit out a strong squadron to go and take him and his men; and at another time it was proposed to invite him home with all his riches, by the offer of his Majesty's pardon. These reports, however, were soon discovered to be groundless, and he was actually starving without a shilling, while he was represented as in the possession of millions. Not to exhaust the patience, or lessen the curiosity of the reader, the facts in Avery's life shall be briefly related.

He was a native of Devonshire (Eng.), and at an early period sent to sea; advanced to the station of a mate in a merchantman, he performed several voyages. It happened previous to the peace of Ryswick, when there existed an alliance between Spain, England, Holland, and other powers, against France, that the French in Martinique carried on a smuggling trade with the Spaniards on the continent of Peru. To prevent their intrusion into the Spanish dominions, a few vessels were commanded to cruise upon that coast, but the French ships were too strong for them; the Spaniards, therefore, came to the resolution of hiring foreigners to act against them. Accordingly, certain merchants of Bristol fitted out two ships of thirty guns, well manned, and provided with every necessary munition, and commanded them to sail for Corunna to receive their orders.

Captain Gibson commanded one of these ships, and Avery appears to have been his mate, in the year 1715. He was a fellow of more cunning than courage, and insinuating himself into the confidence of some of the boldest men in the ship, he represented the immense riches which were to be acquired upon the Spanish coast, and proposed to run off with the ship. The proposal was scarcely made when it was agreed upon, and put in execution at ten o'clock the following evening. Captain Gibson was one of those who mightily love their bottle, and spent much of his time on shore; but he remained on board that night, which did not, however, frustrate their design, because he had taken his usual dose, and so went to bed. The men who were not in the confederacy went also to bed, leaving none upon deck but the conspirators. At the time agreed upon, the long boat of the other ship came, and Avery hailing her in the usual manner, he was answered by the men in her, "Is your drunken boatswain on board?" which was the watchword agreed between them. Avery replying in the affirmative, the boat came alongside with sixteen stout fellows, who joined in the adventure. They next secured the hatches, then softly weighed anchor, and immediately put to sea without bustle or noise. There were several vessels in the bay, besides a Dutchman of forty guns, the captain of which was offered a considerable reward to go in pursuit of Avery, but he declined. When the captain awoke, he rang his bell, and Avery and another conspirator going into the cabin, found him yet half asleep. He inquired, saying, "What is the matter with the ship? does she drive? what weather is it?" supposing that it had been a storm, and that the ship was driven from her anchors. "No, no," answered Avery, "we're at sea, with a fair wind and a good weather." "At sea!" said the captain: "how can that be?" "Come," answered Avery, "don't be in a fright, but put on your clothes, and I'll let you into a secret. You must know that I am captain of this ship now, and this is my cabin, therefore you must walk out; I am bound to Madagascar, with a design of making my own fortune, and that of all the brave fellows joined with me."

The captain, having a little recovered his senses, began to understand his meaning. However, his fright was as great as before, which Avery perceiving, desired him to fear nothing; "for," said he, "if you have a mind to make one of us, we will receive you; and if you turn sober, and attend to business, perhaps in time I may make you one of my lieutenants; if not, here's a boat, and you shall be set on shore." Gibson accepted of the last proposal; and the whole crew being called up to know who was willing to go on shore with the captain, there were only about five or six who chose to accompany him.

Avery proceeded on his voyage to Madagascar, and it does not appear that he captured any vessels upon his way. When arrived at the northeast part of that island, he found two sloops at anchor, which, upon seeing him, slipped their cables and ran themselves ashore, while the men all landed and concealed themselves in the woods. These were two sloops which the men had run off with from the East Indies, and seeing Avery's ship, supposed that he had been sent out after them. Suspecting who they were, he sent some of his men on shore to inform them that they were friends, and to propose a union for their common safety. The sloops' men being well armed, had posted themselves in a wood, and placed sentinels to observe whether the ship's men were landing to pursue them. The sentinels only observing two or three men coming towards them unarmed, did not oppose them. Upon being informed that they were friends, the sentinels conveyed them to the main body, where they delivered their message. They were at first afraid that it was a stratagem to entrap them, but when the messengers assured them that their captain had also run away with his ship, and that a few of their men along with him would meet them unarmed, to consult matters for their common advantage, confidence was established, and they were mutually well pleased, as it added to their strength.

Having consulted what was most proper to be attempted they endeavored to get off the sloops, and hastened to prepare all things, in order to sail for the Arabian coast. Near the river Indus, the man at the mast-head espied a sail, upon which they gave chase; as they came nearer to her, they discovered that she was a tall vessel, and might turn out to be an East Indiaman. She, however, proved a better prize; for when they fired at her she hoisted Mogul colors, and seemed to stand upon her defence. Avery only cannonaded at a distance, when some of his men began to suspect that he was not the hero they had supposed. The sloops, however attacked, the one on the bow, and another upon the quarter of the ship, and so boarded her. She then struck her colors. She was one of the Great Mogul's own ships, and there were in her several of the greatest persons in his court, among whom, it was said, was one of his daughters going upon a pilgrimage to Mecca; and they were carrying with them rich offerings to present at the shrine of Mahomet. It is a well known fact, that the people of the east travel with great magnificence, so that these had along with them all their slaves and attendants, with a large quantity of vessels of gold and silver, and immense sums of money to defray their expenses by land; the spoil therefore which they received from that ship was almost incalculable.

Captain Avery engaging the Great Mogul's Ship

**Captain Avery engaging the Great Mogul's Ship.**

Taking the treasure on board their own ships, and plundering their prize of every thing valuable, they then allowed her to depart. As soon as the Mogul received this intelligence, he threatened to send a mighty army to extirpate the English from all their settlements upon the Indian coast. The East India Company were greatly alarmed, but found means to calm his resentment, by promising to search for the robbers, and deliver them into his hands. The noise which this made over all Europe, gave birth to the rumors that were circulated concerning Avery's greatness.

In the mean time, our adventurers made the best of their way back to Madagascar, intending to make that place the deposit of all their treasure, to build a small fort, and to keep always a few men there for its protection. Avery, however, disconcerted this plan, and rendered it altogether unnecessary.

Captain Avery receiving the three chests of Treasure on board of his Ship.

**Captain Avery receiving the three chests of Treasure on board of his Ship.**

While steering their course, Avery sent a boat to each of the sloops, requesting that the chiefs would come on board his ship to hold a conference. They obeyed, and being assembled, he suggested to them the necessity of securing the property which they had acquired in some safe place on shore, and observed, that the chief difficulty was to get it safe on shore; adding that, if either of the sloops should be attacked alone, they would not be able to make any great resistance, and thus she must either be sunk or taken with all the property on board. That, for his part, his ship was so strong, so well manned, and such a swift-sailing vessel, that he did not think it was possible for any other ship to take or overcome her. Accordingly, he proposed that all their treasure should be sealed up in three chests;–that each of the captains should have keys, and that they should not be opened until all were present;–that the chests should be then put on board his ship, and afterwards lodged in some safe place upon land.

This proposal seemed so reasonable, and so much for the common good, that it was without hesitation agreed to, and all the treasure deposited in three chests, and carried to Avery's ship. The weather being favorable, they remained all three in company during that and the next day; meanwhile Avery, tampering with his men, suggested, that they had now on board what was sufficient to make them all happy; "and what," continued he, "should hinder us from going to some country where we are not known, and living on shore all the rest of our days in plenty?" They soon understood his hint, and all readily consented to deceive the men of the sloops, and fly with all the booty; this they effected during the darkness of the following night. The reader may easily conjecture what were the feelings and indignation of the other two crews in the morning, when they discovered that Avery had made off with all their property.

Avery and his men hastened towards America, and being strangers in that country, agreed to divide the booty, to change their names, and each separately to take up his residence, and live in affluence and honor. The first land they approached was the Island of Providence, then newly settled. It however occurred to them, that the largeness of their vessel, and the report that one had been run off with from the Groine, might create suspicion; they resolved therefore to dispose of their vessel at Providence. Upon this resolution, Avery, pretending that his vessel had been equipped for privateering, and having been unsuccessful, he had orders from the owners to dispose of her to the best advantage, soon found a merchant. Having thus sold his own ship, he immediately purchased a small sloop.

In this he and his companions embarked, and landed at several places in America, where, none suspecting them, they dispersed and settled in the country. Avery, however, had been careful to conceal the greater part of the jewels and other valuable articles, so that his riches were immense. Arriving at Boston, he was almost resolved to settle there, but, as the greater part of his wealth consisted of diamonds, he was apprehensive that he could not dispose of them at that place, without being taken up as a pirate. Upon reflection, therefore, he resolved to sail for Ireland, and in a short time arrived in the northern part of that kingdom, and his men dispersed into several places. Some of them obtained the pardon of King William, and settled in that country.

The wealth of Avery, however, now proved of small service, and occasioned him great uneasiness. He could not offer his diamonds for sale in that country without being suspected. Considering, therefore, what was best to be done, he thought there might be some person at Bristol he could venture to trust. Upon this he resolved, and going into Devonshire, sent to one of his friends to meet him at a town called Bideford. When he had unbosomed himself to him and other pretended friends, they agreed that the safest plan would be to put his effects into the hands of some wealthy merchants, and no inquiry would be made how they came by them. One of these friends told him, he was acquainted with some who were very fit for the purpose, and if he would allow them a handsome commission, they would do the business faithfully. Avery liked the proposal, particularly as he could think of no other way of managing this matter, since he could not appear to act for himself. Accordingly, the merchants paid Avery a visit at Bideford, where, after strong protestations of honor and integrity, he delivered them his effects, consisting of diamonds and some vessels of gold. After giving him a little money for his present subsistence, they departed.

He changed his name, and lived quietly at Bideford, so that no notice was taken of him. In a short time his money was all spent, and he heard nothing from his merchants though he wrote to them repeatedly; at last they sent him a small supply, but it was not sufficient to pay his debts. In short, the remittances they sent him were so trifling, that he could with difficulty exist. He therefore determined to go privately to Bristol, and have an interview with the merchants himself,–where, instead of money, he met with a mortifying repulse; for, when he desired them to come to an account with him, they silenced him by threatening to disclose his character; the merchants thus proving themselves as good pirates on land as he was at sea.

Whether he was frightened by these menaces, or had seen some other person who recognised him, is not known; however, he went immediately to Ireland, and from thence solicited his merchants very strongly for a supply, but to no purpose; so that he was reduced to beggary. In this extremity he was determined to return, and cast himself upon the mercy of these honest Bristol merchants, let the consequence be what it would. He went on board a trading-vessel, and worked his passage over to Plymouth, from whence he travelled on foot to Bideford. He had been there but a few days, when he fell sick and died; not being worth so much as would buy him a coffin!

We shall now turn back and give our readers some account of the other two sloops. Deceiving themselves in the supposition that Avery had outsailed them during the night, they held on their course to the place of rendezvouse; but, arriving there, to their sad disappointment no ship appeared. It was now necessary for them to consult what was most proper to do in their desperate circumstances. Their provisions were nearly exhausted, and both fish and fowl were to be found on shore, yet they were destitute of salt to cure them. As they could not subsist at sea without salt provisions, they resolved to form an establishment upon land. Accordingly making tents of the sails, and using the other materials of the sloops for what purposes they could serve, they encamped upon the shore. It was also a fortunate circumstance, that they had plenty of ammunition and small arms. Here they met with some of their countrymen; and as the digression is short, we will inform our readers how they came to inhabit this place.

Captain George Dew, and Thomas Tew, had received a commission from the Governor of Bermuda to sail for the river Gambia, in Africa, that, with the assistance of the Royal African Company, they might seize the French Factory situated upon that coast. Dew, in a violent storm, not only sprang a mast, but lost sight of his companion. Upon this returned to refit. Instead of proceeding in his voyage, Tew made towards the Cape of Good Hope, doubled that cape, and sailed for the straits of Babel-Mandeb. There he met with a large ship richly laden coming from the Indies, and bound for Arabia. Though she had on board three hundred soldiers, besides seamen, yet Tew had the courage to attack her, and soon made her his prize. It is reported, that by this one prize every man shared near three thousand pounds. Informed by the prisoners that five other ships were to pass that way, Tew would have attacked them, but was prevented by the remonstrances of his quarter-master and others. This difference of opinion terminated in a resolution to abandon the sea, and to settle on some convenient spot on shore; and the island of Madagascar was chosen. Tew, however, and a few others, in a short time went for Rhode Island, and obtained a pardon.

The natives of Madagascar are negroes, but differ from those of Guinea in the length of their hair and in the blackness of their complexion. They are divided into small nations, each governed by its own prince, who carry on a continual war upon each other. The prisoners taken in war are either rendered slaves to the conquerors, sold, or slain, according to pleasure. When the pirates first settled among them, their alliance was much courted by these princes, and those whom they joined were always successful in their wars, the natives being ignorant of the use of fire-arms. Such terror did they carry along with them, that the very appearance of a few pirates in an army would have put the opposing force to flight.

By these means they in a little time became very formidable, and the prisoners whom they took in war they employed in cultivating the ground, and the most beautiful of the women they married; nor were they contented with one, but married as many as they could conveniently maintain. The natural result was, that they separated, each choosing a convenient place for himself, where he lived in a princely style, surrounded by his wives, slaves and dependants. Nor was it long before jarring interests excited them also to draw the sword against each other, and they appeared at the head of their respective forces in the field of battle. In these civil wars their numbers and strength were greatly lessened.

The servant, exalted to the condition of a master, generally becomes a tyrant. These pirates, unexpectedly elevated to the dignity of petty princes, used their power with the most wanton barbarity. The punishment of the very least offence was to be tied to a tree, and instantly shot through the head. The negroes, at length, exasperated by continued oppression, formed the determination of extirpating them in one night; nor was it a difficult matter to accomplish this, since they were now so much divided both in affection and residence. Fortunately, however, for them, a negro woman, who was partial to them, ran twenty miles in three hours, and warning them of their danger, they were united and in arms to oppose the negroes before the latter had assembled. This narrow escape made them more cautious, and induced them to adopt the following system of policy:–

Convinced that fear was not a sufficient protection, and that the bravest man might be murdered by a coward in his bed, they labored to foment wars among the negro princes, while they themselves declined to aid either party. It naturally followed, that those who were vanquished fled to them for protection, and increased their strength. When there was no war, they fomented private discords, and encouraged them to wreak their vengeance against each other; nay, even taught them how to surprise their opponents, and furnished them with fire-arms, with which to dispatch them more effectually and expeditiously. The consequences were, that the murderer was constrained to fly to them for protection, with his wives, children, and kindred. These, from interest, became true friends, as their own safety depended upon the lives of their protectors. By this time the pirates were so formidable, that none of the negro princes durst attack them in open war.

Captain Tew attacks the ship from India.

**Captain Tew attacks the ship from India.**

Pursuing this system of policy, in a short time each chief had his party greatly increased, and they divided like so many tribes, in order to find ground to cultivate, and to choose proper places to build places of residence and erect garrisons of defence. The fears that agitated them were always obvious in their general policy, for they vied with each other in constructing places of safety, and using every precaution to prevent the possibility of sudden danger, either from the negroes or from one another.

A description of one of these dwellings will both show the fears that agitated these tyrants, and prove entertaining to the reader. They selected a spot overgrown with wood, near a river, and raised a rampart or ditch round it, so straight and steep that it was impossible to climb it, more particularly by those who had no scaling ladders. Over that ditch there was one passage into the wood; the dwelling, which was a hut, was built in that part of the wood which the prince thought most secure, but so covered that it could not be discovered until you came near it. But the greatest ingenuity was displayed in the construction of the passage that led to the hut, which was so narrow, that no more than one person could go abreast, and it was contrived in so intricate a manner, that it was a perfect labyrinth; the way going round and round with several small crossways, so that a person unacquainted with it, might walk several hours without finding the hut. Along the sides of these paths, certain large thorns, which grew on a tree in that country, were stuck into the ground with their points outwards; and the path itself being serpentine, as before mentioned, if a man should attempt to approach the hut at night, he would certainly have struck upon these thorns.

A Pirate and his Madagascar wife

***A Pirate and his Madagascar wife.***

Thus like tyrants they lived, dreading, and dreaded by all, and in this state they were found by Captain Woods Rogers, when he went to Madagascar in the Delicia, a ship of forty guns, with the design of purchasing slaves. He touched upon a part of the island at which no ship had been seen for seven or eight years before, where he met with some pirates who had been upon the island above twenty-five years. There were only eleven of the original stock then alive, surrounded with a numerous offspring of children and grandchildren.

They were struck with terror upon the sight of the vessel, supposing that it was a man-of-war sent out to apprehend them; they, therefore, retired to their secret habitations. But when they found some of the ship's crew on shore, without any signs of hostility, and proposing to treat with them for slaves, they ventured to come out of their dwellings attended like princes. Having been so long upon the island, their cloaks were so much worn, that their majesties were extremely out at elbows. It cannot be said that they were ragged, but they had nothing to cover them but the skins of beasts in their natural state, not even a shoe or stocking; so that they resembled the pictures of Hercules in the lion's skin; and being overgrown with beard, and hair upon their bodies, they appeared the most savage figures that the human imagination could well conceive.

The sale of the slaves in their possession soon provided them with more suitable clothes, and all other necessaries, which they received in exchange. Meanwhile, they became very familiar, went frequently on board, and were very eager in examining the inside of the ship, talking very familiarly with the men, and inviting them on shore. Their design was to surprise the ship during the night. They had a sufficient number of men and boats to effect their purpose, but the captain suspecting them, kept so strong a watch upon deck, that they found it in vain to hazard an attempt. When some of the men went on shore, they entered into a plan to seize the ship, but the captain observing their familiarity, prevented any one of his men from speaking to the pirates, and only permitted a confidential person to purchase their slaves. Thus he departed from the island, leaving these pirates to enjoy their savage royalty. One of them had been a waterman upon the Thames, and having committed a murder, fled to the West Indies. The rest had all been foremastmen, nor was there one among them who could either read or write.

Captain Avery's Treasure

***Captain Avery's Treasure.***

**THE REMARKABLE HISTORY OF THE JOASSAMEE PIRATES OF THE PERSIAN GULF.**

*Containing a description of their chief town, Ras El Khyma, and an account of the capture of several European vessels, and the barbarous treatment of their crews.– With interesting details of the several expeditions sent against them, and their final submission to the troops of the English East India Company.*

The line of coast from Cape Mussenndom to Bahrain, on the Arabian side of the Persian Gulf, had been from time immemorial occupied by a tribe of Arabs called Joassamees. These, from local position, were all engaged in maritime pursuits. Some traded in their own small vessels to Bussorah, Bushire, Muscat, and even India; others annually fished in their own boats on the pearl banks of Bahrain; and a still greater number hired themselves out as sailors to navigate the coasting small craft of the Persian Gulf.

The Joassamees at length perceiving that their local position enabled them to reap a rich harvest by plundering vessels in passing this great highway of nations, commenced their piratical career. The small coasting vessels of the gulf, from their defenceless state, were the first object of their pursuit, and these soon fell an easy prey; until, emboldened by success, they directed their views to more arduous enterprises, and having tasted the sweets of plunder in the increase of their wealth, had determined to attempt more promising victories.

About the year 1797, one of the East India Company's vessels of war, the Viper, of ten guns, was lying at anchor in the inner roads of Bushire. Some dows of the Joassamees were at the same moment anchored in the harbor; but as their warfare had hitherto been waged only against what are called native vessels, and they had either feared or respected the British flag, no hostile measures were ever pursued against them by the British ships. The commanders of these dows had applied to the Persian agent of the East India Company there, for a supply of gunpowder and cannon shot for their cruise: and as this man had no suspicions of their intentions, he furnished them with an order to the commanding officer on board for the quantity required. The captain of the Viper was on shore at the time, in the agent's house, but the order being produced to the officer on board, the powder and shot were delivered, and the dows weighed and made sail. The crew of the Viper were at this moment taking their breakfast on deck, and the officers below; when on a sudden, a cannonading was opened on them by two of the dows, who attempted also to board.

A Joassamee Dow in full chase

***A Joassamee Dow in full chase.***

The officers, leaping on deck, called the crew to quarters, and cutting their cable, got sail upon the ship, so as to have the advantage of manoeuvring. A regular engagement now took place between this small cruiser and four dows, all armed with great guns, and full of men. In the contest Lieut. Carruthers, the commanding officer, was once wounded by a ball in the loins; but after girding a handkerchief round his waist, he still kept the deck, till a ball entering his forehead, he fell. Mr. Salter, the midshipman on whom the command devolved, continued the fight with determined bravery, and after a stout resistance, beat them off, chased them some distance out to sea, and subsequently regained the anchorage in safety.

Several years elapsed before the wounds of the first defeat were sufficiently healed to induce a second attempt on vessels under the British flag, though a constant state of warfare was still kept up against the small craft of the gulf. In 1804, the East India Company's cruiser, Fly, was taken by a French privateer, off the Island of Kenn, in the Persian Gulf; but before the enemy boarded her, she ran into shoal water, near that island, and sunk the government dispatches, and some treasure with which they were charged, in about two and a half fathoms of water, taking marks for the recovery of them, if possible, at some future period. The passengers and crew were taken to Bushire where they were set at liberty, and having purchased a country dow by subscription, they fitted her out and commenced their voyage down the gulf, bound for Bombay. On their passage down, as they thought it would be practicable to recover the government packet and treasure sunk off Kenn, they repaired to that island, and were successful, after much exertion, in recovering the former, which being in their estimation of the first importance, as the dispatches were from England to Bombay, they sailed with them on their way thither, without loss of time.

Near the mouth of the gulf, they were captured by a fleet of Joassamee boats, after some resistance, in which several were wounded and taken into their chief port at Ras-el-Khyma. Here they were detained in hope of ransome, and during their stay were shown to the people of the town as curiosities, no similar beings having been before seen there within the memory of man. The Joassamee ladies were so minute in their enquiries, indeed, that they were not satisfied without determining in what respect an uncircumcised infidel differed from a true believer.

When these unfortunate Englishmen had remained for several months in the possession of the Arabs, and no hope of their ransom appeared, it was determined to put them to death, and thus rid themselves of unprofitable enemies. An anxiety to preserve life, however, induced the suggestion, on their parts, of a plan for the temporary prolongation of it, at least. With this view they communicated to the chief of the pirates the fact of their having sunk a quantity of treasure near the island of Kenn, and of their knowing the marks of the spot, by the bearings of objects on shore, with sufficient accuracy to recover it, if furnished with good divers. They offered, therefore, to purchase their own liberty, by a recovery of this money for their captors; and on the fulfillment of their engagement it was solemnly promised to be granted to them.

They soon sailed for the spot, accompanied by divers accustomed to that occupation on the pearl banks of Bahrain; and, on their anchoring at the precise points of bearing taken, they commenced their labors. The first divers who went down were so successful, that all the crew followed in their turns, so that the vessel was at one time almost entirely abandoned at anchor. As the men, too, were all so busily occupied in their golden harvest, the moment appeared favorable for escape; and the still captive Englishmen were already at their stations to overpower the few on board, cut the cable, and make sail. Their motions were either seen or suspected, as the divers repaired on board in haste, and the scheme was thus frustrated. They were now given their liberty as promised, by being landed on the island of Kenn, where, however, no means offered for their immediate escape. The pirates, having at the same time landed themselves on the island, commenced a general massacre of the inhabitants, in which their released prisoners, fearing they might be included, fled for shelter to clefts and hiding places in the rocks. During their refuge here, they lived on such food as chance threw in their way; going out under cover of the night to steal a goat and drag it to their haunts. When the pirates had at length completed their work of blood, and either murdered or driven off every former inhabitant of the island, they quitted it themselves, with the treasure which they had thus collected from the sea and shore. The Englishmen now ventured to come out from their hiding places, and to think of devising some means of escape. Their good fortune in a moment of despair, threw them on the wreck of a boat, near the beach, which was still capable of repair. In searching about the now deserted town, other materials were found, which were of use to them, and sufficient plank and logs of wood for the construction of a raft. These were both completed in a few days, and the party embarked on them in two divisions, to effect a passage to the Persian shore. One of these rafts was lost in the attempt, and all on board her perished; while the raft, with the remainder of the party reached land.

Having gained the main land they now set out on foot towards Bushire, following the line of the coast for the sake of the villages and water. In this they are said to have suffered incredible hardships and privations of every kind. No one knew the language of the country perfectly, and the roads and places of refreshment still less; they were in general destitute of clothes and money, and constantly subject to plunder and imposition, poor as they were. Their food was therefore often scanty, and always of the worst kind; and they had neither shelter from the burning sun of the day, nor from the chilling dews of night.

The Indian sailors, sipakees, and servants, of whom a few were still remaining when they set out, had all dropped off by turns; and even Europeans had been abandoned on the road, in the most affecting way, taking a last adieu of their comrades, who had little else to expect but soon to follow their fate. One instance is mentioned of their having left one who could march no further, at the distance of only a mile from a village; and on returning to the spot on the morrow, to bring him in, nothing was found but his mangled bones, as he had been devoured in the night by jackals. The packet being light was still, however, carried by turns, and preserved through all obstacles and difficulties; and with it they reached at length the island of Busheap, to which they crossed over in a boat from the main. Here they were detained by the Sheikh, but at length he provided them with a boat for the conveyance of themselves and dispatches to Bushire. From this place they proceeded to Bombay, but of all the company only two survived. A Mr. Jowl, an officer of a merchant ship, and an English sailor named Penmel together with the bag of letters and dispatches.

In the following year, two English brigs, the Shannon, Capt. Babcock, and the Trimmer, Capt. Cummings, were on their voyage from Bombay to Bussorah. These were both attacked, near the Islands of Polior and Kenn, by several boats, and after a slight resistance on the part of the Shannon only, were taken possession of, and a part of the crew of each, cruelly put to the sword. Capt. Babcock, having been seen by one of the Arabs to discharge a musket during the contest, was taken by them on shore; and after a consultation on his fate, it was determined that he should forfeit the arm by which this act of resistance was committed. It was accordingly severed from his body by one stroke of a sabre, and no steps were taken either to bind up the wound, or to prevent his bleeding to death. The captain, himself, had yet sufficient presence of mind left, however, to think of his own safety, and there being near him some clarified butter, he procured this to be heated, and while yet warm, thrust the bleeding stump of his arm into it. It had the effect of lessening the effusion of blood, and ultimately of saving a life that would otherwise most probably have been lost. The crew were then all made prisoners, and taken to a port of Arabia, from whence they gradually dispersed and escaped. The vessels themselves were additionally armed, one of them mounting twenty guns, manned with Arab crews, and sent from Ras-el-Khyma to cruise in the gulf, where they committed many piracies.

In the year 1808, the force of the Joassamees having gradually increased, and becoming flushed with the pride of victory, their insulting attacks on the British flag were more numerous and more desperate than ever. The first of these was on the ship Minerva, of Bombay, on her voyage to Bussorah. The attack was commenced by several boats, (for they never cruize singly,) and a spirited resistance in a running fight was kept up at intervals for several days in succession. A favorable moment offered, however, for boarding; the ship was overpowered by numbers, and carried amidst a general massacre. The captain was said to have been cut up into separate pieces, and thrown overboard by fragments; the second mate and carpenter alone were spared, probably to make use of their services; and an Armenian lady, the wife of Lieut. Taylor, then at Bushire, was reserved perhaps for still greater sufferings. But was subsequently ransomed for a large sum.

The Pirates striking off the arm of Capt. Babcock

***The Pirates striking off the arm of Capt. Babcock.***

A few weeks after this, the Sylph, one of the East India Company's cruisers, of sixty tons and mounting eight guns, was accompanying the mission under Sir Hartford Jones, from Bombay, to Persia; when being separated from the rest of the squadron, she was attacked in the gulf by a fleet of dows. These bore down with all the menacing attitude of hostility; but as the commander, Lieut. Graham had received orders from the Bombay government, not to open his fire on any of these vessels until he had been first fired on himself, the ship was hardly prepared for battle, and the colors were not even hoisted to apprise them to what nation she belonged. The dows approached, threw their long overhanging prows across the Sylph's beam, and pouring in a shower of stones on her deck, beat down and wounded almost every one who stood on it. They then boarded, and made the ship an easy prize, before more than a single shot had been fired, and in their usual way, put every one whom they found alive to the sword. Lieut. Graham fell, covered with wounds, down the fore hatchway of his own vessel, where he was dragged by some of the crew into a store room, in which they had secreted themselves, and barricaded the door with a crow-bar from within. The cruiser was thus completely in the possession of the enemy, who made sail on her, and were bearing her off in triumph to their own port, in company with their boats. Soon after, however, the commodore of the squadron in the Neried frigate hove in sight, and perceiving this vessel in company with the dows, judged her to be a prize to the pirates. She accordingly gave them all chase, and coming up with the brig, the Arabs took to their boats and abandoned her. The chase was continued after the dows, but without success.

The Neried Frigate chasing a Fleet of Joassamee Dows

**The Neried Frigate chasing a Fleet of Joassamee Dows.**

These repeated aggressions at length opened the eyes of the East India Government, and an expedition was accordingly assembled at Bombay. The naval force consisted of La Chiffone, frigate, Capt. Wainwright, as commodore. The Caroline of thirty-eight guns; and eight of the East India Company's cruisers, namely, the Mornington, Ternate, Aurora, Prince of Wales, Ariel, Nautilus, Vestal and Fury, with four large transports, and the Stromboli bomb-ketch. The fleet sailed from Bombay in September, and after a long passage they reached Muscat, where it remained for many days to refresh and arrange their future plans; they sailed and soon reached Ras-el-Khyma, the chief port of the pirates within the gulf. Here the squadron anchored abreast of the town, and the troops were landed under cover of the ships and boats. The inhabitants of the town assembled in crowds to repel the invaders; but the firm line, the regular volleys, and the steady charge of the troops at the point of the bayonet, overcame every obstacle, and multiplied the heaps of the slain. A general conflagration was then ordered, and a general plunder to the troops was permitted. The town was set on fire in all parts, and about sixty sail of boats and dows, with the Minerva, a ship which they had taken, then lying in the roads were all burnt and destroyed.

The complete conquest of the place was thus effected with very trifling loss on the part of the besiegers, and some plunder collected; though it was thought that most of the treasure and valuables had been removed into the interior. This career of victory was suddenly damped by the report of the approach of a large body of troops from the interior, and although none of these were seen, this ideal reinforcement induced the besiegers to withdraw. The embarkation took place at daylight in the morning; and while the fleet remained at anchor during the whole of the day, parties were still seen assembling on the shore, displaying their colors, brandishing their spears, and firing muskets from all points; so that the conquest was scarcely as complete as could be wished, since no formal act of submission had yet been shown. The expedition now sailed to Linga, a small port of the Joassamees, and burnt it to the ground. The force had now become separated, the greater portion of the troops being sent to Muscat for supplies, or being deemed unnecessary, and some of the vessels sent on separate services of blockading passages, c. The remaining portion of the blockading squadron consisting of La Chiffone, frigate, and four of the cruisers, the Mornington, Ternate, Nautilus, and Fury, and two transports, with five hundred troops from Linga, then proceeded to Luft, another port of the Joassamees. As the channel here was narrow and difficult of approach, the ships were warped into their stations of anchorage, and a summons sent on shore, as the people had not here abandoned their town, but were found at their posts of defence, in a large and strong castle with many batteries, redoubts, c. The summons being treated with disdain, the troops were landed with Col. Smith at their head; and while forming on the beach a slight skirmish took place with such of the inhabitants of the town, as fled for shelter to the castle. The troops then advanced towards the fortress, which is described to have had walls fourteen feet thick, pierced with loop holes, and only one entrance through a small gate, well cased with iron bars and bolts, in the strongest manner. With a howitzer taken for the occasion, it was intended to have blown this gate open, and to have taken the place by storm; but on reaching it while the ranks opened, and the men sought to surround the castle to seek for some other entrance at the same time, they were picked off so rapidly and unexpectedly from the loop holes above, that a general flight took place, the howitzer was abandoned, even before it had been fired, and both the officers and the troops sought shelter by lying down behind the ridges of sand and little hillocks immediately underneath the castle walls. An Irish officer, jumping up from his hiding place, and calling on some of his comrades to follow him in an attempt to rescue the howitzer, was killed in the enterprise. Such others as even raised their heads to look around them, were picked off by the musketry from above; and the whole of the troops lay therefore hidden in this way, until the darkness of the night favored their escape to the beach, where they embarked after sunset, the enemy having made no sally on them from the fort. A second summons was sent to the chief in the castle, threatening to bombard the town from a nearer anchorage if he did not submit, and no quarter afterwards shown. With the dawn of morning, all eyes were directed to the fortress, when, to the surprise of the whole squadron, a man was seen waving the British Union flag on the summit of its walls. It was lieutenant Hall, who commanded the Fury which was one of the vessels nearest the shore. During the night he had gone on shore alone, taking an union-jack in his hand, and advanced singly to the castle gate. The fortress had already been abandoned by the greater number of the inhabitants, but some few still remained there. These fled at the approach of an individual supposing him to be the herald of those who were to follow. Be this as it may, the castle was entirely abandoned, and the British flag waived on its walls by this daring officer, to the surprise and admiration of all the fleet. The town and fortifications were then taken possession of. After sweeping round the bottom of the gulf, the expedition returned to Muscat.

On the sailing of the fleet from hence, the forces were augmented by a body of troops belonging to the Imaun of Muscat, destined to assist in the recovery of a place called Shenaz, on the coast, taken by the Joassamees. On their arrival at this place, a summons was sent, commanding the fort to surrender, which being refused, a bombardment was opened from the ships and boats, but without producing much effect. On the following morning, the whole of the troops were landed, and a regular encampment formed on the shore, with sand batteries, and other necessary works for a siege. After several days bombardment, in which about four thousand shot and shells were discharged against the fortress, to which the people had fled for refuge after burning down the town, a breach was reported to be practicable, and the castle was accordingly stormed. The resistance still made was desperate; the Arabs fighting as long as they could wield the sword, and even thrusting their spears up through the fragments of towers, in whose ruins they remained irrevocably buried. The loss in killed and wounded was upwards of a thousand men. Notwithstanding that the object of this expedition might be said to be incomplete, inasmuch as nothing less than a *total* extirpation of their race could secure the tranquility of these seas, yet the effect produced by this expedition was such, as to make them reverence or dread the British flag for several years afterwards.

The daring Intrepidity of Lieut. Hall

***The daring Intrepidity of Lieut. Hall.***

At length in 1815, their boats began to infest the entrance to the Red Sea; and in 1816, their numbers had so increased on that coast, that a squadron of them commanded by a chief called Ameer Ibrahim, captured within sight of Mocha, four vessels bound from Surat to that port, richly laden and navigating under the British flag, and the crews were massacred.

A squadron consisting of His Majesty's ship Challenger, Captain Brydges, and the East India Company's cruisers, Mercury, Ariel, and Vestal, were despatched to the chief port of the Joassamees, Ras-el-Khyma. Mr. Buckingham the Great Oriental traveller, accompanied the expedition from Bushire. Upon their arrival at Ras-el-Khyma, a demand was made for the restoration of the four Surat vessels and their cargoes; or in lieu thereof twelve lacks of rupees. Also that the commander of the piratical squadron, Ameer Ibrahim, should be delivered up for punishment. The demand was made by letter, and answer being received, Captain Brydges determined to go on shore and have an interview with the Pirate Chieftain. Mr. Buckingham (says,) He requested me to accompany him on shore as an interpreter. I readily assented. We quitted the ship together about 9 o'clock, and pulled straight to the shore, sounding all the way as we went, and gradually shoaling our water from six to two fathoms, within a quarter of a mile of the beach, where four large dows lay at anchor, ranged in a line, with their heads seaward, each of them mounting several pieces of cannon, and being full of men. On landing on the beach, we found its whole length guarded by a line of armed men, some bearing muskets, but the greater part armed with swords, shields, and spears; most of them were negroes, whom the Joassamees spare in their wars, looking on them rather as property and merchandise, than in the light of enemies. We were permitted to pass this line, and upon our communicating our wish to see the chief, we were conducted to the gate of the principal building, nearly in the centre of the town, and were met by the Pirate Chieftain attended by fifty armed men. I offered him the Mahometan salutation of peace, which he returned without hesitation.

The chief, Hassan ben Rahma, whom we had seen, was a small man, apparently about forty years of age, with an expression of cunning in his looks, and something particularly sarcastic in his smile. He was dressed in the usual Arab garments, with a cashmeer shawl, turban, and a scarlet benish, of the Persian form, to distinguish him from his followers. There were habited in the plainest garments. One of his eyes had been wounded, but his other features were good, his teeth beautifully white and regular, and his complexion very dark.

The town of Ras-el-Khyma stands on a narrow tongue of sandy land, pointing to the northeastward, presenting its northwest edge to the open sea, and its southeast one to a creek, which runs up within it to the southwestward, and affords a safe harbor for boats. There appeared to be no continued wall of defence around it, though round towers and portions of walls were seen in several parts, probably once connected in line, but not yet repaired since their destruction. The strongest points of defence appear to be in a fortress at the northeast angle, and a double round tower, near the centre of the town; in each of which, guns are mounted; but all the other towers appear to afford only shelter for musketeers. The rest of the town is composed of ordinary buildings of unhewn stone, and huts of rushes and long grass, with narrow avenues winding between them. The present number of inhabitants may be computed at ten thousand at least. They are thought to have at present (1816), sixty large boats out from their own port, manned with crews of from eighty, to three hundred men each, and forty other boats that belong to other ports. Their force concentrated, would probably amount to at least one hundred boats and eight thousand fighting men. After several fruitless negociations, the signal was now made to weigh, and stand closer in towards the town. It was then followed by the signal to engage the enemy. The squadron bore down nearly in line, under easy sail, and with the wind right aft, or on shore; the Mercury being on the starboard bow, the Challenger next in order, in the centre, the Vestal following in the same line, and the Ariel completing the division.

A large fleet of small boats were seen standing in from Cape Mussundum, at the same time; but these escaped by keeping closer along shore, and at length passing over the bar and getting into the back water behind the town. The squadron continued to stand on in a direct line towards the four anchored dows, gradually shoaling from the depth of our anchorage to two and a half fathoms, where stream anchors were dropped under foot, with springs on the cables, so that each vessel lay with her broadside to the shore. A fire was now opened by the whole squadron, directed to the four dows. These boats were full of men, brandishing their weapons in the air, their whole number exceeding, probably, six hundred. Some of the shot from the few long guns of the squadron reached the shore, and were buried in the sand; others fell across the bows and near the hulls of the dows to which they were directed; but the cannonades all fell short, as we were then fully a mile from the beach.

The Arab colors were displayed on all the forts; crowds of armed men were assembled on the beach, bearing large banners on poles, and dancing around them with their arms, as if rallying around a sacred standard, so that no sign of submission or conquest was witnessed throughout. The Ariel continued to discharge about fifty shot after all the others had desisted, but with as little avail as before, and thus ended this wordy negociation, and the bloodless battle to which it eventually led.

In 1818, these pirates grew so daring that they made an irruption into the Indian Ocean, and plundered vessels and towns on the islands and coasts. A fleet was sent against them, and intercepted them off Ashlola Island, proceeding to the westward in three divisions; and drove them back into the gulf. The Eden and Psyche fell in with two trankies, and these were so closely pursued that they were obliged to drop a small captured boat they had in tow. The Thetes one day kept in close chase of seventeen vessels, but they were enabled to get away owing to their superior sailing. The cruisers met with the Joassamees seventeen times and were constantly employed in hunting them from place to place.

At length, in 1819, they became such a scourge to commerce that a formidable expedition under the command of Major General Sir W. Grant Keir, sailed against them. It arrived before the chief town in December, and commenced operations. In his despatches Gen. Keir says–

I have the satisfaction to report the town of Ras-el Khyma, after a resistance of six days, was taken possession of this morning by the force under my command.

On the 18th, after completing my arrangements at Muscat, the Liverpool sailed for the rendezvous at Kishme; on the 21st, we fell in with the fleet of the Persian Gulf and anchored off the island of Larrack on the 24th November.

As it appeared probable that a considerable period would elapse before the junction of the ships which were detained at Bombay, I conceived it would prove highly advantageous to avail myself of all the information that could be procured respecting the strength and resources of the pirates we had to deal with.

No time was lost in making the necessary preparations for landing, which was effected the following morning without opposition, at a spot which had been previously selected for that purpose, about two miles to the westward of the town. The troops were formed across the isthmus connecting the peninsula on which the town is situated with the neighboring country, and the whole of the day was occupied in getting the tents on shore, to shelter the men from rain, landing engineers, tools, sand bags, c., and making arrangements preparatory to commencing our approaches the next day. On the morning of the 4th, our light troops were ordered in advance, supported by the pickets, to dislodge the enemy from a bank within nine hundred yards of the outer fort, which was expected to afford good cover for the men. The whole of the light companies of the force under Capt. Backhouse, moved forward, and drove the Arabs with great gallantry from a date grove, and over the bank close under the walls of the fort, followed by the pickets under Major Molesworth, who took post at the sand banks, whilst the European light troops were skirmishing in front. The enemy kept up a sharp fire of musketry and cannon; during these movements, Major Molesworth, a gallant officer was here killed. The troops kept their position during the day, and in the night effected a lodgment within three hundred yards of the southernmost tower, and erected a battery of four guns, together with a mortar battery.

The weather having become rather unfavorable for the disembarkation of the stores required for the siege, but this important object being effected on the morning of the 6th, we were enabled to open three eighteen pounders on the fort, a couple of howitzers, and six pounders were also placed in the battery on the right, which played on the defences of the towers and nearly silenced the enemy's fire, who, during the whole of our progress exhibited a considerable degree of resolution in withstanding, and ingenuity in counteracting our attacks, sallied out at 8 o'clock this evening along the whole front of our entrenchments, crept close up to the mortar battery without being perceived, and entered it over the parapet, after spearing the advance sentries. The party which occupied it were obliged to retire, but being immediately reinforced charged the assailants, who were driven out of the battery with great loss. The enemy repeated his attacks towards morning but was vigorously repulsed. During the seventh every exertion was made to land and bring up the remaining guns and mortars, which was accomplished during the night. They were immediately placed in the battery, together with two twenty-four pounders which were landed from the Liverpool, and in the morning the whole of the ordnance opened on the fort and fired with scarcely any intermission till sunset, when the breach on the curtain was reported nearly practicable and the towers almost untenable. Immediate arrangements were made for the assault, and the troops ordered to move down to the entrenchments by daylight the next morning. The party moved forward about 8 o'clock, and entered the fort through the breaches without firing a shot, and it soon appeared the enemy had evacuated the place. The town was taken possession of and found almost entirely deserted, only eighteen or twenty men, and a few women remaining in their houses.

The expedition next proceeded against Rumps, a piratical town, eight miles north of Ras-el-Khyma, but the inhabitants abandoned the town and took refuge in the hill fort of Zyah, which is situated at the head of a navigable creek nearly two miles from the sea coast. This place was the residence of Hussein Bin Alley, a sheikh of considerable importance among the Joassamee tribes, and a person who from his talents and lawless habits, as well as from the strength and advantageous situation of the fort, was likely to attempt the revival of the piratical system upon the first occasion. It became a desirable object to reduce the power of this chieftain.

On the 18th December, the troops embarked at Ras-el-Khyma, at day break in the boats of the fleet under command of Major Warren, with the 65th regiment and the flank companies of the first and second regiment, and at noon arrived within four miles of their destination. This operation was attended with considerable difficulty and risk, owing to the heavy surf that beat on the shore; and which was the occasion of some loss of ammunition, and of a few boats being upset and stove in.

The Sheikh of Rumps.

***The Sheikh of Rumps.***

At half past three P.M., having refreshed the men, (says Major Warren) we commenced our march, and fording the creek or back water, took up our position at sunset, to the northeastward of the fort, the enemy firing at us as we passed, notwithstanding that our messenger, whom we had previously sent in to summon the Sheikh, was still in the place; and I lost no time in pushing our riflemen and pickets as far forward as I could without exposing them too much to the firing of the enemy, whom I found strongly posted under secure cover in the date tree groves in front of the town. Captain Cocke, with the light company of his battalion, was at the same time sent to the westward, to cut off the retreat of the enemy on that side.

At day break the next morning, finding it necessary to drive the enemy still further in, to get a nearer view of his defences, I moved forward the rifle company of the 65th regiment, and after a considerable opposition from the enemy, I succeeded in forcing him to retire some distance; but not without disputing every inch of ground, which was well calculated for resistance, being intersected at every few yards, by banks and water courses raised for the purpose of irrigation, and covered with date trees. The next morning the riflemen, supported by the pickets, were again called into play, and soon established their position within three and four hundred yards of the town, which with the base of the hill, was so completely surrounded, as to render the escape of any of the garrison now almost impossible. This advantage was gained by a severe loss. Two twenty-four pounders and the two twelves, the landing of which had been retarded by the difficulty of communication with the fleet from which we derived all our supplies, having been now brought on shore, we broke ground in the evening, and notwithstanding the rocky soil, had them to play next morning at daylight.

Aware, however, that the families of the enemy were still in the town, and humanity dictating that some effort should be made to save the innocent from the fate that awaited the guilty; an opportunity was afforded for that purpose by an offer to the garrison of security to their women and children, should they be sent out within the hour; but the infatuated chief, either from an idea that his fort on the hill was not to be reached by our shot, or with the vain hope to gain time by procrastination, returning no answer to our communication, while he detained our messenger; we opened our fire at half past eight in the morning, and such was the precision of the practice, that in two hours we perceived the breach would soon be practicable. I was in the act of ordering the assault, when a white flag was displayed; and the enemy, after some little delay in assembling from the different quarters of the place, marched out without their arms, with Hussein Bin Alley at their head, to the number of three hundred and ninety-eight; and at half past one P.M., the British flags were hoisted on the hill fort and at the Sheikh's house. The women and children to the number of four hundred, were at the same time collected together in a place of security, and sent on board the fleet, together with the men. The service has been short but arduous; the enemy defended themselves with great obstinacy and ability worthy of a better cause.

From two prisoners retaken from the Joassamees, they learnt that the plunder is made a general stock, and distributed by the chief, but in what proportions the deponents cannot say; water is generally very scarce. There is a quantity of fish caught on the bank, upon which and dates they live. There were a few horses, camels, cows, sheep, and goats; the greatest part of which they took with them; they were in general lean, as the sandy plain produces little or no vegetation, except a few dates and cocoa-nut trees. The pirates who abandoned Ras-el-Khyma, encamped about three miles in the interior, ready to retreat into the desert at a moment's warning. The Sheikh of Rumps is an old man, but looks intelligent, and is said to be the man who advises upon all occasions the movements of the different tribes of pirates on the coast, and when he was told that it was the wish of the Company to put a stop to their piracy, and make an honest people of them by encouraging them to trade, seemed to regret much that those intentions were not made known, as they would have been most readily embraced. Rumps is the key to Ras-el-Khyma, and by its strength is defended from a strong banditti infesting the mountains, as also the Bedouin Arabs who are their enemies. A British garrison of twelve hundred men was stationed at Ras-el-Khyma, and a guard-ship. The other places sent in tokens of submission, as driven out of their fortresses on the margin of the sea, they had to contend within with the interior hostile tribes.

The Pirate Stronghold.

*The Pirate Stronghold.*

**THE BARBAROUS CONDUCT AND ROMANTIC DEATH OF THE JOASSAMEE CHIEF, RAHMAH-BEN-JABIR.**

The town of Bushire, on the Persian Gulf is seated in a low peninsula of sand, extending out of the general line of the coast, so as to form a bay on both sides. One of these bays was in 1816, occupied by the fleet of a certain Arab, named Rahmah-ben-Jabir, who has been for more than twenty years the terror of the gulf, and who was the most successful and the most generally tolerated pirate, perhaps, that ever infested any sea. This man by birth was a native of Grain, on the opposite coast, and nephew of the governor of that place. His fellow citizens had all the honesty, however, to declare him an outlaw, from abhorrence of his profession; but he found that aid and protection at Bushire, which his own townsmen denied him. With five or six vessels, most of which were very large, and manned with crews of from two to three hundred each, he sallied forth, and captured whatever he thought himself strong enough to carry off as a prize. His followers, to the number of two thousand, were maintained by the plunder of his prizes; and as the most of these were his own bought African slaves, and the remainder equally subject to his authority, he was sometimes as prodigal of their lives in a fit of anger as he was of his enemies, whom he was not content to slay in battle only, but basely murdered in cold blood, after they had submitted. An instance is related of his having put a great number of his own crew, who used mutinous expressions, into a tank on board, in which they usually kept their water, and this being shut close at the top, the poor wretches were all suffocated, and afterwards thrown overboard. This butcher chief, like the celebrated Djezzar of Acre, affecting great simplicity of dress, manners, and living; and whenever he went out, could not be distinguished by a stranger from the crowd of his attendants. He carried this simplicity to a degree of filthiness, which was disgusting, as his usual dress was a shirt, which was never taken off to be washed, from the time it was first put on till worn out; no drawers or coverings for the legs of any kind, and a large black goat's hair cloak, wrapped over all with a greasy and dirty handkerchief, called the keffeea, thrown loosely over his head. Infamous as was this man's life and character, he was not only cherished and courted by the people of Bushire, who dreaded him, but was courteously received and respectfully entertained whenever he visited the

British Factory. On one occasion (says Mr. Buckingham), at which I was present, he was sent for to give some medical gentlemen of the navy and company's cruisers an opportunity of inspecting his arm, which had been severely wounded. The wound was at first made by grape-shot and splinters, and the arm was one mass of blood about the part for several days, while the man himself was with difficulty known to be alive. He gradually recovered, however, without surgical aid, and the bone of the arm between the shoulder and elbow being completely shivered to pieces, the fragments progressively worked out, and the singular appearance was left of the fore arm and elbow connected to the shoulder by flesh and skin, and tendons, without the least vestige of bone. This man when invited to the factory for the purpose of making an exhibition of his arm, was himself admitted to sit at the table and take some tea, as it was breakfast time, and some of his followers took chairs around him. They were all as disgustingly filthy in appearance as could well be imagined; and some of them did not scruple to hunt for vermin on their skins, of which there was an abundance, and throw them on the floor. Rahmah-ben-Jabir's figure presented a meagre trunk, with four lank members, all of them cut and hacked, and pierced with wounds of sabres, spears and bullets, in every part, to the number, perhaps of more than twenty different wounds. He had, besides, a face naturally ferocious and ugly, and now rendered still more so by several scars there, and by the loss of one eye. When asked by one of the English gentlemen present, with a tone of encouragement and familiarity, whether he could not still dispatch an enemy with his boneless arm, he drew a crooked dagger, or yambeah, from the girdle round his shirt, and placing his left hand, which was sound, to support the elbow of the right, which was the one that was wounded, he grasped the dagger firmly with his clenched fist, and drew it back ward and forward, twirling it at the same time, and saying that he desired nothing better than to have the cutting of as many throats as he could effectually open with his lame hand. Instead of being shocked at the uttering of such a brutal wish, and such a savage triumph at still possessing the power to murder unoffending victims, I knew not how to describe my feelings of shame and sorrow when a loud roar of laughter burst from the whole assembly, when I ventured to express my dissent from the general feeling of admiration for such a man.

Rahmah-ben-Jabir, a Joassamee Chief

**Rahmah-ben-Jabir, a Joassamee Chief.**

This barbarous pirate in the year 1827, at last experienced a fate characteristic of the whole course of his life. His violent aggressions having united the Arabs of Bahrene and Ratiffe against him they blockaded his port of Daman from which Rahmah-ben-Jabir, having left a garrison in the fort under his son, had sailed in a well appointed bungalow, for the purpose of endeavoring to raise a confederacy of his friends in his support. Having failed in this object he returned to Daman, and in spite of the boats blockading the port, succeeded in visiting his garrison, and immediately re-embarked, taking with him his youngest son. On arriving on board his bungalow, he was received by his followers with a salute, which decisive indication of his presence immediately attracted the attention of his opponents, one of whose boats, commanded by the nephew of the Sheikh of Bahrene, proceeded to attack him. A desperate struggle ensued, and the Sheikh finding after some time that he had lost nearly the whole of his crew by the firing of Rahmah's boat, retired for reinforcements. These being obtained, he immediately returned singly to the contest. The fight was renewed with redoubled fury; when at last, Rahmah, being informed (for he had been long blind) that his men were falling fast around him, mustered the remainder of the crew, and issued orders to close and grapple with his opponent. When this was effected, and after embracing his son, he was led with a lighted torch to the magazine, which instantly exploded, blowing his own boat to atoms and setting fire to the Sheikh's, which immediately afterwards shared the same fate. Sheikh Ahmed and few of his followers escaped to the other boats; but only one of Rahmah's brave crew was saved; and it is supposed that upwards of three hundred men were killed in this heroic contest.

Page 71 Illustration

## THE LIFE OF LAFITTE, THE FAMOUS PIRATE OF THE GULF OF MEXICO.

With a History of the Pirates of Barrataria–and an account of their volunteering for the defence of New Orleans; and their daring intrepidity under General Jackson, during the battle of the 8th of January, 1815. For which important service they were pardoned by President Madison.

Jean Lafitte, was born at St. Maloes in France, in 1781, and went to sea at the age of thirteen; after several voyages in Europe, and to the coast of Africa, he was appointed mate of a French East Indiaman, bound to Madras. On the outward passage they encountered a heavy gale off the Cape of Good Hope, which sprung the mainmast and otherwise injured the ship, which determined the captain to bear up for the Mauritius, where he arrived in safety; a quarrel having taken place on the passage out between Lafitte and the captain, he abandoned the ship and refused to continue the voyage. Several privateers were at this time fitting out at this island, and Lafitte was appointed captain of one of these vessels; after a cruise during which he robbed the vessels of other nations, besides those of England, and thus committing piracy, he stopped at the Seychelles, and took in a load of slaves for the Mauritius; but being chased by an English frigate as far north as the equator, he found himself in a very awkward condition; not having provisions enough on board his ship to carry him back to the French Colony. He therefore conceived the bold project of proceeding to the Bay of Bengal, in order to get provisions from on board some English ships. In his ship of two hundred tons, with only two guns and twenty-six men, he attacked and took an English armed schooner with a numerous crew. After putting nineteen of his own crew on board the schooner, he took the command of her and proceeded to cruise upon the coast of Bengal. He there fell in with the Pagoda, a vessel belonging to the English East India Company, armed with twenty-six twelve pounders and manned with one hundred and fifty men. Expecting that the enemy would take him for a pilot of the Ganges, he manoeuvred accordingly. The Pagoda manifested no suspicions, whereupon he suddenly darted with his brave followers upon her decks, overturned all who opposed them, and speedily took the ship. After a very successful cruise he arrived safe at the Mauritius, and took the command of La Confiance of twenty-six guns and two hundred and fifty men, and sailed for the coast of British India. Off the Sand Heads in October, 1807, Lafitte fell in with the Queen East Indiaman, with a crew of near four hundred men, and carrying forty guns; he conceived the bold project of getting possession of her. Never was there beheld a more unequal conflict; even the height of the vessel compared to the feeble privateer augmented the chances against Lafitte; but the difficulty and danger far from discouraging this intrepid sailor, acted as an additional spur to his brilliant valor. After electrifying his crew with a few words of hope and ardor, he manoeuvred and ran on board of the enemy. In this position he received a broadside when close too; but he expected this, and made his men lay flat upon the deck. After the first fire they all rose, and from the yards and tops, threw bombs and grenades into the forecastle of the Indiaman. This sudden and unforeseen attack caused a great havoc. In an instant, death and terror made them abandon a part of the vessel near the mizen-mast. Lafitte, who observed every thing, seized the decisive moment, beat to arms, and forty of his crew prepared to board, with pistols in their hands and daggers held between their teeth. As soon as they got on deck, they rushed upon the affrighted crowd, who retreated to the steerage, and endeavored to defend themselves there. Lafitte thereupon ordered a second division to board, which he headed himself; the captain of the Indiaman was killed, and all were swept away in a moment. Lafitte caused a gun to be loaded with grape, which he pointed towards the place where the crowd was assembled, threatening to exterminate them. The English deeming resistance fruitless, surrendered, and Lafitte hastened to put a stop to the slaughter. This exploit, hitherto unparalleled, resounded through India, and the name of Lafitte became the terror of English commerce in these latitudes.

Lafitte boarding the Queen East Indiaman

***Lafitte boarding the Queen East Indiaman***

As British vessels now traversed the Indian Ocean under strong convoys, game became scarce, and Lafitte determined to visit France; and after doubling the Cape of Good Hope, he coasted up to the Gulf of Guinea, and in the Bight of Benin, took two valuable prizes loaded with gold dust, ivory, and Palm Oil; with this booty he reached St. Maloes in safety. After a short stay at his native place he fitted out a brigantine, mounting twenty guns and one hundred and fifty men, and sailed for Gaudaloupe; amongst the West India Islands, he made several valuable prizes; but during his absence on a cruise the island having been taken by the British, he proceeded to Carthagena, and from thence to Barrataria. After this period, the conduct of Lafitte at Barrataria does not appear to be characterized by the audacity and boldness of his former career; but he had amassed immense sums of booty, and as he was obliged to have dealings with the merchants of the United States, and the West Indies, who frequently owed him large sums, and the cautious dealings necessary to found and conduct a colony of Pirates and Smugglers in the very teeth of a civilized nation, obliged Lafitte to cloak as much as possible his real character.

Lafitte and his crew clearing the decks of the Indiaman.

**Lafitte and his crew clearing the decks of the Indiaman.**

As we have said before, at the period of the taking of Gaudaloupe by the British, most of the privateers commissioned by the government of that island, and which were then on a cruise, not being able to return to any of the West India Islands, made for Barrataria, there to take in a supply of water and provisions, recruit the health of their crews, and dispose of their prizes, which could not be admitted into any of the ports of the United States, we being at that time in peace with Great Britain. Most of the commissions granted to privateers by the French government at Gaudaloupe, having expired sometime after the declaration of the independence of Carthagena, many of the privateers repaired to that port, for the purpose of obtaining from the new government commissions for cruising against Spanish vessels. Having duly obtained their commissions, they in a manner blockaded for a long time all the ports belonging to the royalists, and made numerous captives, which they carried into Barrataria. Under this denomination is comprised part of the coast of Louisiana to the west of the mouths of the Mississippi, comprehended between Bastien bay on the east, and the mouths of the river or bayou la Fourche on the west. Not far from the sea are lakes called the great and little lakes of Barrataria, communicating with one another by several large bayous with a great number of branches. There is also the island of Barrataria, at the extremity of which is a place called the Temple, which denomination it owes to several mounds of shells thrown up there by the Indians. The name of Barrataria is also given to a large basin which extends the whole length of the cypress swamps, from the Gulf of Mexico to three miles above New Orleans. These waters disembogue into the gulf by two entrances of the bayou Barrataria, between which lies an island called Grand Terre, six miles in length, and from two to three miles in breadth, running parallel with the coast. In the western entrance is the great pass of Barrataria, which has from nine to ten feet of water. Within this pass about two leagues from the open sea, lies the only secure harbor on the coast, and accordingly this was the harbor frequented by the *Pirates*, so well known by the name of Barratarians.

At Grand Jerre, the privateers publicly made sale by auction, of the cargoes of their prizes. From all parts of Lower Louisiana, people resorted to Barrataria, without being at all solicitous to conceal the object of their journey. The most respectable inhabitants of the state, especially those living in the country, were in the habit of purchasing smuggled goods coming from Barrataria.

The government of the United States sent an expedition under Commodore Patterson, to disperse the settlement of marauders at Barrataria; the following is an extract of his letter to the secretary of war.

Sir–I have the honor to inform you that I departed from this city on the 11th June, accompanied by Col. Ross, with a detachment of seventy of the 44th regiment of infantry. On the 12th, reached the schooner Carolina, of Plaquemine, and formed a junction with the gun vessels at the Balize on the 13th, sailed from the southwest pass on the evening of the 15th, and at half past 8 o'clock, A.M. on the 16th, made the Island of Barrataria, and discovered a number of vessels in the harbor, some of which shewed Carthagenian colors. At 2 o'clock, perceived the pirates forming their vessels, ten in number, including prizes, into a line of battle near the entrance of the harbor, and making every preparation to offer me battle. At 10 o'clock, wind light and variable, formed the order of battle with six gun boats and the Sea Horse tender, mounting one six pounder and fifteen men, and a launch mounting one twelve pound carronade; the schooner Carolina, drawing too much water to cross the bar. At half past 10 o'clock, perceived several smokes along the coasts as signals, and at the same time a white flag hoisted on board a schooner at the fort, an American flag at the mainmast head and a Carthagenian flag (under which the pirates cruise) at her topping lift; replied with a white flag at my main; at 11 o'clock, discovered that the pirates had fired two of their best schooners; hauled down my white flag and made the *signal for battle*; hoisting with a large white flag bearing the words "Pardon for Deserters"; having heard there was a number on shore from the army and navy. At a quarter past 11 o'clock, two gun boats grounded and were passed agreeably to my previous orders, by the other four which entered the harbor, manned by my barge and the boats belonging to the grounded vessels, and proceeded in to my great disappointment. I perceived that the pirates abandoned their vessels, and were flying in all directions. I immediately sent the launch and two barges with small boats in pursuit of them. At meridian, took possession of all their vessels in the harbor consisting of six schooners and one felucca, cruisers, and prizes of the pirates, one brig, a prize, and two armed schooners under the Carthagenian flag, both in the line of battle, with the armed vessels of the pirates, and apparently with an intention to aid them in any resistance they might make against me, as their crews were at quarters, tompions out of their guns, and matches lighted. Col. Ross at the same time landed, and with his command took possession of their establishment on shore, consisting of about forty houses of different sizes, badly constructed, and thatched with palmetto leaves.

When I perceived the enemy forming their vessels into a line of battle I felt confident from their number and very advantageous position, and their number of men, that they would have fought me; their not doing so I regret; for had they, I should have been enabled more effectually to destroy or make prisoners of them and their leaders; but it is a subject of great satisfaction to me, to have effected the object of my enterprise, without the loss of a man.

The enemy had mounted on their vessels twenty pieces of cannon of different calibre; and as I have since learnt, from eight hundred, to one thousand men of all nations and colors.

Early in the morning of the 20th, the Carolina at anchor, about five miles distant, made the signal of a "strange sail in sight to eastward"; immediately after she weighed anchor, and gave chase the strange sail, standing for Grand Terre, with all sail; at half past 8 o'clock, the chase hauled her wind off shore to escape; sent acting Lieut. Spedding with four boats manned and armed to prevent her passing the harbor; at 9 o'clock A.M., the chase fired upon the Carolina, which was returned; each vessel continued firing during the chase, when their long guns could reach. At 10 o'clock, the chase grounded outside of the bar, at which time the Carolina was from the shoalness of the water obliged to haul her wind off shore and give up the chase; opened a fire upon the chase across the island from the gun vessels. At half past 10 o'clock, she hauled down her colors and was taken possession of. She proved to be the armed schooner Gen. Boliver; by grounding she broke both her rudder pintles and made water; took from her her armament, consisting of one long brass eighteen pounder, one long brass six pounder, two twelve pounders, small arms, c., and twenty-one packages of dry goods. On the afternoon of the 23d, got underway with the whole squadron, in all seventeen vessels, but during the night one escaped, and the next day arrived at New Orleans with my whole squadron.

At different times the English had sought to attack the pirates at Barrataria, in hopes of taking their prizes, and even their armed vessels. Of these attempts of the British, suffice it to instance that of June 23d, 1813, when two privateers being at anchor off Cat Island, a British sloop of war anchored at the entrance of the pass, and sent her boats to endeavor to take the privateers; but they were repulsed with considerable loss.

Such was the state of affairs, when on the 2d Sept., 1814, there appeared an armed brig on the coast opposite the pass. She fired a gun at a vessel about to enter, and forced her to run aground; she then tacked and shortly after came to an anchor at the entrance of the pass. It was not easy to understand the intentions of this vessel, who, having commenced with hostilities on her first appearance now seemed to announce an amicable disposition. Mr. Lafitte then went off in a boat to examine her, venturing so far that he could not escape from the pinnace sent from the brig, and making towards the shore, bearing British colors and a flag of truce. In this pinnace were two naval officers. One was Capt. Lockyer, commander of the brig. The first question they asked was, where was Mr. Lafitte? he not choosing to make himself known to them, replied that the person they inquired for was on shore. They then delivered to him a packet directed to Mr. Lafitte, Barrataria, requesting him to take particular care of it, and to deliver it into Mr. Lafitte's hands. He prevailed on them to make for the shore, and as soon as they got near enough to be in his power, he made himself known, recommending to them at the same time to conceal the business on which they had come. Upwards of two hundred persons lined the shore, and it was a general cry amongst the crews of the privateers at Grand Terre, that those British officers should be made prisoners and sent to New Orleans as spies. It was with much difficulty that Lafitte dissuaded the multitude from this intent, and led the officers in safety to his dwelling. He thought very prudently that the papers contained in the packet might be of importance towards the safety of the country and that the officers if well watched could obtain no intelligence that might turn to the detriment of Louisiana. He now examined the contents of the packet, in which he found a proclamation addressed by Col. Edward Nichalls, in the service of his Brittanic Majesty, and commander of the land forces on the coast of Florida, to the inhabitants of Louisiana. A letter from the same to Mr. Lafitte, the commander of Barrataria; an official letter from the honorable W.H. Percy, captain of the sloop of war Hermes, directed to Lafitte. When he had perused these letters, Capt. Lockyer enlarged on the subject of them and proposed to him to enter into the service of his Brittanic Majesty with the rank of post captain and to receive the command of a 44 gun frigate. Also all those under his command, or over whom he had sufficient influence. He was also offered thirty thousand dollars, payable at Pensacola, and urged him not to let slip this opportunity of acquiring fortune and consideration. On Lafitte's requiring a few days to reflect upon these proposals, Capt. Lockyer observed to him that no reflection could be necessary, respecting proposals that obviously precluded hesitation, as he was a Frenchman and proscribed by the American government. But to all his splendid promises and daring insinuations, Lafitte replied that in a few days he would give a final answer; his object in this procrastination being to gain time to inform the officers of the state government of this nefarious project. Having occasion to go to some distance for a short time, the persons who had proposed to send the British officers prisoners to New Orleans, went and seized them in his absence, and confined both them and the crew of the pinnace, in a secure place, leaving a guard at the door. The British officers sent for Lafitte;

but he, fearing an insurrection of the crews of the privateers, thought it advisable not to see them until he had first persuaded their captains and officers to desist from the measures on which they seemed bent. With this view he represented to the latter that, besides the infamy that would attach to them if they treated as prisoners people who had come with a flag of truce, they would lose the opportunity of discovering the projects of the British against Louisiana.

Early the next morning Lafitte caused them to be released from their confinement and saw them safe on board their pinnace, apologizing the detention. He now wrote to Capt. Lockyer the following letter.

To CAPTAIN LOCKYER.

*Barrataria, 4th Sept.* 1814.

Sir–The confusion which prevailed in our camp yesterday and this morning, and of which you have a complete knowledge, has prevented me from answering in a precise manner to the object of your mission; nor even at this moment can I give you all the satisfaction that you desire; however, if you could grant me a fortnight, I would be entirely at your disposal at the end of that time. This delay is indispensable to enable me to put my affairs in order. You may communicate with me by sending a boat to the eastern point of the pass, where I will be found. You have inspired me with more confidence than the admiral, your superior officer, could have done himself; with you alone, I wish to deal, and from you also I will claim, in due time the reward of the services, which I may render to you. Yours, c.

J. LAFITTE.

His object in writing that letter was, by appearing disposed to accede to their proposals, to give time to communicate the affair to the officers of the state government, and to receive from them instructions how to act, under circumstances so critical and important to the country. He accordingly wrote on the 4th September to Mr. Blanque, one of the representatives of the state, sending him all the papers delivered to him by the British officers with a letter addressed to his excellency, Gov. Claiborne of the state of Louisiana.

To Gov. CLAIBORNE.

*Barrataria, Sept. 4th*, 1814.

Sir–In the firm persuasion that the choice made of you to fill the office of first magistrate of this state, was dictated by the esteem of your fellow citizens, and was conferred on merit, I confidently address you on an affair on which may depend the safety of this country. I offer to you to restore to this state several citizens, who perhaps in your eyes have lost that sacred title. I offer you them, however, such as you could wish to find them, ready to exert their utmost efforts in defence of the country. This point of Louisiana, which I occupy, is of great importance in the present crisis. I tender my services to defend it; and the only reward I ask is that a stop be put to the proscription against me and my adherents, by an act of oblivion, for all that has been done hitherto. I am the stray sheep wishing to return to the fold. If you are thoroughly acquainted with the nature of my offences, I should appear to you much less guilty, and still worthy to discharge the duties of a good citizen. I have never sailed under any flag but that of the republic of Carthagena, and my vessels are perfectly regular in that respect. If I could have brought my lawful prizes into the ports of this state, I should not have employed the illicit means that have caused me to be proscribed. I decline saying more on the subject, until I have the honor of your excellency's answer, which I am persuaded can be dictated only by wisdom. Should your answer not be favorable to my ardent desires, I declare to you that I will instantly leave the country, to avoid the imputation of having cooperated towards an invasion on this point, which cannot fail to take place, and to rest secure in the acquittal of my conscience.

I have the honor to be

your excellency's, c.

J. LAFITTE.

The contents of these letters do honor to Lafitte's judgment, and evince his sincere attachment to the American cause. On the receipt of this packet from Lafitte, Mr. Blanque immediately laid its contents before the governor, who convened the committee of defence lately formed of which he was president; and Mr. Rancher the bearer of Lafitte's packet, was sent back with a verbal answer to desire Lafitte to take no steps until it should be determined what was expedient to be done; the message also contained an assurance that, in the meantime no steps should be taken against him for his past offences against the laws of the United States.

At the expiration of the time agreed on with Captain Lockyer, his ship appeared again on the coast with two others, and continued standing off and on before the pass for several days. But he pretended not to perceive the return of the sloop of war, who tired of waiting to no purpose put out to sea and disappeared.

Lafitte having received a guarantee from General Jackson for his safe passage from Barrataria to New Orleans and back, he proceeded forthwith to the city where he had an interview with Gov. Claiborne and the General. After the usual formalities and courtesies had taken place between these gentlemen, Lafitte addressed the Governor of Louisiana nearly as follows. I have offered to defend for you that part of Louisiana I now hold. But not as an outlaw, would I be its defender. In that confidence, with which you have inspired me, I offer to restore to the state many citizens, now under my command. As I have remarked before, the point I occupy is of great importance in the present crisis. I tender not only my own services to defend it, but those of all I command; and the only reward I ask, is, that a stop be put to the proscription against me and my adherents, by an act of oblivion for all that has been done hitherto.

"My dear sir," said the Governor, who together with General Jackson, was impressed with admiration of his sentiments, "your praiseworthy wishes shall be laid before the council of the state, and I will confer with my August friend here present, upon this important affair, and send you an answer to-morrow." At Lafitte withdrew, the General said farewell; when we meet again, I trust it will be in the ranks of the American army. The result of the conference was the issuing the following order.

Interview between Lafitte, General Jackson, and Governor Claiborne

***Interview between Lafitte, General Jackson, and Governor Claiborne.***

The Governor of Louisiana, informed that many individuals implicated in the offences heretofore committed against the United States at Barrataria, express a willingness at the present crisis to enroll themselves and march against the enemy.

He does hereby invite them to join the standard of the United States and is authorised to say, should their conduct in the field meet the approbation of the Major General, that that officer will unite with the governor in a request to the president of the United States, to extend to each and every individual, so marching and acting, a free and full pardon. These general orders were placed in the hands of Lafitte, who circulated them among his dispersed followers, most of whom readily embraced the conditions of pardon they held out. In a few days many brave men and skillful artillerists, whose services contributed greatly to the safety of the invaded state, flocked to the standard of the United States, and by their conduct, received the highest approbation of General Jackson.

BY THE PRESIDENT OF THE UNITED STATES OF AMERICA.
A PROCLAMATION.

"Among the many evils produced by the wars, which, with little intermission, have afflicted Europe, and extended their ravages into other quarters of the globe, for a period exceeding twenty years, the dispersion of a considerable portion of the inhabitants of different countries, in sorrow and in want, has not been the least injurious to human happiness, nor the least severe in the trial of human virtue.

"It had been long ascertained that many foreigners, flying from the dangers of their own home, and that some citizens, forgetful of their duty, had co-operated in forming an establishment on the island of Barrataria, near the mouth of the river Mississippi, for the purpose of a clandestine and lawless trade. The government of the United States caused the establishment to be broken up and destroyed; and, having obtained the means of designating the offenders of every description, it only remained to answer the demands of justice by inflicting an exemplary punishment.

"But it has since been represented that the offenders have manifested a sincere penitence; that they have abandoned the prosecution of the worst cause for the support of the best, and, particularly, that they have exhibited, in the defence of New Orleans, unequivocal traits of courage and fidelity. Offenders, who have refused to become the associates of the enemy in the war, upon the most seducing terms of invitation; and who have aided to repel his hostile invasion of the territory of the United States, can no longer be considered as objects of punishment, but as objects of a generous forgiveness.

"It has therefore been seen, with great satisfaction, that the General Assembly of the State of Louisiana earnestly recommend those offenders to the benefit of a full pardon; And in compliance with that recommendation, as well as in consideration of all the other extraordinary circumstances in the case, I, *James Madison*, President of the United States of America, do issue this proclamation, hereby granting, publishing and declaring, a free and full pardon of all offences committed in violation of any act or acts of the Congress of the said United States, touching the revenue, trade and navigation thereof, or touching the intercourse and commerce of the United States with foreign nations, at any time before the eighth day of January, in the present year one thousand eight hundred and fifteen, by any person or persons whatsoever, being inhabitants of New Orleans and the adjacent country, or being inhabitants of the said island of Barrataria, and the places adjacent; *Provided*, that every person, claiming the benefit of this full pardon, in order to entitle himself thereto, shall produce a certificate in writing from the governor of the State of Louisiana, stating that such person has aided in the defence of New Orleans and the adjacent country, during the invasion thereof as aforesaid.

"And I do hereby further authorize and direct all suits, indictments, and prosecutions, for fines, penalties, and forfeitures, against any person or persons, who shall be entitled to the benefit of this full pardon, forthwith to be stayed, discontinued and released: All civil officers are hereby required, according to the duties of their respective stations, to carry this proclamation into immediate and faithful execution.

"Done at the City of Washington, the sixth day of February, in the year one thousand eight hundred and fifteen, and of the independence of the United States the thirty-ninth.

"By the President,
"JAMES MADISON
"JAMES MONROE,
"*Acting Secretary of State.*"

The morning of the eighth of January, was ushered in with the discharge of rockets, the sound of cannon, and the cheers of the British soldiers advancing to the attack. The Americans, behind the breastwork, awaited in calm intrepidity their approach. The enemy advanced in close column of sixty men in front, shouldering their muskets and carrying fascines and ladders. A storm of rockets preceded them, and an incessant fire opened from the battery, which commanded the advanced column. The musketry and rifles from the Kentuckians and Tennesseans, joined the fire of the artillery, and in a few moments was heard along the line a ceaseless, rolling fire, whose tremendous noise resembled the continued reverberation of thunder. One of these guns, a twenty-four pounder, placed upon the breastwork in the third embrasure from the river, drew, from the fatal skill and activity with which it was managed, even in the heat of battle, the admiration of both Americans and British; and became one of the points most dreaded by the advancing foe.

Here was stationed Lafitte and his lieutenant Dominique and a large band of his men, who during the continuance of the battle, fought with unparalleled bravery. The British already had been twice driven back in the utmost confusion, with the loss of their commander-in-chief, and two general officers.

Two other batteries were manned by the Barratarians, who served their pieces with the steadiness and precision of veteran gunners. In the first attack of the enemy, a column pushed forward between the levee and river; and so precipitate was their charge that the outposts were forced to retire, closely pressed by the enemy. Before the batteries could meet the charge, clearing the ditch, they gained the redoubt through the embrasures, leaping over the parapet, and overwhelming by their superior force the small party stationed there.

Lafitte, who was commanding in conjunction with his officers, at one of the guns, no sooner saw the bold movement of the enemy, than calling a few of his best men by his side, he sprung forward to the point of danger, and clearing the breastwork of the entrenchments, leaped, cutlass in hand, into the midst of the enemy, followed by a score of his men, who in many a hard fought battle upon his own deck, had been well tried.

Astonished at the intrepidity which could lead men to leave their entrenchments and meet them hand to hand, and pressed by the suddenness of the charge, which was made with the recklessness, skill and rapidity of practised boarders bounding upon the deck of an enemy's vessel, they began to give way, while one after another, two British officers fell before the cutlass of the pirate, as they were bravely encouraging their men. All the energies of the British were now concentrated to scale the breastwork, which one daring officer had already mounted. While Lafitte and his followers, seconding a gallant band of volunteer riflemen, formed a phalanx which they in vain assayed to penetrate.

The British finding it impossible to take the city and the havoc in their ranks being dreadful, made a precipitate retreat, leaving the field covered with their dead and wounded.

General Jackson, in his correspondence with the secretary of war did not fail to notice the conduct of the "Corsairs of Barrataria," who were, as we have already seen, employed in the artillery service. In the course of the campaign they proved, in an unequivocal manner, that they had been misjudged by the enemy, who a short time previous to the invasion of Louisiana, had hoped to enlist them in his cause. Many of them were killed or wounded in the defence of the country. Their zeal, their courage, and their skill, were remarked by the whole army, who could no longer consider such brave men as criminals. In a few days peace was declared between Great Britain and the United States.

The piratical establishment of Barrataria having been broken up and Lafitte not being content with leading an honest, peaceful life, procured some fast sailing vessels, and with a great number of his followers, proceeded to Galvezton Bay, in Texas, during the year 1819; where he received a commission from General Long; and had five vessels generally cruising and about 300 men. Two open boats bearing commissions from General Humbert, of Galvezton, having robbed a plantation on the Marmento river, of negroes, money, c., were captured in the Sabine river, by the boats of the United States schooner Lynx. One of the men was hung by Lafitte, who dreaded the vengeance of the American government. The Lynx also captured one of his schooners, and her prize that had been for a length of time smuggling in the Carmento. One of his cruisers, named the Jupiter, returned safe to Galvezton after a short cruise with a valuable cargo, principally specie; she was the first vessel that sailed under the authority of Texas. The American government well knowing that where Lafitte was, piracy and smuggling would be the order of the day, sent a vessel of war to cruise in the Gulf of Mexico, and scour the coasts of Texas. Lafitte having been appointed governor of Galvezton and one of the cruisers being stationed off the port to watch his motions, it so annoyed him that he wrote the following letter to her commander, Lieutenant Madison.

*To the commandant of the American cruiser, off the port of Galvezton.*

Sir–I am convinced that you are a cruiser of the navy, ordered by your government. I have therefore deemed it proper to inquire into the cause of your living before this port without communicating your intention. I shall by this message inform you, that the port of Galvezton belongs to and is in the possession of the republic of Texas, and was made a port of entry the 9th October last. And whereas the supreme congress of said republic have thought proper to appoint me as governor of this place, in consequence of which, if you have any demands on said government, or persons belonging to or residing in the same, you will please to send an officer with such demands, whom you may be assured will be treated with the greatest politeness, and receive every satisfaction required. But if you are ordered, or should attempt to enter this port in a hostile manner, my oath and duty to the government compels me to rebut your intentions at the expense of my life.

To prove to you my intentions towards the welfare and harmony of your government I send enclosed the declaration of several prisoners, who were taken in custody yesterday, and by a court of inquiry appointed for that purpose, were found guilty of robbing the inhabitants of the United States of a number of slaves and specie. The gentlemen bearing this message will give you any reasonable information relating to this place, that may be required.

Yours, c.

J. LAFITTE.

About this time one Mitchell, who had formerly belonged to Lafitte's gang, collected upwards of one hundred and fifty desperadoes and fortified himself on an island near Barrataria, with several pieces of cannon; and swore that he and all his comrades would perish within their trenches before they would surrender to any man. Four of this gang having gone to New Orleans on a frolic, information was given to the city watch, and the house surrounded, when the whole four with cocked pistols in both hands sallied out and marched through the crowd which made way for them and no person dared to make an attempt to arrest them.

The United States cutter, Alabama, on her way to the station off the mouth of the Mississippi, captured a piratical schooner belonging to Lafitte; she carried two guns and twenty-five men, and was fitted out at New Orleans, and commanded by one of Lafitte's lieutenants, named Le Fage; the schooner had a prize in company and being hailed by the cutter, poured into her a volley of musketry; the cutter then opened upon the privateer and a smart action ensued which terminated in favor of the cutter, which had four men wounded and two of them dangerously; but the pirate had six men killed; both vessels were captured and brought into the bayou St. John. An expedition was now sent to dislodge Mitchell and his comrades from the island he had taken possession of; after coming to anchor, a summons was sent for him to surrender, which was answered by a brisk cannonade from his breastwork. The vessels were warped close in shore; and the boats manned and sent on shore whilst the vessels opened upon the pirates; the boat's crews landed under a galling fire of grape shot and formed in the most undaunted manner; and although a severe loss was sustained they entered the breastwork at the point of the bayonet; after a desperate fight the pirates gave way, many were taken prisoners but Mitchell and the greatest part escaped to the cypress swamps where it was impossible to arrest them. A large quantity of dry goods and specie together with other booty was taken. Twenty of the pirates were taken and brought to New Orleans, and tried before Judge Hall, of the Circuit Court of the United States, sixteen were brought in guilty; and after the Judge had finished pronouncing sentence of death upon the hardened wretches, several of them cried out in open court, *Murder–by God.*

Accounts of these transactions having reached Lafitte, he plainly perceived there was a determination to sweep all his cruisers from the sea; and a war of extermination appeared to be waged against him.

In a fit of desperation he procured a large and fast sailing brigantine mounting sixteen guns and having selected a crew of one hundred and sixty men he started without any commission as a regular pirate determined to rob all nations and neither to give or receive quarter. A British sloop of war which was cruising in the Gulf of Mexico, having heard that Lafitte himself was at sea, kept a sharp look out from the mast head; when one morning as an officer was sweeping the horizon with his glass he discovered a long dark looking vessel, low in the water, but having very tall masts, with sails white as the driven snow. As the sloop of war had the weather gage of the pirate and could outsail her before the wind, she set her studding sails and crowded every inch of canvass in chase; as soon as Lafitte ascertained the character of his opponent, he ordered the awnings to be furled and set his big square-sail and shot rapidly through the water; but as the breeze freshened the sloop of war came up rapidly with the pirate, who, finding no chance of escaping, determined to sell his life as dearly as possible; the guns were cast loose and the shot handed up; and a fire opened upon the ship which killed a number of men and carried away her foretopmast, but she reserved her fire until within cable's distance of the pirate; when she fired a general discharge from her broadside, and a volley of small arms; the broadside was too much elevated to hit the low hull of the brigantine, but was not without effect; the foretopmast fell, the jaws of the main gaff were severed and a large proportion of the rigging came rattling down on deck; ten of the pirates were killed, but Lafitte remained unhurt. The sloop of war entered her men over the starboard bow and a terrific contest with pistols and cutlasses ensued; Lafitte received two wounds at this time which disabled him, a grape shot broke the bone of his right leg and he received a cut in the abdomen, but his crew fought like tigers and the deck was ankle deep with blood and gore; the captain of the boarders received such a tremendous blow on the head from the butt end of a musket, as stretched him senseless on the deck near Lafitte, who raised his dagger to stab him to the heart. But the tide of his existence was ebbing like a torrent, his brain was giddy, his aim faltered and the point descended in the Captain's right thigh; dragging away the blade with the last convulsive energy of a death struggle, he lacerated the wound. Again the reeking steel was upheld, and Lafitte placed his left hand near the Captain's heart, to make his aim more sure; again the dizziness of dissolution spread over his sight, down came the dagger into the captain's left thigh and Lafitte was a corpse.

The upper deck was cleared, and the boarders rushed below on the main deck to complete their conquest. Here the slaughter was dreadful, till the pirates called out for quarter, and the carnage ceased; all the pirates that surrendered were taken to Jamaica and tried before the Admiralty court where sixteen were condemned to die, six were subsequently pardoned and ten executed.

Death of Lafitte, the Pirate

***Death of Lafitte, the Pirate.***

Thus perished Lafitte, a man superior in talent, in knowledge of his profession, in courage, and moreover in physical strength; but unfortunately his reckless career was marked with crimes of the darkest dye.

Page 97 Illustration

**THE LIFE OF CAPTAIN ROBERTS.**

Bartholomew Roberts was trained to a sea-faring life. Among other voyages which he made during the time that he lawfully procured his maintenance, he sailed for the Guinea cost, in November, 1719, where he was taken by the pirate Davis. He was at first very averse to that mode of life, and would certainly have deserted, had an opportunity occurred. It happened to him, however, as to many upon another element, that preferment calmed his conscience, and reconciled him to that which he formerly hated.

Davis having fallen in the manner related, those who had assumed the title of Lords assembled to deliberate concerning the choice of a new commander. There were several candidates, who, by their services, had risen to eminence among their breathren, and each of them thought themselves qualified to bear rule. One addressed the assembled lords, saying, "that the good of the whole, and the maintenance of order, demanded a head, but that the proper authority was deposited in the community at large; so that if one should be elected who did not act and govern for the general good, he could be deposed, and another be substituted in his place."

"We are the original," said he, "of this claim, and should a captain be so saucy as to exceed prescription at any time, why, down with him! It will be a caution, after he is dead, to his successors, to what fatal results any undue assumption may lead; however, it is my advice, while be are sober, to pitch upon a man of courage, and one skilled in navigation,–one who, by his prudence and bravery, seems best able to defend this commonwealth, and ward us from the dangers and tempests of an unstable element, and the fatal consequences of anarchy; and such a one I take Roberts to be: a fellow in all respects worthy of your esteem and favor."

This speech was applauded by all but Lord Simpson, who had himself strong expectations of obtaining the highest command. He at last, in a surly tone, said, he did not regard whom they chose as a commander, provided he was not a papist, for he had conceived a mortal hatred to papists, because his father had been a sufferer in Monmouth's rebellion.

Thus, though Roberts had only been a few weeks among them, his election was confirmed by the Lords and Commons. He, with the best face he could, accepted of the dignity, saying, "that since he had dipped his hands in muddy water, and must be a pirate, it was better being a commander than a private man."

The governor being settled, and other officers chosen in the room of those who had fallen with Davis, it was resolved not to leave this place without revenging his death. Accordingly, thirty men, under the command of one Kennedy, a bold and profligate fellow, landed, and under cover of the fire of the ship, ascended the hill upon which the fort stood. They were no sooner discovered by the Portuguese, than they abandoned the fort, and took shelter in the town. The pirates then entered without opposition, set fire to the fort, and tumbled the guns into the sea.

Not satisfied with this injury, some proposed to land and set the town in flames. Roberts however, reminded them of the great danger to which this would inevitably expose them; that there was a thick wood at the back of the town, where the inhabitants could hide themselves, and that, when their all was at stake, they would make a bolder resistance: and that the burning or destroying of a few houses, would be a small return for their labor, and the loss that they might sustain. This prudent advice had the desired effect, and they contented themselves with lightening the French vessel, and battering down several houses of the town, to show their high displeasure.

Roberts sailed southward, captured a Dutch Guineaman, and, having emptied her of everything they thought proper, returned her to the commander. Two days after, he captured an English ship, and, as the men joined in pirating, emptied and burned the vessel, and then sailed for St. Thomas. Meeting with no prize, he sailed for Anamaboa, and there watered and repaired. Having again put to sea, a vote was taken whether they should sail for the East Indies or for Brazil. The latter place was decided upon, and they arrived there in twenty-eight days.

Upon this coast our rovers cruised for about nine weeks, keeping generally out of sight of land, but without seeing a sail; which discouraged them so, that they determined to leave the station, and steer for the West Indies; and, in order thereto, they stood in to make the land for the taking of their departure, by which means they fell in, unexpectedly, with a fleet of forty-two sail of Portuguese ships, off the Bay of Los Todos Santos, with all their lading in for Lisbon; several of them of good force, who lay there waiting for two men of war of seventy guns each for their convoy. However, Roberts thought it should go hard with him but he would make up his market among them, and thereupon he mixed with the fleet, and kept his men concealed till proper resolutions could be formed; that done, they came close up to one of the deepest, and ordered her to send the master on board quietly, threatening to give them no quarter, if any resistance or signal of distress was made. The Portuguese, being surprised at these threats, and the sudden flourish of cutlasses from the pirates, submitted without a word, and the captain came on board. Roberts saluted him in a friendly manner, telling him that they were gentlemen of fortune, and that their business with him was only to be informed which was the richest ship in that fleet; and if he directed them right, he should be restored to his ship without molestation, otherwise he must expect instant death.

He then pointed to a vessel of forty guns, and a hundred and fifty men; and though her strength was greatly superior to Roberts', yet he made towards her, taking the master of the captured vessel along with him. Coming alongside of her, Roberts ordered the prisoner to ask, "How Seignior Captain did?" and to invite him on board, as he had a matter of importance to impart to him. He was answered, "That he would wait upon him presently." Roberts, however, observing more than ordinary bustle on board, at once concluded they were discovered, and pouring a broadside into her, they immediately boarded, grappled, and took her. She was a very rich prize, laden with sugar, skins, and tobacco, with four thousand moidores of gold, besides other valuable articles.

In possession of so much riches, they now became solicitous to find a safe retreat in which to spend their time in mirth and wantonness. They determined upon a place called the Devil's Island upon the river Surinam, where they arrived in safety, and met with a kind reception from the governor and the inhabitants.

In this river they seized a sloop, which informed them that she had sailed in company with a brigantine loaded with provisions. This was welcome intelligence, as their provisions were nearly exhausted. Deeming this too important a business to trust to foreign hands, Roberts, with forty men in the sloop, gave chase to that sail. In the keenness of the moment, and trusting in his usual good fortune, Roberts supposed that he had only to take a short sail in order to bring in the vessel with her cargo; but to his sad disappointment, he pursued her during eight days, and instead of gaining, was losing way. Under these circumstances, he came to anchor, and sent off the boat to give intelligence of their distress to their companions.

In their extremity of want, they took up part of the floor of the cabin, and patched up a sort of tray with rope-yarns, to paddle on shore to get a little water to preserve their lives. When their patience was almost exhausted, the boat returned, but instead of provisions, brought the unpleasing information, that the lieutenant, one Kennedy, had run off with both the ships.

The misfortune and misery of Roberts were greatly aggravated by reflecting upon his own imprudence and want of foresight, as well as from the baseness of Kennedy and his crew. Impelled by the necessity of his situation, he now began to reflect upon the means he should employ for future support. Under the foolish supposition that any laws, oaths or regulations, could bind those who had bidden open defiance to all divine and human laws, he proceeded to form a code of regulations for the maintenance of order and unity in his little commonwealth.

But present necessity compelled them to action, and with their small sloop they sailed for the West Indies. They were not long before they captured two sloops, which supplied them with provisions, and a few days after, a brigantine, and then proceeded to Barbadoes. When off that island they met a vessel of ten guns, richly laden from Bristol; after plundering, and detaining her three days, they allowed her to prosecute her voyage. This vessel, however, informed the governor of what had befallen them, who sent a vessel of twenty guns and eighty men in quest of the pirates.

That vessel was commanded by one Rogers, who, on the second day of his cruise, discovered Roberts. Ignorant of any vessel being sent after them, they made towards each other. Roberts gave him a gun but instead of striking, the other returned a broadside, with three huzzas. A severe engagement ensued, and Roberts being hard put to it, lightened his vessel and ran off.

Roberts then sailed for the Island of Dominica, where he watered, and was supplied by the inhabitants with provisions, for which he gave them goods in return. Here he met with fifteen Englishmen left upon the island by a Frenchman who had made a prize of their vessel; and they, entering into his service, proved a seasonable addition to his strength.

Though he did not think this a proper place for cleaning, yet as it was absolutely necessary that it should be done, he directed his course to the Granada islands for that purpose. This, however, had well nigh proved fatal to him; for the Governor of Martinique fitted out two sloops to go in quest of the pirates. They, however, sailed to the above-mentioned place, cleaned with unusual despatch, and just left that place the night before the sloops in pursuit of them arrived.

They next sailed for Newfoundland, arriving upon the banks in June, 1720, and entered the harbor of Trepassi, with their black colors flying, drums beating, and trumpets sounding. In that harbor there were no less than twenty-two ships, which the men abandoned upon the sight of the pirates. It is impossible to describe the injury which they did at this place, by burning or sinking the ships, destroying the plantations, and pillaging the houses. Power in the hands of mean and ignorant men renders them wanton, insolent and cruel. They are literally like madmen, who cast firebrands, arrows and death, and say, "Are not we in sport?"

Roberts reserved a Bristol galley from his depredations in the harbor, which he fitted and manned for his own service. Upon the banks he met ten sail of French ships, and destroyed them all, except one of twenty-six guns, which he seized and carried off, and called her the Fortune. Then giving the Bristol galley to the Frenchman, they sailed in quest of new adventures, and soon took several prizes, and out of them increased the number of their own hands. The Samuel, one of these, was a very rich vessel, having some respectable passengers on board, who were roughly used, and threatened with death if they did not deliver up their money and their goods. They stripped the vessel of every article, either necessary for their vessel or themselves, to the amount of eight or nine thousand pounds. They then deliberated whether to sink or burn the Samuel, but in the mean time they discovered a sail, so they left the empty Samuel, and gave the other chase. At midnight they overtook her, and she proved to be the Snow from Bristol; and, because he was an Englishman, they used the master in a cruel and barbarous manner. Two days after, they took the Little York of Virginia, and the Love of Liverpool, both of which they plundered and sent off. In three days they captured three other vessels, removing the goods out of them, sinking one, and sending off the other two.

They next sailed for the West Indies, but provisions growing short, proceeded to St. Christopher's, where, being denied provisions by the governor, they fired on the town, and burnt two ships in the roads. They then repaired to the island of St. Bartholomew, where the governor supplied them with every necessary, and caressed them in the kindest manner. Satiated with indulgence, and having taken in a large stock of everything necessary, they unanimously voted to hasten to the coast of Guinea. In their way they took a Frenchman, and as she was fitter for the pirate service than their own, they informed the captain, that, as "a fair exchange was no robbery," they would exchange sloops with him; accordingly, having shifted their men, they set sail. However, going by mistake out of the track of the trade winds, they were under the necessity of returning to the West Indies.

They now directed their course to Surinam but not having sufficient water for the voyage they were soon reduced to a mouthful of water in the day; their numbers daily diminished by thirst and famine and the few who survived were reduced to the greatest weakness. They at last had not one drop of water or any other liquid, when, to their inexpressible joy, they anchored in seven fathoms of water. This tended to revive exhausted nature and inspire them with new vigour, though as yet they had received no relief. In the morning they discovered land, but at such a distance that their hopes were greatly dampened. The boat was however sent off, and at night returned with plenty of that necessary element. But this remarkable deliverance produced no reformation in the manners of these unfeeling and obdurate men.

Steering their course from that place to Barbadoes, in their way they met with a vessel which supplied them with all necessaries. Not long after, they captured a brigantine, the mate of which joined their association. Having from these two obtained a large supply, they changed their course and watered at Tobago. Informed, however, that there were two vessels sent in pursuit of them, they went to return their compliments to the Governor of Martinique for this kindness.

It was the custom of the Dutch interlopers, when they approached this island to trade with the inhabitants, to hoist their jacks. Roberts knew the signal, and did so likewise. They, supposing that a good market was near, strove who could first reach Roberts. Determined to do them all possible mischief he destroyed them one by one as they came into his power. He only reserved one ship to send the men on shore, and burnt the remainder, to the number of twenty.

Roberts and his crew were so fortunate as to capture several vessels and to render their liquor so plentiful, that it was esteemed a crime against Providence not to be continually drunk. One man, remarkable for his sobriety, along with two others, found an opportunity to set off without taking leave of their friends. But a despatch being sent after them, they were brought back, and in a formal manner tried and sentenced, but one of them was saved by the humorous interference of one of the judges, whose speech was truly worthy of a pirate–while the other two suffered the punishment of death.

Captain Roberts' Crew carousing at Old Calabar River

**Captain Roberts' Crew carousing at Old Calabar River.**

When necessity again compelled them, they renewed their cruising; and, dissatisfied with capturing vessels which only afforded them a temporary supply, directed their course to the Guinea coast to forage for gold. Intoxication rendered them unruly, and the brigantine at last embraced the cover of night to abandon the commodore. Unconcerned at the loss of his companion, Roberts pursued his voyage. He fell in with two French ships, the one of ten guns and sixty-five men, and the other of sixteen guns and seventy-five men. These dastards no sooner beheld the black flag than they surrendered. With these they went to Sierra Leone, constituting one of them a consort, by the name of the Ranger, and the other a store-ship. This port being frequented by the greater part of the traders to that quarter, they remained here six weeks, enjoying themselves in all the splendor and luxury of a piratical life.

After this they renewed their voyage, and having captured a vessel, the greater part of the men united their fortunes with the pirates. On board of one of the ships was a clergyman, whom some of them proposed taking along with them, for no other reason than that they had not a chaplain on board. They endeavored to gain his consent, and assured him that he should want for nothing, and his only work would be, to make punch and say prayers. Depraved, however, as these men were, they did not choose to constrain him to go, but displayed their civility further, by permitting him to carry along with him whatever he called his own. After several cruises, they now went into a convenient harbor at Old Calabar, where they cleaned, refitted, divided their booty, and for a considerable time caroused, to banish care and sober reflection.

According to their usual custom, the time of festivity and mirth was prolonged until the want of means recalled them to reason and exertion. Leaving this port, they cruised from place to place with varied success; but in all their captures, either burning, sinking, or devoting their prizes to their own use, according to the whim of the moment. The Swallow and another man-of-war being sent out expressly to pursue and take Roberts and his fleet, he had frequent and certain intelligence of their destination; but having so often escaped their vigilance, he became rather too secure and fearless. It happened, however, that while he lay off Cape Lopez, the Swallow had information of his being in that place, and made towards him. Upon the appearance of a sail, one of Roberts' ships was sent to chase and take her. The pilot of the Swallow seeing her coming, manoeouvred his vessel so well, that though he fled at her approach, in order to draw her out of the reach of her associates, yet he at his own time allowed her to overtake the man-of-war.

Upon her coming up to the Swallow, the pirate hoisted the black flag, and fired upon her; but how greatly were her crew astonished, when they saw that they had to contend with a man-of-war, and seeing that all resistance was vain, they cried out for quarter, which was granted, and they were made prisoners, having ten men killed and twenty wounded, without the loss or hurt of one of the king's men.

On the 10th, in the morning, the man-of-war bore away to round the cape. Roberts' crew, discerning their masts over the land, went down into the cabin to acquaint him of it, he being then at breakfast with his new guest, captain Hill, on a savoury dish of salmagundy and some of his own beer. He took no notice of it, and his men almost as little, some saying she was a Portuguese ship, others a French slave ship, but the major part swore it was the French Ranger returning; and they were merrily debating for some time on the manner of reception, whether they should salute her or not; but as the Swallow approached nearer, things appeared plainer; and though they who showed any apprehension of danger were stigmatized with the name of cowards, yet some of them, now undeceived, declared it to Roberts, especially one Armstrong, who had deserted from that ship, and knew her well. These Roberts swore at as cowards, who meant to dishearten the men, asking them, if it were so, whether they were afraid to fight or not? In short, he hardly refrained from blows. What his own apprehensions were, till she hauled up her ports and hoisted her proper colors, is uncertain; but then, being perfectly convinced, he slipped his cable, got under sail, ordered his men to arms without any show of timidity, dropping a first-rate oath, that it was a bite, but at the same time resolved, like a gallant rogue, to get clear or die.

There was one Armstrong, as was just mentioned, a deserter from the Swallow, of whom they enquired concerning the trim and sailing of that ship; he told them she sailed best upon the wind, and therefore, if they designed to leave her, they should go before it.

The danger was imminent, and the time very short, to consult about means to extricate himself; his resolution in this strait was as follows: to pass close to the Swallow with all their sails, and receive her broadside before they returned a shot; if disabled by this, or if they could not depend on sailing, then to run on shore at the point, and every one to shift for himself among the negroes; or failing these, to board, and blow up together, for he saw that the greatest part of his men were drunk, passively courageous, and unfit for service.

Roberts, himself, made a gallant figure at the time of the engagement, being dressed in a rich crimson damask waistcoat and breeches, a red feather in his hat, a gold chain round his neck, with a diamond cross hanging to it, a sword in his hand, and two pair of pistols hanging at the end of a silk sling flung over his shoulders, according to the custom of the pirates. He is said to have given his orders with boldness and spirit. Coming, according to what he had purposed, close to the man-of-war, he received her fire, and then hoisted his black flag and returned it, shooting away from her with all the sail he could pack; and had he taken Armstrong's advice to have gone before the wind, he had probably escaped; but keeping his tacks down, either by the wind's shifting, or ill steerage, or both, he was taken aback with his sails, and the Swallow came a second time very nigh to him. He had now, perhaps, finished the fight very desperately, if death, who took a swift passage in a grape shot, had not interposed, and struck him directly on the throat. He settled himself on the tackles of a gun; which one Stephenson, from the helm, observing, ran to his assistance, and not perceiving him wounded, swore at him, and bade him stand up and fight like a man; but when he found his mistake, and that his captain was certainly dead, he burst into tears, and wished the next shot might be his portion. They presently threw him overboard, with his arms and ornaments on, according to his repeated request in his life-time.

This extraordinary man and daring pirate was tall, of a dark complexion, about 40 years of age, and born in Pembrokeshire. His parents were honest and respectable, and his natural activity, courage, and invention, were superior to his education. At a very early period, he, in drinking, would imprecate vengeance upon "the head of him who ever lived to wear a halter." He went willingly into the pirate service, and served three years as a second man. It was not for want of employment, but from a roving, wild, and boisterous turn of mind. It was his usual declaration, that, "In an honest service, there are commonly low wages and hard labor; in this,–plenty, satiety, pleasure and ease, liberty, and power; and who would not balance creditor on this side, when all the hazard that is run for it at worst, is only a sour look or two at choking? No,–a merry life and a short one, shall be my motto!" But it was one favorable trait in his character, that he never forced any man into the pirate service.

The prisoners were strictly guarded while on board, and being conveyed to Cape Coast castle, they underwent a long and solemn trial. The generality of them remained daring and impenitent for some time, but when they found themselves confined within a castle, and their fate drawing near, they changed their course, and became serious, penitent, and fervent in their devotions. Though the judges found no small difficulty in explaining the law, and different acts of parliament, yet the facts were so numerous and flagrant which were proved against them, that there was no difficulty in bringing in a verdict of guilty.

## THE LIFE OF CHARLES GIBBS.

*Containing an Account of his Atrocities committed in the West Indies.*

This atrocious and cruel pirate, when very young became addicted to vices uncommon in youths of his age, and so far from the gentle reproof and friendly admonition, or the more severe chastisement of a fond parent, having its intended effect, it seemed to render him still worse, and to incline him to repay those whom he ought to have esteemed as his best friends and who had manifested so much regard for his welfare, with ingratitude and neglect. His infamous career and ignominious death on the gallows; brought down the "grey hairs of his parents in sorrow to the grave." The poignant affliction which the infamous crimes of children bring upon their relatives ought to be one of the most effective persuasions for them to refrain from vice.

Charles Gibbs was born in the state of Rhode Island, in 1794; his parents and connexions were of the first respectability. When at school, he was very apt to learn, but so refractory and sulky, that neither the birch nor good counsel made any impression on him, and he was expelled from the school.

He was now made to labor on a farm; but having a great antipathy to work, when about fifteen years of age, feeling a great inclination to roam, and like too many unreflecting youths of that age, a great fondness for the sea, he in opposition to the friendly counsel of his parents, privately left them and entered on board the United States sloop-of-war, Hornet, and was in the action when she captured the British sloop-of-war Peacock, off the coast of Pernambuco. Upon the return of the Hornet to the United States, her brave commander, Capt. Lawrence, was promoted for his gallantry to the command of the unfortunate Chesapeake, and to which he was followed by young Gibbs, who took a very distinguished part in the engagement with the Shannon, which resulted in the death of Lawrence and the capture of the Chesapeake. Gibbs states that while on board the Chesapeake the crew previous to the action, were almost in a state of mutiny, growing out of the non payment of the prize money, and that the address of Capt. Lawrence was received by them with coldness and murmurs.

After the engagement, Gibbs became with the survivors of the crew a prisoner of war, and as such was confined in Dartmoor prison until exchanged.

After his exchange, he returned to Boston, where having determined to abandon the sea, he applied to his friends in Rhode Island, to assist him in commencing business; they accordingly lent him one thousand dollars as a capital to begin with. He opened a grocery in Ann Street, near what was then called the *Tin Pot*, a place full of abandoned women and dissolute fellows. As he dealt chiefly in liquor, and had a "*License to retail Spirits*," his drunkery was thronged with customers. But he sold his groceries chiefly to loose girls who paid him in their coin, which, although it answered his purpose, would neither buy him goods or pay his rent, and he found his stock rapidly dwindling away without his receiving any cash to replenish it. By dissipation and inattention his new business proved unsuccessful to him. He resolved to abandon it and again try the sea for a subsistence. With a hundred dollars in his pocket, the remnant of his property, he embarked in the ship John, for Buenos Ayres, and his means being exhausted soon after his arrival there, he entered on board a Buenos Ayrean privateer and sailed on a cruise. A quarrel between the officers and crew in regard to the division of prize money, led eventually to a mutiny; and the mutineers gained the ascendancy, took possession of the vessel, landed the crew on the coast of Florida, and steered for the West Indies, with hearts resolved to make their fortunes at all hazards, and where in a short time, more than twenty vessels were captured by them and nearly *Four Hundred Human Beings Murdered*!

Havana was the resort of these pirates to dispose of their plunder; and Gibbs sauntered about this place with impunity and was acquainted in all the out of the way and bye places of that hot bed of pirates the Regla. He and his comrades even lodged in the very houses with many of the American officers who were sent out to take them. He was acquainted with many of the officers and was apprised of all their intended movements before they left the harbor. On one occasion, the American ship Caroline, was captured by two of their piratical vessels off Cape Antonio. They were busily engaged in landing the cargo, when the British sloop-of-war, Jearus, hove in sight and sent her barges to attack them. The pirates defended themselves for some time behind a small four gun battery which they had erected, but in the end were forced to abandon their own vessel and the prize and fly to the mountains for safety. The Jearus found here twelve vessels burnt to the water's edge, and it was satisfactorily ascertained that their crews, amounting to *one hundred and fifty persons had been murdered.* The crews, if it was thought not necessary otherways to dispose of them were sent adrift in their boats, and frequently without any thing on which they could subsist a single day; nor were all so fortunate thus to escape. "Dead men can tell no tales," was a common saying among them; and as soon as a ship's crew were taken, a short consultation was held; and if it was the opinion of a majority that it would be better to take life than to spare it, a single nod or wink from the captain was sufficient; regardless of age or sex, all entreaties for mercy were then made in vain; they possessed not the tender feelings, to be operated upon by the shrieks and expiring groans of the devoted victims! there was a strife among them, who with his own hands could despatch the greatest number, and in the shortest period of time.

Without any other motives than to gratify their hellish propensities (in their intoxicated moments), blood was not unfrequently and unnecessarily shed, and many widows and orphans probably made, when the lives of the unfortunate victims might have been spared, and without the most distant prospect of any evil consequences (as regarded themselves), resulting therefrom.

Gibbs states that sometime in the course of the year 1819, he left Havana and came to the United States, bringing with him about $30,000. He passed several weeks in the city of New York, and then went to Boston, whence he took passage for Liverpool in the ship Emerald. Before he sailed, however, he has squandered a large part of his money by dissipation and gambling. He remained in Liverpool a few months, and then returned to Boston. His residence in Liverpool at that time is satisfactorily ascertained from another source besides his own confession. A female now in New York was well acquainted with him there, where, she says, he lived like a gentleman, with apparently abundant means of support. In speaking of his acquaintance with this female he says, "I fell in with a woman, who I thought was all virtue, but she deceived me, and I am sorry to say that a heart that never felt abashed at scenes of carnage and blood, was made a child of for a time by her, and I gave way to dissipation to drown the torment. How often when the fumes of liquor have subsided, have I thought of my good and affectionate parents, and of their Godlike advice! But when the little monitor began to move within me, I immediately seized the cup to hide myself from myself, and drank until the sense of intoxication was renewed. My friends advised me to behave myself like a man, and promised me their assistance, but the demon still haunted me, and I spurned their advice."

In 1826, he revisited the United States, and hearing of the war between Brazil and the Republic of Buenos Ayres, sailed from Boston in the brig Hitty, of Portsmouth, with a determination, as he states, of trying his fortune in defence of a republican government. Upon his arrival he made himself known to Admiral Brown, and communicated his desire to join their navy. The admiral accompanied him to the Governor, and a Lieutenant's commission being given him, he joined a ship of 34 guns, called the 'Twenty Fifth of May.' "Here," says Gibbs, "I found Lieutenant Dodge, an old acquaintance, and a number of other persons with whom I had sailed. When the Governor gave me the commission he told me they wanted no cowards in their navy, to which I replied that I thought he would have no apprehension of my cowardice or skill when he became acquainted with me. He thanked me, and said he hoped he should not be deceived; upon which we drank to his health and to the success of the Republic. He then presented me with a sword, and told me to wear that as my companion through the doubtful struggle in which the republic was engaged. I told him I never would disgrace it, so long as I had a nerve in my arm. I remained on board the ship in the capacity of 5th Lieutenant, for about four months, during which time we had a number of skirmishes with the enemy. Having succeeded in gaining the confidence of Admiral Brown, he put me in command of a privateer schooner, mounting two long 24 pounders and 46 men. I sailed from Buenos Ayres, made two good cruises, and returned safely to port. I then bought one half of a new Baltimore schooner, and sailed again, but was captured seven days out, and carried into Rio Janeiro, where the Brazilians paid me my change. I remained there until peace took place, then returned to Buenos Ayres, and thence to New York.

"After the lapse of about a year, which I passed in travelling from place to place, the war between France and Algiers attracted my attention. Knowing that the French commerce presented a fine opportunity for plunder, I determined to embark for Algiers and offer my services to the Dey. I accordingly took passage from New York, in the Sally Ann, belonging to Bath, landed at Barcelona, crossed to Port Mahon, and endeavored to make my way to Algiers. The vigilance of the French fleet prevented the accomplishment of my design, and I proceeded to Tunis. There finding it unsafe to attempt a journey to Algiers across the desert, I amused myself with contemplating the ruins of Carthage, and reviving my recollections of her war with the Romans. I afterwards took passage to Marseilles, and thence to Boston."

An instance of the most barbarous and cold blooded murder of which the wretched Gibbs gives an account in the course of his confessions, is that of an innocent and beautiful female of about 17 or 18 years of age! she was with her parents a passenger on board a Dutch ship, bound from Curracoa to Holland; there were a number of other passengers, male and female, on board, all of whom except the young lady above-mentioned were put to death; her unfortunate parents were inhumanly butchered before her eyes, and she was doomed to witness the agonies and to hear the expiring, heart-piercing groans of those whom she held most dear, and on whom she depended for protection! The life of their wretched daughter was spared for the most nefarious purposes–she was taken by the pirates to the west end of Cuba, where they had a rendezvous, with a small fort that mounted four guns–here she was confined about two months, and where, as has been said by the murderer Gibbs, "she received such treatment, the bare recollection of which causes me to shudder!" At the expiration of the two months she was taken by the pirates on board of one of their vessels, and among whom a consultation was soon after held, which resulted in the conclusion that it would be necessary for their own personal safety, to put her to death! and to her a fatal dose of poison was accordingly administered, which soon proved fatal! when her pure and immortal spirit took its flight to that God, whom, we believe, will avenge her wrongs! her lifeless body was then committed to the deep by two of the merciless wretches with as much unconcern, as if it had been that of the meanest brute! Gibbs persists in the declaration that in this horrid transaction he took no part, that such was his pity for this poor ill-fated female, that he interceded for her life so long as he could do it with safety to his own!

Gibbs carrying the Dutch Girl on board his Vessel

**Gibbs carrying the Dutch Girl on board his Vessel.**

Gibbs in his last visit to Boston remained there but a few days, when he took passage to New Orleans, and there entered as one of the crew on board the brig Vineyard; and for assisting in the murder of the unfortunate captain and mate of which, he was justly condemned, and the awful sentence of death passed upon him! The particulars of the bloody transaction (agreeable to the testimony of Dawes and Brownrigg, the two principal witnesses,) are as follows: The brig Vineyard, Capt. William Thornby, sailed from New Orleans about the 9th of November, for Philadelphia, with a cargo of 112 bales of cotton, 113 hhds. sugar, 54 casks of molasses and 54,000 dollars in specie. Besides the captain there were on board the brig, William Roberts, mate, six seamen shipped at New Orleans, and the cook. Robert Dawes, one of the crew, states on examination, that when, about five days out, he was told that there was money on board, Charles Gibbs, E. Church and the steward then determined to take possession of the brig. They asked James Talbot, another of the crew, to join them. He said no, as he did not believe there was money in the vessel. They concluded to kill the captain and mate, and if Talbot and John Brownrigg would not join them, to kill them also. The next night they talked of doing it, and got their clubs ready. Dawes dared not say a word, as they declared they would kill him if he did; as they did not agree about killing Talbot and Brownrigg, two shipmates, it was put off. They next concluded to kill the captain and mate on the night of November 22, but did not get ready; but, on the night of the 23d, between twelve and one o'clock, as Dawes was at the helm, saw the steward come up with a light and a knife in his hand; he dropt the light and seizing the pump break, struck the captain with it over the head or back of the neck; the captain was sent forward by the blow, and halloed, oh! and murder! once; he was then seized by Gibbs and the cook, one by the head and the other by the heels, and thrown overboard. Atwell and Church stood at the companion way, to strike down the mate when he should come up. As he came up and enquired what was the matter they struck him over the head–he ran back into the cabin, and Charles Gibbs followed him down; but as it was dark, he could not find him–Gibbs came on deck for the light, with which he returned. Dawes' light being taken from him, he could not see to steer, and he in consequence left the helm, to see what was going on below. Gibbs found the mate and seized him, while Atwell and Church came down and struck him with a pump break and a club; he was then dragged upon deck; they called for Dawes to come to them, and as he came up the mate seized his hand, and gave him a death gripe! three of them then hove him overboard, but which three Dawes does not know; the mate when cast overboard was not dead, but called after them twice while in the water! Dawes says he was so frightened that he hardly knew what to do. They then requested him to call Talbot, who was in the forecastle, saying his prayers; he came up and said it would be his turn next! but they gave him some grog, and told him not to be afraid, as they would not hurt him; if he was true to them, he should fare as well as they did. One of those who had been engaged in the bloody deed got drunk, and another became crazy!

Gibbs shooting a comrade

**Gibbs shooting a comrade.**

After killing the captain and mate, they set about overhauling the vessel, and got up one keg of Mexican dollars. They then divided the captain's clothes, and money–about 40 dollars, and a gold watch. Dawes, Talbot and Brownrigg, (who were all innocent of the murder,) were obliged to do as they were commanded–the former, who was placed at the helm, was ordered to steer for Long Island. On the day following, they divided several kegs of the specie, amounting to five thousand dollars each–they made bags and sewed the money up. After this division, they divided the remainder of the money without counting it. On Sunday, when about 15 miles S.S.E. of Southampton Light, they got the boats out and put half the money in each–they then scuttled the vessel and set fire to it in the cabin, and took to the boats. Gibbs, after the murder, took charge of the vessel as captain. From the papers they learnt that the money belonged to Stephen Girard. With the boats they made the land about daylight. Dawes and his three companions were in the long boat; the others, with Atwell, were in the jolly boat–on coming to the bar the boats struck–in the long boat, they threw overboard a trunk of clothes and a great deal of money, in all about 5000 dollars–the jolly boat foundered; they saw the boat fill, and heard them cry out, and saw them clinging to the masts–they went ashore on Barron Island, and buried the money in the sand, but very lightly. Soon after they met with a gunner, whom they requested to conduct them where they could get some refreshments. They were by him conducted to Johnson's (the only man living on the island,) where they staid all night–Dawes went to bed at about 10 o'clock–Jack Brownrigg set up with Johnson, and in the morning told Dawes that he had told Johnson all about the murder. Johnson went in the morning with the steward for the clothes, which were left on the top of the place where they buried the money, but does not believe they took away the money.

Captain Thornby murdered and thrown overboard by Gibbs and the steward

**Captain Thornby murdered and thrown overboard by Gibbs and the steward.**

The prisoners, (Gibbs and Wansley,) were brought to trial at the February term of the United States Court, holden in the city of New York; when the foregoing facts being satisfactorily proved, they were pronounced guilty, and on the 11th March last, the awful sentence of the law was passed upon them in the following affecting and impressive manner:–The Court opened at 11 o'clock, Judge Betts presiding. A few minutes after that hour, Mr. Hamilton, District Attorney, rose and said–May it please the Court, Thomas J. Wansley, the prisoner at the bar, having been tried by a jury of his country, and found guilty of the murder of Captain Thornby, I now move that the sentence of the Court be pronounced upon that verdict.

Gibbs and Wansley burying the Money

**Gibbs and Wansley burying the Money.**

*By the Court.* Thomas J. Wansley, you have heard what has been said by the District Attorney–by the Grand Jury of the South District of New York, you have been arraigned for the wilful murder of Captain Thornby, of the brig Vineyard; you have been put upon your trial, and after a patient and impartial hearing, you have been found Guilty. The public prosecutor now moves for judgment on that verdict; have you any thing to say, why the sentence of the law should not be passed upon you?

*Thomas J. Wansley.* I will say a few words, but it is perhaps of no use. I have often understood that there is a great deal of difference in respect of color, and I have seen it in this Court. Dawes and Brownrigg were as guilty as I am, and these witnesses have tried to fasten upon me greater guilt than is just, for their life has been given to them. You have taken the blacks from their own country, to bring them here to treat them ill. I have seen this. The witnesses, the jury, and the prosecuting Attorney consider me more guilty than Dawes, to condemn me–for otherwise the law must have punished him; he should have had the same verdict, for he was a perpetrator in the conspiracy. Notwithstanding my participating, they have sworn falsely for the purpose of taking my life; they would not even inform the Court, how I gave information of money being on board; they had the biggest part of the money, and have sworn falsely. I have said enough. I will say no more.

*By the Court.* The Court will wait patiently and hear all you have to say; if you have any thing further to add, proceed.

*Wansley* then proceeded. In the first place, I was the first to ship on board the Vineyard at New Orleans, I knew nobody; I saw the money come on board. The judge that first examined me, did not take my deposition down correctly. When talking with the crew on board, said the brig was an old craft, and when we arrived at Philadelphia, we all agreed to leave her. It was mentioned to me that there was plenty of money on board. Henry Atwell said "let's have it." I knew no more of this for some days. Atwell came to me again and asked "what think you of taking the money." I thought it was a joke, and paid no attention to it. The next day he said they had determined to take the brig and money, and that they were the strongest party, and would murder the officers, and he that informed should suffer with them. I knew Church in Boston, and in a joke asked him how it was made up in the ship's company; his reply, that it was he and Dawes. There was no arms on board as was ascertained; the conspiracy was known to the whole company, and had I informed, my life would have been taken, and though I knew if I was found out my life would be taken by law, which is the same thing, so I did not inform. I have committed murder and I know I must die for it.

*By the Court.* If you wish to add any thing further you will still be heard.

*Wansley.* No sir, I believe I have said enough.

The District Attorney rose and moved for judgment on Gibbs, in the same manner as in the case of Wansley, and the Court having addressed Gibbs, in similar terms, concluded by asking what he had to say why the sentence of the law should not now be passed upon him.

*Charles Gibbs* said, I wish to state to the Court, how far I am guilty and how far I am innocent in this transaction. When I left New Orleans, I was a stranger to all on board, except Dawes and Church. It was off Tortugas that Atwell first told me there was money on board, and proposed to me to take possession of the brig. I refused at that time. The conspiracy was talked of for some days, and at last I agreed that I would join. Brownrigg, Dawes, Church, and the whole agreed that they would. A few days after, however, having thought of the affair, I mentioned to Atwell, what a dreadful thing it was to take a man's life, and commit piracy, and recommended him to "abolish," their plan. Atwell and Dawes remonstrated with me; I told Atwell that if ever he would speak of the subject again, I would break his nose. Had I kept to my resolution I would not have been brought here to receive my sentence. It was three days afterwards that the murder was committed. Brownrigg agreed to call up the captain from the cabin, and this man, (pointing to Wansley,) agreed to strike the first blow. The captain was struck and I suppose killed, and I lent a hand to throw him overboard. But for the murder of the mate, of which I have been found guilty, I am innocent–I had nothing to do with that. The mate was murdered by Dawes and Church; that I am innocent of this I commit my soul to that God who will judge all flesh–who will judge all murderers and false swearers, and the wicked who deprive the innocent of his right. I have nothing more to say.

*By the Court.* Thomas J. Wansley and Charles Gibbs, the Court has listened to you patiently and attentively; and although you have said something in your own behalf, yet the Court has heard nothing to affect the deepest and most painful duty that he who presides over a public tribunal has to perform.

You, Thomas J. Wansley, conceive that a different measure of justice has been meted out to you, because of your color. Look back upon your whole course of life; think of the laws under which you have lived, and you will find that to white or black, to free or bond, there is no ground for your allegations; that they are not supported by truth or justice. Admit that Brownrigg and Dawes have sworn falsely; admit that Dawes was concerned with you; admit that Brownrigg is not innocent; admit, in relation to both, that they are guilty, the whole evidence has proved beyond a doubt that you are guilty; and your own words admit that you were an active agent in perpetrating this horrid crime. Two fellow beings who confided in you, and in their perilous voyage called in your assistance, yet you, without reason or provocation, have maliciously taken their lives.

If, peradventure, there was the slightest foundation for a doubt of your guilt, in the mind of the Court, judgment would be arrested, but there is none; and it now remains to the Court to pronounce the most painful duty that devolves upon a civil magistrate. The Court is persuaded of your guilt; it can form no other opinion. Testimony has been heard before the Court and Jury–from that we must form our opinion. We must proceed upon testimony, ascertain facts by evidence of witnesses, on which we must inquire, judge and determine as to guilt or innocence, by that evidence alone. You have been found guilty. You now stand for the last time before an earthly tribunal, and by your own acknowledgments, the sentence of the law falls just on your heads. When men in ordinary cases come under the penalty of the law there is generally some palliative–something to warm the sympathy of the Court and Jury. Men may be led astray, and under the influence of passion have acted under some long smothered resentment, suddenly awakened by the force of circumstances, depriving him of reason, and then they may take the life of a fellow being. Killing, under that kind of excitement, might possibly awaken some sympathy, but that was not your case; you had no provocation. What offence had Thornby or Roberts committed against you? They entrusted themselves with you, as able and trustworthy citizens; confiding implicitly in you; no one act of theirs, after a full examination, appears to have been offensive to you; yet for the purpose of securing the money you coolly determined to take their lives–you slept and deliberated over the act; you were tempted on, and yielded; you entered into the conspiracy, with cool and determined calculation to deprive two human beings of their lives, and it was done.

You, Charles Gibbs, have said that you are not guilty of the murder of Roberts; but were you not there, strongly instigating the murderers on, and without stretching out a hand to save him?–It is murder as much to stand by and encourage the deed, as to stab with a knife, strike with a hatchet, or shoot with a pistol. It is not only murder in law, but in your own feelings and in your own conscience. Notwithstanding all this, I cannot believe that your feelings are so callous, so wholly callous, that your own minds do not melt when you look back upon the unprovoked deeds of yourselves, and those confederated with you.

You are American citizens–this country affords means of instruction to all: your appearance and your remarks have added evidence that you are more than ordinarily intelligent; that your education has enabled you to participate in the advantages of information open to all classes. The Court will believe that when you were young you looked with strong aversion on the course of life of the wicked. In early life, in boyhood, when you heard of the conduct of men, who engaged in robbery–nay more, when you heard of cold blooded murder–how you must have shrunk from the recital. Yet now, after having participated in the advantages of education, after having arrived at full maturity, you stand here as robbers and murderers.

It is a perilous employment of life that you have followed; in this way of life the most enormous crimes that man can commit, are MURDER AND PIRACY. With what detestation would you in early life have looked upon the man who would have raised his hand against his officer, or have committed piracy! yet now you both stand here murderers and pirates, tried and found guilty–you Wansley of the murder of your Captain, and you, Gibbs, of the murder of your Mate. The evidence has convicted you of rising in mutiny against the master of the vessel, for that alone, the law is DEATH!–of murder and robbery on the high seas, for that crime, the law adjudges DEATH–of destroying the vessel and embezzling the cargo, even for scuttling and burning the vessel alone the law is DEATH; yet of all these the evidence has convicted you, and it only remains now for the Court to pass the sentence of the law. It is, that you, Thomas J. Wansley and Charles Gibbs be taken hence to the place of confinement, there to remain in close custody, that thence you be taken to the place of execution, and on the 22d April next, between the hours of 10 and 4 o'clock, you be both publicly hanged by the neck until you are DEAD–and that your bodies be given to the College of Physicians and Surgeons for dissection.

The Court added, that the only thing discretionary with it, was the time of execution; it might have ordered that you should instantly have been taken from the stand to the scaffold, but the sentence has been deferred to as distant a period as prudent–six weeks. But this time has not been granted for the purpose of giving you any hope for pardon or commutation of the sentence;–just as sure as you live till the twenty-second of April, as surely you will suffer death–therefore indulge not a hope that this sentence will be changed!

The Court then spoke of the terror in all men of death!–how they cling to life whether in youth, manhood or old age. What an awful thing it is to die! how in the perils of the sea, when rocks or storms threaten the loss of the vessel, and the lives of all on board, how the crew will labor, night and day, in the hope of escaping shipwreck and death! alluded to the tumult, bustle and confusion of battle–yet even there the hero clings to life. The Court adverted not only to the certainty of their coming doom on earth, but to THINK OF HEREAFTER–that they should seriously think and reflect of their FUTURE STATE! that they would be assisted in their devotions no doubt, by many pious men.

When the Court closed, Charles Gibbs asked, if during his imprisonment, his friends would be permitted to see him. The Court answered that that lay with the Marshal, who then said that no difficulty would exist on that score. The remarks of the Prisoners were delivered in a strong, full-toned and unwavering voice, and they both seemed perfectly resigned to the fate which inevitably awaited them. While Judge Betts was delivering his address to them, Wansley was deeply affected and shed tears–but Gibbs gazed with a steady and unwavering eye, and no sign betrayed the least emotion of his heart. After his condemnation, and during his confinement, his frame became somewhat enfeebled, his face paler, and his eyes more sunken; but the air of his bold, enterprising and desperate mind still remained. In his narrow cell, he seemed more like an object of pity than vengeance–was affable and communicative, and when he smiled, exhibited so mild and gentle a countenance, that no one would take him to be a villain. His conversation was concise and pertinent, and his style of illustration quite original.

Gibbs was married in Buenos Ayres, where he has a child now living. His wife is dead. By a singular concurrence of circumstances, the woman with whom he became acquainted in Liverpool, and who is said at that time to have borne a decent character, was lodged in the same prison with himself. During his confinement he wrote her two letters–one of them is subjoined, to gratify the perhaps innocent curiosity which is naturally felt to know the peculiarities of a man's mind and feelings under such circumstances, and not for the purpose of intimating a belief that he was truly penitent. The reader will be surprised with the apparent readiness with which he made quotations from Scripture.

"BELLEVUE PRISON, March 20, 1831.

"It is with regret that I take my pen in hand to address you with these few lines, under the great embarrassment of my feelings placed within these gloomy walls, my body bound with chains, and under the awful sentence of death! It is enough to throw the strongest mind into gloomy prospects! but I find that Jesus Christ is sufficient to give consolation to the most despairing soul. For he saith, that he that cometh to me I will in no ways cast out. But it is impossible to describe unto you the horror of my feelings. My breast is like the tempestuous ocean, raging in its own shame, harrowing up the bottom of my soul! But I look forward to that serene calm when I shall sleep with Kings and Counsellors of the earth. There the wicked cease from troubling, and there the weary are at rest!–There the prisoners rest together–they hear not the voice of the oppressor; and I trust that there my breast will not be ruffled by the storm of sin–for the thing which I greatly feared has come upon me. I was not in safety, neither had I rest; yet trouble came. It is the Lord, let him do what seemeth to him good. When I saw you in Liverpool, and a peaceful calm wafted across both our breasts, and justice no claim upon us, little did I think to meet you in the gloomy walls of a strong prison, and the arm of justice stretched out with the sword of law, awaiting the appointed period to execute the dreadful sentence. I have had a fair prospect in the world, at last it budded, and brought forth the gallows. I am shortly to mount that scaffold, and to bid adieu to this world, and all that was ever dear to my breast. But I trust when my body is mounted on the gallows high, the heavens above will smile and pity me. I hope that you will reflect on your past, and fly to that Jesus who stands with open arms to receive you. Your character is lost, it is true. When the wicked turneth from the wickedness that they have committed, they shall save their soul alive.

"Let us imagine for a moment that we see the souls standing before the awful tribunal, and we hear its dreadful sentence, depart ye cursed into everlasting fire. Imagine you hear the awful lamentations of a soul in hell. It would be enough to melt your heart, if it was as hard as adamant. You would fall upon your knees and plead for God's mercy, as a famished person would for food, or as a dying criminal would for a pardon. We soon, very soon, must go the way whence we shall ne'er return. Our names will be struck off the records of the living, and enrolled in the vast catalogues of the dead. But may it ne'er be numbered with the damned.–I hope it will please God to set you at your liberty, and that you may see the sins and follies of your life past. I shall now close my letter with a few words which I hope you will receive as from a dying man; and I hope that every important truth of this letter may sink deep in your heart, and be a lesson to you through life.

"Rising griefs distress my soul,
And tears on tears successive roll–
For many an evil voice is near,
To chide my woes and mock my fear–
And silent memory weeps alone,
O'er hours of peace and gladness known.

"I still remain your sincere friend, CHARLES GIBBS."

In another letter which the wretched Gibbs wrote after his condemnation to one who had been his early friend, he writes as follows:–"Alas! it is now, and not until now, that

I have become sensible of my wicked life, from my childhood, and the enormity of the crime, for which I must shortly suffer an ignominious death!–I would to God that I never had been born, or that I had died in my infancy!–the hour of reflection has indeed come, but come too late to prevent justice from cutting me off–my mind recoils with horror at the thoughts of the unnatural deeds of which I have been guilty!–my repose rather prevents than affords me relief, as my mind, while I slumber, is constantly disturbed by frightful dreams of my approaching awful dissolution!"

On Friday, April twenty-second, Gibbs and Wansley paid the penalty of their crimes. Both prisoners arrived at the gallows about twelve o'clock, accompanied by the marshal, his aids, and some twenty or thirty United States' marines. Two clergymen attended them to the fatal spot, where everything being in readiness, and the ropes adjusted about their necks, the Throne of Mercy was fervently addressed in their behalf. Wansley then prayed earnestly himself, and afterwards joined in singing a hymn. These exercises concluded, Gibbs addressed the spectators nearly as follows:

MY DEAR FRIENDS,

My crimes have been heinous–and although I am now about to suffer for the murder of Mr. Roberts, I solemnly declare my innocence of the transaction. It is true, I stood by and saw the fatal deed done, and stretched not forth my arm to save him; the technicalities of the law believe me guilty of the charge–but in the presence of my God–before whom I shall be in a few minutes–I declare I did not murder him.

I have made a full and frank confession to Mr. Hopson, which probably most of my hearers present have already read; and should any of the friends of those whom I have been accessary to, or engaged in the murder of, be now present, before my Maker I beg their forgiveness–it is the only boon I ask–and as I hope for pardon through the blood of Christ, surely this request will not be withheld by man, to a worm like myself, standing as I do, on the very verge of eternity! Another moment, and I cease to exist–and could I find in my bosom room to imagine that the spectators now assembled had forgiven me, the scaffold would have no terrors, nor could the precept which my much respected friend, the marshal of the district, is about to execute. Let me then, in this public manner, return my sincere thanks to him, for his kind and gentlemanly deportment during my confinement. He was to me like a father, and his humanity to a dying man I hope will be duly appreciated by an enlightened community.

My first crime was *piracy*, for which my *life* would pay for forfeit on conviction; no punishment could be inflicted on me further than that, and therefore I had nothing to fear but detection, for had my offences been millions of times more aggravated than they are now, *death* must have satisfied all.

Gibbs having concluded, Wansley began. He said he might be called a pirate, a robber, and a murderer, and he was all of these, but he hoped and trusted God would, through Christ, wash away his aggravated crimes and offences, and not cast him entirely out. His feelings, he said, were so overpowered that he hardly knew how to address those about him, but he frankly admitted the justness of the sentence, and concluded by declaring that he had no hope of pardon except through the atoning blood of his Redeemer, and wished that his sad fate might teach others to shun the broad

road to ruin, and travel in that of virtue, which would lead to honor and happiness in this world, and an immortal crown of glory in that to come.

He then shook hands with Gibbs, the officers, and clergymen–their caps were drawn over their faces, a handkerchief dropped by Gibbs as a signal to the executioner caused the cord to be severed, and in an instant they were suspended in air. Wansley folded his hands before him, soon died with very trifling struggles. Gibbs died hard; before he was run up, and did not again remove them, but after being near two minutes suspended, he raised his right hand and partially removed his cap, and in the course of another minute, raised the same hand to his mouth. His dress was a blue round-about jacket and trousers, with a foul anchor in white on his right arm. Wansley wore a white frock coat, trimmed with black, with trousers of the same color.

After the bodies had remained on the gallows the usual time, they were taken down and given to the surgeons for dissection.

Gibbs was rather below the middle stature, thick set and powerful. The form of Wansley was a perfect model of manly beauty.

Page 136 Illustration

## HISTORY OF THE ADVENTURES, CAPTURE AND EXECUTION OF THE SPANISH PIRATES.

In the Autumn of 1832, there was anchored in the "Man of War Grounds," off the Havana, a clipper-built vessel of the fairest proportions; she had great length and breadth of beam, furnishing stability to bear a large surface of sail, and great depth to take hold of the water and prevent drifting; long, low in the waist, with lofty raking masts, which tapered away till they were almost too fine to be distinguished, the beautiful arrowy sharpness of her bow, and the fineness of her gradually receding quarters, showed a model capable of the greatest speed in sailing. Her low sides were painted black, with one small, narrow ribband of white. Her raking masts were clean scraped, her ropes were hauled taught, and in every point she wore the appearance of being under the control of seamanship and strict discipline. Upon going on board, one would be struck with surprise at the deception relative to the tonnage of the schooner, when viewed at a distance. Instead of a small vessel of about ninety tons, we discover that she is upwards of two hundred; that her breadth of beam is enormous; and that those spars which appeared so light and elegant, are of unexpected dimensions. In the centre of the vessel, between the fore and main masts, there is a long brass thirty-two pounder, fixed upon a carriage revolving in a circle, and so arranged that in bad weather it can be lowered down and housed; while on each side of the deck were mounted guns of smaller calibre.

This vessel was fashioned, at the will of avarice, for the aid of cruelty and injustice; it was an African slaver–the schooner Panda. She was commanded by Don Pedro Gilbert, a native of Catalonia, in Spain, and son of a grandee; a man thirty-six years of age, and exceeding handsome, having a round face, pearly teeth, round forehead, and full black eyes, with beautiful raven hair, and a great favorite with the ladies. He united great energy, coolness and decision, with superior knowledge in mercantile transactions, and the Guinea trade; having made several voyages after slaves. The mate and owner of the Panda was Don Bernardo De Soto, a native of Corunna, Spain, and son, of Isidore De Soto, manager of the royal revenue in said city; he was now twenty-five years of age, and from the time he was fourteen had cultivated the art of navigation, and at the age of twenty-two had obtained the degree of captain in the India service. After a regular examination the correspondent diploma was awarded him. He was married to Donna Petrona Pereyra, daughter of Don Benito Pereyra, a merchant of Corunna. She was at this time just fifteen, and ripening into that slight fullness of form, and roundness of limb, which in that climate mark the early passing from girl into woman. Her complexion was the dark olive tinge of Spain; her eyes jet black, large and lustrous. She had great sweetness of disposition and ingenuousness.

To the strictest discipline De Soto united the practical knowledge of a thorough seaman. But "the master spirit of the whole," was Francisco Ruiz, the carpenter of the Panda. This individual was of the middle size, but muscular, with a short neck. His hair was black and abundant, and projected from his forehead, so that he appeared to look out from under it, like a bonnet. His eyes were dark chestnut, but always restless; his features were well defined; his eye-lashes, jet black. He was familiar with all the out-of-the-way places of the Havana, and entered into any of the dark abodes without ceremony. From report his had been a wild and lawless career. The crew were chiefly Spaniards, with a few Portuguese, South Americans, and half castes. The cook was a young Guinea negro, with a pleasant countenance, and good humored, with a sleek glossy skin, and tatooed on the face; and although entered in the schooner's books as free, yet was a slave. In all there were about forty men. Her cargo was an assorted one, consisting in part of barrels of rum, and gunpowder, muskets, cloth, and numerous articles, with which to purchase slaves.

The Panda sailed from the Havana on the night of the 20th of August; and upon passing the Moro Castle, she was hailed, and asked, "where bound?" She replied, St. Thomas. The schooner now steered through the Bahama channel, on the usual route towards the coast of Guinea; a man was constantly kept at the mast head, on the lookout; they spoke a corvette, and on the morning of the 20th Sept., before light, and during the second mate's watch, a brig was discovered heading to the southward. Capt. Gilbert was asleep at the time, but got up shortly after she was seen, and ordered the Panda to go about and stand for the brig. A consultation was held between the captain, mate and carpenter, when the latter proposed to board her, and if she had any specie to rob her, confine the men below, and burn her. This proposition was instantly acceded to, and a musket was fired to make her heave to.

This vessel was the American brig Mexican, Capt. Butman. She had left the pleasant harbor of Salem, Mass., on the last Wednesday of August, and was quietly pursuing her voyage towards Rio Janeiro. Nothing remarkable had happened on board, says Captain B., until half past two o'clock, in the morning of September 20th, in lat. 38, 0, N., lon. 24, 30, W. The attention of the watch on deck was forcibly arrested by the appearance of a vessel which passed across our stern about half a mile from us. At 4 A.M. saw her again passing across our bow, so near that we could perceive that it was a schooner with a fore top sail and top gallant sail. As it was somewhat dark she was soon out of sight. At daylight saw her about five miles off the weather quarter standing on the wind on the same tack we were on, the wind was light at SSW and we were standing about S.E. At 8 A.M. she was about two miles right to windward of us; could perceive a large number of men upon her deck, and one man on the fore top gallant yard looking out; was very suspicious of her, but knew not how to avoid her. Soon after saw a brig on our weather bow steering to the N.E. By this time the schooner was about three miles from us and four points forward of the beam. Expecting that she would keep on for the brig ahead of us, we tacked to the westward, keeping a little off from the wind to make good way through the water, to get clear of her if possible. She kept on to the eastward about ten or fifteen minutes after we had tacked, then wore round, set square sail, steering directly for us, came down upon us very fast, and was soon within gun shot of us, fired a gun and hoisted patriot colors and backed main topsail. She ran along to windward of us, hailed us to know where we were from, where bound, c. then ordered me to come on board in my boat. Seeing that she was too powerful for us to resist, I accordingly went, and soon as I got along-side of the schooner, five ruffians instantly jumped into my boat, each of them being armed with a large knife, and told me to go on board the brig again; when they got on board they insisted that we had got money, and drew their knives, threatening us with instant death and demanding to know where it was. As soon as they found out where it was they obliged my crew to get it up out of the run upon deck, beating and threatening them at the same time because they did not do it quicker. When they had got it all upon deck, and hailed the schooner, they got out their launch and came and took it on board the schooner, viz: ten boxes containing twenty thousand dollars; then returned to the brig again, drove all the crew into the forecastle, ransacked the cabin, overhauling all the chests, trunks, c. and rifled my pockets, taking my watch, and three doubloons which I had previously put there for safety; robbed the mate of his watch and two hundred dollars in specie, still insisting that there was more money in the hold. Being answered in the negative, they beat me severely over the back, said they knew that there was more, that they should search for it, and if they found any they would cut all our throats. They continued searching about in every part of the vessel for some time longer, but not finding any more specie, they took two coils of rigging, a side of leather, and some other articles, and went on board the schooner, probably to consult what to do with us; for, in eight or ten minutes they came back, apparently in great haste, shut us all below, fastened up the companion way, fore-scuttle and after hatchway, stove our compasses to pieces in the binnacles, cut away tiller-ropes, halliards, braces, and most of our running rigging, cut our sails to pieces badly; took a tub of tarred rope-yarn and what combustibles they could find about deck, put them in the caboose house and set them on fire; then left us, taking with them our boat and colors. When they got alongside of the schooner they scuttled our boat, took in their own, and made sail, steering to the eastward.

As soon as they left us, we got up out of the cabin scuttle, which they had neglected to secure, and extinguished the fire, which if it had been left a few minutes, would have caught the mainsail and set our masts on fire. Soon after we saw a ship to leeward of us steering to the S.E. the schooner being in pursuit of her did not overtake her whilst she was in sight of us.

It was doubtless their intention to burn us up altogether, but seeing the ship, and being eager for more plunder they did not stop fully to accomplish their design. She was a low strait schooner of about one hundred and fifty tons, painted black with a narrow white streak, a large head with the horn of plenty painted white, large maintopmast but no yards or sail on it. Mast raked very much, mainsail very square at the head, sails made with split cloth and all new; had two long brass twelve pounders and a large gun on a pivot amidships, and about seventy men, who appeared to be chiefly Spaniards and mulattoes.

Pirates robbing the brig Mexican of Salem, Mass.

**Pirates robbing the brig Mexican of Salem, Mass.**

The object of the voyage being frustrated by the loss of the specie, nothing now remained but for the Mexican to make the best of her way back to Salem, which she reached in safety. The government of the United States struck with the audacity of this piracy, despatched a cruiser in pursuit of them. After a fruitless voyage in which every exertion was made, and many places visited on the coast of Africa, where it was supposed the rascals might be lurking, the chase was abandoned as hopeless, no clue being found to their "whereabouts."

The Panda after robbing the Mexican, pursued her course across the Atlantic, and made Cape Monte; from this she coasted south, and after passing Cape Palmas entered the Gulf of Guinea, and steered for Cape Lopez which she reached in the first part of November. Cape Lopez de Gonzalves, in lat. 0° 36' 2" south, long. 80° 40' 4" east, is so called from its first discoverer. It is covered with wood but low and swampy, as is also the neighboring country. The extensive bay formed by this cape is fourteen miles in depth, and has several small creeks and rivers running into it. The largest is the river Nazareth on the left point of which is situated King Gula's town the only assemblage of huts in the bay. Here the cargo of the Panda was unloaded, the greater part was entrusted to the king, and with the rest Capt. Gilbert opened a factory and commenced buying various articles of commerce, as tortoise shell, gum, ivory, palm oil, fine straw carpeting, and slaves. After remaining here a short time the crew became sickly and Capt. Gilbert sailed for Prince's Island to recover the health of his crew. Whilst at Prince's Island news arrived of the robbery of the Mexican. And the pirate left with the utmost precipitation for Cape Lopez, and the better to evade pursuit, a pilot was procured; and the vessel carried several miles up the river Nazareth. Soon after the Panda left Prince's Island, the British brig of war, Curlew, Capt. Trotter arrived, and from the description given of the vessel then said to be lying in the Nazareth, Capt. Trotter knew she must be the one, that robbed the Mexican; and he instantly sailed in pursuit. On nearing the coast, she was discovered lying up the river; three boats containing forty men and commanded by Capt. Trotter, started up the river with the sea breeze and flood tide, and colors flying to take the desperadoes; the boats kept in near the shore until rounding a point they were seen from the Panda. The pirates immediately took to their boats, except Francisco Ruiz who seizing a fire brand from the camboose went into the magazine and set some combustibles on fire with the laudable purpose of blowing up the assailants, and then paddled ashore in a canoe. Capt. Trotter chased them with his boats, but could not come up with them, and then boarded the schooner which he found on fire. The first thing he did was to put out the fire which was in the magazine, below the cabin floor; here was found a quantity of cotton and brimstone burning and a slow match ignited and communicating with the magazine, which contained sixteen casks of powder.

The Panda was now warped out of the river and anchored off the negro town of Cape Lopez. Negociations were now entered into for the surrender of the pirates. An officer was accordingly sent on shore to have an interview with the king. He was met on the beach by an ebony chief calling himself duke. "We followed the duke through the extensive and straggling place, frequently buried up to the ankles in sand, from which the vegetation was worn by the constant passing and repassing of the inhabitants. We arrived at a large folding door placed in a high bamboo and palm tree fence, which inclosed the king's establishment, ornamented on our right by two old honeycombed guns, which, although dismounted, were probably, according to the practice of the coast, occasionally fired to attract the attention of passing vessels, and to imply that slaves were to be procured. On the left of the enclosure was a shed, with a large ship's bell suspended beneath, serving as an alarum bell in case of danger, while the remainder was occupied with neatly built huts, inhabited by the numerous wives of the king.

"We sent in to notify him of our arrival; he sent word out that we might remain outside until it suited his convenience. But as such an arrangement did not suit ours, we immediately entered, and found sitting at a table the king. He was a tall, muscular, ugly looking negro, about fifty years of age. We explained the object of our visit, which was to demand the surrender of the white men, who were now concealed in the town, and for permission to pass up the river in pursuit of those who had gone up that way. He now expressed the most violent indignation at our presumption in demanding the pirates, and the interview was broken off by his refusing to deliver up a single man."

We will now return to the pirates. While at Prince's Island, Capt. Gilbert bought a magnificent dressing case worth nearly a thousand dollars and a patent lever watch, and a quantity of tobacco, and provisions, and two valuable cloth coats, some Guinea cloth and black and green paint. The paint, cloth and coats were intended as presents for the African king at Cape Lopez. These articles were all bought with the money taken from the Mexican. After arriving at the Nazareth, $4000 were taken from the trunk, and buried in the yard of a negro prince. Four of the pirates then went to Cape Lopez for $11,000, which had been buried there. Boyga, Castillo, Guzman, and the "State's Evidence," Ferez, were the ones who went. Ferez took the bags out, and the others counted the money; great haste was made as the musquitoes were biting intolerably. $5000 were buried for the captain in canvas bags about two feet deep, part of the money was carried to Nazareth, and from there carried into the mountains and there buried. A consultation was held by Capt. Gilbert, De Soto, and Ruiz, and the latter said, if the money was not divided, "there would be the devil to pay." The money was now divided in a dark room and a lantern used; Capt. Gilbert sat on the floor with the money at his side. He gave the mate about $3000, and the other officers $1000, each; and the crew from $300 to $500, each. The third mate having fled, the captain sent him $1000, and Ruiz carried it to him. When the money was first taken from the Mexican, it was spread out on the companion way and examined to see if there was any gold amongst it; and then put into bags made of dark coarse linen; the boxes were then thrown overboard. After the division of the money the pirates secreted themselves in the woods behind Cape Lopez. Perez and four others procured a boat, and started for Fernando Po; they put their money in the bottom of the boat for ballast, but was thrown overboard, near a rock and afterwards recovered by divers; this was done to prevent detection. The captain, mate, and carpenter had a conversation respecting the attempt of the latter, to blow her up, who could not account for the circumstance, that an explosion had not taken place; they told him he ought to have burst a barrel of powder over the deck and down the stairs to the magazine, loaded a gun, tied a fish line to the lock and pulled it when he came off in the canoe.

View of the Negro village on the river Nazareth, and the Panda at anchor

**View of the Negro village on the river Nazareth, and the Panda at anchor.**

The Panda being manned by Capt. Trotter and an English crew, commenced firing on the town of Cape Lopez, but after firing several shots, a spark communicated with the magazine and she blew up. Several men were killed, and Captain Trotter and the others thrown into the water, when he was made prisoner with several of his crew, by the King, and it required considerable negociations to get them free.

Burying the money on the beach at Cape Lopez

**Burying the money on the beach at Cape Lopez.**

The pirates having gone up the river, an expedition was now equipped to take them if possible. The long-boat and pinnace were instantly armed, and victualled for several weeks, a brass gun was mounted on the bows of each, and awnings fixed up to protect the crew from the extreme heat of the sun by day, and the heavy dews at nightfall. As the sea-breeze and the flood-tide set in, the boats again started and proceeded up the river. It was ascertained the war-canoes were beyond where the Panda was first taken; for fear of an ambuscade great caution was observed in proceeding. "As we approached a point, a single native was observed standing near a hut erected near the river, who, as we approached, beckoned, and called for us to land. We endeavored to do so, but fortunately the water was too shallow to approach near enough.

"We had hardly steered about for the channel, when the man suddenly rushed into the bushes and disappeared. We got into the channel, and continued some time in deep water, but this suddenly shoaled, and the boats grounded near a mangrove, just as we came in sight of a village. Our crew jumped out, and commenced tracking the boat over the sand, and while thus employed, I observed by means of my glass, a crowd of natives, and some of the pirates running down the other side of a low point, apparently with the intention of giving us battle, as they were all armed with spears and muskets."

The men had just succeeded in drawing the boats into deep water, when a great number of canoes were observed coming round the point, and at the same instant another large party running down to launch; some more on the beach, when they joined those already afloat, in all made above twenty-eight canoes, and about one hundred and fifty men. Having collected all their forces, with loud whooping and encouraging shouts to one another, they led towards us with great celerity.

We prepared instantly for battle; the awnings were got down to allow room to use the cutlasses and to load the muskets. The brass guns were loaded with grape shot. They now approached uttering terrific yells, and paddling with all speed. On board the canoes the pirates were loading the guns and encouraging the natives. Bernardo de

Soto and Francisco Ruiz were conspicuous, in manoeuvring the negro boats for battle, and commenced a straggling fire upon the English boats. In them all was still, each man had a cutlass by his side, and a loaded musket in his hand. On arriving within pistol-shot a well directed fire was poured into them, seconded by a discharge of the three pounders; many of the balls took effect, and two of the canoes were sunk. A brisk fire was kept up on both sides; a great number of the negroes were killed, and a few of the pirates; the English loss was small. The negroes now became panic-struck, and some paddled towards the shore, others jumped overboard and swam; the sharks caught several. Captain Gilbert and De Soto were now caught, together with five of the crew; Ruiz and the rest escaped to a village, some ways inland, and with the aid of a telescope it was perceived the negroes were rapidly gathering to renew the combat, urged on by Ruiz and the other pirates; after dislodging them from this village, negociations were entered into by the king of Cape Lopez, who surrendered Ruiz and several men to Captain Trotter. They were carried in the brig Curlew to Fernando Po, and after an examination, were put in irons and conveyed to England, and there put on board the British gun-brig Savage, and arrived in the harbor of Salem on the 26th August, 1834. Her commander, Lieut. Loney, waited upon the authorities of Salem, and after the usual formalities, surrendered the prisoners into their hands–stating that the British Government waived their right to try and punish the prisoners, in favor of the United States, against whom the principal offence had been committed. The pirates were landed at Crowningshield wharf, and taken from thence in carriages to the Town hall; twelve of them, handcuffed in pairs, took their places at the bar. They were all young and middle-aged, the oldest was not over forty. Physiognomically, they were not uncommonly ill looking, in general, although there were exceptions, and they were all clean and wholesome in their appearance. They were now removed to Boston and confined in prison, where one of them, named Manuel Delgarno cut his throat with a piece of glass, thus verifying the old proverb, *that those born to be hung, will never be drown'd!*

On the 11th of November, Don Pedro Gilbert, *Captain*, Don Bernardo de Soto, *Mate*, Francisco Ruiz, *Carpenter*, Nicola Costa, *Cabin-boy,* aged 15, Antonio Ferrer, *Cook*, and Manuel Boyga, Domingo de Guzman, *an Indian*, Juan Antonio Portana, Manuel Castillo, Angel Garcia, Jose Velasquez, and Juan Montenegro, *alias* Jose Basilio de Castro, were arraigned before the Circuit Court of the United States, charged with the crime of Piracy. Joseph Perez appeared as *State's evidence*, and two Portuguese sailors who were shipped on board the Panda at Prince's Island, as witnesses. After a jury was empannelled, Mr. Dunlap, the District Attorney, rose and said–"This is a solemn, and also an unusual scene. Here are twelve men, strangers to our country and to our language, indicted for a heinous offence, and now before you for life or death. They are indicted for a daring crime, and a flagrant violation of the laws, not only of this, but of every other civilized people." He then gave an outline of the commission of the robbery of the Mexican. Numerous witnesses were examined, amongst whom were the captain, mate, and several seamen of the Mexican, who recognized several of the pirates as being the individuals who maltreated them, and took the specie. When Thomas Fuller, one of the crew of the Mexican was called upon to identify Ruiz, he went up to him and struck him a violent blow on the shoulder. Ruiz immediately started up, and with violent gesticulations protested against such conduct, and was joined by his companions. The Court reprimanded the witness severely. The trial occupied *fourteen days*. The counsel for the prisoners were David L. Child, Esq., and George Hillard, Esq., who defended them with great ability. Mr. Child brought to the cause his untiring zeal, his various and profound learning; and exhibited a labour, and *desperation* which showed that he was fully conscious of the weight of the load–the dead lift–he had undertaken to carry. Mr. Hillard concluded his argument, by making an eloquent and affecting appeal to the jury in behalf of the boy Costa and Antonio Ferrer, the cook, and alluded to the circumstance of Bernardo de Soto having rescued the lives of 70 individuals on board the American ship Minerva, whilst on a voyage from Philadelphia to Havana, when captain of the brig Leon.

Explosion of the Panda

**Explosion of the Panda.**

If, gentlemen, said he, you deem with me, that the crew of the Panda, (supposing her to have robbed the Mexican,) were merely servants of the captain, you cannot convict them. But if you do not agree with me, then all that remains for me to do, is to address a few words to you in the way of mercy. It does not seem to me that the good of society requires the death of all these men, the sacrifice of such a hecatomb of human victims, or that the sword of the law should fall till it is clogged with massacre. *Antonio Ferrer* is plainly but a servant. He is set down as a free black in the ship's papers, but that is no proof that he is free. Were he a slave, he would in all probability be represented as free, and this for obvious reasons. He is in all probability a slave, and a native African, as the tattooing on his face proves beyond a doubt. At any rate, he is but a servant. Now will you make misfortune pay the penalty of guilt? Do not, I entreat you, lightly condemn this man to death. Do not throw him in to make up the dozen. The regard for human life is one of the most prominent proofs of a civilized state of society. The Sultan of Turkey may place women in sacks and throw them into the Bosphorus, without exciting more than an hour's additional conversation at Constantinople. But in our country it is different. You well remember the excitement produced by the abduction and death of a single individual; the convulsions which ensued, the effect of which will long be felt in our political institutions. You will ever find that the more a nation becomes civilized, the greater becomes the regard for human life. There is in the eye, the form, and heaven-directed countenance of man, something holy, that forbids he should be rudely touched.

The instinct of life is great. The light of the sun even in chains, is pleasant; and life, though supported but by the damp exhalations of a dungeon, is desirable. Often, too, we cling with added tenacity to life in proportion as we are deprived of all that makes existence to be coveted.

Thomas Fuller striking Ruiz in Court

**Thomas Fuller striking Ruiz in Court.**

"The weariest and most loathed worldly life.
That age, ache, penury and imprisonment
Can lay on Nature, is a Paradise
To that we fear of Death."

Death is a fearful thing. The mere mention of it sometimes blanches the cheek, and sends the fearful blood to the heart. It is a solemn thing to break into the "bloody house of life." Do not, because this man is but an African, imagine that his existence is valueless. He is no drift weed on the ocean of life. There are in his bosom the same social sympathies that animate our own. He has nerves to feel pain, and a heart to throb with human affections, even as you have. His life, to establish the law, or to further the ends of justice, is not required. *Taken*, it is to us of no value; given to him, it is above the price of rubies.

And *Costa*, the cabin boy, only fifteen years of age when this crime was committed–shall he die? Shall the sword fall upon his neck? Some of you are advanced in years–you may have children. Suppose the news had reached you, that your son was under trial for his life, in a foreign country–(and every cabin boy who leaves this port may be placed in the situation of this prisoner,)–suppose you were told that he had been executed, because his captain and officers had violated the laws of a distant land; what would be your feelings? I cannot tell, but I believe the feelings of all of you would be the same, and that you would exclaim, with the Hebrew, "My son! my son! would to God I had died for thee." This boy *has* a father; let the form of that father rise up before you, and plead in your hearts for his offspring. Perhaps he has a mother, and a home. Think of the lengthened shadow that must have been cast over that home by his absence. Think of his mother, during those hours of wretchedness, when she has felt hope darkening into disappointment, next into anxiety, and from anxiety into despair. How often may she have stretched forth her hands in supplication, and asked, even the winds of heaven, to bring her tidings of him who was away? Let the supplications of that mother touch your hearts, and shield their object from the law.

After a luminous charge by Judge Story, the jury retired to agree upon their verdict, and at 9 o'clock the next morning came in with their verdict.

*Clerk*. Gentlemen of the Jury, have you agreed upon your verdict?

*Jury*. We have.

*Clerk*. Who shall speak for you?

*Jury*. Our foreman.

The prisoners were then directed severally to rise as soon as called, and receive the verdict of the jury. The Captain, *Pedro Gilbert*, was the first named. He arose, raised his hand, and regarded the jury with a firm countenance and steady eye.

*Clerk*. Jurors look upon the prisoner; prisoner look upon the jurors. How say you, Gentlemen, is the prisoner at the bar, Pedro Gilbert, guilty or not guilty?

*Foreman*. GUILTY.

The same verdict was pronounced against *De Soto* (the mate) *Ruiz*, (the carpenter,) *Boyga, Castillo, Garcia* and *Montenegro*. But *Costa*, (the cabin-boy,) *Ferrer* (the negro,) *Guzman, Portana*, and *Velasquez*, were declared NOT GUILTY.

After having declared the verdict of the Jury, the Foreman read to the Court the following recommendation to mercy:

"The sympathies of the Jury have been strongly moved in behalf of *Bernardo de Soto*, on account of his generous, noble and self-sacrificing conduct in saving the lives of more than 70 human beings, constituting the passengers and crew of the ship

*Minerva*; and they desire that his case should be presented to the merciful consideration of the Government."

Judge Story replied that the wish of the jury would certainly be complied with both by the Court and the prosecuting officer.

"The appearance and demeanor of Captain Gilbert are the same as when we first saw him; his eye is undimmed, and decision and command yet sit upon his features. We did not discern the slightest alteration of color or countenance when the verdict of the jury was communicated to him; he merely slightly bowed and resumed his seat. With *De Soto* the case was different. He is much altered; has become thinner, and his countenance this morning was expressive of the deepest despondency. When informed of the contents of the paper read by the foreman of the jury, he appeared much affected, and while being removed from the Court, covered his face with his handkerchief."

Immediately after the delivery of the verdict, the acquitted prisoners, on motion of Mr. Hillard, were directed to be discharged, upon which several of the others loudly and angrily expressed their dissatisfaction at the result of the trial. Castillo (*a half-caste*, with an extremely mild and pleasing countenance,) pointed towards heaven, and called upon the Almighty to bear witness that he was innocent; *Ruiz* uttered some words with great vehemence; and *Garcia* said "all were in the same ship; and it was strange that some should be permitted to escape while others were punished." Most of them on leaving the Court uttered some invective against "the *picaro* who had sworn their lives away."

On *Costa*, the cabin boy, (aged 16) being declared "Not Guilty" some degree of approbation was manifested by the audience, but instantly checked by the judge, who directed the officers to take into custody, every one expressing either assent or dissent. We certainly think the sympathy expressed in favor of *Costa* very ill placed, for although we have not deemed ourselves at liberty to mention the fact earlier, his conduct during the whole trial was characterized by the most reckless effrontery and indecorum. Even when standing up to receive the verdict of the jury, his face bore an impudent smile, and he evinced the most total disregard of the mercy which had been extended towards him.

About this time vague rumors reached Corunna, that a Captain belonging to that place, engaged in the Slave Trade, had turned Pirate, been captured, and sent to America with his crew for punishment. Report at first fixed it upon a noted slave-dealer, named Begaro. But the astounding intelligence soon reached Senora de Soto, that her husband was the person captured for this startling crime. The shock to her feelings was terrible, but her love and fortitude surmounted them all; and she determined to brave the terrors of the ocean, to intercede for her husband if condemned, and at all events behold him once more. A small schooner was freighted by her own and husband's father, and in it she embarked for New-York. After a boisterous passage, the vessel reached that port, when she learned her husband had already been tried and condemned to die. The humane people of New-York advised her to hasten on to Washington, and plead with the President for a pardon. On arriving at the capital, she solicited an interview with General Jackson, which was readily granted. From the circumstance of her husband's having saved the lives of seventy Americans, a merciful ear was turned to her solicitations, and a pardon for De Soto was given her, with which she hastened to Boston, and communicated to him the joyful intelligence.

Andrew Jackson, President of the United States of America, to all to whom these presents shall come, *Greeting*: Whereas, at the October Term, 1834, of the Circuit Court of the United States, Bernardo de Soto was convicted of Piracy, and sentenced to be hung on the 11th day of March last from which sentence a respite was granted him for three months, bearing date the third day of March, 1835, also a subsequent one, dated on the fifth day of June, 1835, for sixty days. And whereas the said Bernardo de Soto has been represented as a fit subject for executive clemency–

Now therefore, I, Andrew Jackson, President of the United States of America, in consideration of the premises, divers good and sufficient causes me thereto moving, have pardoned, and hereby do pardon the said Bernardo de Soto, from and after the 11th August next, and direct that he be then discharged from confinement. In testimony whereof I have hereunto subscribed my name, and caused the seal of the United States to be affixed to these presents. Done at the City of Washington the sixth day of July, AD. 1835, and of the independence of the United States and sixtieth. Andrew Jackson.

On the fatal morning of June 11th, 1835, Don Pedro, Juan Montenegro, Manuel Castillo, Angel Garcia and Manuel Boyga, were, agreeably to sentence, summoned to prepare for immediate execution. On the night previous, a mutual agreement had been entered into to commit suicide. Angel Garcia made the first attempt by trying to open the veins of each arm with a piece of glass; but was prevented. In the morning, however, while preparations were making for the execution, Boyga succeeded in inflicting a deep gash on the left side of his neck, with a piece of tin. The officer's eyes had been withdrawn from him scarcely a minute, before he was discovered lying on his pallet, with a convulsive motion of his knees, from loss of blood. Medical aid was at hand, the gash sewed up, but he did not revive. Two Catholic clergymen attended them on the scaffold, one a Spanish priest. They were executed in the rear of the jail. When the procession arrived at the foot of the ladder leading up to the platform of the gallows the Rev. Mr. Varella looking directly at Capt. Gilbert, said, "Spaniards, ascend to heaven." Don Pedro mounted with a quick step, and was followed by his comrades at a more moderate pace, but without the least hesitation. Boyga, unconscious of his situation and destiny, was carried up in a chair, and seated beneath the rope prepared for him. Gilbert, Montenegro, Garcia and Castillo all smiled subduedly as they took their stations on the platform. Soon after Capt. Gilbert ascended the scaffold, he passed over to where the apparently lifeless Boyga was seated in the chair, and kissed him. Addressing his followers, he said, "Boys, we are going to die; but let us be firm, for we are innocent." To Mr. Peyton, the interpreter, he said, "I die innocent, but I'll die like a noble Spaniard. Good bye, brother." The Marshal having read the warrant for their execution, and stated that de Soto was respited *sixty* and Ruiz *thirty* days, the ropes were adjusted round the necks of the prisoners, and a slight hectic flush spread over the countenance of each; but not an eye quailed, nor a limb trembled, not a muscle quivered. The fatal cord was now cut, and the platform fell, by which the prisoners were launched into eternity. After the execution was over, Ruiz, who was confined in his cell, attracted considerable attention, by his maniac shouts and singing. At one time holding up a piece of blanket, stained with Boyga's blood, he gave utterance to his ravings in a sort of recitative, the burden of which was–"This is the red flag my companions died under!"

After the expiration of Ruiz' second respite, the Marshal got two surgeons of the United States Navy, who understood the Spanish language, to attend him in his cell; they, after a patient examination pronounced his madness a counterfeit, and his insanity a hoax. Accordingly, on the morning of Sept. 11th, the Marshal, in company with a Catholic priest and interpreter entered his cell, and made him sensible that longer evasion of the sentence of the law was impossible, and that he must surely die. They informed him that he had but half an hour to live, and retired; when he requested that he might not be disturbed during the brief space that remained to him, and turning his back to the open entrance to his cell, he unrolled some fragments of printed prayers, and commenced reading them to himself. During this interval he neither spoke, nor heeded those who were watching him; but undoubtedly suffered extreme mental agony. At one minute he would drop his chin on his bosom, and stand motionless; at another would press his brow to the wall of his cell, or wave his body from side to side, as if wrung with unutterable anguish. Suddenly, he would throw himself upon his knees on the mattress, and prostrate himself as if in prayer; then throwing his prayers from him, he would clutch his rug in his fingers, and like a child try to double it up, or pick it to pieces. After snatching up his rug and throwing it away again and again, he would suddenly resume his prayers and erect posture, and stand mute, gazing through the aperture that admitted the light of day for upwards of a minute. This scene of imbecility and indecision, of horrible prostration of mind, ceasing in some degree when the Catholic clergyman re-entered his cell.

At 10 o'clock, the prisoner was removed from the prison, and during his progress to the scaffold, though the hue of death was on his face, and he trembled in every joint with fear, he chaunted with a powerful voice an appropriate service from the Catholic ritual. Several times he turned round to survey the heavens which at that moment were clear and bright above him and when he ascended the scaffold after concluding his prayer, he took one long and steadfast look at the sun, and waited in silence his fate. His powers, mental and physical had been suddenly crushed with the appalling reality that surrounded him; his whole soul was absorbed with one master feeling, the dread of a speedy and violent death. He quailed in the presence of the dreadful paraphernalia of his punishment, as much as if he had been a stranger to deeds of blood, and never dealt death to his fellow man as he ploughed the deep, under the black flag of piracy, with the motto of "Rob, Kill, and Burn." After adjusting the rope, a signal was given. The body dropped heavily, and the harsh abrupt shock must have instantly deprived him of sensation, as there was no voluntary action of the hands afterwards. Thus terminated his career of crime in a foreign land without one friend to recognize or cheer him, or a single being to regret his death.

The Spanish Consul having requested that the bodies might not be given to the faculty, they were interred at night under the direction of the Marshal, in the Catholic burial-ground at Charlestown. There being no murder committed with the piracy, the laws of the United States do not authorize the court to order the bodies for dissection.

Ruiz leaving the Panda.
**Ruiz leaving the Panda.**

**THE LIFE OF BENITO DE SOTO THE PIRATE OF THE MORNING STAR.** The following narrative of the career of a desperate pirate who was executed in Gibraltar in the month of January, 1830, is one of two letters from the pen of the author of "the Military Sketch-Book." The writer says Benito de Soto "had been a prisoner in the garrison for nineteen months, during which time the British Government spared neither the pains not expense to establish a full train of evidence against him. The affair had caused the greatest excitement here, as well as at Cadiz, owing to the development of the atrocities which marked the character of this man, and the diabolical gang of which he was the leader. Nothing else is talked of; and a thousand horrors are added to his guilt, which, although he was guilty enough, he has no right to bear. The following is all the authentic information I could collect concerning him. I have drawn it from his trial, from the confession of his accomplices, from the keeper of his prison, and not a little from his own lips. It will be found more interesting than all the tales and sketches furnished in the 'Annuals,' magazines, and other vehicles of invention, from the simple fact–that it is truth and not fiction."

Benito de Soto was a native of a small village near Courna; he was bred a mariner, and was in the guiltless exercise of his calling at Buenos Ayres, in the year 1827. A vessel was there being fitted out for a voyage to the coast of Africa, for the smuggling of slaves; and as she required a strong crew, a great number of sailors were engaged, amongst whom was Soto. The Portuguese of South America have yet a privilege of dealing in slaves on a certain part of the African coast, but it was the intention of the captain of this vessel to exceed the limits of his trade, and to run farther down, so as to take his cargo of human beings from a part of the country which was proscribed, in the certainty of being there enabled to purchase slaves at a much lower rate than he could in the regular way; or, perhaps, to take away by force as many as he could stow away into his ship. He therefore required a considerable number of hands for the enterprise; and in such a traffic, it may be easily conceived, that the morals of the crew could not be a subject of much consideration with the employer. French, Spanish, Portuguese, and others, were entered on board, most of them renegadoes, and they set sail on their evil voyage, with every hope of infamous success.

Those who deal in evil carry along with them the springs of their own destruction, upon which they will tread, in spite of every caution, and their imagined security is but the brink of the pit into which they are to fall. It was so with the captain of this slave-ship. He arrived in Africa, took in a considerable number of slaves, and in order to complete his cargo, went on shore, leaving his mate in charge of the vessel. This mate was a bold, wicked, reckless and ungovernable spirit, and perceiving in Benito de Soto a mind congenial with his own, he fixed on him as a fit person to join in a design he had conceived, of running away with the vessel, and becoming a pirate. Accordingly the mate proposed his plan to Soto, who not only agreed to join in it, but declared that he himself had been contemplating a similar enterprise during the voyage. They both were at once of a mind, and they lost no time in maturing their plot.

Their first step was to break the matter to the other members of the crew. In this they proceeded cautiously, and succeeded so far as to gain over twenty-two of the whole, leaving eighteen who remained faithful to their trust. Every means were used to corrupt the well disposed; both persuasion and threats were resorted to, but without effect, and the leader of the conspiracy, the mate, began to despair of obtaining the desired object. Soto, however, was not so easily depressed. He at once decided on seizing the ship upon the strength of his party: and without consulting the mate, he collected all the arms of the vessel, called the conspirators together, put into each of their possession a cutlass and a brace of pistols, and arming himself in like manner, advanced at the head of the gang, drew his sword, and declared the mate to be the commander of the ship, and the men who joined him part owners. Still, those who had rejected the evil offer remained unmoved; on which Soto ordered out the boats, and pointing to the land, cried out, "There is the African coast; this is our ship–one or the other must be chosen by every man on board within five minutes."

This declaration, although it had the effect of preventing any resistance that might have been offered by the well disposed, to the taking of the vessel, did not change them from their purpose; they still refused to join in the robbery, and entered one by one into the boat, at the orders of Soto, and with but one pair of oars (all that was allowed to them) put off for the shore, from which they were then ten miles distant. Had the weather continued calm, as it was when the boat left the ship, she would have made the shore by dusk; but unhappily a strong gale of wind set in shortly after her departure, and she was seen by Soto and his gang struggling with the billows and approaching night, at such a distance from the land as she could not possibly accomplish while the gale lasted. All on board the ship agreed in opinion that the boat could not live, as they flew away from her at the rate of ten knots an hour, under close reefed topsails, leaving their unhappy messmates to their inevitable fate. Those of the pirates who were lately executed at Cadiz, declared that every soul in the boat perished.

The Pirates carrying rum on shore to purchase slaves

**The Pirates carrying rum on shore to purchase slaves.**

The drunken uproar which that night reigned in the pirate ship was in horrid unison with the raging elements around her; contention and quarrelling followed the brutal ebriety of the pirates; each evil spirit sought the mastery of the others, and Soto's, which was the fiend of all, began to grasp and grapple for its proper place–the head of such a diabolical community.

The mate (now the chief) at once gave the reins to his ruffian tyranny; and the keen eye of Soto saw that he who had fawned with him the day before, would next day rule him with an iron rod. Prompt in his actions as he was penetrating in his judgment, he had no sooner conceived a jealousy of the leader than he determined to put him aside; and as his rival lay in his drunken sleep, Soto put a pistol to his head, and deliberately shot him. For this act he excused himself to the crew, by stating to them that it was in *their* protection he did the act; that *their* interest was the other's death; and concluded by declaring himself their leader, and promising a golden harvest to their future labors, provided they obeyed him. Soto succeeded to the height of his wishes, and was unanimously hailed by the crew as their captain.

On board the vessel, as I before stated, were a number of slaves, and these the pirates had well secured under hatches. They now turned their attention to those half starved, half suffocated creatures;–some were for throwing them overboard, while others, not less cruel, but more desirous of gain, proposed to take them to some port in one of those countries that deal in human beings, and there sell them. The latter recommendation was adopted, and Soto steered for the West Indies, where he received a good price for his slaves. One of those wretched creatures, a boy, he reserved as a servant for himself; and this boy was destined by Providence to be the witness of the punishment of those white men who tore away from their homes himself and his brethren. He alone will carry back to his country the truth of Heaven's retribution, and heal the wounded feelings of broken kindred with the recital of it.

The pirates now entered freely into their villainous pursuit, and plundered many vessels; amongst others was an American brig, the treatment of which forms the *chef d'oeuvre* of their atrocity. Having taken out of this brig all the valuables they could find, they hatched down all hands to the hold, except a black man, who was allowed to remain on deck for the special purpose of affording in his torture an amusing exhibition to Soto and his gang. They set fire to the brig, then lay to, to observe the progress of the flames; and as the miserable African bounded from rope to rope, now climbing to the mast head–now clinging to the shrouds–now leaping to one part of the vessel, and now to another,–their enjoyment seemed raised to its heighest pitch. At length the hatches opened to the devouring element, the tortured victim of their fiendish cruelty fell exhausted into the flames, and the horrid and revolting scene closed amidst the shouts of the miscreants who had caused it.

Of their other exploits, that which ranks next in turpitude, and which led to their overthrow, was the piracy of the Morning Star. They fell in with that vessel near the island Ascension, in the year 1828, as she was on her voyage from Ceylon to England. This vessel, besides a valuable cargo, had on board several passengers, consisting of a major and his wife, an assistant surgeon, two civilians, about five and twenty invalid soldiers, and three or four of their wives. As soon as Benito de Soto perceived the ship, which was at daylight on the 21st of February, he called up all hands, and prepared for attacking her; he was at the time steering on an opposite course to that of the Morning Star. On reconnoitring her, he at first supposed she was a French vessel; but Barbazan, one of his crew, who was himself a Frenchman, assured him the ship was British. "So much the better," exclaimed Soto, in English (for he could speak that language), "we shall find the more booty." He then ordered the sails to be squared, and ran before the wind in chase of his plunder, from which he was about two leagues distant.

The Defensor de Pedro, the name of the pirate ship, was a fast sailer, but owing to the press of canvas which the Morning Star hoisted soon after the pirate had commenced the chase, he did not come up with her so quickly as he had expected: the delay caused great uneasiness to Soto, which he manifested by muttering curses, and restlessness of manner. Sounds of savage satisfaction were to be heard from every mouth but his at the prospect; he alone expressed his anticipated pleasure by oaths, menaces, and mental inquietude. While Barbazan was employed in superintending the clearing of the decks, the arming and breakfasting of the men, he walked rapidly up and down, revolving in his mind the plan of the approaching attack, and when interrupted by any of the crew, he would run into a volley of imprecations. In one instance, he struck his black boy a violent blow with a telescope, because he asked him if he would have his morning cup of chocolate; as soon, however, as he set his studding sails, and perceived that he was gaining on the Morning Star, he became somewhat tranquil, began to eat heartily of cold beef, drank his chocolate at a draught, and coolly sat down on the deck to smoke a cigar.

In less than a quarter of an hour, the pirate had gained considerable on the other vessel. Soto now, without rising from where he sat, ordered a gun, with blank cartridge, to be fired, and the British colors to be hoisted: but finding this measure had not the effect of bringing the Morning Star to, he cried out, "Shot the long gun and give it her point blank." The order was obeyed, but the shot fell short of the intention, on which he jumped up and cursed the fellows for bunglers who had fired the gun. He then ordered them to load with canister shot, and took the match in his own hand. He did not, however, fire immediately, but waited until he was nearly abreast of his victim; then directing the aim himself, and ordering a man to stand by the flag to haul it down, fired with an air that showed he was sure of his mark. He then ran to haul up the Colombian colors, and having done so, cried out through the speaking trumpet, "Lower your boat down this moment, and let your captain come on board with his papers."

During this fearful chase the people on board the Morning Star were in the greatest alarm; but however their apprehensions might have been excited, that courage, which is so characteristic of a British sailor, never for a moment forsook the captain. He boldly carried on sail, and although one of the men fell from a wound, and the ravages of the shot were every where around him, he determined not to strike. But unhappily he had not a single gun on board, and no small arms that could render his courage availing. The tears of the women, and the prudent advice of the passengers overcoming his resolution, he permitted himself to be guided by the general opinion. One of the passengers volunteered himself to go on board the pirate, and a boat was lowered for the purpose. Both vessels now lay to within fifty yards of each other, and a strong hope arose in those on board the Morning Star, that the gentleman who had volunteered to go to the pirate, might, through his exertions, avert, at least, the worst of the dreaded calamity.

Some people here, in their quiet security, have made no scruple of declaring, that the commanding officer of the soldiers on board should not have so tamely yielded to the pirate, particularly as he had his wife along with him, and consequently a misfortune to dread, that might be thought even worse than death: but all who knew the true state of the circumstances, and reflect upon it, will allow that he adopted the only chance of escaping that, which was to be most feared by a husband. The long gun, which was on a pivot in the centre of the pirate ship, could in a few shots sink the Morning Star; and even had resistance been made to the pirates as they boarded her–had they been killed or made prisoners–the result would not be much better. It was evident that the Defensor de Pedro was the best sailer, consequently the Morning Star could not hope to escape; in fact, submission or total destruction was the only choice. The commanding officer, therefore, acted for the best when he recommended the former. There was some slight hope of escaping with life, and without personal abuse, by surrendering, but to contend must be inevitable death.

The gentleman who had gone in a boat to the pirate returned in a short time, exhibiting every proof of the ill treatment he had received from Soto and his crew. It appears that when the villains learned that he was not the captain, they fell upon and beat him, as well as the sailors along with him, in a most brutal manner, and with the most horrid imprecations told him, that if the captain did not instantly come, on his return to the vessel, they would blow the ship out of the water. This report as once decided the captain in the way he was to act. Without hesitation he stepped into the boat, taking with him his second mate, three soldiers and a sailor boy, and proceeded to the pirate. On going on board that vessel, along with the mate, Soto, who stood near the mainmast, with his drawn cutlass in his hand, desired him to approach, while the mate was ordered, by Barbazan, to go to the forecastle. Both these unfortunate individuals obeyed, and were instantly slaughtered.

Soto now ordered six picked men to descend into the boat, amongst whom was Barbazan. To him the leader addressed his orders, the last of which was, to take care to put all in the prize to death, and then sink her.

The six pirates, who proceeded to execute his savage demand, were all armed alike,–they each carried a brace of pistols, a cutlass and a long knife. Their dress was composed of a sort of coarse cotton chequered jacket and trowsers, shirts that were open at the collar, red woollen caps, and broad canvas waistbelts, in which were the pistols and the knives. They were all athletic men, and seemed such as might well be trusted with the sanguinary errand on which they were despatched. While the boat was conveying them, Soto held in his hand a cutlass, reddened with the blood of the murdered captain, and stood scowling on them with silence: while another ruffian, with a lighted match, stood by the long gun, ready to support the boarding, if necessary, with a shot that would sweep the deck.

As the boarders approached the Morning Star, the terror of the females became excessive; they clung to their husbands in despair, who endeavored to allay their fears by their own vain hopes, assuring them that a quiet submission nothing more than the plunder of the vessel was to be apprehended. But a few minutes miserably undeceived them. The pirates rapidly mounted the side, and as they jumped on deck, commenced to cut right and left at all within their reach, uttering at the same time the most dreadful oaths. The females, screaming, hurried to hide themselves below as well as they were able, and the men fell or fled before the pirates, leaving them entire masters of the decks.

The mate begging for his life

**The mate begging for his life.**

When the pirates had succeeded in effectually prostrating all the people on deck, they drove most of them below, and reserved the remainder to assist in their operations. Unless the circumstances be closely examined, it may be wondered how six men could have so easily overcome a crew of English seamen supported by about twenty soldiers with a major at their head:–but it will not appear so surprising, when it is considered that the sailors were altogether unarmed, the soldiers were worn out invalids, and more particularly, that the pirate carried a heavy long gun, ready to sink her victim at a shot. Major Logie was fully impressed with the folly of opposing so powerful and desperate an enemy, and therefore advised submission as the only course for the safety of those under his charge; presuming no doubt that something like humanity might be found in the breasts even of the worst of men. But alas! he was woefully deceived in his estimate of the villains' nature, and felt, when too late, that even death would have been preferable to the barbarous treatment he was forced to endure.

Beaten, bleeding, terrified, the men lay huddled together in the hold, while the pirates proceeded in their work of pillage and brutality. Every trunk was hauled forth, every portable article of value heaped for the plunder; money, plate, charts, nautical instruments, and seven parcels of valuable jewels, which formed part of the cargo; these were carried from below on the backs of those men whom the pirates selected to assist them, and for two hours they were thus employed, during which time Soto stood upon his own deck directing the operations; for the vessels were within a hundred yards of each other. The scene which took place in the cabin exhibited a licentious brutality. The sick officer, Mr. Gibson, was dragged from his berth; the clothes of the other passengers stripped from their backs, and the whole of the cabin passengers driven on deck, except the females, whom they locked up in the round-house on deck, and the steward, who was detained to serve the pirates with wine and eatables. This treatment, no doubt hastened the death of Gibson; the unfortunate gentleman did not long survive it. As the passengers were forced up the cabin ladder, the feelings of Major Logie, it may be imagined, were of the most heart-rending description. In vain did he entreat to be allowed to remain; he was hurried away from even the chance of protecting his defenceless wife, and battened down with the rest in the hold, there to be racked with the fearful apprehensions of their almost certain doom.

The labors of the robbers being now concluded, they sat down to regale themselves, preparatory to the *chef d'oeuvre* of their diabolical enterprise; and a more terrible group of demi-devils, the steward declares, could not be well imagined than commanded his attention at the cabin table. However, as he was a Frenchman, and naturally polite, he acquitted himself of the office of cup-bearer, if not as gracefully, at least as anxiously, as ever did Ganymede herself. Yet, notwithstanding this readiness to serve the visitors in their gastronomic desires, the poor steward felt ill-requited; he was twice frightened into an icicle, and twice thawed back into conscious horror, by the rudeness of those he entertained. In one instance, when he had filled out a sparkling glass for a ruffian, and believed he had quite won the heart of the drinker by the act, he found himself grasped roughly and tightly by the throat, and the point of a knife staring him in the face. It seems the fellow who thus seized him, had felt between his teeth a sharp bit of broken glass, and fancying that something had been put in the wine to poison him, he determined to prove his suspicions by making the steward swallow what remained in the bottle from which the liquor had been drawn, and thus unceremoniously prefaced his command; however, ready and implicit obedience averted further bad consequences. The other instance of the steward's jeopardy was this; when the repast was ended, one of the gentlemen coolly requested him to waive all delicacy, and point out the place in which the captain's money was concealed. He might as well have asked him to produce the philosopher's stone. However, pleading the truth was of no use; his determined requisitor seconded the demand by snapping a pistol at his breast; having missed fire, he recocked, and again presented; but the fatal weapon was struck aside by Barbazan, who reproved the rashness with a threat, and thus averted the steward's impending fate. It was then with feelings of satisfaction he heard himself ordered to go down to the hold, and in a moment he was bolted in among his fellow sufferers.

The ruffians indulged in the pleasures of the bottle for some time longer, and then having ordered down the females, treated them with even less humanity than characterized their conduct towards the others. The screams of the helpless females were heard in the hold by those who were unable to render them assistance, and agonizing, indeed, must those screams have been to their incarcerated hearers! How far the brutality of the pirates was carried in this stage of the horrid proceeding, we can only surmise; fortunately, their lives were spared, although, as it afterwards appeared, the orders of Soto were to butcher every being on board; and it is thought that these orders were not put into action, in consequence of the villains having wasted so much time in drinking, and otherwise indulging themselves; for it was not until the loud voice of their chief was heard to recall them, that they prepared to leave the ship; they therefore contented themselves with fastening the women within the cabin, heaping heavy lumber on the hatches of the hold, and boring holes in the planks of the vessel below the surface of the water, so that in destroying the unhappy people at one swoop, they might make up for the lost time. They then left the ship, sinking fast to her apparently certain fate.

Horrid abuse of the helpless women in the cabin

**Horrid abuse of the helpless women in the cabin.**

It may be reasonably supposed, bad as their conduct was towards the females, and pitiable as was the suffering it produced, that the lives of the whole left to perish were preserved through it; for the ship must have gone down if the women had been either taken out of her or murdered, and those in the hold inevitably have gone with her to the bottom. But by good fortune, the females succeeded in forcing their way out of the cabin, and became the means of liberating the men confined in the hold. When they came on deck, it was nearly dark, yet they could see the pirate ship at a considerable distance, with all her sails set and bearing away from them. They prudently waited, concealed from the possibility of being seen by the enemy, and when the night fell, they crept to the hatchway, and called out to the men below to endeavor to effect their liberation, informing them that the pirate was away and out of sight. They then united their efforts, and the lumber being removed, the hatches gave way to the force below, so that the released captives breathed of hope again. The delightful draught, however, was checked, when the ship was found to contain six feet of water! A momentary collapse took possession of all their newly excited expectations; cries and groans of despair burst forth, but the sailors' energy quickly returned, and was followed by that of the others; they set to work at the pumps, and by dint of labor succeeded in keeping the vessel afloat. Yet to direct her course was impossible; the pirates having completely disabled her, by cutting away her rigging and sawing the masts all the way through. The eye of Providence, however, was not averted from the hapless people, for they fell in with a vessel next day that relieved them from their distressing situation, and brought them to England in safety.

We will now return to Soto, and show how the hand of that Providence that secured his intended victims, fell upon himself and his wicked associates. Intoxicated with their infamous success, the night had far advanced before Soto learned that the people in the Morning Star, instead of being slaughtered, were only left to be drowned. The information excited his utmost rage. He reproached Barbazan, and those who had accompanied them in the boarding, with disobeying his orders, and declared that now there could be no security for their lives. Late as the hour was, and long as he had been steering away from the Morning Star, he determined to put back, in the hope of effectually preventing the escape of those in the devoted vessel, by seeing them destroyed before his eyes. Soto was a follower of the principle inculcated by the old maxim, "Dead men tell no tales;" and in pursuance of his doctrine, lost not a moment in putting about and running back. But it was too late; he could find no trace of the vessel, and so consoled himself with the belief that she was at the bottom of the sea, many fathoms below the ken and cognizance of Admiralty Courts.

Soto, thus satisfied, bent his course to Europe. On his voyage he fell in with a small brig, boarded, plundered, sunk her, and, that he might not again run the hazard of encountering living witnesses of his guilt, murdered the crew, with the exception of one individual, whom he took along with him, on account of his knowledge of the course to Corunna, whither he intended to proceed. But, faithful to his principles of self-protection, as soon as he had made full use of the unfortunate sailor, and found himself in sight of the destined port, he came up to him at the helm, which he held in his hand, "My friend," said he "is that the harbor of Corunna?"–"Yes," was the reply. "Then," rejoined Soto, "You have done your duty well, and I am obliged to you for your services." On the instant he drew a pistol and shot the man; then coolly flung his body overboard, took the helm himself, and steered into his native harbor as little concerned as if he had returned from an honest voyage. At this port he obtained papers in a false name, disposed of a great part of his booty, and after a short stay set out for Cadiz, where he expected a market for the remainder. He had a fair wind until he came within sight of the coast near that city. It was coming on dark and he lay to, expecting to go into his anchorage next morning, but the wind shifted to the westward, and suddenly began to blow a heavy gale; it was right on the land. He luffed his ship as close to the wind as possible, in order to clear a point that stretched outward, and beat off to windward, but his lee-way carried him towards the land, and he was caught when he least expected the trap. The gale increased–the night grew pitchy dark–the roaring breakers were on his lee-beam–the drifting vessel strikes, rebounds, and strikes again–the cry of horror rings through the flapping cordage, and despair is in the eyes of the demon-crew. Helpless they lie amid the wrath of the storm, and the darkened face of Heaven, for the first time, strikes terror on their guilty hearts. Death is before them, but not with a merciful quickness does he approach; hour after hour the frightful vision glares upon them, and at length disappears only to come upon them again in a more dreadful form. The tempest abates, and the sinners were spared for the time.

As the daylight broke they took to their boats, and abandoned the vessel to preserve their lives. But there was no repentance in the pirates; along with the night and the winds went the voice of conscience, and they thought no more of what had passed. They stood upon the beach gazing at the wreck, and the first thought of Soto, was to sell it, and purchase another vessel for the renewal of his atrocious pursuits. With the marked decision of his character, he proposed his intention to his followers, and received their full approbation. The plan was instantly arranged; they were to present themselves as honest, shipwrecked mariners to the authorities at Cadiz; Soto was to take upon himself the office of mate, or *contra maestra,* to an imaginary captain, and thus obtain their sanction in disposing of the vessel. In their assumed character, the whole proceeded to Cadiz, and presented themselves before the proper officers of the marine. Their story was listened to with sympathy, and for a few days every thing went on to their satisfaction. Soto had succeeded so well as to conclude the sale of the wreck with a broker, for the sum of one thousand seven hundred and fifty dollars; the contract was signed, but fortunately the money was not yet paid, when suspicion arose, from some inconsistencies in the pirates' account of themselves, and six of them were arrested by the authorities. Soto and one of his crew instantly disappeared from Cadiz, and succeeded in arriving at the neutral ground before Gibraltar, and six more made their escape to the Carraccas.

None are permitted to enter the fortress of Gibraltar, without permission from the governor, or a passport. Soto and his companion, therefore, took up their quarters at a Posade on the neutral ground, and resided there in security for several days. The busy and daring mind of the former could not long remain inactive; he proposed to his companion to attempt to enter the garrison in disguise and by stealth, but could not prevail upon him to consent. He therefore resolved to go in alone; and his object in doing so was to procure a supply of money by a letter of credit which he brought with him from Cadiz. His companion, more wise than he, chose the safer course; he knew that the neutral ground was not much controllable by the laws either of the Spanish or the English, and although there was not much probability of being discovered, he resolved not to trust to chance in so great a stake as his life; and he proved to have been right in his judgment, for had he gone to Gibraltar, he would have shared the same fate of his chief. This man is the only one of the whole gang, who has not met with the punishment of his crimes, for he succeeded in effecting his escape on board some vessel. It is not even suspected to what country he is gone; but his description, no doubt, is registered. The steward of the Morning Star informed me, that he is a tall, stout man, with fair hair, and fresh complexion, of a mild and gentle countenance, but that he was one of the worst villains of the whole piratical crew. I believe he is stated to be a Frenchman.

Soto secured his admission into the garrison by a false pass, and took up his residence at an inferior tavern in a narrow lane, which runs off the main street of Gibraltar, and is kept by a man of the name of Basso. The appearance of this house suits well with the associations of the worthy Benito's life. I have occasion to pass the door frequently at night, for our barrack, (the Casement,) is but a few yards from it. I never look at the place without feeling an involuntary sensation of horror–the smoky and dirty nooks–the distant groups of dark Spaniards, Moors, and Jews, their sallow countenances made yellow by the fight of dim oil lamps–the unceiled rafters of the rooms above, seen through unshuttered windows and the consciousness of their having covered the atrocious Soto, combine this effect upon me.

In this den the villain remained for a few weeks, and during this time seemed to enjoy himself as if he had never committed a murder. The story he told Basso of his circumstances was, that he had come to Gibraltar on his way to Cadiz from Malaga, and was merely awaiting the arrival of a friend. He dressed expensively–generally wore a white hat of the best English quality, silk stockings, white trowsers, and blue frock coat. His whiskers were large and bushy, and his hair, which was very black, profuse, long and naturally curled, was much in the style of a London preacher of prophetic and anti-poetic notoriety. He was deeply browned with the sun, and had an air and gait expressive of his bold, enterprising, and desperate mind. Indeed, when I saw him in his cell and at his trial, although his frame was attenuated almost to a skeleton, the color of his face a pale yellow, his eyes sunken, and hair closely shorn; he still exhibited strong traces of what he had been, still retained his erect and fearless carriage, his quick, fiery, and malevolent eye, his hurried and concise speech, and his close and pertinent style of remark. He appeared to me such a man as would have made a hero in the ranks of his country, had circumstances placed him in the proper road to fame; but ignorance and poverty turned into the most ferocious robber, one who might have rendered service and been an honor to his sunken country. I should like to hear what the phrenologists say of his head; it appeared to me to be the most peculiar I had ever seen, and certainly, as far as the bump of *destructiveness* went, bore the theory fully out. It is rumored here that the skull has been sent to the *savans* of Edinburg; if this be the case, we shall no doubt be made acquainted with their sage opinions upon the subject, and great conquerors will receive a farther assurance of how much they resemble in their physical natures the greatest murderers.

When I visited the pirate in the Moorish castle where he was confined, he was sitting in his cold, narrow, and miserable cell, upon a pallet of straw, eating his coarse meal from a tin plate. I thought him more an object of pity than vengeance; he looked so worn with disease, so crushed with suffering, yet so affable, frank, and kind in his address; for he happened to be in a communicative mood, a thing that was by no means common with him. He spoke of his long confinement, till I thought the tears were about to start from his eyes, and alluded to his approaching trial with satisfaction; but his predominant characteristic, ferocity, appeared in his small piercing black eyes before I left him, as he alluded to his keeper, the Provost, in such a way that made me suspect his desire for blood was not yet extinguished. When he appeared in court on his trial, his demeanor was quite altered; he seemed to me to have suddenly risen out of the wretch he was in his cell, to all the qualities I had heard of him; he stood erect and unembarrassed; he spoke with a strong voice, attended closely to the proceedings, occasionally examined the witnesses, and at the conclusion protested against the justice of his trial. He sometimes spoke to the guards around him, and sometimes affected an air of carelessness of his awful situation, which, however, did not sit easy upon him. Even here the leading trait of his mind broke forth; for when the interpreter commenced his office, the language which he made use of being pedantic and affected, Soto interrupted him thus, while a scowl sat upon his brow that terrified the man of words: "I don't understand you, man; speak Spai and I'll listen to you." When the dirk that belonged to Mr. Robertso clothes taken from Mr. Gibson, and the pocket book containing the in-... handwriting were placed before him, and proved to have been found in his room, anu when the maid servant of the tavern proved that she found the dirk under his pillow every morning on arranging his bed; and when he was confronted with his own black slave, between two wax lights, the countenance of the villain appeared in its true nature, not depressed nor sorrowful, but vivid and ferocious; and when the patient and dignified governor, Sir George Don, passed the just sentence of the law upon him, he looked daggers at his heart, and assumed a horrid silence, more eloquent than words.

The criminal persisted up to the day before his execution in asserting his innocence, and inveighing against the injustice of his trial, but the certainty of his fate, and the awful voice of religion, at length subdued him. He made an unreserved confession of his guilt, and became truly penitent; gave up to the keeper the blade of a razor which he had secreted between the soles of his shoes for the acknowledged purpose of adding suicide to his crimes, and seemed to wish for the moment that was to send him before his Creator.

I witnessed his execution, and I believe there never was a more contrite man than he appeared to be; yet there were no drivelling fears upon him–he walked firmly at the tail of the fatal cart, gazing sometimes at his coffin, sometimes at the crucifix which he held in his hand. The symbol of divinity he frequently pressed to his lips, repeated the prayers spoken in his ear by the attendant clergyman, and seemed regardless of every thing but the world to come. The gallows was erected beside the water, and fronting the neutral ground. He mounted the cart as firmly as he had walked behind it, and held up his face to Heaven and the beating rain, calm, resigned, but unshaken; and finding the halter too high for his neck, he boldly stepped upon his coffin, and placed his head in the noose, then watching the first turn of the wheels, he murmured "*adios todos*," ["Farewell, all."] and leaned forward to facilitate his fall.

The black slave of the pirate stood upon the battery trembling before his dying master to behold the awful termination of a series of events, the recital of which to his African countrymen, when he shall return to his home, will give them no doubt, a dreadful picture of European civilization. The black boy was acquitted at Cadiz, but the men who had fled to the Carraccas, as well as those arrested after the wreck, were convicted, executed, their limbs severed, and hung on tenter hooks, as a warning to all pirates.

The Rock of Gibraltar

**The Rock of Gibraltar.**

## THE ADVENTURES OF CAPTAIN ROBERT KIDD

The easy access to the harbor of New-York, the number of hiding-places about its waters, and the laxity of its newly organized government, about the year 1695, made it a great rendezvous of pirates, where they might dispose of their booty and concert new depredations. As they brought home with them wealthy lading of all kinds, the luxuries of the tropics, and the sumptuous spoils of the Spanish provinces, and disposed of them with the proverbial carelessness of freebooters, they were welcome visitors to the thrifty traders of New-York. Crews of these desperadoes, therefore, the runagates of every country and every clime, might be seen swaggering in open day about the streets, elbowing its quiet inhabitants, trafficking their rich outlandish plunder at half or quarter price to the wary merchant; and then squandering their prize-money in taverns, drinking, gambling, singing, carousing and astounding the neighborhood with midnight brawl and revelry. At length these excesses rose to such a height as to become a scandal to the provinces, and to call loudly for the interposition of government. Measures were accordingly taken to put a stop to this widely extended evil, and to drive the pirates out of the colonies.

Among the distinguished individuals who lurked about the colonies, was Captain Robert Kidd, [Footnote: His real name was William Kidd.] who in the beginning of King William's war, commanded a privateer in the West Indies, and by his several adventurous actions, acquired the reputation of a brave man, as well as an experienced seaman. But he had now become notorious, as a nondescript animal of the ocean. He was somewhat of a trader, something more of a smuggler, but mostly a pirate. He had traded many years among the pirates, in a little rakish vessel, that could run into all kinds of water. He knew all their haunts and lurking places, and was always hooking about on mysterious voyages.

Upon the good old maxim of "setting a rogue to catch a rogue," Capt. Kidd was recommended by the Lord Bellamont, then governor of Barbadoes, as well as by several other persons, to the government here, as a person very fit to be entrusted to the command of a government ship, and to be employed in cruising upon the pirates, as knowing those seas perfectly well, and being acquainted with all their lurking places; but what reasons governed the politics of those times, I cannot tell, but this proposal met with no encouragement here, though it is certain it would have been of great consequence to the subject, our merchants suffering incredible damages by those robbers.

Upon this neglect, the lord Bellamont and some others, who knew what great captures had been made by the pirates, and what a prodigious wealth must be in their possession, were tempted to fit out a ship at their own private charge, and to give the command of her to Captain Kidd; and to give the thing a greater reputation, as well as to keep their seamen under better command, they procured the king's commission for the said Capt. Kidd, of which the following is an exact copy:

*William Rex,*

"WILLIAM THE THIRD, by the grace of God, King of England, Scotland, France and Ireland, defender of the faith, c. To our trusty and well beloved Capt. ROBERT KIDD, commander of the ship the Adventure galley, or to any other, the commander of the same for the time being, *Greeting*: Whereas we are informed, that Capt. Thomas Too, John Ireland, Capt. Thomas Wake, and Capt. William Maze or Mace, and other subjects, natives or inhabitants of New-York, and elsewhere, in our plantations in America, have associated themselves with divers others, wicked and ill-disposed persons, and do, against the law of nations, commit many and great piracies, robberies and depredations on the seas upon the parts of America, and in other parts, to the great hindrance and discouragement of trade and navigation, and to the great danger and hurt of our loving subjects, our allies, and all others, navigating the seas upon their lawful occasions. Now KNOW YE, that we being desirous to prevent the aforesaid mischiefs, and as much as in us lies, to bring the said pirates, free-booters and sea-rovers to justice, have thought fit, and do hereby give and grant to the said Robert Kidd, (to whom our commissioners for exercising the office of Lord High Admiral of England, have granted a commission as a private man-of-war, bearing date the 11th day of December, 1695,) and unto the commander of the said ship for the time being, and unto the officers, mariners, and others which shall be under your command, full power and authority to apprehend, seize, and take into your custody as well the said Capt. Thomas Too, John Ireland, Capt. Thomas Wake, and Capt. Wm. Maze or Mace, as all such pirates, free-booters, and sea-rovers, being either our subjects, or of other nations associated with them, which you shall meet with upon the seas or coasts of America, or upon any other seas or coasts, with all their ships and vessels, and all such merchandizes, money, goods, and wares as shall be found on board, or with them, in case they shall willingly yield themselves; but if they will not yield without fighting, then you are by force to compel them to yield. And we also require you to bring, or cause to be brought, such pirates, free-booters, or sea-rovers, as you shall seize, to a legal trial, to the end they may be proceeded against according to the law in such cases. And we do hereby command all our officers, ministers, and other our loving subjects whatsoever, to be aiding and assisting to you in the premises. And we do hereby enjoin you to keep an exact journal of your proceedings in execution of the premises, and set down the names of such pirates, and of their officers and company, and the names of such ships and vessels as you shall by virtue of these presents take and seize, and the quantities of arms, ammunition, provision, and lading of such ships, and the true value of the same, as near as you judge. And we do hereby strictly charge and command you, as you will answer the contrary at your peril, that you do not, in any manner, offend or molest our friends or allies, their ships or subjects, by colour or pretence of these presents, or the authority thereby granted. *In witness whereof*, we have caused our great seal of England to be affixed to these presents. Given at our court in Kensington, the 26th day of January, 1695, in the 7th year of our reign."

Capt. Kidd had also another commission, which was called a commission of reprisals; for it being then war time, this commission was to justify him in the taking of French merchant ships, in case he should meet with any; but as this commission is nothing to our present purpose, we shall not burthen the reader with it.

Previous to sailing, Capt. Kidd buried his bible on the sea-shore, in Plymouth Sound; its divine precepts being so at variance with his wicked course of life, that he did not choose to keep a book which condemned him in his lawless career.

With these two commissions he sailed out of Plymouth in May, 1696, in the Adventure galley, of 30 guns, and 80 men; the place he first designed for was New-York; in his voyage thither, he took a French banker, but this was no act of piracy, he having a commission for that purpose, as we have just observed.

When he arrived at New-York, he put up articles for engaging more hands, it being necessary to his ship's crew, since he proposed to deal with a desperate enemy. The terms he offered, were, that every man should have a share of what was taken, reserving for himself and owners forty shares. Upon which encouragement he soon increased his company to 155 men.

Captain Kidd burying his Bible

**Captain Kidd burying his Bible.**

With this company he sailed first for Madeira, where he took in wine and some other necessaries; from thence he proceeded to Bonavista, one of the Cape de Verd Islands, to furnish the ship with salt, and from thence went immediately to St. Jago, another of the Cape de Verd Islands, in order to stock himself with provisions. When all this was done, he bent his course to Madagascar, the known rendezvous of pirates. In his way he fell in with Capt. Warren, commodore of three men of war; he acquainted him with his design, kept them company two or three days, and then leaving them, made the best of his way for Madagascar, where he arrived in February, 1696, just nine months from his departure from Plymouth.

It happened that at this time the pirate ships were most of them out in search of prey; so that according to the best intelligence Capt. Kidd could get, there was not one of them at that time about the island; wherefore, having spent some time in watering his ship and taking in more provisions, he thought of trying his fortune on the coast of Malabar, where he arrived in the month of June following, four months from his reaching Madagascar. Hereabouts he made an unsuccessful cruise, touching sometimes at the island of Mohila, and sometimes at that of Johanna, between Malabar and Madagascar. His provisions were every day wasting, and his ship began to want repair; wherefore, when he was at Johanna, he found means of borrowing a sum of money from some Frenchmen who had lost their ship, but saved their effects, and with this he purchased materials for putting his ship in good repair.

It does not appear all this while that he had the least design of turning pirate; for near Mohila and Johanna both, he met with several Indian ships richly laden, to which he did not offer the least violence, though he was strong enough to have done what he pleased with them; and the first outrage or depredation I find he committed upon mankind, was after his repairing his ship, and leaving Johanna; he touched at a place called Mabbee, upon the Red Sea, where he took some Guinea corn from the natives, by force. After this, he sailed to Bab's Key, a place upon a little island at the entrance of the Red Sea. Here it was that he first began to open himself to his ship's company, and let them understand that he intended to change his measures; for, happening to talk of the Mocha fleet, which was to sail that way, he said, "*We have been unsuccessful hitherto; but courage, my boys, we'll make our fortunes out of this fleet*"; and finding that none of them appeared averse to it, he ordered a boat out, well manned, to go upon the coast to make discoveries, commanding them to take a prisoner and bring him to him, or get intelligence any way they could. The boat returned in a few days, bringing him word, that they saw fourteen or fifteen ships ready to sail, some with English, some with Dutch, and some with Moorish colors.

We cannot account for this sudden change in his conduct, otherwise than by supposing that he first meant well, while he had hopes of making his fortune by taking of pirates; but now weary of ill success, and fearing lest his owners, out of humor at their great expenses, should dismiss him, and he should want employment, and be marked out for an unlucky man; rather, I say, than run the hazard of poverty, he resolved to do his business one way, since he could not do it another.

He therefore ordered a man continually to watch at the mast head, lest this fleet should go by them; and about four days after, towards evening, it appeared in sight, being convoyed by one English and one Dutch man of war. Kidd soon fell in with them, and getting into the midst of them, fired at a Moorish ship which was next him; but the men-of-war taking the alarm, bore down upon Kidd, and firing upon him, obliged him to sheer off, he not being strong enough to contend with them. Now he had begun hostilities, he resolved to go on, and therefore he went and cruised along the coast of Malabar. The first prize he met was a small vessel belonging to Aden; the vessel was Moorish, and the owners were Moorish merchants, but the master was an Englishman; his name was Parker. Kidd forced him and a Portuguese that was called Don Antonio, which were all the Europeans on board, to take on with him; the first he designed as a pilot, and the last as an interpreter. He also used the men very cruelly, causing them to be hoisted up by the arms, and drubbed with a naked cutlass, to force them to discover whether they had money on board, and where it lay; but as they had neither gold nor silver on board, he got nothing by his cruelty; however, he took from them a bale of pepper, and a bale of coffee, and so let them go.

A little time after he touched at Carawar, a place upon the same coast, where, before he arrived, the news of what he had done to the Moorish ship had reached them; for some of the English merchants there had received an account of it from the owners, who corresponded with them; wherefore, as soon as Kidd came in, he was suspected to be the person who committed this piracy; and one Mr. Harvey and Mr. Mason, two of the English factory, came on board and asked for Parker, and Antonio, the Portuguese; but Kidd denied that he knew any such persons, having secured them both in a private place in the hold, where they were kept for seven or eight days, that is, till Kidd sailed from thence.

However, the coast was alarmed, and a Portuguese man-of-war was sent out to cruise. Kidd met with her, and fought her about six hours, gallantly enough; but finding her too strong to be taken, he quitted her; for he was able to run away from her when he would. Then he went to a place called Porca, where he watered his ship and bought a number of hogs of the natives to victual his company.

Soon after this, he came up with a Moorish ship, the master whereof was a Dutchman, called Schipper Mitchell, and chased her under French colors, which they observing hoisted French colors too; when he came up with her, he hailed her in French, and they having a Frenchman on board, answered him in the same language; upon which he ordered them to send their boat on board; they were obliged to do so, and having examined who they were, and from whence they came, he asked the Frenchman who was a passenger, if he had a French pass for himself; the Frenchman gave him to understand that he had. Then he told the Frenchman that he must pass for captain, and by—-, says he, you are the captain; the Frenchman durst not refuse doing as he would have him. The meaning of this was, that he would seize the ship as fair prize, and as if she had belonged to French subjects, according to a commission he had for that purpose; though one would think, after what he had already done, he need not have recourse to a quibble to give his actions a color.

Captain Kidd attacks the Moorish fleet

**Captain Kidd attacks the Moorish fleet.**

In short, he took the cargo, and sold it some time after; yet still he seemed to have some fears upon him, lest these proceedings should have a bad end; for, coming up with a Dutch ship some time after, when his men thought of nothing but attacking her, Kidd opposed it; upon which a mutiny arose, and the majority being for taking the said ship, and arming themselves to man the boat to go and seize her, he told them, such as did, never should come on board him again; which put an end to the design, so that he kept company with the said ship some time, without offering her any violence. However, this dispute was the occasion of an accident, upon which an indictment was grounded against Kidd; for Moor, the gunner, being one day upon deck, and talking with Kidd about the said Dutch ship, some words arose between them, and Moor told Kidd, that he had ruined them all; upon which Kidd, calling him a dog, took up a bucket and struck him with it, which breaking his scull, he died next day.

But Kidd's penitential fit did not last long; for coasting along Malabar, he met with a great number of boats, all of which he plundered. Upon the same coast he also fell in with a Portuguese ship, which he kept possession of a week, and then having taken out of her some chests of India goods, thirty jars of butter, with some wax, iron and a hundred bags of rice, he let her go.

Much about the same time he went to one of the Malabar islands for wood and water, and his cooper being ashore, was murdered by the natives; upon which Kidd himself landed, and burnt and pillaged several of their houses, the people running away; but having taken one, he caused him to be tied to a tree, and commanded one of his men to shoot him; then putting to sea again, he took the greatest prize which fell into his hands while he followed this trade; this was a Moorish ship of 400 tons, richly laden, named the Queda Merchant, the master whereof was an Englishman, by the name of Wright; for the Indians often make use of English or Dutchmen to command their ships, their own mariners not being so good artists in navigation. Kidd chased her under French colors, and having come up with her, he ordered her to hoist out her boat and send on board of him, which being done, he told Wright he was his prisoner; and informing himself concerning the said ship, he understood there were no Europeans on board, except two Dutch and one Frenchman, all the rest being Indians or Armenians, and that the Armenians were part owners of the cargo. Kidd gave the Armenians to understand, that if they would offer anything that was worth his taking for their ransom, he would hearken to it. Upon which, they proposed to pay him 20,000 rupees, not quite $3,000 sterling; but Kidd judged this would be making a bad bargain, wherefore he rejected it, and setting the crew on shore, at different places on the coast, he soon sold as much of the cargo as came to ten thousand pounds. With part of it he also trafficked, receiving in exchange provisions, or such other goods as he wanted; by degrees he disposed of the whole cargo, and when the division was made, it came to about $200 a man; and having reserved forty shares to himself, his dividend amounted to about $8,000 sterling.

The Indians along the coast came on board and trafficked with all freedom, and he punctually performed his bargains, till about the time he was ready to sail; and then thinking he should have no further occasion for them, he made no scruple of taking their goods and setting them on shore, without any payment in money or goods, which they little expected; for as they had been used to deal with pirates, they always found them men of honor in the way of trade; a people, enemies to deceit, and that scorned to rob but in their own way.

Kidd put some of his men on board the Queda Merchant, and with this ship and his own sailed for Madagascar. As soon as he had arrived and cast anchor, there came on board of him a canoe, in which were several Englishmen, who had formerly been well acquainted with Kidd. As soon as they saw him they saluted him, and told him they were informed he was come to take them, and hang them, which would be a little unkind in such an old acquaintance. Kidd soon dissipated their doubts, by swearing he had no such design, and that he was now in every respect their brother, and just as bad as they; and calling for a cup of bomboo, drank their captain's health.

These men belonged to a pirate ship, called the Resolution, formerly the Mocha Merchant, whereof one Capt. Culliford was commander, and which lay at anchor not far from them. Kidd went on board with them, promising them his friendship and assistance, and Culliford in his turn came on board of Kidd; and Kidd, to testify his sincerity in iniquity, finding Culliford in want of some necessaries, made him a present of an anchor and some guns, to fit him out for sea again.

The Adventure galley was now so old and leaky, that they were forced to keep two pumps continually going; wherefore Kidd shifted all the guns and tackle out of her into the Queda Merchant, intending her for his man-of-war; and as he had divided the money before, he now made a division of the remainder of the cargo; soon after which, the greatest part of the company left him, some going on board Capt. Culliford, and others absconding into the country, so that he had not above 40 men left.

He put to sea, and happened to touch at Amboyna, one of the Dutch spice islands, where he was told that the news of his actions had reached England, and that he was there declared a pirate.

The truth of it is, his piracies so alarmed our merchants that some motions were made in parliament, to inquire into the commission that was given him, and the persons who fitted him out. These proceedings seem to lean a little hard upon Lord Bellamont, who thought himself so touched thereby, that he published a justification of himself in a pamphlet, after Kidd's execution. In the meantime it was thought advisable, in order to stop the course of these piracies, to publish a proclamation, offering the king's free pardon to all such pirates as should voluntarily surrender themselves, whatever piracies they had been guilty of, at any time before the last day of April, 1699–that is to say, for all piracies committed eastward of the Cape of Good Hope, to the longitude and meridian of Socatora, and Cape Cormorin; in which proclamation, Avery and Kidd were excepted by name.

When Kidd left Amboyna he knew nothing of this proclamation, for certainly had he had notice of his being excepted in it, he would not have been so infatuated, as to run himself into the very jaws of danger; but relying upon his interest with the lord Bellamont, and fancying that a French pass or two he found on board some of the ships he took, would serve to countenance the matter, and that part of the booty he got would gain him new friends–I say, all these things made him flatter himself that all would be hushed, and that justice would but wink at him. Wherefore he sailed directly for Boston laden with booty, with a crew of swaggering companions at his heels. But no sooner did he show himself in Boston, than the alarm was given of his reappearance, and measures were taken to arrest him. The daring character which Kidd had acquired, however, and the desperate fellows who followed like bull-dogs at his heels, caused a little delay in his arrest. He took advantage of this to bury the greater part of his immense treasure, which has never been found, and then carried a high head about the streets of Boston. He even attempted to defend himself when arrested, but was secured and thrown into prison. Such was the formidable character of this pirate and his crew, that a frigate was sent to convey them to England for trial.

Accordingly a sessions of Admiralty being held at the Old Bailey, in May 1701, Capt. Kidd, Nicholas Churchill, James How, Robert Lumly, William Jenkins, Gabriel Loff, Hugh Parrot, Richard Barlicorn, Abel Owens and Darby Mullins, were arraigned for piracy and robbery on the high seas, and all found guilty except three; these were Robert Lumly, William Jenkins and Richard Barlicorn, who proving themselves to be apprentices to some of the officers of the ship, and producing their indentures in court, were acquitted.

The three above mentioned, though they were proved to be concerned in taking and sharing the ship and goods mentioned in the indictment, yet, as the gentlemen of the long robe rightly distinguished, there was a great difference between their circumstances and the rest; for there must go an intention of the mind and a freedom of the will to the committing an act of felony or piracy. A pirate is not to be understood to be under constraint, but a free agent; for in this case, the bare act will not make a man guilty, unless the will make it so.

Now a servant, it is true, if he go voluntarily, and have his proportion, he must be accounted a pirate, for then he acts upon his own account, and not by compulsion: and these persons, according to the evidence, received their part, but whether they accounted to their masters for their shares afterwards, is the matter in question, and what distinguishes them as free agents, or men that did go under the compulsion of their masters; which being left to the consideration of the jury, they found them *not guilty*.

Kidd was tried upon an indictment of murder also, viz. for killing Moor, the gunner, and found guilty of the same. Nicholas Churchill, and James How pleaded the king's pardon, as having surrendered themselves within the time limited in the proclamation, and Col. Bass, governor of West Jersey, to whom they surrendered, being in court, and called upon, proved the same. However, this plea was overruled by the court, because there being four commissioners named in the proclamation, viz. Capt. Thomas Warren, Israel Hayes, Peter Delannoye, and Christopher Pollard, Esquires, who were appointed commissioners, and sent over on purpose to receive the submissions of such pirates as should surrender, it was adjudged no other person was qualified to receive their surrender, and that they could not be entitled to the benefit of the said proclamation, because they had not in all circumstances complied with the conditions of it.

Darby Mullins urged in his defence, that he served under the king's commission, and therefore could not disobey his commander without incurring great punishments; that whenever a ship or ships went out upon any expedition under the king's commission, the men were never allowed to call their officers to an account, why they did this, or why they did that, because such a liberty would destroy all discipline; that if any thing was done which was unlawful, the officers were to answer it, for the men did no more than their duty in obeying orders. He was told by the court, that acting under the commission justified in what was lawful, but not in what was unlawful. He answered, he stood in need of nothing to justify him in what was lawful, but the case of seamen must be very hard, if they must be brought into such danger for obeying the commands of their officers, and punished for not obeying them; and if they were allowed to dispute the orders, there could be no such thing as command kept up at sea.

This seemed to be the best defence the thing could bear; but his taking a share of the plunder, the seamen's mutinying on board several times, and taking upon them to control the captain, showed there was no obedience paid to the commission; and that they acted in all things according to the custom of pirates and freebooters, which weighing with the jury, they brought him in guilty with the rest.

As to Capt. Kidd's defence, he insisted much on his own innocence, and the villainy of his men. He said, he went out in a laudable employment and had no occasion, being then in good circumstances, to go a pirating; that the men often mutinied against him, and did as they pleased; that he was threatened to be shot in the cabin, and that ninety-five left him at one time, and set fire to his boat, so that he was disabled from bringing his ship home, or the prizes he took, to have them regularly condemned, which he said were taken by virtue of a commission under the broad seal, they having French passes. The captain called one Col. Hewson to his reputation, who gave him an extraordinary character, and declared to the court, that he had served under his command, and been in two engagements with him against the French, in which he fought as well as any man he ever saw; that there were only Kidd's ship and his own against Monsieur du Cass, who commanded a squadron of six sail, and they got the better of him. But this being several years before the facts mentioned in the indictment were committed, proved of no manner of service to the prisoner on his trial.

Captain Kidd hanging in chains

**Captain Kidd hanging in chains.**

As to the friendship shown to Culliford, a notorious pirate, Kidd denied, and said, he intended to have taken him, but his men being a parcel of rogues and villains refused to stand by him, and several of them ran away from his ship to the said pirate. But the evidence being full and particular against him, he was found guilty as before mentioned.

When Kidd was asked what he had to say why sentence should not pass against him, he answered, that *he had nothing to say, but that he had been sworn against by perjured and wicked people*. And when sentence was pronounced, he said, *My Lord, it is a very hard sentence. For my part, I am the most innocent person of them all, only I have been sworn against by perjured persons.*

Wherefore about a week after, Capt. Kidd, Nicholas Churchill, James How, Gabriel Loff, Hugh Parrot, Abel Owen, and Darby Mullins, were executed at Execution Dock, and afterwards hung up in chains, at some distance from each other, down the river, where their bodies hung exposed for many years.

Kidd died hard, for the rope with which he was first tied up broke with his weight and he tumbled to the ground. He was tied up a second time, and more effectually. Hence came the story of Kidd's being twice hung.

Such is Captain Kidd's true history; but it has given birth to an innumerable progeny of traditions. The report of his having buried great treasures of gold and silver which he actually did before his arrest, set the brains of all the good people along the coast in a ferment. There were rumors on rumors of great sums of money found here and there, sometimes in one part of the country sometimes in another; of coins with Moorish inscriptions, doubtless the spoils of his eastern prizes.

Some reported the treasure to have been buried in solitary, unsettled places about Plymouth and Cape Cod; but by degrees, various other parts, not only on the eastern coast but along the shores of the Sound, and even Manhattan and Long Island were gilded by these rumors. In fact the vigorous measures of Lord Bellamont had spread sudden consternation among the pirates in every part of the provinces; they had secreted their money and jewels in lonely out-of-the-way places, about the wild shores of the sea coast, and dispersed themselves over the country. The hand of justice prevented many of them from ever returning to regain their buried treasures, which remain to this day thus secreted, and are irrecoverably lost. This is the cause of those frequent reports of trees and rocks bearing mysterious marks, supposed to indicate the spots where treasure lay hidden; and many have been the ransackings after the pirates' booty. A rocky place on the shores of Long Island, called Kidd's Ledge, has received great attention from the money diggers; but they have not as yet discovered any treasures.

## THE BLOODY CAREER AND EXECUTION OF VINCENT BENAVIDES A PIRATE ON THE WEST COAST OF SOUTH AMERICA.

Vincent Benavides was the son of the gaoler of Quirihue in the district of Conception. He was a man of ferocious manners, and had been guilty of several murders. Upon the breaking out of the revolutionary war, he entered the patriot army as a private soldier; and was a serjeant of grenadiers at the time of the first Chilian revolution. He, however, deserted to the Spaniards, and was taken prisoner in their service, when they sustained, on the plains of Maypo, on the 5th of April, 1818, that defeat which decided their fortunes in that part of America, and secured the independence of Chili. Benavides, his brother, and some other traitors to the Chilian cause, were sentenced to death, and brought forth in the Plaza, or public square of Santiago, in order to be shot. Benavides, though terribly wounded by the discharge, was not killed; but he had the presence of mind to counterfeit death in so perfect a manner, that the imposture was not suspected. The bodies of the traitors were not buried, but dragged away to a distance, and there left to be devoured by the gallinazos or vultures. The serjeant who had the superintendence of this part of the ceremony, had a personal hatred to Benavides, on account of that person having murdered some of his relations; and, to gratify his revenge, he drew his sword, and gave the dead body, (as he thought,) a severe gash in the side, as they were dragging it along. The resolute Benavides had fortitude to bear this also, without flinching or even showing the least indication of life; and one cannot help regretting that so determined a power of endurance had not been turned to a better purpose.

Benavides lay like a dead man, in the heap of carcasses, until it became dark; and then, pierced with shot, and gashed by the sword as he was, he crawled to a neighboring cottage, the inhabitants of which received him with the greatest kindness, and attended him with the greatest care.

The daring ruffian, who knew the value of his own talents and courage, being aware that General San Martin was planning the expedition to Peru, a service in which there would be much of desperation and danger, sent word to the General that he was alive, and invited him to a secret conference at midnight, in the same Plaza in which it was believed Benavides had been shot. The signal agreed upon, was, that they should strike fire three times with their flints, as that was not likely to be answered by any but the proper party, and yet was not calculated to awaken suspicion.

San Martin, alone, and provided with a brace of pistols, met the desperado; and after a long conference, it was agreed that Benavides should, in the mean time, go out against the Araucan Indians; but that he should hold himself in readiness to proceed to Peru, when the expedition suited.

Having procured the requisite passports, he proceeded to Chili, where, having again diverted the Chilians, he succeeded in persuading the commander of the Spanish troops, that he had force sufficient to carry on the war against Chili; and the commander in consequence retired to Valdivia, and left Benavides commander of the whole frontier on the Biobio.

Having thus cleared the coast of the Spanish commander, he went over to the Araucans, or rather, he formed a band of armed robbers, who committed every cruelty, and were guilty of every perfidy in the south of Chili. Whereever Benavides came, his footsteps were marked with blood, and the old men, the women, and the children, were butchered lest they should give notice of his motions.

When he had rendered himself formidable by land, he resolved to be equally powerful upon the sea. He equipped a corsair, with instructions to capture the vessels of all nations; and as Araucan is directly opposite the island of Santa Maria, where vessels put in for refreshment, after having doubled Cape Horn, his situation was well adapted for his purpose. He was but too successful. The first of his prizes was the American ship Hero, which he took by surprise in the night; the second, was the Herculia, a brig belonging to the same country. While the unconscious crew were proceeding, as usual, to catch seals on this island, lying about three leagues from the main land of Arauca, an armed body of men rushed from the woods, and overpowering them, tied their hands behind them, and left them under a guard on the beach. These were no other than the pirates, who now took the Herculia's own boats, and going on board, surprised the captain and four of his crew, who had remained to take care of the brig; and having brought off the prisoners from the beach, threw them all into the hold, closing the hatches over them. They then tripped the vessel's anchor, and sailing over in triumph to Arauca, were received by Benavides, with a salute of musketry fired under the Spanish flag, which it was their chief's pleasure to hoist on that day. In the course of the next night, Benavides ordered the captain and his crew to be removed to a house on shore, at some distance from the town; then taking them out, one by one, he stripped and pillaged them of all they possessed, threatening them the whole time with drawn swords and loaded muskets. Next morning he paid the prisoners a visit and ordered them to the capital, called together the principal people of the town, and desired each to select one as a servant. The captain and four others not happening to please the fancy of any one, Benavides, after saying he would himself take charge of the captain, gave directions, on pain of instant death, that some one should hold themselves responsible for the other prisoners. Some days after this they were called together, and required to serve as soldiers in the pirates army; an order to which they consented, knowing well by what they had already seen, that the consequence of refusal would be fatal.

Benavides, though unquestionably a ferocious savage, was, nevertheless, a man of resource, full of activity, and of considerable energy of character. He converted the whale spears and harpoons into lances for his cavalry, and halberts for his sergeants; and out of the sails he made trowsers for half of his army; the carpenters he set to work making baggage carts and repairing his boats; the armourers he kept perpetually at work, mending muskets, and making pikes; managing in this way, to turn the skill of every one of his prisoners to some useful account. He treated the officers, too, not unkindly, allowed them to live in his house, and was very anxious on all occasions, to have their advice respecting the equipment of his troops.

Upon one occasion, when walking with the captain of the Herculia, he remarked, that his army was now almost complete in every respect, except in one essential particular, and it cut him, he said to the soul, to think of such a deficiency; he had no trumpets for his cavalry, and added, that it was utterly impossible to make the fellows believe themselves dragoons, unless they heard a blast in their ears at every turn; and neither men nor horses would ever do their duty properly, if not roused to it by the sound of a trumpet; in short he declared, some device must be hit upon to supply this equipment. The captain, willing to ingratiate himself with the pirate, after a little reflection, suggested to him, that trumpets might easily be made of copper sheets on the bottoms of the vessels he had taken. "Very true," cried the delighted chief, "how came I not to think of that before?" Instantly all hands were employed in ripping off the copper, and the armourers being set to work under his personal superintendence, the whole camp, before night, resounded with the warlike blasts of the cavalry.

The captain of the ship, who had given him the brilliant idea of the copper trumpets, had by these means, so far won upon his good will and confidence, as to be allowed a considerable range to walk on. He of course, was always looking out for some plan of escape, and at length an opportunity occurring, he, with the mate of the Ocean, and nine of his crew, seized two whale boats, imprudently left on the banks of the river, and rowed off. Before quitting the shore, they took the precaution of staving all the other boats, to prevent pursuit, and accordingly, though their escape was immediately discovered, they succeeded in getting so much the start of the people whom Benavides sent in pursuit of them, that they reached St. Mary's Island in safety. Here they caught several seals upon which they subsisted very miserably till they reached Valparaiso. It was in consequence of their report of Benavides proceedings made to Sir Thomas Hardy, the commander-in-chief, that he deemed it proper to send a ship to rescue if possible, the remaining unfortunate captives at Arauca.

Benavides having manned the Herculia, it suited the mate, (the captain and crew being detained as hostages,) to sail with the brig to Chili, and seek aid from the Spanish governor. The Herculia returned with a twenty-four pounder, two field-pieces, eleven Spanish officers, and twenty soldiers, together with the most flattering letters and congratulations to the worthy ally of his Most Catholic Majesty. Soon after this he captured the Perseverance, English whaler, and the American brig Ocean, bound for Lima, with several thousand stand of arms on board. The captain of the Herculia, with the mate of the Ocean, and several men, after suffering great hardships, landed at Valparaiso, and gave notice of the proceedings of Benavides; and in consequence, Sir Thomas Hardy directed Captain Hall to proceed to Arauca with the convoy, to set the captives free, if possible.

It was for the accomplishment of this service that Capt. Hall sailed from Valparaiso; and he called at Conception on his way, in order to glean information respecting the pirate. Here the Captain ascertained that Benavides was between two considerable bodies of Chilian force, on the Chilian side of the Biobio, and one of those bodies between him and the river.

Having to wait two days at Conception for information, Captain Hall occupied them in observing the place; the country he describes as green and fertile, and having none of the dry and desert character of the environs of Valparaiso. Abundance of vegetables, wood, and also coals, are found on the shores of the bay.

On the 12th of October, the captain heard of the defeat of Benavides, and his flight, alone, across the Biobio into the Araucan country; and also that two of the Americans whom he had taken with him had made their escape, and were on board the Chacabuco. As these were the only persons who could give Captain Hall information respecting the prisoners of whom he was in quest, he set out in search of the vessel, and after two days' search, found her at anchor near the island of Mocha. From thence he learned that the captain of the Ocean, with several English and American seamen had been left at Arauca, when Benavides went on his expedition, and he sailed for that place immediately.

He was too late, however; the Chilian forces had already made a successful attack, and the Indians had fled, setting fire to the town and the ships. The Indians, who were in league with the Chilians, were every way as wild as those who arrayed themselves under Benavides. Capt. Hall, upon his return to Conception, though dissuaded from it by the governor, visited the Indian encampment.

When the captain and his associates entered the courtyard, they observed a party seated on the ground, round a great tub of wine, who hailed their entrance with loud shouts, or rather yells, and boisterously demanded their business; to all appearance very little pleased with the interruption. The interpreter became alarmed, and wished them to retire; but this the captain thought imprudent, as each man had his long spear close at hand, resting against the eaves of the house. Had they attempted to escape they must have been taken, and possibly sacrificed, by these drunken savages. As their best chance seemed to lie in treating them without any show of distrust, they advanced to the circle with a good humored confidence, which appeased them considerably. One of the party rose and embraced them in the Indian fashion, which they had learned from the gentlemen who had been prisoners with Benavides. After this ceremony they roared out to them to sit down on the ground, and with the most boisterous hospitality, insisted on their drinking with them; a request which they cheerfully complied with. Their anger soon vanished, and was succeeded by mirth and satisfaction, which speedily became as outrageous as their displeasure had been at first. Seizing a favorable opportunity, Captain Hall stated his wish to have an interview with their chief, upon which a message was sent to him; but he did not think fit to show himself for a considerable time, during which they remained with the party round the tub, who continued swilling their wine like so many hogs. Their heads soon became affected, and their obstreperous mirth increasing every minute, the situation of the strangers became by no means agreeable.

At length Peneleo's door opened, and the chief made his appearance; he did not condescend, however, to cross the threshold, but leaned against the door post to prevent falling, being by some degrees more drunk than any of his people. A more finished picture of a savage cannot be conceived. He was a tall, broad shouldered man; with a prodigiously large head, and a square-shaped bloated face, from which peeped out two very small eyes, partly hid by an immense superfluity of black, coarse, oily, straight hair, covering his cheeks, hanging over his shoulders, and rendering his head somewhat the shape and size of a bee-hive. Over his shoulders was thrown a poncho of coarse blanket stuff. He received them very gruffly, and appeared irritated and sulky at having been disturbed; he was still more offended when he learned that they wished to see his captive. They in vain endeavored to explain their real views; but he grunted out his answer in a tone and manner which showed them plainly that he neither did, nor wished to understand them.

Whilst in conversation with Peneleo, they stole an occasional glance at his apartment. By the side of the fire burning in the middle of the floor, was seated a young Indian woman, with long black hair reaching to the ground; this, they conceived, could be no other than one of the unfortunate persons they were in search of; and they were somewhat disappointed to observe, that the lady was neither in tears, nor apparently very miserable; they therefore came away impressed with the unsentimental idea, that the amiable Peneleo had already made some impression on her young heart.

Two Indians, who were not so drunk as the rest, followed them to the outside of the court, and told them that several foreigners had been taken by the Chilians in the battle near Chilian, and were now safe. The interpreter hinted to them that this was probably invented by these cunning people, on hearing their questions in the court; but he advised them, as a matter of policy, to give them each a piece of money, and to get away as far as they could.

Captain Hall returned to Conception on the 23d of October, reached Valparaiso on the 26th, and in two weeks thereafter, the men of whom he was in search, made their appearance.

The bloody career of Benavides now drew near to a close. The defeat on the Chilian side of the Biobio, and the burning of Arauca with the loss of his vessels, he never recovered. At length, in the end of December 1821, discovering the miserable state to which he was reduced, he entreated the Intendant of Conception, that he might be received on giving himself up along with his partisans. This generous chief accepted his offer, and informed the supreme government; but in the meantime Benavides embarked in a launch, at the mouth of the river Lebo, and fled, with the intention of joining a division of the enemy's army, which he supposed to be at some one of the ports on the south coast of Peru. It was indeed absurd to expect any good faith from such an intriguer; for in his letters at this time, he offered his services to Chili and promised fidelity, while his real intention was still to follow the enemy. He finally left the unhappy province of Conception, the theatre of so many miserable scenes, overwhelmed with the misery which he had caused, without ever recollecting that it was in that province that he had first drawn his breath.

His despair in the boat made his conduct insupportable to those who accompanied him, and they rejoiced when they were obliged to put into the harbor of Topocalma in search of water of which they had run short. He was now arrested by some patriotic individuals. From the notorious nature of his crimes, alone, even the most impartial stranger would have condemned him to the last punishment; but the supreme government wished to hear what he had to say for himself, and ordered him to be tried according to the laws. It appearing on his trial that he had placed himself beyond the laws of society, such punishment was awarded him as any one of his crimes deserved. As a pirate, he merited death, and as a destroyer of whole towns, it became necessary to put him to death in such a manner as might satisfy outraged humanity, and terrify others who should dare to imitate him. In pursuance of the sentence passed upon him, he was dragged from the prison in a pannier tied to the tail of a mule, and was hanged in the great square; his head and hands were afterwards cut off, in order to their being placed upon high poles, to point out the places of his horrid crimes, Santa Juona, Tarpellanca and Arauca.

The head of Benavides stuck on a pole

**The head of Benavides stuck on a pole.**

Page 215 Illustration

## THE LIFE OF CAPTAIN DAVIS

*With an account of his surprising the Fort at Gambia.*

Davis was born in Monmouthshire, and, from a boy, trained to the sea. His last voyage from England was in the sloop Cadogan from Bristol, in the character of chief mate. This vessel was captured by the pirate England, upon the Guinea coast, whose companions plundered the crew, and murdered the captain, as is related in England's life.

Upon the death of Captain Skinner, Davis pretended that he was urged by England to become a pirate, but that he resolutely refused. He added, that England, pleased with his conduct, had made him captain in room of Skinner, giving him a sealed paper, which he was not to open until he was in a certain latitude, and then expressly to follow the given directions. When he arrived in the appointed place, he collected the whole crew, and solemnly read his sealed instructions, which contained a generous grant of the ship and all her stores to Davis and his crew, requesting them to go to Brazil, and dispose of the cargo to the best advantage, and make an equal division of the money.

Davis then commanded the crew to signify whether they were inclined to follow that mode of life, when, to his astonishment and chagrin, the majority positively refused. Then, in a transport of rage, he desired them to go where they would.

Knowing that part of the cargo was consigned to merchants in Barbadoes, they directed their course to that place. When arrived there, they informed the merchants of the unfortunate death of Skinner, and of the proposal which had been made to them. Davis was accordingly seized, and committed to prison, but he having never been in the pirate service, nothing could be proved to condemn him, and he was discharged without a trial. Convinced that he could never hope for employment in that quarter after this detection, he went to the island of Providence, which he knew to be a rendezvous for pirates. Upon his arrival there, he was grievously disappointed, because the pirates who frequented that place had just accepted of his majesty's pardon, and had surrendered.

Captain Rogers having equipped two sloops for trade, Davis obtained employment in one of these, called the Buck. They were laden with European goods to a considerable value, which they were to sell or exchange with the French and Spanish. They first touched at the island of Martinique, belonging to the French, and Davis knowing that many of the men were formerly in the pirate service, enticed them to seize the master, and to run off with the sloop. When they had effected their purpose, they hailed the other ship, in which they knew that there were many hands ripe for rebellion, and coming to, the greater part joined Davis. Those who did not choose to adhere to them were allowed to remain in the other sloop, and continue their course, after Davis had pillaged her of what things he pleased.

In full possession of the vessel and stores and goods, a large bowl of punch was made; under its exhilarating influence, it was proposed to choose a commander, and to form their future mode of policy. The election was soon over, and a large majority of legal votes were in favor of Davis, and no scrutiny demanded, Davis was declared duly elected. He then drew up a code of laws, to which he himself swore, and required the same bond of alliance from all the rest of the crew. He then addressed them in a short and appropriate speech, the substance of which was, a proclamation of war with the whole world.

They next consulted, what part would be most convenient to clean the vessel, and it was resolved to repair to Coxon's Hole, at the east end of the island of Cuba, where they could remain in perfect security, as the entrance was so narrow that one ship could keep out a hundred.

They, however, had no small difficulty in cleaning their vessel, as there was no carpenter among them. They performed that laborious task in the best manner they could, and then made to the north side of Hispaniola. The first sail they met with was a French ship of twelve guns, which they captured; and while they were plundering her, another appeared in view. Enquiring of the Frenchmen, they learned that she was a ship of twenty-four guns and sixty men. Davis proposed to his crew to attack her, assuring them that she would prove a rich prize. This appeared to the crew such a hazardous enterprise, that they were rather adverse to the measure. But he acquainted them that he had conceived a stratagem that he was confident would succeed; they might, therefore, safely leave the matter to his management. He then commenced chase, and ordered his prize to do the same. Being a better sailer, he soon came up with the enemy, and showed his black colors. With no small surprise at his insolence in coming so near them, they commanded him to strike. He replied, that he was disposed to give them employment until his companion came up, who was able to contend with them; meanwhile assuring them that, if they did not strike to him, it would most certainly fare the worse for them: then giving them a broadside, he received the same in return.

When the other pirate ship drew near, they, according to the directions of Davis, appeared upon deck in white shirts, which making an appearance of numbers, the Frenchman was intimidated, and struck. Davis ordered the captain with twenty of his men to come on board, and they were all put in irons except the captain. He then despatched four of his men to the other ship, and calling aloud to them, desired that his compliments should be given to the captain, with a request to send a sufficient number of hands to go on board their new prize, to see what they had got in her. At the same time, he gave them a written paper with their proper instructions, even to nail up the small guns, to take out all the arms and powder, and to go every man on board the new prize. When his men were on board her, he ordered the greater part of the prisoners to be removed into the empty vessels, and by this means secured himself from any attempt to recover their ship.

During three days, these three vessels sailed in company, but finding that his late prize was a heavy sailer, he emptied her of everything that he stood in need of, and then restored her to the captain with all his men. The French captain was so much enraged at being thus miserably deceived, that, upon the discovery of the stratagem, he would have thrown himself overboard, had not his men prevented him.

Captain Davis then formed the resolution of parting with the other prize-ship also, and soon afterwards steered northward, and took a Spanish sloop. He next directed his course towards the western islands, and from Cape de Verd islands cast anchor at St. Nicholas, and hoisted English colors. The Portuguese supposed that he was a privateer, and Davis going on shore was hospitably received, and they traded with him for such articles as they found most advantageous. He remained here five weeks, and he and half of his crew visited the principal town of the island. Davis, from his appearing in the dress of a gentleman, was greatly caressed by the Portuguese, and nothing was spared to entertain and render him and his men happy. Having amused themselves during a week, they returned to the ship, and allowed the other half of the crew to visit the capital, and enjoy themselves in like manner. Upon their return, they cleaned their ship and put to sea, but four of the men were so captivated with the ladies and the luxuries of the place, that they remained in the island, and one of them married and settled there.

Davis now sailed for Bonavista, and perceiving nothing in that harbor steered for the Isle of May. Arrived there, he found several vessels in the harbor, and plundered them of whatever he found necessary. He also received a considerable reinforcement of men, the greater part of whom entered willingly into the piratical service. He likewise made free with one of the ships, equipped her for his own purpose, and called her the King James. Davis next proceeded to St. Jago to take in water. Davis, with some others going on shore to seek water, the governor came to inquire who they were, and expressed his suspicion of their being pirates. Upon this, Davis seemed highly affronted, and expressed his displeasure in the most polite but determined manner. He, however, hastened on board, informed his men, and suggested the possibility of surprising the fort during the night. Accordingly, all his men being well armed, they advanced to the assault; and, from the carelessness of the guards, they were in the garrison before the inhabitants were alarmed. Upon the discovery of their danger, they took shelter in the governor's house, and fortified it against the pirates: but the latter throwing in some grando shells, ruined the furniture, and killed several people.

The alarm was circulated in the morning, and the country assembled to attack them; but, unwilling to stand a siege, the pirates dismounted the guns, pillaged the fort, and fled to their ships.

When at sea, they mustered their hands, and found that they were seventy strong. They then consulted among themselves what course they should steer, and were divided in opinion; but by a majority it was carried to sail for Gambia, on the coast of Guinea. Of this opinion was the captain, who having been employed in that trade, was acquainted with the coast; and informed his companions, that there was always a large quantity of money deposited in that castle, and he was confident, if the matter was entrusted to him, he should successfully storm that fort. From their experience of his former prudence and courage, they cheerfully submitted to his direction, in the full assurance of success.

Arrived at Gambia, he ordered all his men below, except just so many as were necessary to work the vessel, that those from the fort, seeing so few hands, might have no suspicion that she was any other than a trading vessel. He then ran under the fort and cast anchor, and having ordered out the boat, manned with six men indifferently dressed, he, with the master and doctor, dressed themselves like gentlemen, in order that the one party might look like foremastmen, and the other like merchants. In rowing ashore, he instructed his men what to say if any questions were put to them by the garrison.

On reaching land, the party was conducted by a file of musqueteers into the fort, and kindly received by the governor, who enquired what they were, and whence they came? They replied, that they were from Liverpool, and bound for the river Senegal, to trade for gum and elephants teeth; but that they were chased on that coast by two French men-of-war, and narrowly escaped being taken. "We were now disposed," continued Davis, "to make the best of our voyage, and would willingly trade here for slaves." The governor then inquired what were the principal articles of their cargo. They replied, that they were iron and plate, which were necessary articles in that place. The governor then said, that he would give them slaves for all their cargo; and asked if they had any European liquor on board. They answered, that they had a little for their own use, but that he should have a hamper of it. He then treated them with the greatest civility, and desired them all to dine with him. Davis answered, that as he was commander of the vessel, it would be necessary for him to go down to see if she were properly moored, and to give some other directions; but that these gentlemen might stay, and he would return before dinner, and bring the hamper with him.

While in the fort, his eyes were keenly employed to discover the position of the arms, and how the fort might most successfully be surprised. He discovered that there was a sentry standing near a guard-house, in which there were a quantity of arms heaped up in a corner, and that a considerable number of small arms were in the governor's hall. When he went on board, he ordered some hands on board a sloop lying at anchor, lest, hearing any bustle they should come to the aid of the castle; then desiring his men to avoid too much liquor, and to be ready when he should hoist the flag from the walls, to come to his assistance, he proceeded to the castle.

Having taken these precautions and formed these arrangements, he ordered every man who was to accompany him to arm himself with two pair of pistols, which he himself also did, concealed under their clothes. He then directed them to go into the guard-room, and fall into conversation, and immediately upon his firing a pistol out of the governor's window, to shut the men up, and secure the arms in the guard-room.

When Davis arrived, dinner not being ready, the governor proposed that they should pass the time in making a bowl of punch. Davis's boatswain attending him, had an opportunity of visiting all parts of the house, and observing their strength. He whispered his intelligence to his master, who being surrounded by his own friends, and seeing the governor unattended by any of his retinue, presented a pistol to the breast of the latter, informing him that he was a dead man, unless he should surrender the fort and all its riches. The governor, thus taken by surprise, was compelled to submit; for Davis took down all the pistols that hung in the hall, and loaded them. He then fired his pistol out of the window. His men flew like lions, presented their pistols to the soldiers, and while some carried out the arms, the rest secured the military, and shut them all up in the guard-house, placing a guard on the door. Then one of them struck the union flag on the top of the castle, which the men from the vessel perceiving, rushed to the combat, and in an instant were in possession of the castle, without tumult or bloodshed.

Davis then harrangued the soldiers, many of whom enlisted with him; and those who declined, he put on board the small ships, and to prevent the necessity of a guard, or the possibility of escape, carried off the sails, rigging and cables.

That day being spent in feasting and rejoicing, the castle saluting the ship, and the ship the castle, on the day following they proceeded to examine the contents of their prize. They, however, were greatly disappointed in their expectations, a large sum of money having been sent off a few days before. But they found money to the amount of about two thousand pounds in gold, and many valuable articles of different kinds. They carried on board their vessel whatever they deemed useful, gave several articles to the captain and crew of the small vessel, and allowed them to depart, while they dismounted the guns, and demolished the fortifications.

After doing all the mischief that their vicious minds could possibly devise, they weighed anchor; but in the mean time, perceiving a sail bearing towards them with all possible speed, they hastened to prepare for her reception, and made towards her. Upon her near approach they discovered that she was a French pirate of fourteen guns and sixty-four men, the one half French, and the other half negroes.

The Frenchman was in high expectation of a rich prize, but when he came nearer, he suspected, from the number of her guns and men, that she was a small English man-of-war; he determined, notwithstanding, upon the bold attempt of boarding her, and immediately fired a gun, and hoisted his black colors: Davis immediately returned the compliment. The Frenchman was highly gratified at this discovery; both hoisted out their boats, and congratulated each other. Mutual civilities and good offices passed, and the French captain proposed to Davis to sail down the coast with him, in order to look out for a better ship, assuring him that the very first that could be captured should be his, as he was always willing to encourage an industrious brother.

They first touched at Sierra Leone, where they espied a large vessel, and Davis being the swifter sailer, came first up with him. He was not a little surprised that she did not endeavor to make off, and began to suspect her strength. When he came alongside of her, she fired a whole broadside, and hoisted black colors. Davis did the same, and fired a gun to leeward. The satisfaction of these brothers in iniquity was mutual, at having thus acquired so much additional strength and ability to undertake more formidable adventures. Two days were devoted to mirth and song, and upon the third, Davis and Cochlyn, the captain of the new confederate, agreed to go in the French pirate ship to attack the fort. When they approached, the men in the fort, apprehensive of their character and intentions, fired all the guns upon them at once. The ship returned the fire, and afforded employment until the other two ships arrived, when the men in the fort seeing such a number on board, lost courage, and abandoned the fort to the mercy of the robbers.

They took possession, remained there seven weeks, and cleaned their vessels. They then called a council of war, to deliberate concerning future undertakings, when it was resolved to sail down the coast in company; and, for the greater regularity and grandeur, Davis was chosen Commodore. That dangerous enemy, strong drink, had well nigh, however, sown the seeds of discord among these affectionate brethren. But Davis, alike prepared for council or for war, addressed them to the following purport: "Hear ye, you Cochlyn and La Boise, (which was the name of the French captain) I find, by strengthening you, I have put a rod into your hands to whip myself; but I am still able to deal with you both: however, since we met in love, let us part in love; for I find that three of a trade can never agree long together." Upon this, the other two went on board of their respective ships, and steered different courses.

Davis held down the coast, and reaching Cape Appolonia he captured three vessels, two English and one Scottish, plundered them, and allowed them to proceed. In five days after he met with a Dutchman of thirty guns and ninety men. She gave Davis a broadside, and killed nine of his men; a desperate engagement ensued, which continued from one o'clock at noon until nine next morning, when the Dutchman struck.

Davis equipped her for the pirate service, and called her "The Rover." With his two ships he sailed for the bay of Anamaboa, which he entered about noon, and took several vessels which were there waiting to take in negroes, gold, and elephants' teeth. Davis made a present of one of these vessels to the Dutch captain and his crew, and allowed them to go in quest of their fortune. When the fort had intelligence that they were pirates, they fired at them, but without any effect; Davis fired also, and hoisted the black colors, but deemed it prudent to depart.

The next day after he left Anamaboa, the man at the mast-head discovered a sail. It may be proper to inform our readers, that, according to the laws of pirates, the man who first discovers a vessel, is entitled to the best pair of pistols in the ship, and such is the honor attached to these, that a pair of them has been known to sell for thirty pounds.

Davis pursued that vessel, which, being between him and the shore, labored hard to run aground. Davis perceiving this, got between her and the land, and fired a broadside at her, when she immediately struck. She proved to be a very rich prize, having on board the Governor of Acra, with all his substance, going to Holland. There was in money to the amount of fifteen thousand pounds, besides a large quantity of merchant goods, and other valuable articles.

Before they reached the Isle of Princes, the St. James sprang a leak, so that the men and the valuable articles were removed into Davis's own ship. When he came in sight of the fort he hoisted English colors. The Portuguese, seeing a large ship sailing towards the shore, sent a sloop to discover her character and destination. Davis informed them, that he was an English man-of-war, sent out in search of some pirates which they had heard were in this quarter. Upon this, he was piloted into the port, and anchored below the guns at the fort. The governor was happy to have Englishmen in his harbor; and to do honor to Davis, sent down a file of musqueteers to escort him into the fort, while Davis, the more to cover his design, ordered nine men, according to the custom of the English, to row him on shore.

Davis also took the opportunity of cleaning and preparing all things for renewing his operations. He, however, could not contentedly leave the fort, without receiving some of the riches of the island. He formed a scheme to accomplish his purpose, and communicated the same to his men. He design was to make the governor a present of a few negroes in return for his kindness; then to invite him, with a few of the principal men and friars belonging to the island, to dine on board his ship, and secure them all in irons, until each of them should give a large ransom. They were accordingly invited, and very readily consented to go: and deeming themselves honored by his attention, all that were invited, would certainly have gone on board. Fortunately however, for them, a negro, who was privy to the horrible plan of Davis, swam on shore during the night, and gave information of the danger to the governor.

Retreat of the Pirates and Death of Captain Davis

**Retreat of the Pirates and Death of Captain Davis.**

The governor occupied the whole night in strengthening the defences and posting the men in the most advantageous places. Soon after day-break, the pirates, with Captain Davis at their head were discovered landing from the boats; and quickly marched across the open space toward the fort. A brisk fire was opened upon them from the fort, which they returned in a spirited manner. At length, a hand grenade, thrown from the wooden veranda of the fort killed three of the pirates; but several of the Portuguese were killed. The veranda of the fort being of wood and very dry, it was set fire to by the pirates. This was a great advantage to the attacking party, who could now distinguish those in the fort without their being so clearly seen themselves; but at this moment Captain Davis fell, mortally wounded by a musket ball in his belly. The fall of their chief, and the determined resistance of those in the fort, checked the impetuosity of the assailants. They hesitated, and at last retreated, bearing away with them their wounded commander. The Portuguese cheered, and led on by the governor, now became the assailants. Still the pirates' retreat was orderly; they fired and retired rank behind rank successively. They kept the Portuguese at bay until they had arrived at the boats, when a charge was made and a severe conflict ensued. But the pirates had lost too many men; and without their Captain, felt dispirited. As they lifted Davis into the boat in his dying agonies he fired his pistols at his pursuers. They now pulled with all their might to escape from the muskets of the Portuguese, who followed them along the banks of the river, annoying them in their retreat to the vessel. And those on board, who expected to hoist in treasure had to receive naught but their wounded comrades and dead commander.

Page 229 Illustration

## AUTHENTIC HISTORY OF THE MALAY PIRATES OF THE INDIAN OCEAN.

*With a Narrative of the Expedition against the Inhabitants of Quallah Battoo, commanded by Commodore Downes.*

A glance at the map of the East India Islands will convince us that this region of the globe must, from its natural configuration and locality; be peculiarly liable to become the seat of piracy. These islands form an immense cluster, lying as if it were in the high road which connects the commercial nations of Europe and Asia with each other, affording a hundred fastnesses from which to waylay the traveller. A large proportion of the population is at the same time confined to the coasts or the estuaries of rivers; they are fishermen and mariners; they are barbarous and poor, therefore rapacious, faithless and sanguinary. These are circumstances, it must be confessed, which militate strongly to beget a piratical character. It is not surprising, then, that the Malays should have been notorious for their depredations from our first acquaintance with them.

Among the tribes of the Indian Islands, the most noted for their piracies are, of course, the most idle, and the least industrious, and particularly such as are unaccustomed to follow agriculture or trade as regular pursuits. The agricultural tribes of Java, and many of Sumatra, never commit piracy at all; and the most civilized inhabitants of Celebes are very little addicted to this vice.

Among the most confirmed pirates are the true Malays, inhabiting the small islands about the eastern extremity of the straits of Malacca, and those lying between Sumatra and Borneo, down to Billitin and Cavimattir. Still more noted than these, are the inhabitants of certain islands situated between Borneo and the Phillipines, of whom the most desperate and enterprising are the Soolos and Illanoons, the former inhabiting a well known group of islands of the same name, and the latter being one of the most numerous nations of the great island of Magindando. The depredations of the proper Malays extend from Junkceylon to Java, through its whole coast, as far as Grip to Papir and Kritti, in Borneo and the western coast of Celebes. In another direction they infest the coasting trade of the Cochin Chinese and Siamese nations in the Gulf of Siam, finding sale for their booty, and shelter for themselves in the ports of Tringham, Calantan and Sahang. The most noted piratical stations of these people are the small islands about Lingin and Rhio, particularly Galang, Tamiang and Maphar. The chief of this last has seventy or eighty proas fit to undertake piratical expeditions.

The Soolo pirates chiefly confine their depredations to the Phillipine Islands, which they have continued to infest, with little interruption, for near three centuries, in open defiance of the Spanish authorities, and the numerous establishments maintained to check them. The piracies of the Illanoons, on the contrary, are widely extended, being carried on all the way from their native country to the Spice Islands, on one side, and to the Straits of Malacca on the other. In these last, indeed, they have formed, for the last few years, two permanent establishments; one of these situated on Sumatra, near Indragiri, is called Ritti, and the other a small island on the coast of Linga, is named Salangut. Besides those who are avowed pirates, it ought to be particularly noticed that a great number of the Malayan princes must be considered as accessories to their crimes, for they afford them protection, contribute to their outfit, and often share in their booty; so that a piratical proa is too commonly more welcome in their harbours than a fair trader.

The Malay piratical proas are from six to eight tons burden, and run from six to eight fathoms in length. They carry from one to two small guns, with commonly four swivels or rantakas to each side, and a crew of from twenty to thirty men. When they engage, they put up a strong bulwark of thick plank; the Illanoon proas are much larger and more formidable, and commonly carry from four to six guns, and a proportionable number of swivels, and have not unfrequently a double bulwark covered with buffalo hides; their crews consist of from forty to eighty men. Both, of course, are provided with spears, krisses, and as many fire arms as they can procure. Their modes of attack are cautious and cowardly, for plunder and not fame is their object. They lie concealed under the land, until they find a fit object and opportunity. The time chosen is when a vessel runs aground, or is becalmed, in the interval between the land and sea breezes. A vessel underway is seldom or never attacked. Several of the marauders attack together, and station themselves under the bows and quarters of a ship when she has no longer steerage way, and is incapable of pointing her guns. The action continues often for several hours, doing very little mischief; but when the crew are exhausted with the defence, or have expended their ammunition, the pirates take this opportunity of boarding in a mass. This may suggest the best means of defence. A ship, when attacked during a calm, ought, perhaps, rather to stand on the defensive, and wait if possible the setting in of the sea breeze, than attempt any active operations, which would only fatigue the crew, and disable them from making the necessary defence when boarding is attempted. Boarding netting, pikes and pistols, appear to afford effectual security; and, indeed, we conceive that a vessel thus defended by resolute crews of Europeans or Americans stand but little danger from any open attack of pirates whatsoever; for their guns are so ill served, that neither the hull or the rigging of a vessel can receive much damage from them, however much protracted the contest. The pirates are upon the whole extremely impartial in the selection of their prey, making little choice between natives and strangers, giving always, however, a natural preference to the most timid, and the most easily overcome.

When an expedition is undertaken by the Malay pirates, they range themselves under the banner of some piratical chief noted for his courage and conduct. The native prince of the place where it is prepared, supplies the adventurers with arms, ammunition and opium, and claims as his share of the plunder, the female captives, the cannon, and one third of all the rest of the booty.

In Nov. 1827, a principal chief of pirates, named Sindana, made a descent upon Mamoodgoo with forty-five proas, burnt three-fourths of the campong, driving the rajah with his family among the mountains. Some scores of men were killed, and 300 made prisoners, besides women and children to half that amount. In December following, when I was there, the people were slowly returning from the hills, but had not yet attempted to rebuild the campong, which lay in ashes. During my stay here (ten weeks) the place was visited by two other piratical chiefs, one of which was from Kylie, the other from Mandhaar Point under Bem Bowan, who appeared to have charge of the whole; between them they had 134 proas of all sizes.

Among the most desperate and successful pirates of the present day, Raga is most distinguished. He is dreaded by people of all denominations, and universally known as the "prince of pirates." For more than seventeen years this man has carried on a system of piracy to an extent never before known; his expeditions and enterprises would fill a large volume. They have invariably been marked with singular cunning and intelligence, barbarity, and reckless inattention to the shedding of human blood. He has emissaries every where, and has intelligence of the best description. It was about the year 1813 Raga commenced operations on a large scale. In that year he cut off three English vessels, killing the captains with his own hands. So extensive were his depredations about that time that a proclamation was issued from Batavia, declaring the east coast of Borneo to be under strict blockade. Two British sloops of war scoured the coast. One of which, the Elk, Capt. Reynolds, was attacked during the night by Raga's own proa, who unfortunately was not on board at the time. This proa which Raga personally commanded, and the loss of which he frequently laments, carried eight guns and was full of his best men.

A Piratical Proa in Full Chase

**A Piratical Proa in Full Chase.**

An European vessel was faintly descried about three o'clock one foggy morning; the rain fell in torrents; the time and weather were favorable circumstances for a surprise, and the commander determined to distinguish himself in the absence of the Rajah Raga, gave directions to close, fire the guns and board. He was the more confident of success, as the European vessel was observed to keep away out of the proper course on approaching her. On getting within about an hundred fathoms of the Elk they fired their broadside, gave a loud shout, and with their long oars pulled towards their prey. The sound of a drum beating to quarters no sooner struck the ear of the astonished Malays than they endeavored to get away: it was too late; the ports were opened, and a broadside, accompanied with three British cheers, gave sure indications of their fate. The captain hailed the Elk, and would fain persuade him it was a mistake. It was indeed a mistake, and one not to be rectified by the Malayan explanation. The proa was sunk by repeated broadsides, and the commanding officer refused to pick up any of the people, who, with the exception of five were drowned; these, after floating four days on some spars, were picked up by a Pergottan proa, and told the story to Raga, who swore anew destruction to every European he should henceforth take. This desperado has for upwards of seventeen years been the terror of the Straits of Macassar, during which period he has committed the most extensive and dreadful excesses sparing no one. Few respectable families along the coast of Borneo and

Celebes but have to complain of the loss of a proa, or of some number of their race; he is not more universally dreaded than detested; it is well known that he has cut off and murdered the crews of more than forty European vessels, which have either been wrecked on the coasts, or entrusted themselves in native ports. It is his boast that twenty of the commanders have fallen by his hands. The western coast of Celebes, for about 250 miles, is absolutely lined with proas belonging principally to three considerable rajahs, who act in conjunction with Raga and other pirates. Their proas may be seen in clusters of from 50, 80, and 100 (at Sediano I counted 147 laying on the sand at high water mark in parallel rows,) and kept in a horizontal position by poles, completely ready for the sea. Immediately behind them are the campongs, in which are the crews; here likewise are kept the sails, gunpowder, c. necessary for their equipment. On the very summits of the mountains, which in many parts rise abruptly from the sea, may be distinguished innumerable huts; here reside people who are constantly on the lookout. A vessel within ten miles of the shore will not probably perceive a single proa, yet in less than two hours, if the tide be high, she may be surrounded by some hundreds. Should the water be low they will push off during the night. Signals are made from mountain to mountain along the coast with the utmost rapidity; during the day time by flags attached to long bamboos; at night, by fires. Each chief sends forth his proas, the crews of which, in hazardous cases, are infuriated with opium, when they will most assuredly take the vessel if she be not better provided than most merchantmen.

Mr. Dalton, who went to the Pergottan river in 1830 says, "whilst I remained here, there were 71 proas of considerable sizes, 39 of which were professed pirates. They were anchored off the point of a small promontory, on which the rajah has an establishment and bazaar. The largest of these proas belonged to Raga, who received by the fleet of proas, in which I came, his regular supplies of arms and ammunition from Singapore. Here nestle the principal pirates, and Raga holds his head quarters; his grand depot was a few miles farther up. Rajah Agi Bota himself generally resides some distance up a small river which runs eastward of the point; near his habitation stands the principal bazaar, which would be a great curiosity for an European to visit if he could only manage to return, which very few have. The Raga gave me a pressing invitation to spend a couple of days at his country house, but all the Bugis' nacodahs strongly dissuaded me from such an attempt. I soon discovered the cause of their apprehension; they were jealous of Agi Bota, well knowing he would plunder me, and considered every article taken by him was so much lost to the Sultan of Coti, who naturally would expect the people to reserve me for his own particular plucking. When the fact was known of an European having arrived in the Pergottan river, this amiable prince and friend of Europeans, impatient to seize his prey, came immediately to the point from his country house, and sending for the nacodah of the proa, ordered him to land me and all my goods instantly. An invitation now came for me to go on shore and amuse myself with shooting, and look at some rare birds of beautiful plumage which the rajah would give me if I would accept of them; but knowing what were his intentions, and being well aware that I should be supported by all the Bugis' proas from Coti, I feigned sickness, and requested that the birds might be sent on board. Upon this Agi Bota, who could no longer restrain himself, sent off two boats of armed men, who robbed me of many articles, and would certainly have forced me on shore, or murdered me in the proa had not a signal been made to the Bugis' nacodahs, who immediately came with their people, and with spears and krisses, drove the rajah's people overboard. The nacodahs, nine in number, now went on shore, when a scene of contention took place showing clearly the character of this chief. The Bugis from Coti explained, that with regard to me it was necessary to be particularly circumspect, as I was not only well known at Singapore, but the authorities in that settlement knew that I was on board the Sultan's proa, and they themselves were responsible for my safety. To this circumstance alone I owe my life on several occasions, as in the event of any thing happening to me, every nacodah was apprehensive of his proa being seized on his return to Singapore; I was therefore more peculiarly cared for by this class of men, and they are powerful. The rajah answered the nacodahs by saying, I might be disposed of as many others had been, and no further notice taken of the circumstance; he himself would write to Singapore that I had been taken by an alligator, or bitten by a snake whilst out shooting; and as for what property I might have in the proa he would divide it with the Sultan of Coti. The Bugis, however, refused to listen to any terms, knowing the Sultan of Coti would call him to an account for the property, and the authorities of Singapore for my life. Our proa, with others, therefore dropped about four miles down the river, where we took in fresh water. Here we remained six days, every argument being in vain to entice me on shore. At length the Bugis' nacodahs came to the determination to sail without passes, which brought the rajah to terms. The proas returned to the point, and I was given to understand I might go on shore in safety. I did so, and was introduced to the rajah whom I found under a shed, with about 150 of his people; they were busy gambling, and had the appearance of what they really are, a ferocious set of banditti. Agi Bota is a good looking man, about forty years of age, of no education whatever; he divides his time between gaming, opium and cockfighting; that is in the interval of his more serious and profitable employment, piracy and rapine. He asked me to produce what money I had about me; on seeing only ten rupees, he remarked that it was not worth while to win so small a sum, but that if I would fight cocks with him he would lend me as much money as I wanted, and added it was beneath his dignity to fight under fifty reals a battle. On my saying it was contrary to an Englishman's religion to bet wagers, he dismissed me; immediately after the two rajahs produced their cocks and commenced fighting for one rupee a side. I was now obliged to give the old Baudarre five rupees to take some care of me, as whilst walking about, the people not only thrust their hands into my pockets, but pulled the buttons from my clothes. Whilst sauntering behind the rajah's campong I caught sight of an European woman, who on perceiving herself observed, instantly ran into one of the houses, no doubt dreading the consequences of being recognized. There are now in the house of Agi Bota two European women; up the country there are others, besides several men. The Bugis, inimical to the rajah, made no secret of the fact; I had heard of it on board the proa, and some person in the bazaar confirmed the statement. On my arrival, strict orders had been given to the inhabitants to put all European articles out of sight. One of my servants going into the bazaar, brought me such accounts as induced me to visit it. In one house were the following articles: four Bibles, one in English, one in Dutch, and two in the Portuguese languages; many articles of wearing apparel, such as jackets and trowsers, with the buttons altered to suit the natives; pieces of shirts tagged to other parts of dress; several broken instruments, such as quadrants, spy glasses (two,) binnacles, with pieces of ship's sails, bolts and hoops; a considerable variety of gunner's and carpenter's tools, stores, c. In another shop were two pelisses of faded lilac color; these were of modern cut and fashionably made. On enquiring how they became possessed of these articles, I was told they were some wrecks of European vessels on which no people were found, whilst others made no scruple of averring that they were formerly the property of people who had died in the country. All the goods in the bazaar belonged to the rajah, and were sold on his account; large quantities were said to be in his house up the river; but on all hands it was admitted Raga and his followers had by far the largest part of what was taken. A Mandoor, or head of one of the campongs, showed me some women's stockings, several of which were marked with the letters S.W.; also two chemises, one with the letters S.W.; two flannel petticoats, a miniature portrait frame (the picture was in the rajah's house,) with many articles of dress of both sexes. In consequence of the strict orders given on the subject I could see no more; indeed there were both difficulty and danger attending these inquiries. I particularly wanted to obtain the miniature picture, and offered the Mandoor fifty rupees if he could procure it; he laughed at me, and pointing significantly to his kris, drew one hand across my throat, and then across his own, giving me to understand such would be the result to us both on such an application to the rajah. It is the universal custom of the pirates, on this coast, to sell the people for slaves immediately on their arrival, the rajah taking for himself a few of the most useful, and receiving a percentage upon the purchase money of the remainder, with a moiety of the vessel and every article on board. European vessels are taken up the river, where they are immediately broken up. The situation of European prisoners is indeed dreadful in a climate like this, where even the labor of natives is intolerable; they are compelled to bear all the drudgery, and allowed a bare sufficiency of rice and salt to eat."

It is utterly impossible for Europeans who have seen these pirates at such places as Singapore and Batavia, to form any conception of their true character. There they are under immediate control, and every part of their behaviour is a tissue of falsehood and deception. They constantly carry about with them a smooth tongue, cringing demeanor, a complying disposition, which always asserts, and never contradicts; a countenance which appears to anticipate the very wish of the Europeans, and which so generally imposes upon his understanding, that he at once concludes them to be the best and gentlest of human beings; but let the European meet them in any of their own campongs, and a very different character they will appear. The character and treacherous proceeding narrated above, and the manner of cutting off vessels and butchering their crews, apply equally to all the pirates of the East India Islands, by which many hundred European and American vessels have been surprised and their crews butchered.

On the 7th of February, 1831, the ship Friendship, Capt. Endicott, of Salem (Mass.,) was captured by the Malays while lying at Quallah Battoo, on the coast of Sumatra. In the forenoon of the fatal day, Capt. Endicott, Mr. Barry, second mate, and four of the crew, it seems went on shore as usual, for the purpose of weighing pepper, expecting to obtain that day two boat loads, which had been promised them by the Malays. After the first boat was loaded, they observed that she delayed some time in passing down the river, and her crew being composed of Malays, was supposed by the officers to be stealing pepper from her, and secreting it in the bushes. In consequence of this conjecture, two men were sent off to watch them, who on approaching the boat, saw five or six Malays leap from the jungle, and hurry on board of her. The former, however, supposed them to be the boat's crew, as they had seen an equal number quit her previous to their own approach. In this they were mistaken, as will subsequently appear. At this time a brig hove in sight, and was seen standing towards Soo Soo, another pepper port, distant about five miles. Capt. Endicott, on going to the beach to ascertain whether the brig had hoisted any colors, discovered that the boat with pepper had approached within a few yards of the Friendship, manned with an unusual number of natives.

It appears that when the pepper boats came alongside of the Friendship, as but few of the hands could work at a time, numbers of the Malays came on board, and on being questioned by Mr. Knight, the first officer, who was in the gangway, taking an account of the pepper, as to their business, their reply was, that they had come to see the vessel. Mr. Knight ordered them into their boat again, and some of them obeyed, but only to return immediately to assist in the work of death, which was now commenced by attacking Mr. Knight and the rest of the crew on board. The crew of the vessel being so scattered, it was impossible to concentrate their force so as to make a successful resistance. Some fell on the forecastle, one in the gangway, and Mr. Knight fell upon the quarter deck, severely wounded by a stab in the back while in the act of snatching from the bulwarks a boarding pike with which to defend himself.

The two men who were taking the pepper on a stage, having vainly attempted to get on board to the assistance of their comrades, were compelled to leap into the sea. One of them, Charles Converse, of Salem, being severely wounded, succeeded in swimming to the bobstays, to which he clung until taken on board by the natives, and from some cause he was not afterwards molested. His companion, John Davis, being unable to swim, drifted with the tide near the *boat tackle*, or *davit falls*, the blocks being overhauled down near the water; one of these he laid hold of, which the Malays perceiving, dropped their boat astern and despatched him! the cook sprang into a canoe along side, and in attempting to push off she was capsized; and being unable to swim, he got on the bottom, and paddled ashore with his hands, where he was made prisoner. Gregory, an Italian, sought shelter in the foretop-gallant cross-trees, where he was fired at several times by the Malays with the muskets of the Friendship, which were always kept loaded and ready for use while on the coast.

Three of the crew leaped into the sea, and swam to a point of land near a mile distant, to the northward of the town; and, unperceived by the Malays on shore, pursued their course to the northward towards Cape Felix, intending to go to the port of Annalaboo, about forty-five miles distant. Having walked all night, they found themselves, on the following morning, near the promontory, and still twenty-five miles distant from Annalaboo.

When Mr. Endicott, Mr. Barry, and the four seamen arrived at the beach, they saw the crew jumping into the sea; the truth now, with all its horrors, flashed upon his mind, that the vessel was attacked, and in an instant they jumped on board the boat and pushed off; at the same time a friendly rajah named Po Adam, sprang into the boat; he was the proprietor of a port and considerable property at a place called Pulo Kio, but three miles distant from the mouth of the river Quallah Battoo. More business had been done by the rajah during the eight years past than by any other on the pepper coast; he had uniformly professed himself friendly to the Americans, and he has generally received the character of their being honest. Speaking a little English as he sprang into the boat, he exclaimed, "Captain, you got trouble; Malay kill you, he kill Po Adam too!" Crowds of Malays assembled on both sides of the river, brandishing their weapons in a menacing manner, while a ferry boat, manned with eight or ten of the natives, armed with spears and krisses, pushed off to prevent the officers' regaining their ship. The latter exhibited no fear, and flourished the cutlass of Po Adam in a menacing manner from the bows of the boat; it so intimidated the Malays that they fled to the shore, leaving a free passage to the ship; but as they got near her they found that the Malays had got entire possession of her; some of them were promenading the deck, others were making signals of success to the people on shore, while, with the exception of one man aloft, not an individual of the crew could be seen. Three Malay boats, with about fifty men, now issued from the river in the direction of the ship, while the captain and his men, concluding that their only hope of recovering their vessel was to obtain assistance from some other ships, directed their course towards Muchie, where they knew that several American vessels were lying at anchor. Three American captains, upon hearing the misfortunes of their countrymen, weighed anchor immediately for Quallah Battoo, determined, if possible, to recover the ship. By four o'clock on the same day they gained an anchorage off that place; the Malays, in the meantime, had removed on shore every moveable article belonging to the ship, including specie, besides several cases of opium, amounting in all to upwards of thirty thousand dollars. This was done on the night of the 9th, and on the morning of the 10th, they contrived to heave in the chain cable, and get the anchor up to the bows; and the ship was drifting finely towards the beach, when the cable, not being stopped abaft the bitts, began suddenly to run out with great velocity; but a bight having by accident been thrown forward of the windlass, a riding turn was the consequence, and the anchor, in its descent, was suddenly checked about fifteen fathoms from the hawse. A squall soon after coming on, the vessel drifted obliquely towards the shore, and grounded upon a coral reef near half a mile to the southward of the town. The next day, having obtained a convenient anchorage, a message was sent by a friendly Malay who came on board at Soo Soo, demanding the restoration of the ship. The rajah replied that he would not give her up, but that they were welcome to take her if they could; a fire was now opened upon the Friendship by the vessels, her decks were crowded with Malays, who promptly returned the fire, as did also the forts on shore. This mode of warfare appeared undecisive, and it was determined to decide the contest by a close action. A number of boats being manned and armed with about thirty officers and men, a movement was made to carry the ship by boarding. The Malays did not wait the approach of this determined attack, but all deserted the vessel to her lawful owners, when she was taken possession of and warped out into deep water. The appearance of the ship, at the time she was boarded, beggars all description; every part of her bore ample testimony of the scene of violence and destruction with which she had been visited. The objects of the voyage were abandoned, and the Friendship returned to the United States. The public were unanimous in calling for a redress of the unparalleled outrage on the lives and property of citizens of the United States. The government immediately adopted measures to punish so outrageous an act of piracy by despatching the frigate Potomac, Commodore Downs, Commander. The Potomac sailed from New York the 24th of August, 1831, after touching at Rio Janeiro and the Cape of Good Hope. She anchored off Quallah Battoo in February 1832, disguised as a Danish ship, and came to in merchantman style, a few men being sent aloft, dressed in red and blue flannel shirts, and one sail being clewed up and furled at a time. A reconnoitering party were sent on shore disguised as pepper dealers, but they returned without being able to ascertain the situations of the forts. The ship now presented a busy scene; it was determined to commence an attack upon the town the next morning, and every necessary preparation was accordingly made, muskets were cleaned, cartridge-boxes buckled on, cutlasses examined and put in order, c.

At twelve o'clock at night, all hands were called, those assigned to take part in the expedition were mustered, when Lieut. Shubrick, the commander of the detachment, gave them special orders; when they entered the boats and proceeded to the shore, where they effected a landing near the dawn of day, amid a heavy surf, about a mile and a half to the north of the town, undiscovered by the enemy, and without any serious accident having befallen them, though several of the party were thoroughly drenched by the beating of the surf, and some of their ammunition was injured.

The troops then formed and took up their line of march against the enemy, over a beach of deep and heavy sand. They had not proceeded far before they were discovered by a native at a distance, who ran at full speed to give the alarm. A rapid march soon brought them up with the first fort, when a division of men, under the command of Lieut. Hoff, was detached from the main body, and ordered to surround it. The first fort was found difficult of access, in consequence of a deep hedge of thorn-bushes and brambles with which it was environed. The assault was commenced by the pioneers, with their crows and axes, breaking down the gates and forcing a passage. This was attended with some difficulty, and gave the enemy time for preparation. They raised their warwhoop, and resisted most manfully, fighting with spears, sabres, and muskets. They had also a few brass pieces in the fort, but they managed them with so little skill as to produce no effect, for the balls uniformly whizzed over the heads of our men. The resistance of the Malays was in vain, the fort was stormed, and soon carried; not, however, till almost every individual in it was slain. Po Mahomet, a chief of much distinction, and who was one of the principal persons concerned in the outrage on the Friendship was here slain; the mother of Chadoolah, another rajah, was also slain here; another woman fell at this port, but her rank was not ascertained; she fought with the spirit of a desperado. A seaman had just scaled one of the ramparts, when he was severely wounded by a blow received from a weapon in her hands, but her life paid the forfeit of her daring, for she was immediately transfixed by a bayonet in the hands of the person whom she had so severely injured. His head was wounded by a javelin, his thumb nearly cut off by a sabre, and a ball was shot through his hat.

Lieutenants Edson and Ferret proceeded to the rear of the town, and made a bold attack upon that fort, which, after a spirited resistance on the part of the Malays, surrendered. Both officers and marines here narrowly escaped with their lives. One of the natives in the fort had trained his piece in such a manner as to rake their whole body, when he was shot down by a marine while in the very act of applying a match to it. The cannon was afterwards found to have been filled with bullets. This fort, like the former, was environed with thick jungle, and great difficulty had been experienced in entering it. The engagement had now become general, and the alarm universal. Men, women and children were seen flying in every direction, carrying the few articles they were able to seize in the moments of peril, and some of the men were cut down in the flight. Several of the enemy's proas, filled with people, were severely raked by a brisk fire from the six pounder, as they were sailing up the river to the south of the town, and numbers of the natives were killed. The third and most formidable fort was now attacked, and it proved the most formidable, and the co-operation of the several divisions was required for its reduction; but so spirited was the fire poured into it that it was soon obliged to yield, and the next moment the American colors were seen triumphantly waving over its battlements. The greater part of the town was reduced to ashes. The bazaar, the principal place of merchandize, and most of the private dwellings were consumed by fire. The triumph had now been completed over the Malays; ample satisfaction had been taken for their outrages committed upon our own countrymen, and the bugle sounded the return of the ship's forces; and the embarkation was soon after effected. The action had continued about two hours and a half, and was gallantly sustained both by officers and men, from its commencement to its close. The loss on the part of the Malays was near a hundred killed, while of the Americans only two lost their lives. Among the spoils were a Chinese gong, a Koran, taken at Mahomet's fort, and several pieces of rich gold cloth. Many of the men came off richly laden with spoils which they had taken from the enemy, such as rajah's scarfs, gold and silver chunam boxes, chains, ear rings and finger rings, anklets and bracelets, and a variety of shawls, krisses richly hilted and with gold scabbards, and a variety of other ornaments. Money to a considerable amount was brought off. That nothing should be left undone to have an indelible impression on the minds of these people, of the power of the United States to inflict punishment for aggressions committed on her commerce, in seas however distant, the ship was got underway the following morning, and brought to, with a spring on her cable, within less than a mile of the shore, when the larboard side was brought to bear nearly upon the site of the town. The object of the Commodore, in this movement, was not to open an indiscriminate or destructive fire upon the town and inhabitants of Quallah Battoo, but to show them the irresistible power of thirty-two pound shot, and to reduce the fort of Tuca de Lama, which could not be reached on account of the jungle and stream of water, on the morning before, and from which a fire had been opened and continued during the embarkation of the troops on their return to the ship. The fort was very soon deserted, while the shot was cutting it to pieces, and tearing up whole cocoa-trees by the roots. In the afternoon a boat came off from the shore, bearing a flag of truce to the Commodore, beseeching him, in all the practised forms of submission of the east, that he would grant them peace, and cease to fire his big guns. Hostilities now ceased, and the Commodore informed them that the objects of his government in sending him to their shores had now been consummated in the punishment of the guilty, who had committed their piracies on the Friendship. Thus ended the intercourse with Quallah Battoo. The Potomac proceeded from this place to China, and from thence to the Pacific Ocean; after looking to the interests of the American commerce in those parts she arrived at Boston in 1834, after a three years' absence.

**THE ADVENTURES OF CAPTAIN CONDENT**

Captain Condent was a Plymouth man born, but we are as yet ignorant of the motives and time of his first turning pirate. He was one of those who thought fit to retire from Providence, on Governor Rogers' arrival at that island, in a sloop belonging to Mr. Simpson, of New York, a Jew merchant, of which sloop he was then quarter-master. Soon after they left the island, an accident happened on board, which put the whole crew into consternation. They had among them an Indian man, whom some of them had beaten; in revenge, he got most of the arms forward into the hold, and designed to blow up the sloop; upon which, some advised scuttling the deck, and throwing grenade shells down, but Condent said that was too tedious and dangerous, since the fellow might fire through the deck and kill several of them. He, therefore, taking a pistol in one hand, and his cutlass in the other, leaped into the hold. The Indian discharged a piece at him, which broke his arm; but, however, he ran up and shot the Indian. When he was dead, the crew hacked him to pieces, and the gunner, ripping up his belly and tearing out his heart, broiled and eat it.

After this, they took a merchantman called the Duke of York; and some disputes arising among the pirates, the captain, and one half of the company, went on board the prize; the other half, who continued in the sloop, chose Condent captain. He shaped his course for the Cape-de Verd Islands, and in his way took a merchant ship from Madeira, laden with wine, and bound for the West Indies, which he plundered and let go; then coming to the Isle of May, one of the said islands, he took the whole salt fleet, consisting of about 20 sail. Wanting a boom, he took out the mainmast of one of these ships to supply the want. Here he took upon himself the administration of justice, inquiring into the manner of the commanders' behaviour to their men, and those against whom complaint was made, he whipped and pickled. He took what provision and other necessaries he wanted, and having augmented his company by volunteers and forced men, he left the ships and sailed to St. Jago, where he took a Dutch ship, which had formerly been a privateer. This proved also an easy prize, for he fired but one broadside, and clapping her on board, carried her without resistance, for the captain and several men were killed, and some wounded by his great shot.

The ship proving for his purpose, he gave her the name of the Flying Dragon, went on board with his crew, and made a present of his sloop to a mate of an English prize, whom he had forced with him. From hence he stood away for the coast of Brazil, and in his cruize took several Portuguese ships, which he plundered and let go.

After these he fell in with the Wright galley, Capt. John Spelt, commander, hired by the South Sea company, to go to the coast of Angola for slaves, and thence to Buenos Ayres. This ship he detained a considerable time, and the captain being his townsman, treated him very civilly. A few days after he took Spelt, he made prize of a Portuguese, laden with bale goods and stores. He rigged the Wright galley anew, and put on board of her some of the goods. Soon after he had discharged the Portuguese, he met with a Dutch East Indiaman of 28 guns, whose captain was killed the first broadside, and took her with little resistance, for he had hoisted the pirate's colors on board Spelt's ship.

Capt. Condent leaping into the hold, to attack the Indian.

**Capt. Condent leaping into the hold, to attack the Indian.**

He now, with three sail, steered for the island of Ferdinando, where he hove down and cleaned the Flying Dragon. Having careened, he put 11 Dutchmen on board Capt. Spelt, to make amends for the hands he had forced from him, and sent him away, making him a present of the goods he had taken from the Portuguese ship. When he sailed himself, he ordered the Dutch to stay at Ferdinando 24 hours after his departure; threatening, if he did not comply, to sink his ship, if he fell a second time into his hands, and to put all the company to the sword. He then stood for the coast of Brazil, where he met a Portuguese man of war of 70 guns, which he came up with. The Portuguese hailed him, and he answered, *from London, bound to Buenos Ayres.* The Portuguese manned his shrouds and cheered him, when Condent fired a broadside, and a smart engagement ensued for the space of three glasses; but Condent finding himself over-matched, made the best of his way, and being the best sailer, got off.

A few days after, he took a vessel of the same nation, who gave an account that he had killed above forty men in the Guarda del Costa, beside a number wounded. He kept along the coast to the southward, and took a French ship of 18 guns, laden with wine and brandy, bound for the South Sea, which he carried with him into the River of Platte. He sent some of his men ashore to kill some wild cattle, but they were taken by the crew of a Spanish man-of-war. On their examination before the captain, they said they were two Guinea ships, with slaves belonging to the South Sea company, and on this story were allowed to return to their boats. Here five of his forced men ran away with his canoe; he plundered the French ship, cut her adrift, and she was stranded. He proceeded along the Brazil coast, and hearing a pirate ship was lost upon it, and the pirates imprisoned, he used all the Portuguese who fell into his hands, who were many, very barbarously, cutting off their ears and noses; and as his master was a papist, when they took a priest, they made him say mass at the mainmast, and would afterwards get on his back and ride him about the decks, or else load and drive him like a beast. He from this went to the Guinea coast, and took Capt. Hill, in the Indian Queen.

The Pirates riding the Priests about deck

**The Pirates riding the Priests about deck.**

In Luengo Bay he saw two ships at anchor, one a Dutchman of 44 guns, the other an English ship, called the Fame, Capt. Bowen, commander. They both cut and ran ashore; the Fame was lost, but the Dutch ship the pirate got off and took with him. When he was at sea again, he discharged Captain Hill, and stood away for the East Indies. Near the Cape he took an Ostend East-Indiaman, of which Mr. Nash, a noted merchant of London, was supercargo. Soon after he took a Dutch East-Indiaman, discharged the Ostender, and made for Madagascar. At the Isle of St. Mary, he met with some of Capt. Halsey's crew, whom he took on board with other stragglers, and shaped his course for the East-Indies, and in the way, at the island of Johanna, took, in company with two other pirates he met at St. Mary's, the Cassandra East-Indiaman, commanded by Capt. James Macraigh. He continued his course for the East-Indies, where he made a very great booty; and returning, touched at the island of Mascarenhas, where he met with a Portuguese ship of 70 guns, with the viceroy of Goa on board. This ship he made prize of, and hearing she had money on board, they would allow of no ransom, but carried her to the coast of Zanguebar, where was a Dutch fortification, which they took and plundered, razed the fort, and carried off several men voluntarily. From hence they stood for St. Mary's, where they shared their booty, broke up their company, and settled among the natives. Here a snow came from Bristol, which they obliged to carry a petition to the governor of Mascarenhas for a pardon, though they paid the master very generously. The governor returned answer he would take them into protection if they would destroy their ships, which they agreed to, and accordingly sunk the Flying Dragon, c. Condent and some others went to Mascarenhas, where Condent married the governor's sister-in-law, and remained some time; but, as I have been credibly informed, he is since come to France, settled at St. Maloes, and drives a considerable trade as a merchant.

## THE LIFE OF CAPTAIN EDWARD LOW.

This ferocious villain was born in Westminster, and received an education similar to that of the common people in England. He was by nature a pirate; for even when very young he raised contributions among the boys of Westminster, and if they declined compliance, a battle was the result. When he advanced a step farther in life, he began to exert his ingenuity at low games, and cheating all in his power; and those who pretended to maintain their own right, he was ready to call to the field of combat.

He went to sea in company with his brother, and continued with him for three or four years. Going over to America, he wrought in a rigging-house at Boston for some time. He then came home to see his mother in England, returned to Boston, and continued for some years longer at the same business. But being of a quarrelsome temper, he differed with his master, and went on board a sloop bound for the Bay of Honduras.

While there, he had the command of a boat employed in bringing logwood to the ship. In that boat there were twelve men well armed, to be prepared for the Spaniards, from whom the wood was taken by force. It happened one day that the boat came to the ship just a little before dinner was ready, and Low desired that they might dine before they returned. The captain, however, ordered them a bottle of rum, and requested them to take another trip, as no time was to be lost. The crew were enraged, particularly Low, who took up a loaded musket and fired at the captain, but missing him, another man was shot, and they ran off with the boat. The next day they took a small vessel, went on board her, hoisted a black flag, and declared war with the whole world.

In their rovings, Low met with Lowther, who proposed that he should join him, and thus promote their mutual advantage. Having captured a brigantine, Low, with forty more, went on board her; and leaving Lowther, they went to seek their own fortune.

Their first adventure was the capture of a vessel belonging to Amboy, out of which they took the provisions, and allowed her to proceed. On the same day they took a sloop, plundered her, and permitted her to depart. The sloop went into Black Island, and sent intelligence to the governor that Low was on the coast. Two small vessels were immediately fitted out, but, before their arrival, Low was beyond their reach. After this narrow escape, Low went into port to procure water and fresh provisions; and then renewed his search of plunder. He next sailed into the harbor of Port Rosemary, where were thirteen ships, but none of them of any great strength. Low hoisted the black flag, assuring them that if they made any resistance they should have no quarter; and manning their boat, the pirates took possession of every one of them, which they plundered and converted to their own use. They then put on board a schooner ten guns and fifty men, named her the Fancy, and Low himself went on board of her, while Charles Harris was constituted captain of the brigantine. They also constrained a few of the men to join them, and sign their articles.

After an unsuccessful pursuit of two sloops from Boston, they steered for the Leeward Islands, but in their way were overtaken by a terrible hurricane. The search for plunder gave place to the most vigorous exertion to save themselves. On board the brigantine, all hands were at work both day and night; they were under the necessity of throwing overboard six of her guns, and all the weighty provisions. In the storm, the two vessels were separated, and it was some time before they again saw each other.

After the storm, Low went into a small island west of the Carribbees, refitted his vessels, and got provision for them in exchange of goods. As soon as the brigantine was ready for sea, they went on a cruise until the Fancy should be prepared, and during that cruise, met with a vessel which had lost all her masts in the storm, which they plundered of goods to the value of 1000*l*. and returned to the island. When the Fancy was ready to sail, a council was held what course they should next steer. They followed the advice of the captain, who thought it not safe to cruise any longer to the leeward, lest they should fall in with any of the men-of-war that cruised upon that coast, so they sailed for the Azores.

The good fortune of Low was now singular; in his way thither he captured a French ship of 34 guns, and carried her along with him. Then entering St. Michael's roads, he captured seven sail, threatening with instant death all who dared to oppose him. Thus, by inspiring terror, without firing a single gun, he became master of all that property. Being in want of water and fresh provisions, Low sent to the governor demanding a supply, upon condition of releasing the ships he had taken, otherwise he would commit them to the flames. The request was instantly complied with, and six of the vessels were restored. But a French vessel being among them, they emptied her of guns and all her men except the cook, who, they said, being a greasy fellow, would fry well; they accordingly bound the unfortunate man to the mast, and set the ship on fire.

The next who fell in their way was Captain Carter, in the Wright galley; who, because he showed some inclination to defend himself, was cut and mangled in a barbarous manner. There were also two Portuguese friars, whom they tied to the foremast, and several times let them down before they were dead, merely to gratify their own ferocious dispositions. Meanwhile, another Portuguese, beholding this cruel scene, expressed some sorrow in his countenance, upon which one of the wretches said he did not like his looks, and so giving him a stroke across the body with his cutlass, he fell upon the spot. Another of the miscreants, aiming a blow at a prisoner, missed his aim, and struck Low upon the under jaw. The surgeon was called, and stitched up the wound; but Low finding fault with the operation, the surgeon gave him a blow which broke all the stiches, and left him to sew them himself. After he had plundered this vessel, some of them were for burning her, as they had done the Frenchman; but instead of that, they cut her cables, rigging, and sails to pieces, and sent her adrift to the mercy of the waves.

The Cruelties practised by Captain Low

**The Cruelties practised by Captain Low.**

They next sailed for the island of Madeira, and took up a fishing boat with two old men and a boy. They detained one of them, and sent the other on shore with a flag of truce, requesting the governor to send them a boat of water, else they would hang the other man at the yard arm. The water was sent, and the man dismissed.

They next sailed for the Canary Islands, and there took several vessels; and being informed that two small galleys were daily expected, the sloop was manned and sent in quest of them. They, however, missing their prey, and being in great want of provision, went into St. Michael's in the character of traders, and being discovered, were apprehended, and the whole crew conducted to the castle, and treated according to their merits.

Meanwhile, Low's ship was overset upon the careen and lost, so that, having only the Fancy schooner remaining, they all, to the number of a hundred, went on board her, and set sail in search of new spoils. They soon met a rich Portuguese vessel, and after some resistance captured her. Low tortured the men to constrain them to inform him where they had hid their treasures. He accordingly discovered that, during the chase, the captain had hung a bag with eleven thousand moidores out of the cabin window, and that, when they were taken, he had cut the rope, and allowed it to fall into the sea. Upon this intelligence, Low raved and stormed like a fury, ordered the captain's lips to be cut off and broiled before his eyes, then murdered him and all his crew.

The Captain of the Portuguese Ship cutting away the Bag of Moidores

**The Captain of the Portuguese Ship cutting away the Bag of Moidores.**

After this bloody action, the miscreants steered northward, and in their course seized several vessels, one of which they burned, and plundering the rest, allowed them to proceed. Having cleaned in one of the islands, they then sailed for the bay of Honduras. They met a Spaniard coming out of the bay, which had captured five Englishmen and a pink, plundered them, and brought away the masters prisoners. Low hoisted Spanish colors, but, when he came near, hung out the black flag, and the Spaniard was seized without resistance. Upon finding the masters of the English vessels in the hold, and seeing English goods on board, a consultation was held, when it was determined to put all the Spaniards to the sword. This was scarcely resolved upon, when they commenced with every species of weapons to massacre every man, and some flying from their merciless hands into the waves, a canoe was sent in pursuit of those who endeavored to swim on shore. They next plundered the Spanish vessel, restored the English masters to their respective vessels, and set the Spaniard on fire.

Low's next cruise was between the Leeward Islands and the main land, where, in a continued course of prosperity, he successively captured no less than nineteen ships of different sizes, and in general treated their crews with a barbarity unequalled even among pirates. But it happened that the Greyhound, of twenty guns and one hundred and twenty men, was cruising upon that coast. Informed of the mischief these miscreants had done, the Greyhound went in search of them. Supposing they had discovered a prize, Low and his crew pursued them, and the Greyhound, allowing them to run after her until all things were ready to engage, turned upon the two sloops.

One of these sloops was called the Fancy, and commanded by Low himself, and the other the Ranger, commanded by Harris; both hoisted their piratical colors, and fired each a gun. When the Greyhound came within musket shot, she hauled up her mainsail, and clapped close upon a wind, to keep the pirates from running to leeward, and then engaged. But when the rogues found whom they had to deal with, they edged away under the man-of-war's stern, and the Greyhound standing after them, they made a running fight for about two hours; but little wind happening, the sloops gained from her, by the help of their oars; upon which the Greyhound left off firing, turned all hands to her own oars, and at three in the afternoon came up with them. The pirates hauled upon a wind to receive the man-of-war, and the fight was immediately renewed, with a brisk fire on both sides, till the Ranger's mainyard was shot down. Under these circumstances, Low abandoned her to the enemy, and fled.

The conduct of Low was surprising in this adventure, because his reputed courage and boldness had hitherto so possessed the minds of all people, that he became a terror even to his own men; but his behaviour throughout this whole action showed him to be a base cowardly villain; for had Low's sloop fought half so briskly as Harris' had done (as they were under a solemn oath to do,) the man-of-war, in the opinion of some present, could never have hurt them.

Nothing, however, could lessen the fury, or reform the manners, of that obdurate crew. Their narrow escape had no good effect upon them, and with redoubled violence they renewed their depredations and cruelties. The next vessel they captured, was eighty miles from land. They used the master with the most wanton cruelty, then shot him dead, and forced the crew into the boat with a compass, a little water, and a few biscuits, and left them to the mercy of the waves; they, however, beyond all expectation, got safe to shore.

Low proceeded in his villainous career with too fatal success. Unsatisfied with satiating their avarice and walking the common path of wickedness, those inhuman wretches, like to Satan himself, made mischief their sport, cruelty their delight, and the ruin and murder of their fellow men their constant employment. Of all the piratical crews belonging to the English nation, none ever equalled Low in barbarity. Their mirth and their anger had the same effect. They murdered a man from good humor, as well as from anger and passion. Their ferocious disposition seemed only to delight in cries, groans, and lamentations. One day Low having captured Captain Graves, a Virginia man, took a bowl of punch in his hand, and said, "Captain, here's half this to you." The poor gentleman was too much touched with his misfortunes to be in a humor for drinking, he therefore modestly excused himself. Upon this Low cocked and presented a pistol in the one hand, and his bowl in the other, saying, "Either take the one or the other."

Low next captured a vessel called the Christmas, mounted her with thirty-four guns, went on board her himself, assumed the title of admiral, and hoisted the black flag. His next prize was a brigantine half manned with Portuguese, and half with English. The former he hanged, and the latter he thrust into their boat and dismissed, while he set fire to the vessel. The success of Low was unequalled, as well as his cruelty; and during a long period he continued to pursue his wicked course with impunity.

All wickedness comes to an end and Low's crew at last rose against him and he was thrown into a boat without provisions and abandoned to his fate. This was because Low murdered the quarter-master while he lay asleep. Not long after he was cast adrift a French vessel happened along and took him into Martinico, and after a quick trial by the authorities he received short shift on a gallows erected for his benefit.

Low presenting a Pistol and Bowl of Punch

**Low presenting a Pistol and Bowl of Punch.**

## LIFE AND ADVENTURES OF CAPTAIN EDWARD ENGLAND

This adventurer was mate of a sloop that sailed from Jamaica, and was taken by Captain Winter, a pirate, just before the settlement of the pirates at Providence island. After the pirates had surrendered to his Majesty's pardon, and Providence island was peopled by the English government, Captain England sailed to Africa. There he took several vessels, particularly the Cadogan, from Bristol, commanded by one Skinner. When the latter struck to the pirate, he was ordered to come on board in his boat. The person upon whom he first cast his eye, proved to be his old boatswain, who stared him in the face, and accosted him in the following manner: "Ah, Captain Skinner, is it you? the only person I wished to see: I am much in your debt, and I shall pay you all in your own coin." The poor man trembled in every joint, and dreaded the event, as he well might. It happened that Skinner and his old boatswain, with some of his men, had quarrelled, so that he thought fit to remove them on board a man-of-war, while he refused to pay them their wages. Not long after, they found means to leave the man-of-war, and went on board a small ship in the West Indies. They were taken by a pirate, and brought to Providence, and from thence sailed as pirates with Captain England. Thus accidentally meeting their old captain, they severely revenged the treatment they had received.

After the rough salutation which has been related, the boatswain called to his comrades, laid hold of Skinner, tied him fast to the windlass, and pelted him with glass bottles until they cut him in a shocking manner, then whipped him about the deck until they were quite fatigued, remaining deaf to all his prayers and entreaties; and at last, in an insulting tone, observed, that as he had been a good master to his men, he should have an easy death, and upon this shot him through the head.

The Pirates pelting Captain Skinner with Glass Bottles

**The Pirates pelting Captain Skinner with Glass Bottles.**

Having taken such things out of the ship as they stood most in need of, she was given to Captain Davis in order to try his fortune with a few hands.

Captain England, some time after, took a ship called the Pearl, for which he exchanged his own sloop, fitted her up for piratical service, and called her the Royal

James. In that vessel he was very fortunate, and took several ships of different sizes and different nations. In the spring of 1719, the pirates returned to Africa, and beginning at the river Gambia, sailed down the coast to Cape Corso, and captured several vessels. Some of them they pillaged, and allowed to proceed, some they fitted out for the pirate service, and others they burned.

Leaving our pirate upon this coast, the Revenge and the Flying King, two other pirate vessels, sailed for the West Indies, where they took several prizes, and then cleared and sailed for Brazil. There they captured some Portuguese vessels; but a large Portuguese man-of-war coming up to them, proved an unwelcome guest. The Revenge escaped, but was soon lost upon that coast. The Flying King in despair run ashore. There were then seventy on board, twelve of whom were slain, and the remainder taken prisoners. The Portuguese hanged thirty-eight of them.

Captain England, whilst cruising upon that coast, took the Peterborough of Bristol, and the Victory. The former they detained, the latter they plundered and dismissed. In the course of his voyage, England met with two ships, but these taking shelter under Cape Corso Castle, he unsuccessfully attempted to set them on fire. He next sailed down to Whydah road, where Captain La Bouche had been before England, and left him no spoil. He now went into the harbor, cleaned his own ship, and fitted up the Peterborough, which he called the Victory. During several weeks the pirates remained in this quarter, indulging in every species of riot and debauchery, until the natives, exasperated with their conduct, came to an open rupture, when several of the negroes were slain, and one of their towns set on fire by the pirates.

Leaving that port, the pirates, when at sea, determined by vote to sail for the East Indies, and arrived at Madagascar. After watering and taking in some provisions they sailed for the coast of Malabar. This place is situated in the Mogul Empire, and is one of its most beautiful and fertile districts. It extends from the coast of Canora to Cape Comorin. The original natives are negroes; but a mingled race of Mahometans, who are generally merchants, have been introduced in modern times. Having sailed almost round the one half of the globe, literally seeking whom they might devour, our pirates arrived in this hitherto untried and prolific field for their operations.

Not long after their settlement at Madagascar, they took a cruise, in which they captured two Indian vessels and a Dutchman. They exchanged the latter for one of their own, and directed their course again to Madagascar. Several of their hands were sent on shore with tents and ammunition, to kill such beasts and venison as the island afforded. They also formed the resolution to go in search of Avery's crew, which they knew had settled upon the island; but as their residence was upon the other side of the island, the loss of time and labour was the only fruit of their search.

They tarried here but a very short time, then steered their course to Johanna, and coming out of that harbor, fell in with two English vessels and an Ostend ship, all Indiamen, which, after a most desperate action, they captured. The particulars of this extraordinary action are related in the following letter from Captain Mackra.

"*Bombay, November 16th*, 1720.

"We arrived on the 25th of July last, in company with the Greenwich, at Johanna, an island not far from Madagascar. Putting in there to refresh our men, we found fourteen pirates who came in their canoes from the Mayotta, where the pirate ship to which they belonged, viz. the Indian Queen, two hundred and fifty tons, twenty-eight guns, and ninety men, commanded by Captain Oliver de la Bouche, bound from the Guinea coast to the East Indies, had been bulged and lost. They said they left the captain and forty of their men building a new vessel, to proceed on their wicked designs. Captain Kirby and I concluding that it might be of great service to the East India Company to destroy such a nest of rogues, were ready to sail for that purpose on the 17th of August, about eight o'clock in the morning, when we discovered two pirates standing into the bay Johanna, one of thirty-four, and the other of thirty-six guns. I immediately went on board the Greenwich, where they seemed very diligent in preparation for an engagement, and I left Captain Kirby with mutual promises of standing by each other. I then unmoored, got under sail, and brought two boats a-head to row me close to the Greenwich; but he being open to a valley and a breeze, made the best of his way from me; which an Ostender in our company, of twenty-two guns, seeing, did the same, though the captain had promised heartily to engage with us, and I believe would have been as good as his word, if Captain Kirby had kept his. About half an hour after twelve, I called several times to the Greenwich to bear down to our assistance, and fired a shot at him, but to no purpose; for though we did not doubt but he would join us, because, when he got about a league from us he brought his ship to and looked on, yet both he and the Ostender basely deserted us, and left us engaged with barbarous and inhuman enemies, with their black and bloody flags hanging over us, without the least appearance of ever escaping, but to be cut to pieces. But God in his good providence determined otherwise; for, notwithstanding their superiority, we engaged them both about three hours; during which time the biggest of them received some shot betwixt wind and water, which made her keep off a little to stop her leaks. The other endeavored all she could to board us, by rowing with her oars, being within half a ship's length of us above an hour; but by good fortune we shot all her oars to pieces, which prevented them, and by consequence saved our lives.

"About four o'clock most of the officers and men posted on the quarter-deck being killed and wounded, the largest ship making up to us with diligence, being still within a cable's length of us, often giving us a broadside; there being now no hopes of Captain Kirby's coming to our assistance, we endeavored to run a-shore; and though we drew four feet of water more than the pirate, it pleased God that he stuck fast on a higher ground than happily we fell in with; so was disappointed a second time from boarding us. Here we had a more violent engagement than before: all my officers and most of my men behaved with unexpected courage; and, as we had a considerable advantage by having a broadside to his bow, we did him great damage; so that had Captain Kirby come in then, I believe we should have taken both the vessels, for we had one of them sure; but the other pirate (who was still firing at us,) seeing the Greenwich did not offer to assist us, supplied his consort with three boats full of fresh men. About five in the evening the Greenwich stood clear away to sea, leaving us struggling hard for life, in the very jaws of death; which the other pirate that was afloat, seeing, got a warp out, and was hauling under our stern.

"By this time many of my men being killed and wounded, and no hopes left us of escaping being all murdered by enraged barbarous conquerors, I ordered all that could to get into the long-boat, under the cover of the smoke of our guns; so that, with what some did in boats, and others by swimming, most of us that were able, got ashore by seven o'clock. When the pirates came aboard, they cut three of our wounded men to pieces. I with some of my people made what haste I could to King's-town, twenty-five miles from us, where I arrived next day, almost dead with the fatigue and loss of blood, having been sorely wounded in the head by a musket-ball.

"At this town I heard that the pirates had offered ten thousand dollars to the country people to bring me in, which many of them would have accepted, only they knew the king and all his chief people were in my interest. Meantime, I caused a report to be spread that I was dead of my wounds, which much abated their fury. About ten days after, being pretty well recovered, and hoping the malice of our enemies was nigh over, I began to consider the dismal condition we were reduced to; being in a place where we had no hopes of getting a passage home, all of us in a manner naked, not having had time to bring with us either a shirt or a pair of shoes, except what we had on. Having obtained leave to go on board the pirates with a promise of safety, several of the chief of them knew me, and some of them had sailed with me, which I found to be of great advantage; because, notwithstanding their promise, some of them would have cut me to pieces, and all that would not enter with them, had it not been for their chief captain, Edward England, and some others whom I knew. They talked of burning one of their ships, which we had so entirely disabled as to be no farther useful to them, and to fit the Cassandra in her room; but in the end I managed the affair so well, that they made me a present of the said shattered ship, which was Dutch built, and called the Fancy; her burden was about three hundred tons. I procured also a hundred and twenty-nine bales of the Company's cloth, though they would not give me a rag of my own clothes.

"They sailed the 3rd of September; and I, with jury-masts, and such old sails as they left me, made a shift to do the like on the 8th, together with forty-three of my ship's crew, including two passengers and twelve soldiers; having no more than five tuns of water aboard. After a passage of forty-eight days, I arrived here on the 26th of October, almost naked and starved, having been reduced to a pint of water a-day, and almost in despair of ever seeing land, by reason of the calms we met with between the coast of Arabia and Malabar.

"We had in all thirteen men killed and twenty-four wounded; and we were told that we destroyed about ninety or a hundred of the pirates. When they left us, they were about three hundred whites, and eighty blacks, on both ships. I am persuaded, had our consort the Greenwich done his duty, we had destroyed both of them, and got two hundred thousand pounds for our owners and selves; whereas the loss of the Cassandra may justly be imputed to his deserting us. I have delivered all the bales that were given me into the Company's warehouse, for which the governor and council have ordered me a reward. Our governor, Mr. Boon, who is extremely kind and civil to me, had ordered me home with the packet; but Captain Harvey, who had a prior promise, being come in with the fleet, goes in my room. The governor had promised me a country voyage to help to make up my losses, and would have me stay and accompany him to England next year."

Captain Mackra was certainly in imminent danger, in trusting himself and his men on board the pirate ship, and unquestionably nothing but the desperate circumstances in which he was placed could have justified so hazardous a step. The honor and influence of Captain England, however, protected him and his men from the fury of the crew, who would willingly have wreaked their vengeance upon them.

It is pleasing to discover any instance of generosity or honor among such an abandoned race, who bid defiance to all the laws of honor, and, indeed, are regardless of all laws human and divine. Captain England was so steady to Captain Mackra, that he informed him, it would be with no small difficulty and address that he would be able to preserve him and his men from the fury of the crew, who were greatly enraged at the resistance which had been made. He likewise acquainted him, that his influence and authority among them was giving place to that of Captain Taylor, chiefly because the dispositions of the latter were more savage and brutal. They therefore consulted between them what was the best method to secure the favor of Taylor, and keep him in good humor. Mackra made the punch to flow in great abundance, and employed every artifice to soothe the mind of that ferocious villain.

A single incident was also very favorable to the unfortunate captain. It happened that a pirate, with a prodigious pair of whiskers, a wooden leg, and stuck round with pistols, came blustering and swearing upon the quarter deck, inquiring "where was Captain Mackra." He naturally supposed that this barbarous-looking fellow would be his executioner; but, as he approached, he took the captain by the hand, swearing "that he was an honest fellow, and that he had formerly sailed with him, and would stand by him; and let him see the man that would touch him." This terminated the dispute, and Captain Taylor's disposition was so ameliorated with punch, that he consented that the old pirate ship, and so many bales of cloth, should be given to Mackra, and then sank into the arms of intoxication. England now pressed Mackra to hasten away, lest the ruffian, upon his becoming sober, should not only retract his word, but give liberty to the crew to cut him and his men to pieces.

But the gentle temper of Captain England, and his generosity towards the unfortunate Mackra, proved the organ of much calamity to himself. The crew, in general, deeming the kind of usage which Mackra had received, inconsistent with piratical policy, they circulated a report, that he was coming against them with the Company's force. The result of these invidious reports was to deprive England of his command, and to excite these cruel villains to put him on shore, with three others, upon the island of Mauritius. If England and his small company had not been destitute of every necessary, they might have made a comfortable subsistence here, as the island abounds with deer, hogs, and other animals. Dissatisfied, however, with their solitary situation, Captain England and his three men exerted their industry and ingenuity, and formed a small boat, with which they sailed to Madagascar, where they subsisted upon the generosity of some more fortunate piratical companions.

Captain Mackra, and the Pirate with a wooden leg

**Captain Mackra, and the Pirate with a wooden leg.**

Captain Taylor detained some of the officers and men belonging to Captain Mackra, and having repaired their vessel, sailed for India. The day before they made land, they espied two ships to the eastward, and supposing them to be English, Captain Taylor ordered one of the officers of Mackra's ship to communicate to him the private signals between the Company's ships, swearing that if he did not do so immediately, he would cut him into pound pieces. But the poor man being unable to give the information demanded, was under the necessity of enduring their threats. Arrived at the vessels, they found that they were two Moorish ships, laden with horses. The pirates brought the captains and merchants on board, and tortured them in a barbarous manner, to constrain them to tell where they had hid their treasure. They were, however, disappointed; and the next morning they discovered land, and at the same time a fleet on shore plying to windward. In this situation they were at a considerable loss how to dispose of their prizes. To let them go would lead to their discovery, and thus defeat the design of their voyage; and it was a distressing matter to sink the men and the horses, though many of them were for adopting that measure. They, however, brought them to anchor, threw all the sails overboard, and cut one of the masts half through.

While they lay at anchor, and were employed in taking in water, one of the above-mentioned fleet moved towards them with English colors, and was answered by the pirate with a red ensign; but they did not hail each other. At night they left the Muscat ships, and sailed after the fleet. About four next morning, the pirates were in the midst of the fleet, but seeing their vast superiority, were greatly at a loss what method to adopt. The Victory had become leaky, and their hands were so few in number, that it only remained for them to deceive, if possible, the English squadron. They were unsuccessful in gaining any thing out of that fleet, and had only the wretched satisfaction of burning a single galley. They however that day seized a galliot laden with cotton, and made inquiry of the men concerning the fleet. They protested that they had not seen a ship since they left Gogo, and earnestly implored their mercy; but, instead of treating them with lenity, they put them to the rack, in order to extort farther confession. The day following, a fresh easterly wind blew hard, and rent the galliot's sails; upon this the pirates put her company into a boat, with nothing but a try-sail, no provisions, and only four gallons of water, and, though they were out of sight of land, left them to shift for themselves.

It may be proper to inform our readers, that one Angria, an Indian prince, of considerable territory and strength, had proved a troublesome enemy to Europeans, and particularly to the English. Calaba was his principal fort, situated not many leagues from Bombay, and he possessed an island in sight of the port, from whence he molested the Company's ships. His art in bribing the ministers of the Great Mogul, and the shallowness of the water, that prevented large ships of war from approaching, were the principal causes of his safety.

The Bombay fleet, consisting of four grabs, the London and the Candois, and two other ships, with a galliot, having an additional thousand men on board for this enterprise, sailed to attack a fort belonging to Angria upon the Malabar coast. Though their strength was great, yet they were totally unsuccessful in their enterprise. It was this fleet returning home that our pirates discovered upon the present occasion. Upon the sight of the pirates, the commodore of the fleet intimated to Mr. Brown, the general, that as they had no orders to fight, and had gone upon a different purpose, it would be improper for them to engage. Informed of the loss of this favorable opportunity of destroying the robbers, the governor of Bombay was highly enraged, and giving the command of the fleet to Captain Mackra, ordered him to pursue and engage them wherever they should be found.

The pirates having barbarously sent away the galliot with her men, they arrived southward, and between Goa and Carwar they heard several guns, so that they came to anchor, and sent their boat to reconnoitre, which returned next morning with the intelligence of two grabs, lying at anchor in the road. They accordingly weighed, ran towards the bay, and in the morning were discovered by the grabs, who had just time to run under India-Diva castle for protection. This was the more vexatious to the pirates, as they were without water; some of them, therefore, were for making a descent upon the island, but that measure not being generally approved, they sailed towards the south, and took a small ship, which had only a Dutchman and two Portuguese on board. They sent one of these on shore to the captain, to inform him that, if he would give them some water and fresh provisions, he might have his vessel returned. He replied that, if they would give him possession over the bar, he would comply with their request. But, suspecting the integrity of his design, they sailed for Lacca Deva islands, uttering dreadful imprecations against the captain.

Disappointed in finding water at these islands, they sailed to Malinda island, and sent their boats on shore, to discover if there was any water, or if there were any inhabitants.. They returned with the information, that there was abundance of water, that the houses were only inhabited by women and children, the men having fled at the appearance of the ships. They accordingly hastened to supply themselves with water, used the defenceless women in a brutal manner, destroyed many of their fruit-trees, and set some of their houses on fire.

While off the island, they lost several of their anchors by the rockiness of the ground; and one day, blowing more violently than usual, they were forced to take to sea, leaving several people and most of the water-casks; but when the gale was over, they returned to take in their men and water. Their provisions being nearly exhausted, they resolved to visit the Dutch at Cochin. After sailing three days, they arrived off Tellechery, and took a small vessel belonging to Governor Adams, and brought the master on board, very much intoxicated, who informed them of the expedition of Captain Mackra. This intelligence raised their utmost indignation. "A villain!" said they, "to whom we have given a ship and presents, to come against us! he ought to be hanged; and since we cannot show our resentment to him, let us hang the dogs his people, who wish him well, and would do the same, if they were clear." "If it be in my power," said the quarter-master, "both masters and officers of ships shall be carried with us for the future, only to plague them. Now, England, we mark him for this."

They proceeded to Calicut, and attempting to cut out a ship, were prevented by some guns placed upon the shore. One of Captain Mackra's officers was under deck at this time, and was commanded both by the captain and the quarter-master to tend the braces on the booms, in hopes that a shot would take him before they got clear. He was about to have excused himself, but they threatened to shoot him; and when he expostulated, and claimed their promise to put him on shore, he received an unmerciful beating from the quarter-master; Captain Taylor, to whom that duty belonged, being lame in his hands.

The day following they met a Dutch galliot, laden with limestone, bound for Calicut, on board of which they put one Captain Fawkes; and some of the crew interceding for Mackra's officer, Taylor and his party replied, "If we let this dog go, who has overheard our designs and resolutions, he will overset all our well-advised resolutions, and particularly this supply we are seeking for at the hands of the Dutch."

When they arrived at Cochin, they sent a letter on shore by a fishing-boat, entered the road, and anchored, each ship saluting the fort with eleven guns, and receiving the same number in return. This was the token of their welcome reception, and at night a large boat was sent, deeply laden with liquors and all kinds of provisions, and in it a servant of John Trumpet, one of their friends, to inform them that it would be necessary for them to run farther south, where they would be supplied both with provisions and naval stores.

They had scarcely anchored at the appointed place, when several canoes, with white and black inhabitants, came on board, and continued without interruption to perform all the good offices in their power during their stay in that place. In particular, John Trumpet brought a large boat of arrack, and sixty bales of sugar, as a present from the governor and his daughter; the former receiving in return a table-clock, and the other a gold watch, the spoil of Captain Mackra's vessel. When their provisions were all on board, Trumpet was rewarded with about six or seven thousand pounds, was saluted with three cheers, and eleven guns; and several handsfull of silver were thrown into the boat, for the men to gather at pleasure.

There being little wind that night, they remained at anchor, and in the morning were surprised with the return of Trumpet, bringing another boat equally well stored with provisions, with chests of piece-goods and ready-made clothes, and along with him the fiscal of the place. At noon they espied a sail towards the south, and immediately gave chase, but she outsailed them, and sheltered under the fort of Cochin. Informed that they would not be molested in taking her from under the castle, they sailed towards her, but upon the fort firing two guns, they ran off for fear of more serious altercation, and returning, anchored in their former station. They were too welcome visitants to be permitted to depart, so long as John Trumpet could contrive to detain them. With this view he informed them, that in a few days a rich vessel, commanded by the Governor of Bombay's brother, was to pass that way.

That government is certainly in a wretched state, which is under the necessity of trading with pirates, in order to enrich itself; nor will such a government hesitate by what means an injury can be repaired, or a fortune gained. Neither can language describe the low and base principles of a government which could employ such a miscreant as John Trumpet in its service. He was a tool in the hands of the government of Cochin; and, as the dog said in the fable, "What is done by the master's orders, is the master's action;" or, as the same sentiment is, perhaps, better expressed in the legal axiom; "Qui facit per alium facit per se."

While under the direction of Trumpet, some proposed to proceed directly to Madagascar, but others were disposed to wait until they should be provided with a store ship. The majority being of the latter opinion, they steered to the south, and seeing a ship on shore were desirous to get near her, but the wind preventing, they separated, the one sailing northward and the other southward, in hopes of securing her when she should come out, whatever direction she might take. They were now, however, almost entrapped in the snare laid for them. In the morning, to their astonishment and consternation, instead of being called to give chase, five large ships were near, which made a signal for the pirates to bear down. The pirates were in the greatest dread lest it should be Captain Mackra, of whose activity and courage they had formerly sufficient proof. The pirate ships, however, joined and fled with all speed from the fleet. In three hours' chase none of the fleet gained upon them, except one grab. The remainder of the day was calm, and, to their great consolation, the next day this dreaded fleet was entirely out of sight.

Their alarm being over, they resolved to spend the Christmas in feasting and mirth, in order to drown care, and to banish thought. Nor did one day suffice, but they continued their revelling for several days, and made so free with their fresh provisions, that in their next cruise they were put upon short allowance; and it was entirely owing to the sugar and other provisions that were in the leaky ship that they were preserved from absolute starvation.

In this condition they reached the island of Mauritius, refitted the Victory, and left that place with the following inscription written upon one of the walls: "Left this place on the 5th of April, to go to Madagascar for Limos." This they did lest any visit should be paid to the place during their absence. They, however, did not sail directly for Madagascar, but the island of Mascarius, where they fortunately fell in with a Portuguese of seventy guns, lying at anchor. The greater part of her guns had been thrown overboard, her masts lost, and the whole vessel disabled by a storm; she therefore, became an easy prey to the pirates. Conde de Ericeira, Viceroy of Goa, who went upon the fruitless expedition against Angria the Indian, and several passengers, were on board. Besides other valuable articles and specie, they found in her diamonds to the amount of four millions of dollars. Supposing that the ship was an Englishman, the Viceroy came on board next morning, was made prisoner, and obliged to pay two thousand dollars as a ransom for himself and the other prisoners. After this he was sent ashore, with an express engagement to leave a ship to convey him and his companions to another port.

Meanwhile, the pirates received intelligence that a vessel was to the leeward of the island, which they pursued and captured. But instead of performing their promise to the Viceroy, which they could easily have done, they sent the Ostender along with some of their men to Madagascar, to inform their friends of their success, with instructions to prepare masts for the prize; and they soon followed, carrying two thousand negroes in the Portuguese vessel.

Madagascar is an island larger than Great Britain, situated upon the eastern coast of Africa, abounding with all sorts of provisions, such as oxen, goats, sheep, poultry, fish, citrons, oranges, tamarinds, dates, cocoa-nuts, bananas, wax, honey, rice, cotton, indigo, and all other fruits common in that quarter of the globe; ebony of which lances are made, gums of several kinds, and many other valuable productions. Here, in St. Augustine's bay, the ships sometimes stop to take in water, when they make the inner passage to India, and do not intend to stop at Johanna.

When the Portuguese ship arrived there, they received intelligence that the Ostender had taken advantage of an hour when the men were intoxicated, had risen upon them, and carried the ship to Mozambique, from whence the governor ordered her to Goa.

The pirates now divided their plunder, receiving forty-two diamonds per man, or in smaller proportion according to their magnitude. A foolish jocular fellow, who had received a large diamond of the value of forty-two, was highly displeased, and so went and broke it in pieces, exclaiming, that he had many more shares than either of them. Some, contended with their treasure, and unwilling to run the risk of losing what they possessed, and perhaps their lives also, resolved to remain with their friends at Madagascar, under the stipulation that the longest livers should enjoy all the booty. The number of adventurers being now lessened, they burned the Viceroy, cleaned the Cassandra, and the remainder went on board her under the command of Taylor, whom we must leave for a little while, in order to give an account of the squadron which arrived in India in 1721.

When the commodore arrived at the Cape, he received a letter that had been written by the Governor of Pondicherry to the Governor of Madras, informing him that the pirates were strong in the Indian seas; that they had eleven sail, and fifteen hundred men; but adding, that many of them retired about that time to Brazil and Guinea, while others fortified themselves at Madagascar, Mauritius, Johanna, and Mohilla; and that a crew under the command of Condin, in a ship called the Dragon, had captured a vessel with thirteen lacks of rupees on board, and having divided their plunder, had taken up their residence with their friends at Madagascar.

Upon receiving this intelligence, Commodore Matthews sailed for these islands, as the most probable place of success. He endeavored to prevail on England, at St. Mary's, to communicate to him what information he could give respecting the pirates; but England declined, thinking that this would be almost to surrender at discretion. He then took up the guns of the Jubilee sloop that were on board, and the men-of-war made several cruises in search of the pirates, but to no purpose. The squadron was then sent down to Bombay, was saluted by the fort, and after these exploits returned home.

The pirate, Captain Taylor, in the Cassandra, now fitted up the Portuguese man-of-war, and resolved upon another voyage to the Indies; but, informed that four men-of-war had been sent after the pirates in that quarter, he changed his determination, and sailed for Africa. Arrived there, they put in a place near the river Spirito Sancto, on the coast of Monomotapa. As there was no correspondence by land, nor any trade carried on by sea to this place, they thought that it would afford a safe retreat. To their astonishment, however, when they approached the shore, it being in the dusk of the evening, they were accosted by several shot. They immediately anchored, and in the morning saw that the shot had come from a small fort of six guns, which they attacked and destroyed.

This small fort was erected by the Dutch East India Company a few weeks before, and committed to the care of 150 men, the one half of whom had perished by sickness or other causes. Upon their petition, sixteen of these were admitted into the society of the pirates; and the rest would also have been received, had they not been Dutchmen, to whom they had a rooted aversion.

In this place they continued during four months, refitting their vessels, and amusing themselves with all manner of diversions, until the scarcity of their provisions awakened them to industry and exertion. They, however, left several parcels of goods to the starving Dutchmen, which Mynheer joyfully exchanged for provisions with the next vessel that touched at that fort.

Leaving that place, they were divided in opinion what course to steer; some went on board the Portuguese prize, and, sailing for Madagascar, abandoned the pirate life; and others going on board the Cassandra, sailed for the Spanish West Indies. The Mermaid man-of-war, returning from a convoy, got near the pirates, and would have attacked them, but a consultation being held, it was deemed inexpedient, and thus the pirates escaped. A sloop was, however, dispatched to Jamaica with the intelligence, and the Lancaster was sent after them; but they were some days too late, the pirates having, with all their riches, surrendered to the Governor of Portobello.

## ACCOUNT OF THE LYNN PIRATES

*And Thomas Veal, who was buried in his cave by the Great Earthquake.*

In the year 1658 there was a great earthquake in New-England. Some time previous, on one pleasant evening, a little after sunset, a small vessel was seen to anchor near the mouth of Saugus river. A boat was presently lowered from her side, into which four men descended, and moved up the river a considerable distance, when they landed, and proceeded directly into the woods. They had been noticed by only a few individuals; but in those early times, when the people were surrounded by danger, and easily susceptible of alarm, such an incident was well calculated to awaken suspicion, and in the course of the evening the intelligence was conveyed to many houses. In the morning, the people naturally directed their eyes toward the shore, in search of the strange vessel–but she was gone, and no trace could be found either of her or her singular crew. It was afterwards ascertained that, on the morning one of the men at the Iron Works, on going into the foundry, discovered a paper, on which was written, that if a quantity of shackles, handcuffs, hatchets, and other articles of iron manufacture, were made and deposited, with secrecy, in a certain place in the woods, which was particularly designated, an amount of silver, to their full value, would be found in their place. The articles were made in a few days, and placed in conformity with the directions. On the next morning they were gone, and the money was found according to the promise; but though a watch had been kept, no vessel was seen. Some months afterwards, the four men returned, and selected one of the most secluded and romantic spots in the woods of Saugus, for their abode. The place of their retreat was a deep narrow valley, shut in on two sides by craggy, precipitous rocks, and shrouded on the others by thick pines, hemlocks and cedars, between which there was only one small spot, to which the rays of the sun at noon could penetrate. On climbing up the rude and almost perpendicular steps of the rock on either side, the eye could command a full view of the bay on the south, and a prospect of a considerable portion of the surrounding country. The place of their retreat has ever since been called the Pirates' Glen, and they could not have selected a spot on the coast for many miles, more favorable for the purposes both of concealment and observation. Even at this day, when the neighborhood has become thickly peopled, it is still a lonely and desolate place, and probably not one in a hundred of the inhabitants has ever descended into its silent and gloomy recess. There the pirates built a small hut, made a garden, and dug a well, the appearance of which is still visible. It has been supposed that they buried money; but though people have dug there, and in many other places, none has ever been found. After residing there some time, their retreat became known, and one of the king's cruizers appeared on the coast. They were traced to their glen, and three of them were taken, and carried to England, where it is probable they were executed. The other, whose name was Thomas Veal, escaped to a rock in the woods, about two miles to the north, in which was a spacious cavern, where the pirates had previously deposited some of their plunder. There the fugitive fixed his residence, and practised the trade of a shoemaker, occasionally coming down to the village to obtain articles of sustenance. He continued his residence till the great earthquake in 1658, when the top of the rock was loosened, and crushed down into the mouth of the cavern, enclosing the unfortunate inmate in its unyielding prison. It has ever since been called the Pirate's Dungeon. A part of the cavern is still open, and is much visited by the curious.

This rock is situated on a lofty range of thickly wooded hills, and commands an extensive view of the ocean, for fifty miles both north and south. A view from the top of it, at once convinces the beholder that it would be impossible to select a place more convenient for the haunt of a gang of pirates; as all vessels bound in and out of the harbors of Boston, Salem, and the adjacent ports, can be distinctly seen from its summit. Saugus river meanders among the hills a short distance to the south, and its numerous creeks which extend among thick bushes, would afford good places to secrete boats, until such time as the pirates descried a sail, when they could instantly row down the river, attack and plunder them, and with their booty return to the cavern. This was evidently their mode of procedure. On an open space in front of the rock are still to be seen distinct traces of a small garden spot, and in the corner is a small well, full of stones and rubbish; the foundation of the wall round the garden remains, and shows that the spot was of a triangular shape, and was well selected for the cultivation of potatoes and common vegetables. The aperture in the rock is only about five feet in height, and extends only fifteen feet into the rock. The needle is strongly attracted around this, either by the presence of magnetic iron ore or some metallic substance buried in the interior.

The Pirates' Glen, which is some distance from this, is one of Nature's wildest and most picturesque spots, and the cellar of the pirate's hut remains to the present time, as does a clear space, which was evidently cultivated at some remote period.

The Dungeon Rock and Pirate's Cave, at Lynn, Mass.

**The Dungeon Rock and Pirate's Cave, at Lynn, Mass.**

## HISTORY OF THE LADRONE PIRATES

*And their Depredations on the Coast of China: with an Account of the Enterprises and Victories of Mistress Ching, a Female Pirate.*

The Ladrones as they were christened by the Portuguese at Macao, were originally a disaffected set of Chinese, that revolted against the oppression of the Mandarins. The first scene of their depredations was the Western coast, about Cochin China, where they began by attacking small trading vessels in row boats, carrying from thirty to forty men each. They continued this system of piracy, and thrived and increased in numbers under it, for several years. At length the fame of their success, and the oppression and horrid poverty and want that many of the lower orders of Chinese labored under, had the effect of augmenting their bands with astonishing rapidity. Fishermen and other destitute classes flocked by hundreds to their standard, and their audacity growing with their numbers, they not merely swept the coast, but blockaded all the rivers and attacked and took several large government war junks, mounting from ten to fifteen guns each.–These junks being added to their shoals of boats, the pirates formed a tremendous fleet, which was always along shore, so that no small vessel could safely trade on the coast. When they lacked prey on the sea, they laid the land under tribute. They were at first accustomed to go on shore and attack the maritime villages, but becoming bolder, like the Buccaneers, made long inland journeys, and surprised and plundered even large towns.

An energetic attempt made by the Chinese government to destroy them, only increased their strength; for in their first encounter with the pirates, twenty-eight of the Imperial junks struck, and the remaining twelve saved themselves, by a precipitate retreat.

The captured junks, fully equipped for war, were a great acquisition to the robbers, whose numbers now increased more rapidly than ever. They were in their plenitude of power in the year 1809, when Mr. Glasspoole had the misfortune to fall into their hands, at which time that gentleman supposed their force to consist of 70,000 men, navigating eight hundred large vessels, and one thousand small ones, including row boats. They were divided into six large squadrons, under different flags;–the red, the yellow, the green, the blue, the black and the white. "These wasps of the Ocean," as a Chinese historian calls them, were further distinguished by the names of their respective commanders: by these commanders a certain *Ching-yih* had been the most distinguished by his valor and conduct. By degrees, Ching obtained almost a supremacy of command over the whole united fleet; and so confident was this robber in his strength and daily augmenting means, that he aspired to the dignity of a king, and went so far as openly to declare his patriotic intention of hurling the present Tartar family from the throne of China, and of restoring the ancient Chinese dynasty. But unfortunately for the ambitious pirate, he perished in a heavy gale, and instead of placing a sovereign on the Chinese throne, he and his lofty aspirations were buried in the yellow sea. And now comes the most remarkable passage in the history of these pirates–remarkable with any class of men, but doubly so among the Chinese, who entertain more than the general oriental opinion of the inferiority of the fair sex. On the death of *Ching-yih,* his legitimate wife had sufficient influence over the freebooters to induce them to recognize her authority in the place of her deceased husband's, and she appointed one *Paou* as her lieutenant and prime minister, and provided that she should be considered the mistress or commander-in-chief of the united squadrons.

This *Paou* had been a poor fisher-boy, picked up with his father at sea, while fishing, by *Ching-yih,* whose good will and favor he had the fortune to captivate, and by whom, before that pirate's death, he had been made a captain. Instead of declining under the rule of a woman, the pirates became more enterprising than ever. Ching's widow was clever as well as brave, and so was her lieutenant Paou. Between them they drew up a code of law for the better regulation of the freebooters.

In this it was decreed, that if any man went privately on shore, or did what they called "transgressing the bars," he should have his ears slit in the presence of the whole fleet; a repetition of the same unlawful act, was death! No one article, however trifling in value, was to be privately subtracted from the booty or plundered goods. Every thing they took was regularly entered on the register of their stores. The following clause of Mistress *Ching's* code is still more delicate. No person shall debauch at his pleasure captive women, taken in the villages and open places, and brought on board a ship; he must first request the ship's purser for permission, and then go aside in the ship's hold. To use violence, against any woman, or to wed her, without permission, shall be punished with death.

By these means an admirable discipline was maintained on board the ships, and the peasantry on shore never let the pirates want for gunpowder, provisions, or any other necessary. On a piratical expedition, either to advance or retreat without orders, was a capital offence. Under these philosophical institutions, and the guidance of a woman, the robbers continued to scour the China sea, plundering every vessel they came near. The Great War Mandarin, Kwolang-lin sailed from the Bocca Tigris into the sea to fight the pirates. Paou gave him a tremendous drubbing, and gained a splendid victory. In this battle which lasted from morning to night, the Mandarin Kwolang-lin, a desperate fellow himself, levelled a gun at Paou, who fell on the deck as the piece went off; his disheartened crew concluded it was all over with him. But Paou was quick eyed. He had seen the unfriendly intention of the mandarin, and thrown himself down. The Great Mandarin was soon after taken with fifteen junks; three were sunk. The pirate lieutenant would have dealt mercifully with him, but the fierce old man suddenly seized him by the hair on the crown of his head, and grinned at him, so that he might provoke him to slay him. But even then Paou spoke kindly to him. Upon this he committed suicide, being seventy years of age.

After several victories and reverses, the Chinese historian says our men-of-war escorting some merchant ships, happened to meet the pirate chief nicknamed "The Jewel of the Crew" cruising at sea. The traders became exceedingly frightened, but our commander said,–This not being the flag of the widow Ching-yih, we are a match for them, therefore we will attack and conquer them. Then ensued a battle; they attacked each other with guns and stones, and many people were killed and wounded. The fighting ceased towards evening, and began again next morning. The pirates and the men-of-war were very close to each other, and they boasted mutually about their strength and valor. The traders remained at some distance; they saw the pirates mixing gunpowder in their beverage,–they looked instantly red about the face and the eyes, and then fought desperately. This fighting continued three days and nights incessantly; at last, becoming tired on both sides, they separated.

To understand this inglorious bulletin, the reader must remember that many of the combatants only handled bows and arrows, and pelted stones, and that Chinese powder and guns are both exceedingly bad. The pathos of the conclusion does somewhat remind one of the Irishman's despatch during the American war,–"It was a bloody battle while it lasted; and the searjent of marines lost his cartouche box."

The Admiral Ting River was sent to sea against them. This man was surprised at anchor by the ever vigilant Paou, to whom many fishermen and other people on the coast, must have acted as friendly spies. Seeing escape impossible, and that his officers stood pale and inactive by the flag-staff, the Admiral conjured them, by their fathers and mothers, their wives and children, and by the hopes of brilliant reward if they succeeded, and of vengeance if they perished, to do their duty, and the combat began. The Admiral had the good fortune, at the onset, of killing with one of his great guns the pirate captain, "The Jewel of the Crew." But the robbers swarmed thicker and thicker around him, and when the dreaded Paou lay him by the board, without help or hope, the Mandarin killed himself. An immense number of his men perished in the sea, and twenty-five vessels were lost. After his defeat, it was resolved by the Chinese Government to cut off all their supplies of food, and starve them out. All vessels that were in port were ordered to remain there, and those at sea, or on the coast ordered to return with all speed. But the pirates, full of confidence, now resolved to attack the harbors themselves, and to ascend the rivers, which are navigable for many miles up the country, and rob the villages. The consternation was great when the Chinese saw them venturing above the government forts.

The pirates separated: Mistress Ching plundering in one place, Paou in another, and O-po-tae in another, c.

It was at this time that Mr. Glasspoole had the ill fortune to fall into their power. This gentlemen, then an officer in the East India Company's ship the Marquis of Ely, which was anchored under an island about twelve miles from Macao, was ordered to proceed to the latter place with a boat to procure a pilot. He left the ship in one of the cutters, with seven British seamen well armed, on the 17th September, 1809. He reached Macao in safety, and having done his business there and procured a pilot, returned towards the ship the following day. But, unfortunately, the ship had weighed anchor and was under sail, and in consequence of squally weather, accompanied with thick fogs, the boat could not reach her, and Mr. Glasspoole and his men and the pilot were left at sea, in an open boat. "Our situation," says that gentleman, "was truly distressing–night closing fast, with a threatening appearance, blowing fresh, with a hard rain and a heavy sea; our boat very leaky, without a compass, anchor, or provisions, and drifting fast on a lee-shore, surrounded with dangerous rocks, and inhabited by the most barbarous pirates."

After suffering dreadfully for three whole days, Mr. Glasspoole, by the advice of the pilot, made for a narrow channel, where he presently discovered three large boats at anchor, which, on seeing the English boat, weighed and made sail towards it. The pilot told Mr. Glasspoole they were Ladrones, and that if they captured the boat, they would certainly put them all to death! After rowing tremendously for six hours they escaped these boats, but on the following morning falling in with a large fleet of the pirates, which the English mistook for fishing-boats, they were captured.

"About twenty savage-looking villains," says Mr. Glasspoole, "who were stowed at the bottom of the boat, leaped on board us. They were armed with a short sword in either hand, one of which they layed upon our necks, and pointed the other to our breasts, keeping their eyes fixed on their officer, waiting his signal to cut or desist. Seeing we were incapable of making any resistance, the officer sheathed his sword, and the others immediately followed his example. They then dragged us into their boat, and carried us on board one of their junks, with the most savage demonstrations of joy, and, as we supposed, to torture and put us to a cruel death."

When on board the junk they rifled the Englishmen, and brought heavy chains to chain them to the deck.

"At this time a boat came, and took me, with one of my men and an interpreter, on board the chief's vessel. I was then taken before the chief. He was seated on deck, in a large chair, dressed in purple silk, with a black turban on. He appeared to be about thirty years of age, a stout commanding-looking man. He took me by the coat, and drew me close to him; then questioned the interpreter very strictly, asking who we were, and what was our business in that part of the country. I told him to say we were Englishmen in distress, having been four days at sea without provisions. This he would not credit, but said we were bad men, and that he would put us all to death; and then ordered some men to put the interpreter to the torture until he confessed the truth. Upon this occasion, a Ladrone, who had been once to England and spoke a few words of English, came to the chief, and told him we were really Englishmen, and that we had plenty of money, adding that the buttons on my coat were gold. The chief then ordered us some coarse brown rice, of which we made a tolerable meal, having eaten nothing for nearly four days, except a few green oranges. During our repast, a number of Ladrones crowded round us, examining our clothes and hair, and giving us every possible annoyance. Several of them brought swords, and laid them on our necks, making signs that they would soon take us on shore, and cut us in pieces, which I am sorry to say was the fate of some hundreds during my captivity. I was now summoned before the chief, who had been conversing with the interpreter: he said I must write to my captain, and tell him, if he did not send an hundred thousand dollars for our ransom, in ten days he would put us all to death."

After vainly expostulating to lessen the ransom, Mr. Glasspoole wrote the letter, and a small boat came alongside and took it to Macao.

Early in the night the fleet sailed, and anchored about one o'clock the following day in a bay under the island of Lantow, where the head admiral of Ladrones (our acquaintance Paou) was lying at anchor, with about two hundred vessels and a Portuguese brig they had captured a few days before, and the captain and part of the crew of which they had murdered. Early the next morning, a fishing-boat came to inquire if they had captured an European boat; they came to the vessel the English were in.

"One of the boatmen spoke a few words of English, and told me he had a Ladrone-pass, and was sent by our captain in search of us; I was rather surprised to find he had no letter. He appeared to be well acquainted with the chief, and remained in his cabin smoking opium, and playing cards all the day. In the evening I was summoned with the interpreter before the chief. He questioned us in a much milder tone, saying, he now believed we were Englishmen, a people he wished to be friendly with; and that if our captain would lend him seventy thousand dollars till he returned from his cruise up the river, he would repay him, and send us all to Macao. I assured him it was useless writing on these terms, and unless our ransom was speedily settled, the English fleet would sail, and render our enlargement altogether ineffectual. He remained determined, and said if it were not sent, he would keep us, and make us fight, or put us to death. I accordingly wrote, and gave my letter to the man belonging to the boat before mentioned. He said he could not return with an answer in less than five days. The chief now gave me the letter I wrote when first taken. I have never been able to ascertain his reasons for detaining it, but suppose he dared not negociate for our ransom without orders from the head admiral, who I understood was sorry at our being captured. He said the English ships would join the Mandarins and attack them."

While the fleet lay here, one night the Portuguese who were left in the captured brig murdered the Ladrones that were on board of her, cut the cables, and fortunately escaped through the darkness of the night.

"At day-light the next morning, the fleet, amounting to above five hundred sail of different sizes, weighed, to proceed on their intended cruise up the rivers, to levy contributions on the towns and villages. It is impossible to describe what were my feelings at this critical time, having received no answers to my letters, and the fleet under-way to sail–hundreds of miles up a country never visited by Europeans, there to remain probably for many months, which would render all opportunities for negotiating for our enlargement totally ineffectual; as the only method of communication is by boats that have a pass from the Ladrones, and they dare not venture above twenty miles from Macao, being obliged to come and go in the night, to avoid the Mandarins; and if these boats should be detected in having any intercourse with the Ladrones, they are immediately put to death, and all their relations, though they had not joined in the crime, share in the punishment, in order that not a single person of their families should be left to imitate their crimes or avenge their death."

The following is a very touching incident in Mr. Glasspoole's narrative.

"Wednesday the 26th of September, at day-light, we passed in sight of our own ships, at anchor under the island of Chun Po. The chief then called me, pointed to the ships, and told the interpreter to tell us to look at them, for we should never see them again! About noon we entered a river to the westward of the Bogue. Three or four miles from the entrance we passed a large town situated on the side of a beautiful hill, which is tributary to the Ladrones; the inhabitants saluted them with songs as they passed."

After committing numerous minor robberies, "The Ladrones now prepared to attack a town with a formidable force, collected in row-boats from the different vessels. They sent a messenger to the town, demanding a tribute of ten thousand dollars annually, saying, if these terms were not complied with, they would land, destroy the town, and murder all the inhabitants: which they would certainly have done, had the town laid in a more advantageous situation for their purpose; but being placed out of the reach of their shot, they allowed them to come to terms. The inhabitants agreed to pay six thousand dollars, which they were to collect by the time of our return down the river. This finesse had the desired effect, for during our absence they mounted a few guns on a hill, which commanded the passage, and gave us in lieu of the dollars, a warm salute on our return.

"October the 1st, the fleet weighed in the night, dropped by the tide up the river, and anchored very quietly before a town surrounded by a thick wood. Early in the morning the Ladrones assembled in row-boats, and landed; then gave a shout, and rushed into the town, sword in hand. The inhabitants fled to the adjacent hills, in numbers apparently superior to the Ladrones. We may easily imagine to ourselves the horror with which these miserable people must be seized, on being obliged to leave their homes, and everything dear to them. It was a most melancholy sight to see women in tears, clasping their infants in their arms, and imploring mercy for them from those brutal robbers! The old and the sick, who were unable to fly, or make resistance, were either made prisoners or most inhumanly butchered! The boats continued passing and repassing from the junks to the shore, in quick succession, laden with booty, and the men besmeared with blood! Two hundred and fifty women and several children, were made prisoners, and sent on board different vessels. They were unable to escape with the men, owing to that abominable practice of cramping their feet; several of them were not able to move without assistance. In fact, they might all be said to totter, rather than walk. Twenty of these poor women were sent on board the vessel I was in; they were hauled on board by the hair, and treated in a most savage manner. When the chief came on board, he questioned them respecting the circumstances of their friends, and demanded ransoms accordingly, from six thousand to six hundred dollars each. He ordered them a berth on deck, at the after part of the vessel, where they had nothing to shelter them from the weather, which at this time was very variable–the days excessively hot, and the nights cold, with heavy rains. The town being plundered of everything valuable, it was set on fire, and reduced to ashes by the morning. The fleet remained here three days, negotiating for the ransom of the prisoners, and plundering the fish-tanks and gardens. During all this time, the Chinese never ventured from the hills, though there were frequently not more than a hundred Ladrones on shore at a time, and I am sure the people on the hills exceeded ten times that number.

"On the 10th we formed a junction with the Black-squadron, and proceeded many miles up a wide and beautiful river, passing several ruins of villages that had been destroyed by the Black-squadron. On the 17th, the fleet anchored abreast four mud batteries, which defended a town, so entirely surrounded with wood, that it was impossible to form any idea of its size. The weather was very hazy, with hard squalls of rain. The Ladrones remained perfectly quiet for two days. On the third day the forts commenced a brisk fire for several hours: the Ladrones did not return a single shot, but weighed in the night and dropped down the river. The reasons they gave for not attacking the town, or returning the fire, were, that Joss had not promised them success. They are very superstitious, and consult their idol on all occasions. If his omens are good, they will undertake the most daring enterprises. The fleet now anchored opposite the ruins of the town where the women had been made prisoners. Here we remained five or six days, during which time about an hundred of the women were ransomed; the remainder were offered for sale amongst the Ladrones, for forty dollars each. The woman is considered the lawful wife of the purchaser, who would be put to death if he discarded her. Several of them leaped overboard and drowned themselves, rather than submit to such infamous degradation.

"Mei-ying, the wife of Ke-choo-yang, was very beautiful, and a pirate being about to seize her by the head, she abused him exceedingly. The pirate bound her to the yard-arm; but on abusing him yet more, the pirate dragged her down and broke two of her teeth, which filled her mouth and jaws with blood. The pirate sprang up again to bind her. Ying allowed him to approach, but as soon as he came near her, she laid hold of his garments with her bleeding mouth, and threw both him and herself into the river, where they were drowned. The remaining captives of both sexes were after some months liberated, on having paid a ransom of fifteen thousand leang or ounces of silver.

"The fleet then weighed," continues Mr. Glasspoole, "and made sail down the river, to receive the ransom from the town before-mentioned. As we passed the hill, they fired several shot at us, but without effect. The Ladrones were much exasperated, and determined to revenge themselves; they dropped out of reach of their shot, and anchored. Every junk sent about a hundred men each on shore, to cut paddy, and destroy their orange-groves, which was most effectually performed for several miles down the river. During our stay here, they received information of nine boats lying up a creek, laden with paddy; boats were immediately despatched after them. Next morning these boats were brought to the fleet; ten or twelve men were taken in them. As these had made no resistance, the chief said he would allow them to become Ladrones, if they agreed to take the usual oaths before Joss. Three or four of them refused to comply, for which they were punished in the following cruel manner: their hands were tied behind their backs, a rope from the masthead rove through their arms, and hoisted three or four feet from the deck, and five or six men flogged them with their rattans twisted together till they were apparently dead; then hoisted them up to the mast-head, and left them hanging nearly an hour, then lowered them down, and repeated the punishment, till they died or complied with the oath.

"On the 28th of October, I received a letter from Captain Kay, brought by a fisherman, who had told him he would get us all back for three thousand dollars. He advised me to offer three thousand, and if not accepted, extend it to four; but not farther, as it was bad policy to offer much at first: at the same time assuring me we should be liberated, let the ransom be what it would. I offered the chief the three thousand, which he disdainfully refused, saying he was not to be played with; and unless they sent ten thousand dollars, and two large guns, with several casks of gunpowder, he would soon put us to death. I wrote to Captain Kay, and informed him of the chief's determination, requesting, if an opportunity offered, to send us a shift of clothes, for which it may be easily imagined we were much distressed, having been seven weeks without a shift; although constantly exposed to the weather, and of course frequently wet.

"On the first of November, the fleet sailed up a narrow river, and anchored at night within two miles of a town called Little Whampoa. In front of it was a small fort, and several Mandarin vessels lying in the harbor. The chief sent the interpreter to me, saying, I must order my men to make cartridges and clean their muskets, ready to go on shore in the morning. I assured the interpreter I should give the men no such orders, that they must please themselves. Soon after the chief came on board, threatening to put us all to a cruel death if we refused to obey his orders. For my own part I remained determined, and advised the men not to comply, as I thought by making ourselves useful we should be accounted too valuable. A few hours afterwards he sent to me again, saying, that if myself and the quarter-master would assist them at the great guns, that if also the rest of the men went on shore and succeeded in taking the place, he would then take the money offered for our ransom, and give them twenty dollars for every Chinaman's head they cut off. To these proposals we cheerfully acceded, in hopes of facilitating our deliverance.

"The Mandarin vessels continued firing, having blocked up the entrance of the harbor to prevent the Ladrone boats entering. At this the Ladrones were much exasperated, and about three hundred of them swam on shore, with a short sword lashed close under each arm; they then ran along the banks of the river till they came abreast of the vessels, and then swam off again and boarded them. The Chinese thus attacked, leaped overboard, and endeavored to reach the opposite shore; the Ladrones followed, and cut the greater number of them to pieces in the water. They next towed the vessels out of the harbor, and attacked the town with increased fury. The inhabitants fought about a quarter of an hour, and then retreated to an adjacent hill, from which they were soon driven with great slaughter. After this the Ladrones returned, and plundered the town, every boat leaving it with lading. The Chinese on the hills perceiving most of the boats were off, rallied, and retook the town, after killing near two hundred Ladrones. One of my men was unfortunately lost in this dreadful massacre! The Ladrones landed a second time, drove the Chinese out of the town, then reduced it to ashes, and put all their prisoners to death, without regarding either age or sex! I must not omit to mention a most horrid (though ludicrous) circumstance which happened at this place. The Ladrones were paid by their chief ten dollars for every Chinaman's head they produced. One of my men turning the corner of a street was met by a Ladrone running furiously after a Chinese; he had a drawn sword in his hand, and two Chinaman's heads which he had cut off, tied by their tails, and slung round his neck. I was witness myself to some of them producing five or six to obtain payment!

"On the 4th of November an order arrived from the admiral for the fleet to proceed immediately to Lantow, where he was lying with only two vessels, and three Portuguese ships and a brig constantly annoying him; several sail of Mandarin vessels were daily expected. The fleet weighed and proceeded towards Lantow. On passing the island of Lintin, three ships and a brig gave chase to us. The Ladrones prepared to board; but night closing we lost sight of them: I am convinced they altered their course and stood from us. These vessels were in the pay of the Chinese Government, and styled themselves the Invincible Squadron, cruising in the river Tigris to annihilate the Ladrones!

"On the fifth, in the morning, the red squadron anchored in a bay under Lantow; the black squadron stood to the eastward. In the afternoon of the 8th of November, four ships, a brig, and a schooner came off the mouth of the bay. At first the pirates were much alarmed, supposing them to be English vessels come to rescue us. Some of them threatened to hang us to the mast-head for them to fire at; and with much difficulty we persuaded them that they were Portuguese. The Ladrones had only seven junks in a fit state for action; these they hauled outside, and moored them head and stern across the bay, and manned all the boats belonging to the repairing vessels ready for boarding. The Portuguese observing these manoeuvres hove to, and communicated by boats. Soon afterwards they made sail, each ship firing her broadside as she passed, but without effect, the shot falling far short. The Ladrones did not return a single shot, but waved their colors, and threw up rockets, to induce them to come further in, which they might easily have done, the outside junks lying in four fathoms water, which I sounded myself: though the Portuguese in their letters to Macao lamented there was not sufficient water for them to engage closer, but that they would certainly prevent their escaping before the Mandarin fleet arrived!

A Ladrone Pirate, cutting off the Heads of the Chinese

**A Ladrone Pirate, cutting off the Heads of the Chinese.**

"On the 20th of November, early in the morning, discovered an immense fleet of Mandarin vessels standing for the bay. On nearing us, they formed a line, and stood close in; each vessel, as she discharged her guns, tacked to join the rear and reload. They kept up a constant fire for about two hours, when one of their largest vessels was blown up by a firebrand thrown from a Ladrone junk; after which they kept at a more respectful distance, but continued firing without intermission till the 21st at night, when it fell calm. The Ladrones towed out seven large vessels, with about two hundred row-boats to board them: but a breeze springing up, they made sail and escaped. The Ladrones returned into the bay, and anchored. The Portuguese and Mandarins followed, and continued a heavy cannonading during that night and the next day. The vessel I was in had her foremast shot away, which they supplied very expeditiously by taking a mainmast from a smaller vessel.

On the 23d, in the evening, it again fell calm; the Ladrones towed out fifteen junks in two divisions, with the intention of surrounding them, which was nearly effected, having come up with and boarded one, when a breeze suddenly sprang up. The captured vessel mounted twenty-two guns. Most of her crew leaped overboard; sixty or seventy were taken, immediately cut to pieces, and thrown into the river. Early in the morning the Ladrones returned into the bay, and anchored in the same situation as before. The Portuguese and Mandarins followed, keeping up a constant fire. The Ladrones never returned a single shot, but always kept in readiness to board, and the Portuguese were careful never to allow them an opportunity.

"On the 28th, at night they sent eight fire-vessels, which, if properly constructed, must have done great execution, having every advantage they could wish for to effect their purpose; a strong breeze and tide directed into the bay, and the vessels lying so close together, that it was impossible to miss them. On their first appearance, the Ladrones gave a general shout, supposing them to be Mandarin vessels on fire, but were very soon convinced of their mistake. They came very regularly into the centre of the fleet, two and two, burning furiously; one of them came alongside of the vessel I was in, but they succeeded in booming her off. She appeared to be a vessel of about thirty tons; her hold was filled with straw and wood, and there were a few small boxes of combustibles on her deck, which exploded alongside of us without doing any damage. The Ladrones, however, towed them all on shore, extinguished the fire, and broke them up for firewood. The Portuguese claim the credit of constructing these destructive machines, and actually sent a despatch to the Governor of Macao, saying they had destroyed at least one-third of the Ladrone's fleet, and hoped soon to effect their purpose by totally annihilating them!

"On the 29th of November, the Ladrones being all ready for sea, they weighed and stood boldly out, bidding defiance to the invincible squadron and imperial fleet, consisting of ninety-three war-junks, six Portuguese ships, a brig, and a schooner. Immediately after the Ladrones weighed, they made all sail. The Ladrones chased them two or three hours, keeping up a constant fire; finding they did not come up with them, they hauled their wind, and stood to the eastward. Thus terminated the boasted blockade, which lasted nine days, during which time the Ladrones completed all their repairs. In this action not a single Ladrone vessel was destroyed, and their loss was about thirty or forty men. An American was also killed, one of three that remained out of eight taken in a schooner. I had two very narrow escapes: the first, a twelve pounder shot fell within three or four feet of me; another took a piece out of a small brass-swivel on which I was standing. The chief's wife frequently sprinkled me with garlick-water, which they considered an effectual charm against shot. The fleet continued under sail all night, steering towards the eastward. In the morning they anchored in a large bay surrounded by lofty and barren mountains. On the 2d of December I received a letter from Lieutenant Maughn, commander of the Honorable Company's cruiser Antelope, saying that he had the ransom on board, and had been three days cruising after us, and wished me to settle with the chief on the securest method of delivering it. The chief agreed to send us in a small gun-boat till we came within sight of the Antelope; then the compradore's boat was to bring the ransom and receive us. I was so agitated at receiving this joyful news, that it was with difficulty I could scrawl about two or three lines to inform Lieutenant Maughn of the arrangements I had made. We were all so deeply affected by the gratifying tidings, that we seldom closed our eyes, but continued watching day and night for the boat.

"On the 6th she returned with Lieutenant Maughn's answer, saying, he would respect any single boat; but would not allow the fleet to approach him. The chief, then, according to his first proposal, ordered a gun-boat to take us, and with no small degree of pleasure we left the Ladrone fleet about four o'clock in the afternoon. At one P.M. saw the Antelope under all sail, standing towards us. The Ladrone boat immediately anchored, and dispatched the compradore's boat for the ransom, saying, that if she approached nearer they would return to the fleet; and they were just weighing when she shortened sail, and anchored about two miles from us. The boat did not reach her till late in the afternoon, owing to the tide's being strong against her. She received the ransom and left the Antelope just before dark. A Mandarin boat that had been lying concealed under the land, and watching their manoeuvres, gave chace to her, and was within a few fathoms of taking her, when she saw a light, which the Ladrones answered, and the Mandarin hauled off. Our situation was now a critical one; the ransom was in the hands of the Ladrones, and the compradore dare not return with us for fear of a second attack from the Mandarin boat. The Ladrones would not wait till morning, so we were obliged to return with them to the fleet. In the morning the chief inspected the ransom, which consisted of the following articles: two bales of superfine cloth; two chests of opium; two casks of gunpowder, and a telescope; the rest in dollars. He objected to the telescope not being new; and said he should detain one of us till another was sent, or a hundred dollars in lieu of it. The compradore, however, agreed with him for the hundred dollars. Every thing being at length settled, the chief ordered two gun-boats to convey us near the Antelope; we saw her just before dusk, when the Ladrone boats left us. We had the inexpressible pleasure of arriving on board the Antelope at seven, P.M., where we were most cordially received, and heartily congratulated on our safe and happy deliverance from a miserable captivity, which we had endured for eleven weeks and three days.

(Signed) "RICHARD GLASSPOOLE. *China, December 8th.* 1809."

"The Ladrones have no settled residence on shore, but live constantly in their vessels. The after-part is appropriated to the captain and his wives; he generally has five or six. With respect to the conjugal rights they are religiously strict; no person is allowed to have a woman on board, unless married to her according to their laws. Every man is allowed a small berth, about four feet square, where he stows with his wife and family. From the number of souls crowded in so small a space, it must naturally be supposed they are horridly dirty, which is evidently the case, and their vessels swarm with all kinds of vermin. Rats in particular, which they encourage to breed, and eat as great delicacies; in fact, there are very few creatures they will not eat. During our captivity we lived three weeks on caterpillars boiled with rice. They are much addicted to gambling, and spend all their leisure hours at cards and smoking opium."

The War Junks of the Ladrones

**The War Junks of the Ladrones.**

At the time of Mr. Glasspoole's liberation, the pirates were at the height of their power; after such repeated victories over the Mandarin ships, they had set at nought the Imperial allies–the Portuguese, and not only the coast, but the rivers of the celestial empire seemed to be at their discretion–and yet their formidable association did not many months survive this event. It was not, however, defeat that reduced it to the obedience of the laws. On the contrary, that extraordinary woman, the widow of Ching-yih, and the daring Paou, were victorious and more powerful than ever, when dissensions broke out among the pirates themselves. Ever since the favor of the chieftainess had elevated Paou to the general command, there had been enmity and altercations between him and the chief O-po-tae, who commanded one of the flags or divisions of the fleet; and it was only by the deference and respect they both owed to Ching-yih's widow, that they had been prevented from turning their arms against each other long before.

At length, when the brave Paou was surprised and cooped up by a strong blockading force of the Emperor's ships, O-po-tae showed all his deadly spite, and refused to obey the orders of Paou, and even of the chieftainess, which were, that he should sail to the relief of his rival.

Paou, with his bravery and usual good fortune, broke through the blockade, but when he came in contact with O-po-tae, his rage was too violent to be restrained.

O-po-tae at first pleaded that his means and strength had been insufficient to do what had been expected of him, but concluded by saying,–"Am I bound to come and join the forces of Paou?"

"Would you then separate from us!" cried Paou, more enraged than ever.

O-po-tae answered: "I will not separate myself."

Paou:–"Why then do you not obey the orders of the wife of Ching-yih and my own? What is this else than separation, that you do not come to assist me, when I am surrounded by the enemy? I have sworn it that I will destroy thee, wicked man, that I may do away with this soreness on my back."

The summons of Paou, when blockaded, to O-po-tae was in language equally figurative:–"I am harassed by the Government's officers outside in the sea; lips and teeth must help one another, if the lips are cut away the teeth will feel cold. How shall I alone be able to fight the Government forces? You should therefore come at the head of your crew, to attack the Government squadron in the rear. I will then come out of my station and make an attack in front; the enemy being so taken in the front and rear, will, even supposing we cannot master him, certainly be thrown into disorder."

The angry words of Paou were followed by others, and then by blows. Paou, though at the moment far inferior in force, first began the fight, and ultimately sustained a sanguinary defeat, and the loss of sixteen vessels. Our loathing for this cruel, detestable race, must be increased by the fact, that the victors massacred all their prisoners–or three hundred men!

This was the death-blow to the confederacy which had so long defied the Emperor's power, and which might have effected his dethronement. O-po-tae dreading the vengeance of Paou and his mistress, Ching-yih's widow, whose united forces would have quintupled his own, gained over his men to his views, and proffered a submission to Government, on condition of free pardon, and a proper provision for all.

The petition of the pirates is so curious a production, and so characteristic of the Chinese, that it deserves to be inserted at length. "It is my humble opinion that all robbers of an overpowering force, whether they had their origin from this or any other cause, have felt the humanity of Government at different times. Leang-sham, who three times plundered the city, was nevertheless pardoned, and at last made a minister of state. Wakang often challenged the arms of his country, and was suffered to live, and at last made a corner-stone of the empire. Joo-ming pardoned seven times Mang-hwo; and Kwan-kung three times set Tsaou-tsaou at liberty. Ma-yuen pursued not the exhausted robbers; and Yo-fei killed not those who made their submission. There are many instances of such transactions both in former and recent times, by which the country was strengthened, and government increased its power. We now live in a very populous age; some of us could not agree with their relations, and were driven out like noxious weeds. Some, after having tried all they could, without being able to provide for themselves, at last joined bad society. Some lost their property by shipwrecks; some withdrew into this watery empire to escape from punishment. In such a way those who in the beginning were only three or five, were in the course of time increased to a thousand or ten thousand, and so it went on increasing every year. Would it not have been wonderful if such a multitude, being in want of their daily bread, had not resorted to plunder and robbery to gain their subsistence, since they could not in any other manner be saved from famine? It was from necessity that the laws of the empire were violated, and the merchants robbed of their goods. Being deprived of our land and of our native places, having no house or home to resort to, and relying only on the chances of wind and water, even could we for a moment forget our griefs, we might fall in with a man-of-war, who with stones, darts, and guns, would knock out our brains! Even if we dared to sail up a stream and boldly go on with anxiety of mind under wind, rain, and stormy weather, we must everywhere prepare for fighting. Whether we went to the east, or to the west, and after having felt all the hardships of the sea, the night dew was our only dwelling, and the rude wind our meal. But now we will avoid these perils, leave our connexions, and desert our comrades; we will make our submission. The power of Government knows no bounds; it reaches to the islands in the sea, and every man is afraid, and sighs. Oh we must be destroyed by our crimes, none can escape who opposeth the laws of Government. May you then feel compassion for those who are deserving of death; may you sustain us by your humanity!"

The Government that had made so many lamentable displays of its weakness, was glad to make an unreal parade of its mercy. It was but too happy to grant all the conditions instantly, and, in the fulsome language of its historians, "feeling that compassion is the way of heaven–that it is the right way to govern by righteousness–it therefore redeemed these pirates from destruction, and pardoned their former crimes."

O-po-tae, however, had hardly struck his free flag, and the pirates were hardly in the power of the Chinese, when it was proposed by many that they should all be treacherously murdered. The governor happened to be more honorable and humane, or probably, only more politic than those who made this foul proposal–he knew that such a bloody breach of faith would for ever prevent the pirates still in arms from voluntary submitting; he knew equally well, even weakened as they were by O-po-tae's defection, that the Government could not reduce them by force, and he thought by keeping his faith with them, he might turn the force of those who had submitted against those who still held out, and so destroy the pirates with the pirates. Consequently the eight thousand men, it had been proposed to cut off in cold blood, were allowed to remain uninjured, and their leader, O-po-tae, having changed his name to that of Hoe-been, or, "The Lustre of Instruction," was elevated to the rank of an imperial officer.

The widow of Ching-yih, and her favorite Paou, continued for some months to pillage the coast, and to beat the Chinese and the Mandarins' troops and ships, and seemed almost as strong as before the separation of O-po-tae's flag. But that example was probably operating in the minds of many of the outlaws, and finally the lawless heroine herself, who was the spirit that kept the complicate body together, seeing that O-po-tae had been made a government officer, and that he continued to prosper, began also to think of making her submission.

"I am," said she, "ten times stronger than O-po-tae, and government will perhaps, if I submit, act towards me as they have done with O-po-tae."

A rumor of her intentions having reached shore, the Mandarin sent off a certain Chow, a doctor of Macao, "Who," says the historian, "being already well acquainted with the pirates, did not need any introduction," to enter on preliminaries with them.

When the worthy practitioner presented himself to Paou, that friend concluded he had been committing some crime, and had come for safety to that general *refugium peccatorum,* the pirate fleet.

The Doctor explained, and assured the chief, that if he would submit, Government was inclined to treat him and his far more favorably and more honorably than O-po-tae. But if he continued to resist, not only a general arming of all the coast and the rivers, but O-po-tae was to proceed against him.

At this part of his narrative our Chinese historian is again so curious, that I shall quote his words at length.

"When Fei-heung-Chow came to Paou, he said: 'Friend Paou, do you know why I come to you?'"

"Paou.–'Thou hast committed some crime and comest to me for protection?'"

"Chow.–'By no means.'"

"Paou.–'You will then know how it stands concerning the report about our submission, if it is true or false?'"

"Chow.–'You are again wrong here, Sir. What are you in comparison with O-po-tae?'"

"Paou.–'Who is bold enough to compare me with O-po-tae?'"

"Chow.–'I know very well that O-po-tae could not come up to you, Sir; but I mean only, that since O-po-tae has made his submission, since he has got his pardon and been created a Government officer,–how would it be, if you with your whole crew should also submit, and if his Excellency should desire to treat you in the same manner, and to give you the same rank as O-po-tae? Your submission would produce more joy to Government than the submission of O-po-tae. You should not wait for wisdom to act wisely; you should make up your mind to submit to the Government with all your followers. I will assist you in every respect, it would be the means of securing your own happiness and the lives of all your adherents.'"

"Chang-paou remained like a statue without motion, and Fei-heung Chow went on to say: 'You should think about this affair in time, and not stay till the last moment. Is it not clear that O-po-tae, since you could not agree together, has joined Government. He being enraged against you, will fight, united with the forces of the Government, for your destruction; and who could help you, so that you might overcome your enemies? If O-po-tae could before vanquish you quite alone, how much more can he now when he is united with Government? O-po-tae will then satisfy his hatred against you, and you yourself will soon be taken either at Wei-chow or at Neaou-chow. If the merchant-vessels of Hwy-chaou, the boats of Kwang-chow, and all the fishing-vessels, unite together to surround and attack you in the open sea, you will certainly have enough to do. But even supposing they should not attack you, you will soon feel the want of provisions to sustain you and all your followers. It is always wisdom to provide before things happen; stupidity and folly never think about future events. It is too late to reflect upon events when things have happened; you should, therefore, consider this matter in time!'"

Paou was puzzled, but after being closeted for some time with his mistress, Ching-yih's widow, who gave her high permission for him to make arrangements with Doctor Chow, he said he would repair with his fleet to the Bocca Tigris, and there communicate personally with the organs of Government.

After two visits had been paid to the pirate-fleets by two inferior Mandarins, who carried the Imperial proclamation of free pardon, and who, at the order of Ching-yih's widow, were treated to a sumptuous banquet by Paou, the Governor-general of the province went himself in one vessel to the pirates' ships, that occupied a line of ten *le* off the mouth of the river.

As the governor approached, the pirates hoisted their flags, played on their instruments, and fired their guns, so that the smoke rose in clouds, and then bent sail to meet him. On this the dense population that were ranged thousands after thousands along the shore, to witness the important reconciliation, became sorely alarmed, and the Governor-general seems to have had a strong inclination to run away. But in brief space of time, the long dreaded widow of Ching-yih, supported by her Lieutenant Paou, and followed by three other of her principal commanders, mounted the side of the governor's ship, and rushed through the smoke to the spot where his excellency was stationed; where they fell on their hands and knees, shed tears, knocked their heads on the deck before him, and received his gracious pardon, and promised for future kind treatment. They then withdrew satisfied, having promised to give in a list of their ships, and of all else they possessed, within three days.

But the sudden apparition of some large Portuguese ships, and some Government war-junks, made the pirates suspect treachery. They immediately set sail, and the negociations were interrupted for several days.

They were at last concluded by the boldness of their female leader. "If the Governor-general," said this heroine, "a man of the highest rank, could come to us quite alone, why should not I, a mean woman, go to the officers of Government? If there be danger in it, I take it all on myself; no person among you need trouble himself about me–my mind is made up, and I will go to Canton!"

Paou said–"If the widow of Ching-yih goes, we must fix a time for her return. If this pass without our obtaining any information, we must collect all our forces, and go before Canton: this is my opinion as to what ought to be done; comrades, let me hear yours!"

The pirates, then, struck with the intrepidity of their chieftainess, and loving her more than ever, answered, "Friend Paou, we have heard thy opinion, but we think it better to wait for the news here, on the water, than to send the wife of Ching-yih alone to be killed." Nor would they allow her to leave the fleet.

Matters were in this state of indecision, when the two inferior Mandarins who had before visited the pirates, ventured out to repeat their visit. These officers protested no treachery had been intended, and pledged themselves, that if the widow of Ching-yih would repair to the Governor, she would be kindly received, and every thing settled to their hearts' satisfaction.

With this, in the language of our old ballads, upspoke Mrs. Ching. "You say well, gentlemen! and I will go myself to Canton with some other of our ladies, accompanied by you!" And accordingly, she and a number of the pirates' wives with their children, went fearlessly to Canton, arranged every thing, and found they had not been deceived. The fleet soon followed. On its arrival every vessel was supplied with pork and with wine, and every man (in lieu it may be supposed, of his share of the vessels, and plundered property he resigned) received at the same time a bill for a certain quantity of money. Those who wished it, could join the military force of Government for pursuing the remaining pirates; and those who objected, dispersed and withdrew into the country. "This is the manner in which the great red squadron of the pirates was pacified."

The valiant Paou, following the example of his rival O-po-tae, entered into the service of Government, and proceeded against such of his former associates and friends as would not accept the pardon offered them. There was some hard fighting, but the two renegadoes successively took the chief Shih Url, forced the redoubtable captain, styled "The scourge of the Eastern Ocean" to surrender himself, drove "Frog's Meal," another dreadful pirate, to Manilla, and finally, and within a few months, destroyed or dissipated the "wasps of the ocean" altogether.

I have already noticed the marked intention of the Chinese historian, to paint the character of Paou in a poetical or epic manner. When describing the battle with Shih-Url, he says:–

"They fought from seven o'clock in the morning till one at noon, burnt ten vessels, and killed an immense number of the pirates. Shih-Url was so weakened that he could scarcely make any opposition. On perceiving this through the smoke, Paou mounted on a sudden the vessel of the pirate, and cried out: 'I Chang Paou am come,' and at the same moment he cut some pirates to pieces; the remainder were then hardly dealt with. Paou addressed himself in an angry tone to Shih-Url, and said: 'I advise you to submit: will you not follow my advice? what have you to say?' Shih-Url was struck with amazement, and his courage left him. Paou advanced and bound him, and the whole crew were then taken captives."

"From that period," says our Chinese historian, in conclusion, "ships began to pass and repass in tranquillity. All became quiet on the rivers, and tranquil on the four seas. People lived in peace and plenty. Men sold their arms and bought oxen to plough their fields; they buried sacrifices, said prayers on the tops of the hills, and rejoiced themselves by singing behind screens during day-time"–and (grand climax to all!) the Governor of the province, in consideration of his valuable services in the pacification of the pirates, was allowed by an edict of the "Son of Heaven," to wear peacocks' feathers with two eyes!

**THE LIFE OF CAPTAIN LEWIS.**

Captain Lewis was at an early age associated with pirates. We first find him a boy in company with the pirate Banister, who was hanged at the yard arm of a man-of-war, in sight of Port Royal, Jamaica. This Lewis and another boy were taken with him, and brought into the island hanging by the middle at the mizen peak. He had a great aptitude for languages, and spoke perfectly well that of the Mosquil Indians, French, Spanish, and English. I mention our own, because it is doubted whether he was French or English, for we cannot trace him back to his origin. He sailed out of Jamaica till he was a lusty lad, and was then taken by the Spaniards at the Havana, where he tarried some time; but at length he and six more ran away with a small canoe, and surprised a Spanish periagua, out of which two men joined them, so that they were now nine in company. With this periagua they surprised a turtling sloop, and forced some of the hands to take on with them; the others they sent away in the periagua.

He played at this small game, surprising and taking coasters and turtlers, till with forced men and volunteers he made up a company of 40 men. With these he took a large pink built ship, bound from Jamaica to the bay of Campeachy, and after her, several others bound to the same place; and having intelligence that there lay in the bay a fine Bermuda built brigantine of 10 guns, commanded by Captain Tucker, he sent the captain of the pink to him with a letter, the purport of which was, that he wanted such a brigantine, and if he would part with her, he would pay him 10,000 pieces of eight; if he refused this, he would take care to lie in his way, for he was resolved, either by fair or foul means to have the vessel. Captain Tucker, having read the letter, sent for the masters of vessels then lying in the bay, and told them, after he had shown the letter, that if they would make him up 54 men, (for there were about ten Bermuda sloops,) he would go out and fight the pirates. They said no, they would not hazard their men, they depended on their sailing, and every one must take care of himself as well as he could.

The Pirate Banister, hanging at the Yard Arm

**The Pirate Banister, hanging at the Yard Arm.**

However, they all put to sea together, and spied a sail under the land, which had a breeze while they lay becalmed. Some said he was a turtler; others, the pirate, and so it proved; for it was honest Captain Lewis, who putting out his oars, got in among them. Some of the sloops had four guns, some two, some none. Joseph Dill had two, which he brought on one side, and fired smartly at the pirate, but unfortunately one of them split, and killed three men. Tucker called to all the sloops to send him men, and he would fight Lewis, but to no purpose; nobody came on board him. In the mean while a breeze sprung up, and Tucker, trimming his sails, left them, who all fell a prey to the pirate; into whom, however, he fired a broadside at going off. One sloop, whose master I will not name, was a very good sailer, and was going off; but Lewis firing a shot, brought her to, and he lay by till all the sloops were visited and secured. Then Lewis sent on board him, and ordered the master into his sloop. As soon as he was on board, he asked the reason of his lying by, and betraying the trust his owners had reposed in him, which was doing like a knave and coward, and he would punish him accordingly; *for*, said he, *you might have got off, being so much a better sailer than my vessel.* After this speech, he fell upon him with a rope's end, and then snatching up his cane, drove him about the decks without mercy. The master, thinking to pacify him, told him he had been out trading in that sloop several months, and had on board a good quantity of money, which was hid, and which, if he would send on board a black belonging to the owners, he would discover to him. This had not the desired effect, but one quite contrary; for Lewis told him he was a rascal and villain for this discovery, and he would pay him for betraying his owners, and redoubled his strokes. However, he sent and took the money and negro, who was an able sailor. He took out of his prizes what he had occasion for, forty able negro sailors, and a white carpenter. The largest sloop, which was about ninety tons, he took for his own use, and mounted her with 12 guns. His crew was now about eighty men, whites and blacks.

The Master Caned by Captain Lewis

**The Master Caned by Captain Lewis.**

After these captures, he cruised in the Gulf of Florida, laying in wait for the West India homeward bound ships that took the leeward passage, several of which, falling into his hands, were plundered by him, and released. From hence he went to the coast of Carolina, where he cleaned his sloop, and a great many men whom he had forced, ran away from him. However, the natives traded with him for rum and sugar, and brought him all he wanted, without the government's having any knowledge of him, for he had got into a very private creek; though he was very much on his guard, that he might not be surprised from the shore.

From Carolina he cruised on the coast of Virginia, where he took and plundered several merchantmen, and forced several men, and then returned to the coast of Carolina, where he did abundance of mischief. As he had now an abundance of French on board, who had entered with him, and Lewis, hearing the English had a design to maroon them, he secured the men he suspected, and put them in a boat, with all the other English, ten leagues from shore, with only ten pieces of beef, and sent them away, keeping none but French and negroes. These men, it is supposed, all perished in the sea.

From the coast of Carolina he shaped his course for the banks of Newfoundland, where he overhauled several fishing vessels, and then went into Trinity Harbor in Conception Bay, where there lay several merchantmen, and seized a 24 gun galley, called the Herman. The commander, Captain Beal, told Lewis, if he would send his quarter master ashore he would furnish him with necessaries. He being sent ashore, a council was held among the masters, the consequence of which was, the seizing the quarter master, whom they carried to Captain Woodes Rogers. He chained him to a sheet anchor which was ashore, and planted guns at the point, to prevent the pirate getting out, but to little purpose; for the people at one of these points firing too soon, Lewis quitted the ship, and, by the help of oars and the favor of the night, got out in his sloop, though she received many shot in her hull. The last shot that was fired at the pirate did him considerable damage.

He lay off and on the harbor, swearing he would have his quarter master, and intercepted two fishing shallops, on board of one of which was the captain of the galley's brother. He detained them, and sent word, if his quarter master did not immediately come off, he would put all his prisoners to death. He was sent on board without hesitation. Lewis and the crew inquired how he had been used, and he answered, very civilly. "It's well," said the pirate, "for had you been ill treated, I would have put all these rascals to the sword." They were dismissed, and the captain's brother going over the side, the quarter master stopped him, saying, he must drink the gentlemen's health ashore, particularly Captain Rogers' and, whispering him in the ear, told him, if they had known of his being chained all night, he would have been cut in pieces, with all his men. After this poor man and his shallop's company were gone, the quarter master told the usage he had met with, which enraged Lewis, and made him reproach his quarter master, whose answer was, that he did not think it just the innocent should suffer for the guilty.

The masters of the merchantmen sent to Capt. Tudor Trevor, who lay at St. John's in the Sheerness man-of-war. He immediately got under sail, and missed the pirate but four hours. She kept along the coast and made several prizes, French and English, and put into a harbor where a French ship lay making fish. She was built at the latter end of the war, for a privateer, was an excellent sailer, and mounted 24 guns. The commander hailed him: the pirate answered, *from Jamaica with rum and sugar*. The

Frenchman bid him go about his business; that a pirate sloop was on the coast, and he might be the rogue; if he did not immediately sheer off, he would fire a broadside into him. He went off and lay a fortnight out at sea, so far as not to be descried from shore, with resolution to have the ship. The Frenchman being on his guard, in the meanwhile raised a battery on the shore, which commanded the harbor. After a fortnight, when he was thought to be gone off, he returned, and took two of the fishing shallops belonging to the Frenchman, and manning them with pirates, they went in. One shallop attacked the battery; the other surprised, boarded and carried the ship, just as the morning star appeared, for which reason he gave her that name. In the engagement the owner's son was killed, who made the voyage out of curiosity only. The ship being taken, seven guns were fired, which was the signal, and the sloop came down and lay alongside the ship. The captain told him he supposed he only wanted his liquor; but Lewis made answer he wanted his ship, and accordingly hoisted all his ammunition and provision into her. When the Frenchman saw they would have his ship, he told her trim, and Lewis gave him the sloop; and excepting what he took for provision, all the fish he had made. Several of the French took on with him, who, with others, English and French, had by force or voluntarily, made him up 200 men.

From Newfoundland he steered for the coast of Guinea, where he took a great many ships, English, Dutch and Portuguese. Among these ships was one belonging to Carolina, commanded by Capt. Smith. While he was in chase of this vessel a circumstance occurred, which made his men believe he dealt with the devil; his fore and main top-mast being carried away, he, Lewis, running up the shrouds to the maintop, tore off a handful of hair, and throwing it into the air used this expression, *good devil, take this till I come*. And it was observed, that he came afterwards faster up with the chase than before the loss of his top-masts.

Captain Lewis giving a lock of his hair to the Devil

**Captain Lewis giving a lock of his hair to the Devil.**

Smith being taken, Lewis used him very civilly, and gave him as much or more in value than he took from him, and let him go, saying, he would come to Carolina when he had made money on the coast, and would rely on his friendship.

They kept some time on the coast, when they quarrelled among themselves, the French and English, of which the former were more numerous, and they resolved to part. The French therefore chose a large sloop newly taken, thinking the ship's bottom, which was not sheathed, damaged by the worms. According to this agreement they took on board what ammunition and provision they thought fit out of the ship, and put off, choosing one Le Barre captain. As it blew hard, and the decks were encumbered, they came to an anchor under the coast, to stow away their ammunition, goods, c. Lewis told his men they were a parcel of rogues, and he would make them refund; accordingly he run alongside, his guns being all loaded and new primed, and ordered him to cut away his mast or he would sink him. Le Barre was obliged to obey. Then he ordered them all ashore. They begged the liberty of carrying their arms, goods, c. with them, but he allowed them only their small arms and cartridge boxes. Then he brought the sloop alongside, put every thing on board the ship, and sunk the sloop.

Le Barre and the rest begged to be taken on board. However, though he denied them, he suffered Le Barre and some few to come, with whom he and his men drank plentifully. The negroes on board Lewis told him the French had a plot against him. He answered, he could not withstand his destiny; for the devil told him in the great cabin he should be murdered that night.

In the dead of the night, the rest of the French came on board in canoes, got into the cabin and killed Lewis. They fell on the crew; but, after an hour and a half's dispute, the French were beaten off, and the quarter master, John Cornelius, an Irishman, succeeded Lewis.

–"He was the mildest manner'd man,
That ever scuttled ship or cut a throat;
With such true breeding of a gentleman,
You never could discern his real thought.
Pity he loved an adventurous life's variety,
He was so great a loss to good society."

## THE LIFE, CAREER AND DEATH OF CAPTAIN THOMAS WHITE.

He was born at Plymouth, where his mother kept a public house. She took great care of his education, and when he was grown up, as he had an inclination to the sea, procured him the king's letter. After he had served some years on board a man-of-war, he went to Barbadoes, where he married, got into the merchant service, and designed to settle in the island. He had the command of the Marygold brigantine given him, in which he made two successful voyages to Guinea and back to Barbadoes. In his third, he had the misfortune to be taken by a French pirate, as were several other English ships, the masters and inferior officers of which they detained, being in want of good artists. The brigantine belonging to White, they kept for their own use, and sunk the vessel they before sailed in; but meeting with a ship on the Guinea coast more fit for their purpose, they went on board her and burnt the brigantine.

It is not my business here to give an account of this French pirate, any farther than Capt. White's story obliges me, though I beg leave to take notice of their barbarity to the English prisoners, for they would set them up as a butt or mark to shoot at; several of whom were thus murdered in cold blood, by way of diversion.

White was marked out for a sacrifice by one of these villains, who, for what reason I know not, had sworn his death, which he escaped thus. One of the crew, who had a friendship for White, knew this fellow's design to kill him in the night, and therefore advised him to lie between him and the ship's side, with intention to save him; which indeed he did, but was himself shot dead by the murderous villain, who mistook him for White.

After some time cruising along the coast, the pirates doubled the Cape of Good Hope, and shaped their course for Madagascar, where, being drunk and mad, they knocked their ship on the head, at the south end of the island, at a place called by the natives Elexa. The country thereabouts was governed by a king, named Mafaly.

When the ship struck, Capt. White, Capt. Boreman, (born in the Isle of Wight, formerly a lieutenant of a man-of-war, but in the merchant service when he fell into the hands of the pirates,) Capt. Bowen and some other prisoners got into the long-boat, and with broken oars and barrel staves, which they found in the bottom of the boat, paddled to Augustin Bay, which is about 14 or 15 leagues from the wreck, where they landed, and were kindly received by the king of Bavaw, (the name of that part of the island) who spoke good English.

They stayed here a year and a half at the king's expense, who gave them a plentiful allowance of provision, as was his custom to all white men, who met with any misfortune on his coast. His humanity not only provided for such, but the first European vessel that came in, he always obliged to take in the unfortunate people, let the vessel be what it would; for he had no notion of any difference between pirates and merchants.

At the expiration of the above term, a pirate brigantine came in, on board which the king obliged them to enter, or travel by land to some other place, which they durst not do; and of two evils chose the least, that of going on board the pirate vessel, which was commanded by one William Read, who received them very civilly.

This commander went along the coast, and picked up what Europeans he could meet with. His crew, however, did not exceed 40 men. He would have been glad of taking some of the wrecked Frenchmen, but for the barbarity they had used towards the English prisoners. However, it was impracticable, for the French pretending to lord it over the natives, whom they began to treat inhumanly, were set upon by them, one half of their number cut off, and the other half made slaves.

Read, with this gang, and a brigantine of 60 tons, steered his course for the Persian Gulf, where they met a grab, (a one masted vessel) of about 200 tons, which was made a prize. They found nothing on board but bale goods, most of which they threw overboard in search of gold, and to make room in the vessel; but as they learned afterwards, they threw over, in their search, what they so greedily hunted after, for there was a considerable quantity of gold concealed in one of the bales they tossed into the sea!

In this cruise Capt. Read fell ill and died, and was succeeded by one James. The brigantine being small, crazy and worm-eaten, they shaped their course for the island of Mayotta, where they took out the masts of the brigantine, fitted up the grab, and made a ship of her. Here they took in a quantity of fresh provisions, which are in this island very plentiful and very cheap, and found a twelve-oared boat, which formerly belonged to the Ruby East Indiaman, which had been lost there.

They stayed here all the monsoon time, which is about six months; after which they resolved for Madagascar. As they came in with the land, they spied a sail coming round from the east side of the island. They gave chase on both sides, so that they soon met. They hailed each other and receiving the same answer from each vessel, viz. *from the seas,* they joined company.

This vessel was a small French ship, laden with liquors from Martinico, first commanded by one Fourgette, to trade with the pirates for slaves, at Ambonavoula, on the east side of the island, in the latitude of 17 deg. 30 min. and was by them taken after the following manner.

The pirates, who were headed by George Booth, now commander of the ship, went on board, (as they had often done,) to the number of ten, and carried money with them under pretence of purchasing what they wanted. This Booth had formerly been gunner of a pirate ship, called the Dolphin. Capt. Fourgette was pretty much upon his guard, and searched every man as he came over the side, and a pair of pocket pistols were found upon a Dutchman, who was the first that entered. The captain told him that *he was a rogue, and had a design upon his ship*, and the pirates pretended to be so angry with this fellow's offering to come on board with arms, that they threatened to knock him on the head, and tossing him roughly into the boat, ordered him ashore, though they had before taken an oath on the Bible, either to carry the ship, or die in the undertaking.

They were all searched, but they however contrived to get on board four pistols, which were all the arms they had for the enterprise, though Fourgette had 20 hands on board, and his small arms on the awning, to be in readiness.

The captain invited them into the cabin to dinner, but Booth chose to dine with the petty officer, though one Johnson, Isaac and another, went down. Booth was to give the watchword, which was *hurrah*. Standing near the awning, and being a nimble fellow, at one spring he threw himself upon it, drew the arms to him, fired his pistol among the men, one of whom he wounded, (who jumping overboard was lost) and gave the signal.

Three, I said, were in the cabin, and seven upon deck, who with handspikes and the arms seized, secured the ship's crew. The captain and his two mates, who were at dinner in the cabin, hearing the pistol, fell upon Johnson, and stabbed him in several places with their forks, but they being silver, did him no great damage. Fourgette snatched his piece, which he snapped at Isaac's breast several times, but it would not go off. At last, finding his resistance vain, he submitted, and the pirates set him, and those of his men who would not join them, on shore, allowing him to take his books, papers, and whatever else he claimed as belonging to himself; and besides treating him very humanely, gave him several casks of liquor, with arms and powder, to purchase provisions in the country.

I hope this digression, as it was in a manner needful, will be excused. I shall now proceed.

After they had taken in the Dolphin's company, which were on the island, and increased their crew, by that means, to the number of 80 hands, they sailed to St. Mary's, where Capt. Mosson's ship lay at anchor, between the island and the main. This gentleman and his whole ship's company had been cut off at the instigation of Ort-Vantyle, a Dutchman of New-York.

Out of her they took water casks and other necessaries; which having done, they designed for the river Methelage, on the west side of Madagascar, in the lat. of 16 degrees or thereabouts, to salt up provisions and to proceed to the East Indies, cruise off the islands of St. John, and lie in wait for the Moor ships from Mocha.

In their way to Methelage they fell in (as I have said) with the pirate, on board of which was Capt. White. They joined company, came to an anchor together in the above named river, where they had cleaned, salted and took in their provisions, and were ready to go to sea, when a large ship appeared in sight, and stood into the same river.

The pirates knew not whether she was a merchantman or man-of-war. She had been the latter, belonging to the French king, and could mount 50 guns; but being taken by the English, she was bought by some London merchants, and fitted out from that port to slave at Madagascar, and go to Jamaica. The captain was a young, inexperienced man, who was put in with a nurse.

The pirates sent their boats to speak with them, but the ship firing at them, they concluded it a man of war, and rowed ashore; the grab standing in, and not keeping her wind so well as the French built ship, run among a parcel of mangroves, and a stump piercing her bottom, she sunk: the other run aground, let go her anchor, and came to no damage, for the tide of flood fetched her off.

The captain of the Speaker, for that was the name of the ship which frightened the pirates, was not a little vain of having forced these two vessels ashore, though he did not know whether they were pirates or merchantmen, and could not help expressing himself in these words: "How will my name ring on the exchange, when it is known I have run two pirates aground;" which gave handle to a satirical return from one of his men after he was taken, who said, "Lord! how our captain's name will ring on the exchange, when it is heard, he frightened two pirate ships ashore, and was taken by their two boats afterwards."

When the Speaker came within shot, she fired several times at the two vessels; and when she came to anchor, several more into the country, which alarmed the negroes, who, acquainting their king, he would allow him no trade, till the pirates living ashore, and who had a design on his ship, interceded for them, telling the king, they were their countrymen, and what had happened was through a mistake, it being a custom among them to fire their guns by way of respect, and it was owing to the gunner of the ship's negligence that they fired shot.

The captain of the Speaker sent his purser ashore, to go up the country to the king, who lived about 24 miles from the coast, to carry a couple of small arms inlaid with gold, a couple of brass blunderbusses, and a pair of pistols, as presents, and to require trade. As soon as the purser was ashore, he was taken prisoner, by one Tom Collins, a Welshman, born in Pembroke, who lived on shore, and had belonged to the Charming Mary, of Barbadoes, which went out with a commission but was converted to a pirate. He told the purser he was his prisoner, and must answer the damage done to two merchants who were slaving. The purser answered, that he was not commander; that the captain was a hot rash youth, put into business by his friends, which he did not understand; but however, satisfaction should be made. He was carried by Collins on board Booth's ship, where, at first, he was talked to in pretty strong terms; but after a while very civilly used, and the next morning sent up to the king with a guide, and peace made for him.

The king allowed them trade, and sent down the usual presents, a couple of oxen between twenty and thirty people laden with rice, and as many more with the country liquor, called *toke*.

The captain then settled the factory on the shore side, and began to buy slaves and provisions. The pirates were among them, and had opportunities of sounding the men, and knowing in what posture the ship lay. They found by one Hugh Man, belonging to the Speaker, that there were not above 40 men on board, and that they had lost the second mate and 20 hands in the long boat, on the coast, before they came into this harbor, but that they kept a good look out, and had their guns ready primed. However, he, for a hundred pounds, undertook to wet all the priming, and assist in taking the ship.

After some days the captain of the Speaker came on shore, and was received with great civility by the heads of the pirates, having agreed before to make satisfaction. In a day or two after, he was invited by them to eat a barbacued shoat, which invitation he accepted. After dinner, Capt. Bowen, who was, I have already said, a prisoner on board the French pirate, but now become one of the fraternity, and master of the grab, went out, and returned with a case of pistols in his hand, and told the Captain of the Speaker, whose name I won't mention, that he was his prisoner. He asked, upon what account? Bowen answered, "they wanted his ship, his was a good one, and they were resolved to have her, to make amends for the damage he had done them."

Hugh Man wetting the Priming of the Guns.

**Hugh Man wetting the Priming of the Guns.**

In the mean while his boat's crew, and the rest of his men ashore, were told by others of the pirates, who were drinking with them, that they were also prisoners: some of them answered, *Zounds, we don't trouble our heads what we are, let's have t'other bowl of punch.*

A watchword was given, and no boat to be admitted on board the ship. This word, which was for that night, *Coventry*, was known to them. At 8 o'clock they manned the twelve-oared boat, and the one they found at Mayotta, with 24 men, and set out for the ship. When they were put off, the captain of the Speaker desired them to come back, as he wanted to speak with them. Capt. Booth asked what he wanted! He said, "they could never take his ship." "Then," said Booth, "we'll die in or alongside of her."–"But," replied the captain, "if you will go with safety, don't board on the larboard side, for there is a gun out of the steerage loaded with partridge, which will clear the decks." They thanked him, and proceeded.

When they were near the ship they were hailed, and the answer was, *the Coventry*. "All well," said the mate, "get the lights over the side;" but spying the second boat, he asked what boat that was? One answered it was a raft of water, another that it was a boat of beef; this disagreement in the answers made the mate suspicious, who cried out–*Pirates, take to your arms my lads*, and immediately clapped a match to a gun, which, as the priming was before wet by the treachery of Hugh Man, only fizzed. They boarded in the instant, and made themselves masters of her, without the loss of a man on either side.

The next day they put necessary provisions on board the French built ship, and gave her to the captain of the Speaker, and those men who would go off with him, among whom was Man, who had betrayed his ship; for the pirates had both paid him the 100*l* agreed, and kept his secret. The captain having thus lost his ship, sailed in that which the pirates gave him, for Johanna, where he fell ill and died with grief.

The pirates having here victualled, they sailed for the Bay of St. Augustine, where they took in between 70 and 80 men, who had belonged to the ship Alexander, commanded by Capt. James, a pirate. They also took up her guns, and mounted the Speaker with 54, which made up their number, and 240 men, besides slaves, of which they had about 20.

From hence they sailed for the East Indies, but stopped at Zanguebar for fresh provisions, where the Portuguese had once a settlement, but now inhabited by Arabians. Some of them went ashore with the captain to buy provisions. The captain was sent for by the governor, who went with about 14 in company. They passed through the guard, and when they had entered the governor's house, they were all cut off; and, at the same time, others who were in different houses of the town were set upon, which made them fly to the shore. The long-boat, which lay off a grappling, was immediately put in by those who looked after her. There were not above half a dozen of the pirates who brought their arms ashore, but they plied them so well, for they were in the boat, that most of the men got into her. The quarter-master ran down sword in hand, and though he was attacked by many, he behaved himself so well, that he got into a little canoe, put off, and reached the long-boat.

In the interim, the little fort the Arabians had, played upon the ship, which returned the salute very warmly. Thus they got on board, with the loss of Captain Booth and 20 men, and set sail for the East Indies. When they were under sail, they went to voting for a new captain, and the quarter-master, who had behaved so well in the last affair with the Arabians, was chosen; but he declining all command the crew made choice of Bowen for captain, Pickering to succeed him as master, Samuel Herault, a Frenchman, for quarter-master, and Nathaniel North for captain quarter-master.

Things being thus settled, they came to the mouth of the Red Sea, and fell in with 13 sail of Moor ships, which they kept company with the greater part of the day, but afraid to venture on them, as they took them for Portuguese men-of-war. At length part were for boarding, and advised it. The captain though he said little, did not seem inclined, for he was but a young pirate, though an old commander of a merchantman. Those who pushed for boarding, then desired Captain Boreman, already mentioned, to take the command; but he said he would not be a usurper; that nobody was more fit for it than he who had it; that for his part he would stand by his fuzil, and went forward to the forecastle with such as would have him take the command, to be ready to board; on which the captain's quarter-master said, if they were resolved to engage, their captain, (whose representative he was) did not want resolution; therefore ordered them to get their tacks on board (for they had already made a clear ship) and get ready for boarding; which they accordingly did, and coming up with the sternmost ship, they fired a broadside into her, which killed two Moors, clapped her on board and carried her; but night coming on, they made only this prize, which yielded them $500 per man. From hence they sailed to the coast of Malabar. The adventures of these pirates on this coast are already set down in Captain Bowen's life, to which I refer the reader, and shall only observe, that Captain White was all this time before the mast, being a forced man from the beginning.

Bowen's crew dispersing, Captain White went to Methelage, where he lived ashore with the king, not having an opportunity of getting off the island, till another pirate ship, called the Prosperous, commanded by one Howard, who had been bred a lighterman on the river Thames, came in. This ship was taken at Augustin, by some pirates from shore, and the crew of their long-boat, which joined them, at the instigation of one Ranten, boatswain's mate, who sent for water. They came on board in the night and surprised her, though not without resistance, in which the captain and chief mate were killed, and several others wounded.

Those who were ashore with Captain White, resolving to enter in this ship, determined him to go also, rather than be left alone with the natives, hoping, by some accident or other, to have an opportunity of returning home. He continued on board this ship, in which he was made quarter-master, till they met with, and all went on board of Bowen, as is set down in his life, in which ship he continued after Bowen left them. At Port Dolphin he went *off* in the boats to fetch some of the crew left ashore, the ship being blown to sea the night before. The ship not being able to get in, and he supposing her gone to the west side of the island, as they had formerly proposed, he steered that course in his boat with 26 men. They touched at Augustin, expecting the ship, but she not appearing in a week, the time they waited, the king ordered them to be gone, telling them they imposed on him with lies, for he did not believe they had any ship: however he gave them fresh provision: they took in water, and made for Methelage. Here as Captain White was known to the king, they were kindly received, and staid about a fortnight in expectation of the ship, but she not appearing they raised their boat a streak, salted the provision the king gave them, put water aboard, and stood for the north end of the island, designing to go round, believing their ship might be at the island of St. Mary. When they came to the north end, the current, which sets to the N.W. for eight months in the year, was so strong they found it impossible to get round. Wherefore they got into a harbor, of which there are many for small vessels. Here they stayed about three weeks or a month, when part of the crew were for burning the boat, and travelling over land to a black king of their acquaintance, whose name was Reberimbo, who lived at a place called Manangaromasigh, in lat. 15 deg. or thereabouts. As this king had been several times assisted by the whites in his wars, he was a great friend to them. Captain White dissuaded them from this undertaking, and with much ado, saved the boat; but one half of the men being resolved to go by land, they took what provisions they thought necessary, and set out. Captain White, and those who staid with him, conveyed them a day's journey, and then returning, he got into the boat with his companions, and went back to Methelage, fearing these men might return, prevail with the rest, and burn the boat.

The Murder of the Captain and Chief Mate

**The Murder of the Captain and Chief Mate.**

Here he built a deck on his boat, and lay by three months, in which time there came in three pirates with a boat, who had formerly been trepanned on board the Severn and Scarborough men-of-war, which had been looking for pirates on the east side; from which ships they made their escape at Mohila, in a small canoe to Johanna, and from Johanna to Mayotta, where the king built them the boat which brought them to Methelage. The time of the current's setting with violence to the N.W. being over, they proceeded together in White's boat (burning that of Mayotta) to the north end, where the current running yet too strong to get round, they went into a harbor and staid there a month, maintaining themselves with fish and wild hogs, of which there was a great plenty. At length, having fine weather, and the strength of the current abating, they got round; and after sailing about 40 miles on the east side, they went into a harbor, where they found a piece of a jacket, which they knew belonged to one of those men who had left them to go over land. He had been a forced man, and a ship carpenter. This they supposed he had torn to wrap round his feet; that part of the country being barren and rocky. As they sailed along this coast, they came to anchor in convenient harbors every night, till they got as far as Manangaromasigh, where king Reberimbo resided, where they went in to inquire for their men, who left them at the north end, and to recruit with provisions. The latter was given them, but they could get no information of their companions.

From hence they went to the island of St. Mary, where a canoe came off to them with a letter directed to any white man. They knew it to be the hand of one of their former shipmates. The contents of this letter was to advise them to be on their guard, and not trust too much to the blacks of this place, they having been formerly treacherous. They inquired after their ship, and were informed, that the company had given her to the Moors, who were gone away with her, and that they themselves were settled at Ambonavoula, about 20 leagues to the southward of St. Mary, where they lived among the negroes as so many sovereign princes.

One of the blacks, who brought off the letter went on board their boat, carried them to the place called Olumbah, a point of land made by a river on one side, and the sea on the other, where twelve of them lived together in a large house they had built, and fortified with about twenty pieces of cannon.

The rest of them were settled in small companies of about 12 or 14 together, more or less, up the said river, and along the coast, every nation by itself, as the English, French, Dutch, c. They made inquiry of their consorts after the different prizes which belonged to them, and they found all very justly laid by to be given them, if ever they returned, as were what belonged to the men who went over land. Captain White, hankering after home, proposed going out again in the boat; for he was adverse to settling with them; and many others agreed to go under his command; and if they could meet with a ship to carry them to Europe, to follow their old vocation. But the others did not think it reasonable he should have the boat, but that it should be set to sale for the benefit of the company. Accordingly it was set up, and Captain White bought it for 400 pieces of eight, and with some of his old consorts, whose number was increased by others of the ship's crew, he went back the way he had come to Methelage. Here he met with a French ship of about 50 tons, and 6 guns, which had been taken by some pirates who lived at Maratan, on the east side of the island, and some of the Degrave East-Indiaman's crew, to whom the master of her refused a passage to Europe; for as he had himself been a pirate, and quarter-master to Bowen, in the Speaker, he apprehended their taking away his ship. War then existing between England and France, he thought they might do it without being called in question as pirates. The pirates who had been concerned in taking Herault's ship, for that was his name, had gone up the country, and left her to the men belonging to the Degrave, who had fitted her up, cleaned and tallowed her, and got in some provision, with a design to go to the East-Indies, that they might light on some ship to return to their own country.

Captain White, finding these men proposed joining him, and going round to Ambonavoula, to make up a company, it was agreed upon, and they unanimously chose him commander. They accordingly put to sea, and stood away round the south end of the island, and touched at Don Mascarenhas, where he took in a surgeon, and stretching over again to Madagascar, fell in with Ambonavoula, and made up his complement of 60 men. From hence he shaped his course for the island of Mayotta, where he cleaned his ship, and waited for the season to go into the Red Sea. His provisions being taken in, the time proper, and the ship well fitted, he steered for Babel-Mandeb, and running into a harbor, waited for the Mocha ships.

He here took two grabs laden with provisions, and having some small money and drugs aboard. These he plundered of what was for his turn, kept them a fortnight by him, and let them go. Soon after they espied a lofty ship, upon which they put to sea; but finding her European built, and too strong to attempt, for it was a Dutchman, they gave over the chase, and were glad to shake them off, and return to their station. Fancying they were here discovered, from the coast of Arabia, or that the grabs had given information of them they stood over for the Ethiopian shore, keeping a good look out for the Mocha ships. A few days after, they met with a large ship of about 1000 tons and 600 men, called the Malabar, which they chased, kept company with her all night, and took in the morning, with the loss of only their boatswain, and two or three men wounded. In taking this ship, they damaged their own so much, by springing their foremast, carrying away their bowsprit, and beating in part of their upper works that they did not think her longer fit for their use. They therefore filled her away with prisoners, gave them provision and sent them away.

Some days after this, they espied a Portuguese man-of war of 44 guns, which they chased, but gave it over by carrying away their maintopmast, so that they did not speak with her, for the Portuguese took no notice of them. Four days after they had left this man-of-war, they fell in with a Portuguese merchantman, which they chased with English colors flying. The chase, taking White for an English man-of-war or East-Indiaman, made no sail to get from him, but on his coming up, brought to, and sent his boat on board with a present of sweet-meats for the English captain. His boat's crew was detained, and the pirates getting into his boat with their arms, went on board and fired on the Portuguese, who being surprised, asked if war was broke out between England and Portugal? They answered in the affirmative, but the captain could not believe them. However they took what they liked, and kept him with them.

After two days they met with the Dorothy, an English ship, Captain Penruddock, commander, coming from Mocha. They exchanged several shots in the chase, but when they came along side of her, they entered their men, and found no resistance, she being navigated by Moors, no Europeans, except the officers being on board. On a vote, they gave Captain Penruddock (from whom they took a considerable quantity of money) the Portuguese ship and cargo, with what bale he pleased to take out of his own, bid him go about his business, and make what he could of her. As to the English ship, they kept her for their own use.

Soon after they plundered the Malabar ship, out of which they took as much money as came to $200 sterling a man, but missed 50,000 sequins, which were hid in a jar under a cow's stall, kept for the giving milk to the Moor supercargo, an ancient man. They then put the Portuguese and Moor prisoners on board the Malabar, and sent them about their business. The day after they had sent them away, one Captain Benjamin Stacy, in a ketch of 6 guns fell into their hands. They took what money he had, and what goods and provisions they wanted. Among the money were 500 dollars, a silver mug, and two spoons belonging to a couple of children on board, who were under the care of Stacy. The children took on for their loss, and the captain asked the reason of their tears, was answered by Stacy, and the above sum and plate was all the children had to bring them up. Captain White made a speech to his men, and told them it was cruel to rob the innocent children; upon which, by unanimous consent, all was restored to them again. Besides, they made a gathering among themselves, and made a present to Stacy's mate, and other of his inferior officers, and about 120 dollars to the children. They then discharged Stacy and his crew, and made the best of their way out of the Red Sea.

They came into the bay of Defarr, where they found a ketch at anchor, which the people had made prize of, by seizing the master and boat's crew ashore. They found a French gentleman, one Monsieur Berger, on board, whom they carried with them, took out about 2000 dollars, and sold the ketch to the chief ashore for provisions.

Hence they sailed for Madagascar, but touched at Mascarenhas, where several of them went ashore with their booty, about $1200 a man. Here taking in fresh provisions, White steered for Madagascar, and fell in with Hopeful Point where they shared their goods, and took up settlements ashore, where White built a house, bought cattle, took off the upper deck of ship, and was fitting her up for the next season. When she was near ready for sea, Captain John Halsey, who had made a broken voyage, came in with a brigantine, which being a more proper vessel for their turn, they desisted from working on the ship, and those who had a mind for fresh adventures, went on board Halsey, among whom Captain White entered before the mast.

At his return to Madagascar, White was taken ill of a flux, which in about five or six months ended his days. Finding his time was drawing nigh, he made his will, left several legacies, and named three men of different nations, guardian to a son he had by a woman in the country, requiring he might be sent to England with the money he left him, by the first English ship, to be brought up in the Christian religion, in hopes that he might live a better man than his father. He was buried with the same ceremony they used at the funerals of their companions, which is mentioned in the account of Halsey. Some years after, an English ship touching there, the guardians faithfully discharged their trust, and put him on board with the captain, who brought up the boy with care, acting by him as became a man of probity and honor.

## THE LIFE, ATROCITIES, AND BLOODY DEATH OF BLACK BEARD.

Edward Teach was a native of Bristol, and having gone to Jamaica, frequently sailed from that port as one of the crew of a privateer during the French war. In that station he gave frequent proofs of his boldness and personal courage; but he was not entrusted with any command until Captain Benjamin Hornigold gave him the command of a prize which he had taken.

In the spring of 1717, Hornigold and Teach sailed from Providence for the continent of America, and on their way captured a small vessel with 120 barrels of flour, which they put on board their own vessel. They also seized two other vessels; from one they took some gallons of wine, and from the other, plunder to a considerable value. After cleaning upon the coast of Virginia, they made a prize of a large French Guineaman bound to Martinique, and Teach obtaining the command of her, went to the island of Providence, and surrendered to the king's clemency.

Teach now began to act an independent part. He mounted his vessel with forty guns, and named her "The Queen Anne's Revenge." Cruising near the island of St. Vincent, he took a large ship, called the Great Allan, and after having plundered her of what he deemed proper, set her on fire. A few days after, Teach encountered the Scarborough man-of-war, and engaged her for some hours; but perceiving his strength and resolution, she retired, and left Teach to pursue his depredations. His next adventure was with a sloop of ten guns, commanded by Major Bonnet, and these two men co-operated for some time: but Teach finding him unacquainted with naval affairs, gave the command of Bonnet's ship to Richards, one of his own crew, and entertained Bonnet on board his own vessel. Watering at Turniff, they discovered a sail, and Richards with the Revenge slipped her cable, and ran out to meet her. Upon seeing the black flag hoisted, the vessel struck, and came-to under the stern of Teach the commodore. This was the Adventure from Jamaica. They took the captain and his men on board the great ship, and manned his sloop for their own service.

Weighing from Turniff, where they remained during a week, and sailing to the bay, they found there a ship and four sloops. Teach hoisted his flag, and began to fire at them, upon which the captain and his men left their ship and fled to the shore. Teach burned two of these sloops, and let the other three depart.

They afterwards sailed to different places, and having taken two small vessels, anchored off the bar of Charleston for a few days. Here they captured a ship bound for England, as she was coming out of the harbor. They next seized a vessel coming out of Charleston, and two pinks coming into the same harbor, together with a brigantine with fourteen negroes. The audacity of these transactions, performed in sight of the town, struck the inhabitants with terror, as they had been lately visited by some other notorious pirates. Meanwhile, there were eight sail in the harbor, none of which durst set to sea for fear of falling into the hands of Teach. The trade of this place was totally interrupted, and the inhabitants were abandoned to despair. Their calamity was greatly augmented from this circumstance, that a long and desperate war with the natives had just terminated, when they began to be infested by these robbers.

Teach having detained all the persons taken in these ships as prisoners, they were soon in great want of medicines, and he had the audacity to demand a chest from the governor. This demand was made in a manner not less daring than insolent. Teach sent Richards, the captain of the Revenge, with Mr. Marks, one of the prisoners, and several others, to present their request. Richards informed the governor, that unless their demand was granted, and he and his companions returned in safety, every prisoner on board the captured ships should instantly be slain, and the vessels consumed to ashes.

During the time that Mr. Marks was negotiating with the governor, Richards and his associates walked the streets at pleasure, while indignation flamed from every eye against them, as the robbers of their property, and the terror of their country. Though the affront thus offered to the Government was great and most audacious, yet, to preserve the lives of so many men, they granted their request, and sent on board a chest valued at three or four hundred pounds.

Teach, as soon as he received the medicines and his fellow pirates, pillaged the ships of gold and provisions, and then dismissed the prisoners with their vessels. From the bar of Charleston they sailed to North Carolina. Teach now began to reflect how he could best secure the spoil, along with some of the crew who were his favorites. Accordingly, under pretence of cleaning, he ran his vessel on shore, and grounded; then ordered the men in Hands' sloop to come to his assistance, which they endeavoring to do, also ran aground, and so they were both lost. Then Teach went into the tender with forty hands, and upon a sandy island, about a league from shore, where there was neither bird no beast, nor herb for their subsistence, he left seventeen of his crew, who must inevitably have perished, had not Major Bonnet received intelligence of their miserable situation, and sent a long-boat for them. After this barbarous deed. Teach, with the remainder of his crew, went and surrendered to the governor of North Carolina, retaining all the property which had been acquired by his fleet.

The temporary suspension of the depredations of Black Beard, for so he was now called, did not proceed from a conviction of his former errors, or a determination to reform, but to prepare for future and more extensive exploits. As governors are but men, and not unfrequently by no means possessed of the most virtuous principles, the gold of Black Beard rendered him comely in the governor's eyes, and, by his influence, he obtained a legal right to the great ship called "The Queen Anne's Revenge." By order of the governor, a court of vice-admiralty was held at Bath-town, and that vessel was condemned as a lawful prize which he had taken from the Spaniards, though it was a well-known fact that she belonged to English merchants. Before he entered upon his new adventures, he married a young woman of about sixteen years of age, the governor himself attending the ceremony. It was reported that this was only his fourteenth wife, about twelve of whom were yet alive; and though this woman was young and amiable, he behaved towards her in a manner so brutal, that it was shocking to all decency and propriety, even among his abandoned crew of pirates.

In his first voyage, Black Beard directed his course to the Bermudas, and meeting with two or three English vessels, emptied them of their stores and other necessaries, and allowed them to proceed. He also met with two French vessels bound for Martinique, the one light, and the other laden with sugar and cocoa: he put the men on board the latter into the former, and allowed her to depart. He brought the freighted vessel into North Carolina, where the governor and Black Beard shared the prizes. Nor did their audacity and villany stop here. Teach and some of his abandoned crew waited upon his excellency, and swore that they had seized the French ship at sea, without a soul on board; therefore a court was called, and she was condemned, the honorable governor received sixty hogsheads of sugar for his share, his secretary twenty, and the pirates the remainder. But as guilt always inspires suspicion, Teach was afraid that some one might arrive in the harbor who might detect the roguery: therefore, upon pretence that she was leaky, and might sink, and so stop up the entrance to the harbor where she lay, they obtained the governor's liberty to drag her into the river, where she was set on fire, and when burnt down to the water, her bottom was sunk, that so she might never rise in judgment against the governor and his confederates.

The crews of Black Beard's and Vane's vessels carousing on the coast of Carolina

**The crews of Black Beard's and Vane's vessels carousing on the coast of Carolina.**

Black Beard now being in the province of Friendship, passed several months in the river, giving and receiving visits from the planters; while he traded with the vessels which came to that river, sometimes in the way of lawful commerce, and sometimes in his own way. When he chose to appear the honest man, he made fair purchases on equal barter; but when this did not suit his necessities, or his humor, he would rob at pleasure, and leave them to seek their redress from the governor; and the better to cover his intrigues with his excellency, he would sometimes outbrave him to his face, and administer to him a share of that contempt and insolence which he so liberally bestowed upon the rest of the inhabitants of the province.

But there are limits to human insolence and depravity. The captains of the vessels who frequented that river, and had been so often harrassed and plundered by Black Beard, secretly consulted with some of the planters what measures to pursue, in order to banish such an infamous miscreant from their coasts, and to bring him to deserved punishment. Convinced from long experience, that the governor himself, to whom it belonged, would give no redress, they represented the matter to the governor of Virginia, and entreated that an armed force might be sent from the men-of-war lying there, either to take or to destroy those pirates who infested their coast.

Upon this representation, the Governor of Virginia consulted with the captains of the two men-of-war as to the best measures to be adopted. It was resolved that the governor should hire two small vessels, which could pursue Bleak Beard into all his inlets and creeks; that they should be manned from the men-of-war, and the command given to Lieutenant Maynard, an experienced and resolute officer. When all was ready for his departure, the governor called an assembly, in which it was resolved to issue a proclamation, offering a great reward to any who, within a year, should take or destroy any pirate.

Upon the 17th of November, 1717, Maynard left James's river in quest of Black Beard, and on the evening of the 21st came in sight of the pirate. This expedition was fitted out with all possible expedition and secrecy, no boat being permitted to pass that might convey any intelligence, while care was taken to discover where the pirates were lurking. His excellency the governor of Bermuda, and his secretary, however, having obtained information of the intended expedition, the latter wrote a letter to Black Beard, intimating, that he had sent him four of his men, who were all he could meet within or about town, and so bade him be on his guard. These men were sent from Bath-town to the place where Black Beard lay, about the distance of twenty leagues.

The hardened and infatuated pirate, having been often deceived by false intelligence, was the less attentive to this information, nor was he convinced of its accuracy until he saw the sloops sent to apprehend him. Though he had then only twenty men on board, he prepared to give battle. Lieutenant Maynard arrived with his sloops in the evening, and anchored, as he could not venture, under cloud of night, to go into the place where Black Beard lay. The latter spent the night in drinking with the master of a trading-vessel, with the same indifference as if no danger had been near. Nay, such was the desperate wickedness of this villain, that, it is reported, during the carousals of that night, one of his men asked him, "In case any thing should happen to him during the engagement with the two sloops which were waiting to attack him in the morning, whether his wife knew where he had buried his money?" when he impiously replied, "That nobody but himself and the devil knew where it was, and the longest liver should take all."

In the morning Maynard weighed, and sent his boat to sound, which coming near the pirate, received her fire. Maynard then hoisted royal colors, and made directly towards Black Beard with every sail and oar. In a little time the pirate ran aground, and so also did the king's vessels. Maynard lightened his vessel of the ballast and water, and made towards Black Beard. Upon this he hailed him in his own rude style, "D–n you for villains, who are you, and from whence come you?" The lieutenant answered, "You may see from our colors we are no pirates." Black Beard bade him send his boat on board, that he might see who he was. But Maynard replied, "I cannot spare my boat, but I will come on board of you as soon as I can with my sloop." Upon this Black Beard took a glass of liquor and drank to him, saying, "I'll give no quarter nor take any from you." Maynard replied, "He expected no quarter from him, nor should he give him any."

During this dialogue the pirate's ship floated, and the sloops were rowing with all expedition towards him. As she came near, the pirate fired a broadside, charged with all manner of small shot, which killed or wounded twenty men. Black Beard's ship in a little after fell broadside to the shore; one of the sloops called the Ranger, also fell astern. But Maynard finding that his own sloop had way, and would soon be on board of Teach, ordered all his men down, while himself and the man at the helm, who he commanded to lie concealed, were the only persons who remained on deck. He at the same time desired them to take their pistols, cutlasses, and swords, and be ready for action upon his call, and, for greater expedition, two ladders were placed in the hatchway. When the king's sloop boarded, the pirate's case-boxes, filled with powder, small shot, slugs, and pieces of lead and iron, with a quick-match in the mouth of them, were thrown into Maynard's sloop. Fortunately, however, the men being in the hold, they did small injury on the present occasion, though they are usually very destructive. Black Beard seeing few or no hands upon deck, cried to his men that they were all knocked on the head except three or four; "and therefore," said he, "let us jump on board, and cut to pieces those that are alive."

Death of Black Beard.

**Death of Black Beard.**

Upon this, during the smoke occasioned by one of these case-boxes, Black Beard, with fourteen of his men, entered, and were not perceived until the smoke was dispelled. The signal was given to Maynard's men, who rushed up in an instant. Black Beard and the lieutenant exchange shots, and the pirate was wounded; they then engaged sword in hand, until the sword of the lieutenant broke, but fortunately one of his men at that instant gave Black Beard a terrible wound in the neck and throat. The most desperate and bloody conflict ensued:–Maynard with twelve men, and Black Beard with fourteen. The sea was dyed with blood all around the vessel, and uncommon bravery was displayed upon both sides. Though the pirate was wounded by the first shot from Maynard, though he had received twenty cuts, and as many shots, he fought with desperate valor; but at length, when in the act of cocking his pistol, fell down dead. By this time eight of his men had fallen, and the rest being wounded, cried out for quarter, which was granted, as the ringleader was slain. The other sloop also attacked the men who remained in the pirate vessels, until they also cried out for quarter. And such was the desperation of Black Beard, that, having small hope of escaping, he had placed a negro with a match at the gunpowder door, to blow up the ship the moment that he should have been boarded by the king's men, in order to involve the whole in general ruin. That destructive broadside at the commencement of the action, which at first appeared so unlucky, was, however, the means of their preservation from the intended destruction.

Maynard severed the pirate's head from his body, suspended it upon his bowsprit-end, and sailed to Bath-town, to obtain medical aid for his wounded men. In the pirate sloop several letters and papers were found, which Black Beard would certainly have destroyed previous to the engagement, had he not determined to blow her up upon his being taken, which disclosed the whole villainy between the honorable governor of Bermuda and his honest secretary on the one hand, and the notorious pirate on the other, who had now suffered the just punishment of his crimes.

Black Beard's Head on the end of the Bowsprit

**Black Beard's Head on the end of the Bowsprit.**

Scarcely was Maynard returned to Bath-town, when he boldly went and made free with the sixty hogsheads of sugar in the possession of the governor, and the twenty in that of his secretary.

After his men had been healed at Bath-town, the lieutenant proceeded to Virginia, with the head of Black Beard still suspended on his bowsprit-end, as a trophy of his victory, to the great joy of all the inhabitants. The prisoners were tried, condemned, and executed; and thus all the crew of that infernal miscreant, Black Beard, were destroyed, except two. One of these was taken out of a trading-vessel, only the day before the engagement, in which he received no less than seventy wounds, of all which he was cured. The other was Israel Hands, who was master of the Queen Anne's Revenge; he was taken at Bath-town, being wounded in one of Black Beard's savage humors. One night Black Beard, drinking in his cabin with Hands, the pilot, and another man, without any pretence, took a small pair of pistols, and cocked them under the table; which being perceived by the man, he went on deck, leaving the captain, Hands, and the pilot together. When his pistols were prepared, he extinguished the candle, crossed his arms, and fired at his company. The one pistol did no execution, but the other wounded Hands in the knee. Interrogated concerning the meaning of this, he answered with an imprecation, "That if he did not now and then kill one of them, they would forget who he was." Hands was eventually tried and condemned, but as he was about to be executed, a vessel arrived with a proclamation prolonging the time of his Majesty's pardon, which Hands pleading, he was saved from a violent and shameful death.

In the commonwealth of pirates, he who goes the greatest length of wickedness, is looked upon with a kind of envy amongst them, as a person of a most extraordinary gallantry; he is therefore entitled to be distinguished by some post, and, if such a one has but courage, he must certainly be a great man. The hero of whom we are writing was thoroughly accomplished in this way, and some of his frolics of wickedness were as extravagant as if he aimed at making his men believe he was a devil incarnate. Being one day at sea, and a little flushed with drink; "Come," said he, "let us make a hell of our own, and try how long we can bear it." Accordingly he, with two or three others, went down into the hold, and closing up all the hatches, filled several pots full of brimstone, and other combustible matter; they then set it on fire, and so continued till they were almost suffocated, when some of the men cried out for air; at length he opened the hatches, not a little pleased that he had held out the longest.

Those of his crew who were taken alive, told a story which may appear a little incredible. That once, upon a cruise, they found out that they had a man on board more than their crew; such a one was seen several days amongst them, sometimes below, and sometimes upon deck, yet no man in the ship could give any account who he was, or from whence he came; but that he disappeared a little before they were cast away in their great ship, and, it seems, they verily believed it was the devil.

One would think these things should have induced them to reform their lives; but being so many reprobates together, they encouraged and spirited one another up in their wickedness, to which a continual course of drinking did not a little contribute. In Black Beard's journal, which was taken, there were several memoranda of the following nature, all written with his own hand.–"Such a day, rum all out;–our company somewhat sober;–a d–d confusion amongst us!–rogues a plotting;–great talk of separation. So I looked sharp for a prize;–such a day took one, with a great deal of liquor on board; so kept the company hot, d–d hot, then all things went well again."

We shall close the narrative of this extraordinary man's life by an account of the cause why he was denominated Black Beard. He derived this name from his long black beard, which, like a frightful meteor, covered his whole face, and terrified all America more than any comet that had ever appeared. He was accustomed to twist it with ribbon in small quantities, and turn them about his ears. In time of action he wore a sling over his shoulders with three brace of pistols. He stuck lighted matches under his hat, which appeared on both sides of his face and eyes, naturally fierce and wild, made him such a figure that the human imagination cannot form a conception of a fury more terrible and alarming; and if he had the appearance and look of a fury, his actions corresponded with that character.

## THE EXPLOITS, ARREST, AND EXECUTION OF CAPTAIN CHARLES VANE.

Charles Vane was one of those who stole away the silver which the Spaniards had fished up from the wrecks of the galleons in the Gulf of Florida, and was at Providence when governor Rogers arrived there with two men-of-war.

All the pirates who were then found at this colony of rogues, submitted and received certificates of their pardon, except Captain Vane and his crew; who, as soon as they saw the men-of-war enter, slipped their cable, set fire to a prize they had in the harbor, sailed out with their piratical colors flying, and fired at one of the men-of-war, as they went off from the coast.

Two days after, they met with a sloop belonging to Barbadoes, which they took, and kept the vessel for their own use, putting aboard five and twenty hands, with one Yeates the commander. In a day or two they fell in with a small interloping trader, with a quantity of Spanish pieces of eight aboard, bound for Providence, which they also took along with them. With these two sloops, Vane went to a small island and cleaned; where he shared the booty, and spent some time in a riotous manner.

About the latter end of May 1718, Vane and his crew sailed, and being in want of provisions, they beat up for the Windward Islands. In the way they met with a Spanish sloop, bound from Porto Rico to the Havana, which they burnt, stowed the Spaniards into a boat, and left them to get to the island by the blaze of their vessel. Steering between St. Christopher's and Anguilla, they fell in with a brigantine and a sloop, freighted with such cargo as they wanted; from whom they got provisions for sea-store.

Sometime after this, standing to the northward, in the track the old English ships take in their voyage to the American colonies, they took several ships and vessels, which they plundered of what they thought fit, and then let them pass.

About the latter end of August, with his consort Yeates, came off South Carolina, and took a ship belonging to Ipswich, laden with logwood. This was thought convenient enough for their own business, and therefore they ordered their prisoners to work, and threw all the lading overboard; but when they had more than half cleared the ship, the whim changed, and they would not have her; so Coggershall, the captain of the captured vessel, had his ship again, and he was suffered to pursue his voyage home. In this voyage the pirates took several ships and vessels, particularly a sloop from Barbadoes, a small ship from Antigua, a sloop belonging to Curaçoa, and a large brigantine from Guinea, with upwards of ninety negroes aboard. The pirates plundered them all and let them go, putting the negroes out of the brigantine aboard Yeates' vessel.

Captain Vane always treated his consort with very little respect, and assumed a superiority over him and his crew, regarding the vessel but as a tender to his own: this gave them disgust; for they thought themselves as good pirates, and as great rogues as the best of them; so they caballed together, and resolved, the first opportunity, to leave the company, and accept of his majesty's pardon, or set up for themselves; either of which they thought more honorable than to be the servants to Vane: the putting aboard so many negroes, where there were so few hands to take care of them, aggravated the matter, though they thought fit to conceal or stifle their resentment at that time.

In a day or two, the pirates lying off at anchor, Yeates in the evening slipped his cable, and put his vessel under sail, standing into the shore; which when Vane saw, he was highly provoked, and got his sloop under sail to chase his consort. Vane's brigantine sailing best, he gained ground of Yeates, and would certainly have come up with them, had he had a little longer run; but just as he got over the bar, when Vane came within gun-shot of him, he fired a broadside at his old friend, and so took his leave.

Yeates came into North Eddisto river, about ten leagues to the southward of Charleston, and sent an express to the governor, to know if he and his comrades might have the benefit of his majesty's pardon; promising that, if they might, they would surrender themselves to his mercy, with the sloops and negroes. Their request being granted, they all came up, and received certificates; and Captain Thompson, from whom the negroes were taken, had them all restored to him, for the use of his owners.

Vane cruised some time off the bar, in hopes to catch Yeates at his coming out again, but therein he was disappointed; however, he there took two ships from Charleston, which were bound home to England. It happened just at this time, that two sloops well manned and armed, were equipped to go after a pirate, which the governor of South Carolina was informed lay then in Cape Fear river cleaning: but Colonel Rhet, who commanded the sloops, meeting with one of the ships that Vane had plundered, going back over the bar for such necessaries as had been taken from her, and she giving the Colonel an account of being taken by the pirate Vane, and also, that some of her men, while they were prisoners on board of him, had heard the pirates say they should clean in one of the rivers to the southward, he altered his first design, and instead of standing to the northward, in pursuit of the pirate in Cape Fear river, turned to the southward after Vane, who had ordered such reports to be given out, on purpose to put any force that should come after him upon a wrong scent; for he stood away to the northward, so that the pursuit proved to be of no effect. Colonel Rhet's speaking with this ship was the most unlucky thing that could have happened, because it turned him out of the road which, in all probability, would have brought him into the company of Vane, as well as of the pirate he went after, and so they might have been both destroyed; whereas, by the Colonel's going a different way, he not only lost the opportunity of meeting with one, but if the other had not been infatuated, and lain six weeks together at Cape Fear, he would have missed him likewise; however, the Colonel having searched the rivers and inlets, as directed, for several days without success, at length sailed in prosecution of his first design, and met with the pirate accordingly, whom he fought and took.

Captain Vane went into an inlet to the northward, where he met with Captain Teach, otherwise Black Beard, whom he saluted (when he found who he was) with his great guns loaded with shot: it being the custom among pirates when they meet, to do so, though they are wide of one another: Black Beard answered the salute in the same manner, and mutual civilities passed between them some days, when, about the beginning of October, Vane took leave, and sailed farther to the northward.

On the 23d of October, off Long Island, he took a small brigantine bound from Jamaica to Salem in New England, besides a little sloop: they rifled the brigantine, and sent her away. From thence they resolved on a cruise between Cape Meise and Cape Nicholas, where they spent some time without seeing or speaking with any vessel, till the latter end of November; they then fell in with a ship, which it was expected would have struck as soon as their black colors were hoisted; but instead of this she discharged a broadside upon the pirate, and hoisted French colors, which showed her to be a French man-of-war. Vane desired to have nothing more to say to her, but trimmed his sails, and stood away from the Frenchman; however, Monsieur having a mind to be better informed who he was, set all his sails and crowded after him. During this chase the pirates were divided in their resolution what to do. Vane, the captain, was for making off as fast as he could, alleging that the man-of-war was too strong for them to cope with; but one John Rackam, their quarter-master, and who was a kind of check upon the captain, rose up in defence of a contrary opinion, saying, "that though she had more guns, and a greater weight of metal, they might board her, and then the best boys would carry the day." Rackam was well seconded, and the majority was for boarding; but Vane urged, "that it was too rash and desperate an enterprise, the man-of-war appearing to be twice their force, and that their brigantine might be sunk by her before they could reach to board her." The mate, one Robert Deal, was of Vane's opinion, as were about fifteen more, and all the rest joined with Rackam the quarter-master. At length the captain made use of his power to determine this dispute, which in these cases is absolute and uncontrollable, by their own laws, viz., the captain's absolute right of determining in all questions concerning fighting, chasing, or being chased; in all other matters whatsoever the captain being governed by a majority; so the brigantine having the heels, as they term it, of the Frenchman, she came clear off.

But the next day, the captain's conduct was obliged to stand the test of a vote, and a resolution passed against his honor and dignity, which branded him with the name of coward, deposed him from the command, and turned him out of the company with marks of infamy; and with him went all those who did not vote for boarding the French man-of-war. They had with them a small sloop that had been taken by them some time before, which they gave to Vane and the discarded members; and that they might be in a condition to provide for themselves by their own honest endeavors, they let them have a sufficient quantity of provisions and ammunition.

John Rackam was voted captain of the brigantine in Vane's room, and he proceeded towards the Carribbee Islands, where we must leave him, till we have finished our history of Charles Vane.

The sloop sailed for the bay of Honduras, and Vane and his crew put her in as good a condition as they could by the way, that they might follow their old trade. They cruised two or three days off the northwest part of Jamaica, and took a sloop and two perriaguas, all the men of which entered with them: the sloop they kept, and Robert Deal was appointed captain.

On the 16th of December, the two sloops came into the bay, where they found only one vessel at anchor. She was called the Pearl of Jamaica, and got under sail at the sight of them; but the pirate sloops coming near Rowland, and showing no colors, he gave them a gun or two, whereupon they hoisted the black flag, and fired three guns each at the Pearl. She struck, and the pirates took possession, and carried her away to a small island called Barnacho, where they cleaned. By the way they met with a sloop from Jamaica, as she was going down to the bay, which they also took.

In February, Vane sailed from Barnacho, for a cruise; but, some days after he was out, a violent tornado overtook him, which separated him from his consort, and, after two days' distress, threw his sloop upon a small uninhabited island, near the bay of Honduras, where she staved to pieces, and most of her men were drowned: Vane himself was saved, but reduced to great straits for want of necessaries, having no opportunity to get any thing from the wreck. He lived here some weeks, and was supported chiefly by fishermen, who frequented the island with small crafts from the main, to catch turtles and other fish.

Vane arrested by Captain Holford

**Vane arrested by Captain Holford.**

While Vane was upon this island, a ship put in there from Jamaica for water, the captain of which, one Holford, an old buccaneer, happened to be Vane's acquaintance. He thought this a good opportunity to get off, and accordingly applied to his old friend: but Holford absolutely refused him, saying to him, "Charles, I shan't trust you aboard my ship, unless I carry you as a prisoner, for I shall have you caballing with my men, knocking me on the head, and running away with my ship pirating." Vane made all the protestations of honor in the world to him; but, it seems, Captain Holford was too intimately acquainted with him, to repose any confidence at all in his words or oaths. He told him, "He might easily find a way to get off, if he had a mind to it:–I am going down the bay," said he, "and shall return hither in about a month, and if I find you upon the island when I come back, I'll carry you to Jamaica, and there hang you." "How can I get away?" answered Vane. "Are there not fishermen's dories upon the beach? Can't you take one of them?" replied Holford. "What!" said Vane, "would you have me steal a dory then?" "Do you make it a matter of conscience," replied Holford, "to steal a dory, when you have been a common robber and pirate, stealing ships and cargoes, and plundering all mankind that fell in your way! Stay here if you are so squeamish?" and he left him to consider of the matter.

After Captain Holford's departure, another ship put into the same island, in her way home, for water; none of the company knowing Vane, he easily passed for another man, and so was shipped for the voyage. One would be apt to think that Vane was now pretty safe, and likely to escape the fate which his crimes had merited; but here a cross accident happened that ruined all. Holford returning from the bay, was met by this ship, and the captains being very well acquainted with each other, Holford was invited to dine aboard, which he did. As he passed along to the cabin, he chanced to cast his eye down into the hold, and there saw Charles Vane at work: he immediately spoke to the captain, saying, "Do you know whom you have got aboard there?" "Why," said he, "I have shipped a man at such an island, who was cast away in a trading sloop, and he seems to be a brisk hand." "I tell you," replied Captain Holford, "it is Vane the notorious pirate." "If it be he," cried the other, "I won't keep him." "Why then," said Holford, "I'll send and take him aboard, and surrender him at Jamaica." This being agreed upon, Captain Holford, as soon as he returned to his ship, sent his boat with his mate, armed, who coming to Vane, showed him a pistol, and told him he was his prisoner. No man daring to make opposition, he was brought aboard and put into irons; and when Captain Holford arrived at Jamaica, he delivered up his old acquaintance to justice, at which place he was tried, convicted, and executed, as was some time before, Vane's consort, Robert Deal, who was brought thither by one of the men-of-war. It is clear from this how little ancient friendship will avail a great villain, when he is deprived of the power that had before supported and rendered him formidable.

Page 372 Illustration

**THE WEST INDIA PIRATES**

Containing Accounts of their Atrocities, Manners of Living, c., with proceedings of the Squadron under Commodore Porter in those seas, the victory and death of Lieutenant Allen, the interesting Narrative of Captain Lincoln, c.

Those innumerable groups of islands, keys and sandbanks, known as the West-Indies, are peculiarly adapted from their locality and formation, to be a favorite resort for pirates; many of them are composed of coral rocks, on which a few cocoa trees raise their lofty heads; where there is sufficient earth for vegetation between the interstices of the rocks, stunted brushwood grows. But a chief peculiarity of some of the islands, and which renders them suitable to those who frequent them as pirates, are the numerous caves with which the rocks are perforated; some of them are above high-water mark, but the majority with the sea water flowing in and out of them, in some cases merely rushing in at high-water filling deep pools, which are detached from each other when the tide recedes, in others with a sufficient depth of water to allow a large boat to float in. It is hardly necessary to observe how convenient the higher and dry caves are as receptacles for articles which are intended to be concealed, until an opportunity occurs to dispose of them. The Bahamas, themselves are a singular group of isles, reefs and quays; consisting of several hundred in number, and were the chief resort of pirates in old times, but now they are all rooted from them; they are low and not elevated, and are more than 600 miles in extent, cut up into numerous intricate passages and channels, full of sunken rocks and coral reefs. They afforded a sure retreat to desperadoes. Other islands are full of mountain fastnesses, where all pursuit can be eluded. Many of the low shores are skirted, and the islands covered by the mangrove, a singular tree, shooting fresh roots as it grows, which, when the tree is at its full age, may be found six or eight feet from the ground, to which the shoots gradually tend in regular succession; the leaf is very thick and stiff and about eight inches long and nine wide, the interval between the roots offer secure hiding places for those who are suddenly pursued. Another circumstance assists the pirate when pursued.–As the islands belong to several different nations, when pursued from one island he can pass to that under the jurisdiction of another power. And as permission must be got by those in pursuit of him, from the authorities of the island to land and take him, he thus gains time to secrete himself. A tropical climate is suited to a roving life, and liquor as well as dissolute women being in great abundance, to gratify him during his hours of relaxation, makes this a congenial region for the lawless.

A Piratical Vessel destroying a Merchant Ship

**A Piratical Vessel destroying a Merchant Ship.**

The crews of pirate vessels in these seas are chiefly composed of Spaniards, Portuguese, French, Mulattoes, Negroes, and a few natives of other countries. The island of Cuba is the great nest of pirates at the present day, and at the Havana, piracy is as much tolerated as any other profession. As the piracies committed in these seas, during a single year, have amounted to more than fifty, we shall give only a few accounts of the most interesting.

In November 1821, the brig Cobbessecontee, Captain Jackson, sailed from Havana, on the morning of the 8th for Boston, and on the evening of the same day, about four miles from the Moro, was brought to by a piratical sloop containing about 30 men. A boat from her, with 10 men, came alongside, and soon after they got on board commenced plundering. They took nearly all the clothing from the captain and mate–all the cooking utensils and spare rigging–unrove part of the running rigging–cut the small cable–broke the compasses–cut the mast's coats to pieces–took from the captain his watch and four boxes cigars–and from the cargo three bales cochineal and six boxes cigars. They beat the mate unmercifully, and hung him up by the neck under the maintop. They also beat the captain severely–broke a large broad sword across his back, and ran a long knife through his thigh, so that he almost bled to death. Captain Jackson saw the sloop at Regla the day before.

Captain Jackson informs us, and we have also been informed by other persons from the Havana, that this system of piracy is openly countenanced by some of the inhabitants of that place–who say that it is a retaliation on the Americans for interfering against the Slave Trade.

About this time the ship Liverpool Packet, Ricker, of Portsmouth, N.H., was boarded off Cape St. Antonio, Cuba, by two piratical schooners; two barges containing thirty or forty men, robbed the vessel of every thing movable, even of her *flags*, rigging, and a boat which happened to be afloat, having a boy in it, which belonged to the ship. They held a consultation whether they should murder the crew, as they had done before, or not–in the mean time taking the ship into anchoring ground. On bringing her to anchor, the crew saw a brig close alongside, burnt to the water's edge, and three dead bodies floating near her. The pirates said they had burnt the brig the day before, and *murdered all the crew!*–and intended doing the same with them. They said "look at the turtles (meaning the dead bodies) you will soon be the same." They said the vessel was a Baltimore brig, which they had robbed and burnt, and murdered the crew as before stated, of which they had little doubt. Captain Ricker was most shockingly bruised by them. The mate was hung till he was supposed to be dead, but came to, and is now alive. They told the captain that they belonged in Regla, and should kill them all to prevent discovery.

In 1822, the United States had several cruisers among the West-India islands, to keep the pirates in check. Much good was done but still many vessels were robbed and destroyed, together with their crews. This year the brave Lieutenant Allen fell by the hand of pirates; he was in the United States schooner Alligator, and receiving intelligence at Matanzas, that several vessels which had sailed from that port, had been taken by the pirates, and were then in the bay of Lejuapo. He hastened to their assistance. He arrived just in time to save five sail of vessels which he found in possession of a gang of pirates, 300 strong, established in the bay of Lejuapo, about 15 leagues east of this. He fell, pierced by two musket balls, in the van of a division of boats, attacking their principal vessel, a fine schooner of about eighty tons, with a long eighteen pounder on a pivot, and four smaller guns, *with the bloody flag nailed to the mast.* Himself, Captain Freeman of Marines, and twelve men, were in the boat, much in advance of his other boats, and even took possession of the schooner, after a desperate resistance, which nothing but a bravery almost too daring could have overcome. The pirates, all but one, escaped by taking to their boats and jumping overboard, before the Alligator's boat reached them. Two other schooners escaped by the use of their oars, the wind being light.

Captain Allen survived about four hours, during which his conversation evinced a composure and firmness of mind, and correctness of feeling, as honorable to his character, and more consoling to his friends, than even the dauntless bravery he before exhibited.

The surgeon of the Alligator in a letter to a friend, says, "He continued giving orders and conversing with Mr. Dale and the rest of us, until a few minutes before his death, with a degree of cheerfulness that was little to be expected from a man in his condition. He said he wished his relatives and his country to know that he had fought well, and added that he died in peace and good will towards all the world, and hoped for his reward in the next."

Lieutenant Allen had but few equals in the service. He was ardently devoted to the interest of his country, was brave, intelligent, and accomplished in his profession. He displayed, living and dying, a magnanimity that sheds lustre on his relatives, his friends, and his country.

Horrid Piracy and Murder by a Mexican privateer.

**Horrid Piracy and Murder by a Mexican "privateer."**

About this time Captain Lincoln fell into the hands of the pirates, and as his treatment shows the peculiar habits and practices of these wretches, we insert the very interesting narrative of the captain.

The schooner Exertion, Captain Lincoln, sailed from Boston, bound for Trinidad de Cuba, Nov. 13th, 1821, with the following crew; Joshua Bracket, mate; David Warren, cook; and Thomas Young, Francis De Suze, and George Reed, seamen.

The cargo consisted of flour, beef, pork, lard, butter, fish, beans, onions, potatoes, apples, hams, furniture, sugar box shooks, c., invoiced at about eight thousand dollars. Nothing remarkable occurred during the passage, except much bad weather, until my capture, which was as follows:–

Monday, December 17th, 1821, commenced with fine breezes from the eastward. At daybreak saw some of the islands northward of Cape Cruz, called Keys–stood along northwest; every thing now seemed favorable for a happy termination of our voyage. At 3 o'clock, P.M., saw a sail coming round one of the Keys, into a channel called Boca de Cavolone by the chart, nearly in latitude 20° 55' north, longitude 79° 55' west, she made directly for us with all sails set, sweeps on both sides (the wind being light) and was soon near enough for us to discover about forty men on her deck, armed with muskets, blunderbusses, cutlasses, long knives, dirks, c., two carronades, one a twelve, the other a six pounder; she was a schooner, wearing the Patriot flag (blue, white and blue) of the Republic of Mexico. I thought it not prudent to resist them, should they be pirates, with a crew of seven men, and only five muskets; accordingly ordered the arms and ammunition to be immediately stowed away in as secret a place as possible, and suffer her to speak us, hoping and believing that a republican flag indicated both honor and friendship from those who wore it, and which we might expect even from Spaniards. But how great was my astonishment, when the schooner having approached very near us, hailed in English, and ordered me to heave my boat out immediately and come on board of her with my papers.–Accordingly my boat was hove out, but filled before I could get into her.–I was then ordered to tack ship and lay by for the pirates' boat to board me; which was done by Bolidar, their first lieutenant, with six or eight Spaniards armed with as many of the before mentioned weapons as they could well sling about their bodies. They drove me into the boat, and two of them rowed me to their privateer (as they called their vessel), where I shook hands with their commander, Captain Jonnia, a Spaniard, who before looking at my papers, ordered

Bolidar, his lieutenant, to follow the Mexican in, back of the Key they had left, which was done. At 6 o'clock, P.M., the Exertion was anchored in eleven feet water, near this vessel, and an island, which they called Twelve League Key (called by the chart Key Largo), about thirty or thirty-five leagues from Trinidad. After this strange conduct they began examining my papers by a Scotchman who went by the name of Nickola, their sailing master.–He spoke good English, had a countenance rather pleasing, although his beard and mustachios had a frightful appearance–his face, apparently full of anxiety, indicated something in my favor; he gave me my papers, saying "take good care of them, for I am afraid you have fallen into bad hands." The pirates' boat was then sent to the Exertion with more men and arms; a part of them left on board her; the rest returning with three of my crew to their vessel; viz., Thomas Young, Thomas Goodall, and George Reed–they treated them with something to drink, and offered them equal shares with themselves, and some money, if they would enlist, but they could not prevail on them. I then requested permission to go on board my vessel which was granted, and further requested Nickola should go with me, but was refused by the captain, who vociferated in a harsh manner, "No, No, No." accompanied with a heavy stamp upon the deck. When I got on board, I was invited below by Bolidar, where I found they had emptied the case of liquors, and broken a cheese to pieces and crumbled it on the table and cabin floor; the pirates, elated with their prize (as they called it), had drank so much as to make them desperately abusive. I was permitted to lie down in my berth; but, reader, if you have ever been awakened by a gang of armed, desperadoes, who have taken possession of your habitation in the midnight hour, you can imagine my feelings.–Sleep was a stranger to me, and anxiety was my guest. Bolidar, however, pretended friendship, and flattered me with the prospect of being soon set at liberty. But I found him, as I suspected, a consummate hypocrite; indeed, his very looks indicated it. He was a stout and well built man, of a dark, swarthy complexion, with keen, ferocious eyes, huge whiskers, and beard under his chin and on his lips, four or five inches long; he was a Portuguese by birth, but had become a naturalized Frenchman–had a wife, if not children (as I was told) in France, and was well known there as commander of a first rate privateer. His appearance was truly terrific; he could talk some English, and had a most lion-like voice.

Tuesday, 18th.–Early this morning the captain of the pirates came on board the Exertion; took a look at the cabin stores, and cargo in the state rooms, and then ordered me back with him to his vessel, where he, with his crew, held a consultation for some time respecting the cargo. After which, the interpreter, Nickola, told me that "the captain had, or pretended to have, a commission under General Traspelascus, commander-in-chief of the republic of Mexico, authorizing him to take all cargoes whatever of provisions, bound to any royalist Spanish port–that my cargo being bound to an enemy's port, must be condemned; but that the vessel should be given up and be put into a fair channel for Trinidad, where I was bound." I requested him to examine the papers thoroughly, and perhaps he would be convinced to the contrary, and told him my cargo was all American property taken in at Boston, and consigned to an American gentleman, agent at Trinidad. But the captain would not take the trouble, but ordered both vessels under way immediately, and commenced beating up amongst the Keys through most of the day, the wind being very light. They now sent their boats on board the Exertion for stores, and commenced plundering her of bread, butter, lard, onions, potatoes, fish, beans, c., took up some sugar box shocks that were on deck, and found the barrels of apples; selected the best of them and threw the rest overboard. They inquired for spirits, wine, cider, c. and were told "they had already taken all that was on board." But not satisfied they proceeded to search the state rooms and forcastle, ripped up the floor of the later and found some boxes of bottled cider, which they carried to their vessel, gave three cheers, in an exulting manner to me, and then began drinking it with such freedom, that a violent quarrel arose between officers and men, which came very near ending in bloodshed. I was accused of falsehood, for saying they had got all the liquors that were on board, and I thought they had; the truth was, I never had any bill of lading of the cider, and consequently had no recollection of its being on board; yet it served them as an excuse for being insolent. In the evening peace was restored and they sung songs. I was suffered to go below for the night, and they placed a guard over me, stationed at the companion way.

Wednesday, 19th, commenced with moderate easterly winds, beating towards the northeast, the pirate's boats frequently going on board the Exertion for potatoes, fish, beans, butter, c. which were used with great waste and extravagance. They gave me food and drink, but of bad quality, more particularly the victuals, which was wretchedly cooked. The place assigned me to eat was covered with dirt and vermin. It appeared that their great object was to hurt my feelings with threats and observations, and to make my situation as unpleasant as circumstances would admit. We came to anchor near a Key, called by them Brigantine, where myself and mate were permitted to go on shore, but were guarded by several armed pirates. I soon returned to the Mexican and my mate to the Exertion, with George Reed, one of my crew; the other two being kept on board the Mexican. In the course of this day I had considerable conversation with Nickola, who appeared well disposed towards me. He lamented most deeply his own situation, for he was one of those men, whose early good impressions were not entirely effaced, although confederated with guilt. He told me "those who had taken me were no better than pirates, and their end would be the halter; but," he added, with peculiar emotion, "I will never be hung as a pirate," showing me a bottle of laudanum which he had found in my medicine chest, saying, "If we are taken, that shall cheat the hangman, before we are condemned." I endeavored to get it from him, but did not succeed. I then asked him how he came to be in such company, as he appeared to be dissatisfied. He stated, that he was at New Orleans last summer, out of employment, and became acquainted with one Captain August Orgamar, a Frenchman, who had bought a small schooner of about fifteen tons, and was going down to the bay of Mexico to get a commission under General Traspelascus, in order to go a privateering under the patriot flag. Capt. Orgamar made him liberal offers respecting shares, and promised him a sailing master's berth, which he accepted and embarked on board the schooner, without sufficiently reflecting on the danger of such an undertaking. Soon after she sailed from Mexico, where they got a commission, and the vessel was called Mexican. They made up a complement of twenty men, and after rendering the General some little service, in transporting his troops to a place called —- proceeded on a cruise; took some small prizes off Campeachy; afterwards came on the south coast of Cuba, where they took other small prizes, and the one which we were now on board of. By this time the crew were increased to about forty, nearly one half Spaniards, the others Frenchmen and Portuguese. Several of them had sailed out of ports in the United States with American protections; but, I confidently believe, none are natives, especially of the northern states. I was careful in examining the men, being desirous of knowing if any of my countrymen were among this wretched crew; but am satisfied there were none, and my Scotch friend concurred in the opinion. And now, with a new vessel, which was the prize of these plunderers, they sailed up Manganeil bay; previously, however, they fell in with an American schooner, from which they bought four barrels of beef, and paid in tobacco. At the Bay was an English brig belonging to Jamaica, owned by Mr. John Louden of that place. On board of this vessel the Spanish part of the crew commenced their depredations as pirates, although Captain Orgamar and Nickola protested against it, and refused any participation; but they persisted, and like so many ferocious blood-hounds, boarded the brig, plundered the cabin, stores, furniture, captain's trunk, c., took a hogshead of rum, one twelve pound carronade, some rigging and sails. One of them plundered the chest of a sailor, who made some resistance, so that the Spaniard took his cutlass, and beat and wounded him without mercy. Nickola asked him "why he did it?" the fellow answered, "I will let you know," and took up the cook's axe and gave him a cut on the head, which nearly deprived him of life. Then they ordered Captain Orgamar to leave his vessel, allowing him his trunk and turned him ashore, to seek for himself. Nickola begged them to dismiss him with his captain, but no, no, was the answer; for they had no complete navigator but him. After Captain Orgamar was gone, they put in his stead the present brave (or as I should call him cowardly) Captain Jonnia, who headed them in plundering the before mentioned brig, and made Bolidar their first lieutenant, and then proceeded down among those Keys or Islands, where I was captured. This is the amount of what my friend Nickola told me of their history.

Saturday, 22d.–Both vessels under way standing to the eastward, they ran the Exertion aground on a bar, but after throwing overboard most of her deck load of shooks, she floated off; a pilot was sent to her, and she was run into a narrow creek between two keys, where they moored her head and stern along side of the mangrove trees, set down her yards and topmasts, and covered her mast heads and shrouds with bushes to prevent her being seen by vessels which might pass that way. I was then suffered to go on board my own vessel, and found her in a very filthy condition; sails torn, rigging cut to pieces, and every thing in the cabin in waste and confusion. The swarms of moschetoes and sand-flies made it impossible to get any sleep or rest. The pirate's large boat was armed and manned under Bolidar, and sent off with letters to a merchant (as they called him) by the name of Dominico, residing in a town called Principe, on the main island of Cuba. I was told by one of them, who could speak English, that Principe was a very large and populous town, situated at the head of St. Maria, which was about twenty miles northeast from where we lay, and the Keys lying around us were called Cotton Keys.–The captain pressed into his service Francis de Suze, one of my crew, saying that he was one of his countrymen. Francis was very reluctant in going, and said to me, with tears in his eyes, "I shall do nothing but what I am obliged to do, and will not aid in the least to hurt you or the vessel; I am very sorry to leave you." He was immediately put on duty and Thomas Goodall sent back to the Exertion.

Sunday, 23d.–Early this morning a large number of the pirates came on board of the Exertion, threw out the long boat, broke open the hatches, and took out considerable of the cargo, in search of rum, gin, c., still telling me "I had some and they would find it," uttering the most awful profaneness. In the afternoon their boat returned with a perough, having on board the captain, his first lieutenant and seven men of a patriot or piratical vessel that was chased ashore at Cape Cruz by a Spanish armed brig. These seven men made their escape in said boat, and after four days, found our pirates and joined them; the remainder of the crew being killed or taken prisoners.

Monday, 24th.–Their boat was manned and sent to the before-mentioned town.–I was informed by a line from Nickola, that the pirates had a man on board, a native of Principe, who, in the garb of a sailor, was a partner with Dominico, but I could not get sight of him. This lets us a little into the plans by which this atrocious system of piracy has been carried on. Merchants having partners on board of these pirates! thus pirates at sea and robbers on land are associated to destroy the peaceful trader. The willingness exhibited by the seven above-mentioned men, to join our gang of pirates, seems to look like a general understanding among them; and from there being merchants on shore so base as to encourage the plunder and vend the goods, I am persuaded there has been a systematic confederacy on the part of these unprincipled desperadoes, under cover of the patriot flag; and those on land are no better than those on the sea. If the governments to whom they belong know of the atrocities committed (and I have but little doubt they do) they deserve the execration of all mankind.

Thursday, 27th.–A gang of the pirates came and stripped our masts of the green bushes, saying, "she appeared more like a sail than trees"–took one barrel of bread and one of potatoes, using about one of each every day. I understood they were waiting for boats to take the cargo; for the principal merchant had gone to Trinidad.

Sunday, 30th.–The beginning of trouble! This day, which peculiarly reminds Christians of the high duties of compassion and benevolence, was never observed by these pirates. This, of course, we might expect, as they did not often know when the day came, and if they knew it, it was spent in gambling. The old saying among seamen, "no Sunday off soundings," was not thought of; and even this poor plea was not theirs, for they were on soundings and often at anchor.–Early this morning, the merchant, as they called him, came with a large boat for the cargo. I was immediately ordered into the boat with my crew, not allowed any breakfast, and carried about three miles to a small island out of sight of the Exertion, and left there by the side of a little pond of thick, muddy water, which proved to be very brackish, with nothing to eat but a few biscuits. One of the boat's men told us the merchant was afraid of being recognized, and when he had gone the boat would return for us; but we had great reason to apprehend they would deceive us, and therefore passed the day in the utmost anxiety. At night, however, the boats came and took us again on board the Exertion; when, to our surprise and astonishment, we found they had broken open the trunks and chests, and taken all our wearing apparel, not even leaving a shirt or pair of pantaloons, nor sparing a small miniature of my wife which was in my trunk. The little money I and my mate had, with some belonging to the owners, my mate had previously distributed about the cabin in three or four parcels, while I was on board the pirate, for we dare not keep it about us; one parcel in a butter pot they did not discover.–Amidst the hurry with which I was obliged to go to the before-mentioned island, I fortunately snatched by vessel's papers, and hid them in my bosom, which the reader will find was a happy circumstance for me. My writing desk, with papers, accounts, c., all Mr. Lord's letters (the gentlemen to whom my cargo was consigned) and several others were taken and maliciously destroyed. My medicine chest, which I so much wanted, was kept for their own use. What their motive could be to take my papers I could not imagine, except they had hopes of finding bills of lading for some Spaniards, to clear them from piracy. Mr. Bracket had some notes and papers of consequence to him, which shared the same fate. My quadrant, charts, books and bedding were not yet taken, but I found it impossible to hide them, and they were soon gone from my sight.

A Cave in the Caicos group of the West India Islands

**A Cave in the Caicos group of the West India Islands.**

Tuesday, January 1st, 1822–A sad new-year's day to me. Before breakfast orders came for me to cut down the Exertion's railing and bulwarks on one side, for their vessel to heave out by, and clean her bottom. On my hesitating a little they observed with anger, "very well, captain, suppose you no do it quick, we do it for you." Directly afterwards another boat full of armed men came along side; they jumped on deck with swords drawn, and ordered all of us into her immediately; I stepped below, in hopes of getting something which would be of service to us; but the captain hallooed, "Go into the boat directly or I will fire upon you." Thus compelled to obey, we were carried, together with four Spanish prisoners, to a small, low island or key of sand in the shape of a half moon, and partly covered with mangrove trees; which was about one mile from and in sight of my vessel. There they left nine of us, with a little bread, flour, fish, lard, a little coffee and molasses; two or three kegs of water, which was brackish; an old sail for a covering, and a pot and some other articles no way fit to cook in. Leaving us these, which were much less than they appear in the enumeration, they pushed off, saying, "we will come to see you in a day or two." Selecting the best place, we spread the old sail for an awning; but no place was free from flies, moschetoes, snakes, the venomous skinned scorpion, and the more venomous santipee. Sometimes they were found crawling inside of our pantaloons, but fortunately no injury was received. This afternoon the pirates hove their vessel out by the Exertion and cleaned one side, using her paints, oil, c. for that purpose. To see my vessel in that situation and to think of our prospects was a source of the deepest distress. At night we retired to our tent; but having nothing but the cold damp ground for a bed, and the heavy dew of night penetrating the old canvass–the situation of the island being fifty miles from the usual track of friendly vessels, and one hundred and thirty-five from Trinidad–seeing my owner's property so unjustly and wantonly destroyed–considering my condition, the hands at whose mercy I was, and deprived of all hopes, rendered sleep or rest a stranger to me.

Friday, 4th.–Commenced with light winds and hot sun, saw a boat coming from the Exertion, apparently loaded; she passed between two small Keys to northward, supposed to be bound for Cuba. At sunset a boat came and inquired if we wanted anything, but instead of adding to our provisions, took away our molasses, and pushed off. We found one of the Exertion's water casks, and several pieces of plank, which we carefully laid up, in hopes of getting enough to make a raft.

Saturday, 5th.–Pirates again in sight, coming from the eastward; they beat up along side their prize, and commenced loading. In the afternoon Nickola came to us, bringing with him two more prisoners, which they had taken in a small sail boat coming from Trinidad to Manganeil, one a Frenchman, the other a Scotchman, with two Spaniards, who remained on board the pirate, and who afterwards joined them. The back of one of these poor fellows was extremely sore, having just suffered a cruel beating from Bolidar, with the broad side of a cutlass. It appeared, that when the officer asked him "where their money was, and how much," he answered, "he was not certain but believed they had only two ounces of gold"–Bolidar furiously swore he said "ten," and not finding any more, gave him the beating. Nickola now related to me a singular fact; which was, that the Spanish part of the crew were determined to shoot him; that they tied him to the mast, and a man was appointed for the purpose; but Lion, a Frenchman, his particular friend, stepped up and told them, if they shot him they must shoot several more; some of the Spaniards sided with him, and he was released. Nickola told me, the reason for such treatment was, that he continually objected to their conduct towards me, and their opinion if he should escape, they would be discovered, as he declared he would take no prize money. While with us he gave me a letter written in great haste, which contains some particulars respecting the cargo;–as follows:–

*January 4th,* 1822.

Sir,–We arrived here this morning, and before we came to anchor, had five canoes alongside ready to take your cargo, part of which we had in; and as I heard you express a wish to know what they took out of her, to this moment, you may depend upon this account of Jamieson for quality and quantity; if I have the same opportunity you will have an account of the whole. The villain who bought your cargo is from the town of Principe, his name is Dominico, as to that it is all that I can learn; they have taken your charts aboard the schooner Mexican, and I suppose mean to keep them, as the other captain has agreed to act the same infamous part in the tragedy of his life. Your clothes are here on board, but do not let me flatter you that you will get them back; it may be so, and it may not. Perhaps in your old age, when you recline with ease in a corner of your cottage, you will have the goodness to drop a tear of pleasure to the memory of him, whose highest ambition should have been to subscribe himself, though devoted to the gallows, your friend,

Excuse haste. NICKOLA MONACRE.

Sunday, 6th.–The pirates were under way at sunrise, with a full load of the Exertion's cargo, going to Principe again to sell a second freight, which was done readily for cash. I afterwards heard that the flour only fetched five dollars per barrel, when it was worth at Trinidad thirteen; so that the villain who bought my cargo at Principe, made very large profits by it.

Tuesday, 8th.–Early this morning the pirates in sight again, with fore top sail and top gallant sail set; beat up along side of the Exertion and commenced loading; having, as I supposed, sold and discharged her last freight among some of the inhabitants of Cuba. They appeared to load in great haste; and the song, "O he oh," which echoed from one vessel to the other, was distinctly heard by us. How wounding was this to me! How different was this sound from what it would have been, had I been permitted to pass unmolested by these lawless plunderers, and been favored with a safe arrival at the port of my destination, where my cargo would have found an excellent sale. Then would the "O he oh," on its discharging, have been a delightful sound to me. In the afternoon she sailed with the perough in tow, both with a full load, having chairs, which was part of the cargo, slung at her quarters.

Monday, 14th.–They again hove in sight, and beat up as usual, along-side their prize. While passing our solitary island, they laughed at our misery, which was almost insupportable–looking upon us as though we had committed some heinous crime, and they had not sufficiently punished us; they hallooed to us, crying out "Captain, Captain," accompanied with obscene motions and words, with which I shall not blacken these pages–yet I heard no check upon such conduct, nor could I expect it among such a gang, who have no idea of subordination on board, except when in chase of vessels, and even then but very little. My resentment was excited at such a malicious outrage, and I felt a disposition to revenge myself, should fortune ever favor me with an opportunity. It was beyond human nature not to feel and express some indignation at such treatment.–Soon after, Bolidar, with five men, well armed, came to us; he having a blunderbuss, cutlass, a long knife and pair of pistols–but for what purpose did he come? He took me by the hand, saying, "Captain, me speak with you, walk this way." I obeyed, and when at some distance from my fellow prisoners, (his men following) he said, "the captain send me for your *wash*" I pretended not to understand what he meant, and replied, "I have no clothes, nor any soap to wash with–you have taken them all," for I had kept my watch about me, hoping they would not discover it. He demanded it again as before; and was answered, "I have nothing to wash;" this raised his anger, and lifting his blunderbuss, he roared out, "what the d–l you call him that make clock? give it me." I considered it imprudent to contend any longer, and submitted to his unlawful demand. As he was going off, he gave me a small bundle, in which was a pair of linen drawers, sent to me by Nickola, and also the Rev. Mr. Brooks' "Family Prayer Book." This gave me great satisfaction. Soon after, he returned with his captain, who had one arm slung up, yet with as many implements of war, as his diminutive wicked self could conveniently carry; he told me (through an interpreter who was his prisoner.) "that on his cruize he had fallen in with two Spanish privateers, and beat them off; but had three of his men killed, and himself wounded in the arm"–Bolidar turned to me and said, "it is a d–n lie"–which words proved to be correct, for his arm was not wounded, and when I saw him again, which was soon afterwards, he had forgotten to sling it up. He further told me, "after tomorrow you shall go with your vessel, and we will accompany you towards Trinidad." This gave me some new hopes, and why I could not tell. They then left us without rendering any assistance.–This night we got some rest.

Tuesday, 15th. The words "go after tomorrow," were used among our Spanish fellow prisoners, as though that happy tomorrow would never come–in what manner it came will soon be noticed.

Friday, 18th commenced with brighter prospects of liberty than ever. The pirates were employed in setting up our devoted schooner's shrouds, stays, c. My condition now reminded me of the hungry man, chained in one corner of a room, while at another part was a table loaded with delicious food and fruits, the smell and sight of which he was continually to experience, but alas! his chains were never to be loosed that he might go and partake–at almost the same moment they were thus employed, the axe was applied with the greatest dexterity to both her masts and I saw them fall over the side! Here fell my hopes–I looked at my condition, and then thought of home.–Our Spanish fellow prisoners were so disappointed and alarmed that they recommended hiding ourselves, if possible, among the mangrove trees, believing, as they said, we should now certainly be put to death; or, what was worse, compelled to serve on board the Mexican as pirates. Little else it is true, seemed left for us; however, we kept a bright look out for them during the day, and at night "an anchor watch" as we called it, determined if we discovered their boats coming towards us, to adopt the plan of hiding, although starvation stared us in the face–yet preferred that to instant death. This night was passed in sufficient anxiety–I took the first watch.

Saturday, 19th.–The pirate's largest boat came for us–it being day-light, and supposing they could see us, determined to stand our ground and wait the result. They ordered us all into the boat, but left every thing else; they rowed towards the Exertion–I noticed a dejection of spirits in one of the pirates, and inquired of him where they were going to carry us? He shook his head and replied, "I do not know." I now had some hopes of visiting my vessel again–but the pirates made sail, ran down, took us in tow and stood out of the harbor. Bolidar afterwards took me, my mate and two of my men on board and gave us some coffee. On examination I found they had several additional light sails, made of the Exertion's. Almost every man, a pair of canvas trousers; and my colors cut up and made into belts to carry their money about them. My jolly boat was on deck, and I was informed, all my rigging was disposed of. Several of the pirates had on some of my clothes, and the captain one of my best shirts, a cleaner one, than I had ever seen him have on before.–He kept at a good distance from me, and forbid my friend Nickola's speaking to me.–I saw from the companion way in the captain's cabin my quadrant, spy glass and other things which belonged to us, and observed by the compass, that the course steered was about west by south,–distance nearly twenty miles, which brought them up with a cluster of islands called by some "Cayman Keys." Here they anchored and caught some fish, (one of which was named *guard fish*) of which we had a taste. I observed that my friend Mr. Bracket was somewhat dejected, and asked him in a low voice, what his opinion was with respects to our fate? He answered, "I cannot tell you, but it appears to me the worst is to come." I told him that I hoped not, but thought they would give us our small boat and liberate the prisoners. But mercy even in this shape was not left-for us. Soon after, saw the captain and officers whispering for some time in private conference. When over, their boat was manned under the commond of Bolidar, and went to one of those Islands or Keys before mentioned. On their return, another conference took place–whether it was a jury upon our lives we could not tell. I did not think conscience could be entirely extinguished in the human breast, or that men could become fiends. In the afternoon, while we knew not the doom which had been fixed for us, the captain was engaged with several of his men in gambling, in hopes to get back some of the five hundred dollars, they said, he lost but a few nights before; which had made his unusually fractious. A little before sunset he ordered all the prisoners into the large boat, with a supply of provisions and water, and to be put on shore. While we were getting into her, one of my fellow prisoners, a Spaniard, attempted with tears in his eyes to speak to the captain, but was refused with the answer. "I'll have nothing to say to any prisoner, go into the boat." In the mean time Nickola said to me, "My friend, I will give you your book," (being Mr. Colman's Sermons,) "it is the only thing of yours that is in my possession; I dare not attempt any thing more." But the captain forbid his giving it to me, and I stepped into the boat–at that moment Nickola said in a low voice, "never mind, I may see you again before I die." The small boat was well armed and manned, and both set off together for the island, where they had agreed to leave us to perish! The scene to us was a funereal scene. There were no arms in the prisoners boat, and, of course, all attempts to relieve ourselves would have been throwing our lives away, as Bolidar was near us, well armed. We were rowed about two miles north-easterly from the pirates, to a small low island, lonely and desolate. We arrived about sunset; and for the support of us eleven prisoners, they only left a ten gallon keg of water, and perhaps a few quarts, in another small vessel, which was very poor; part of a barrel of flour, a small keg of lard, one ham and some salt fish; a small kettle and an old broken pot; an old sail for a covering, and a small mattress and blanket, which was thrown out as the boats hastened away. One of the prisoners happened to have a little coffee in his pocket, and these comprehended all our means of sustaining life, and for what length of time we knew not. We now felt the need of water, and our supply was comparatively nothing. A man may live nearly twice as long without food, as without water. Look at us now, my friends, left benighted on a little spot of sand in the midst of the ocean, far from the usual track of vessels, and every appearance of a violent thunder tempest, and a boisterous night. Judge of my feelings, and the circumstances which our band of sufferers now witnessed. Perhaps you can and have pitied us. I assure you, we were very wretched; and to paint the scene, is not within my power. When the boats were moving from the shore, on recovering myself a little, I asked Bolidar, "If he was going to leave us so?"–he answered, "no, only two days–we go for water and wood, then come back, take you." I requested him to give us bread and other stores, for they had plenty in the boat, and at least one hundred barrels of flour in the Mexican. "No, no, suppose to-morrow morning me come, me give you bread," and hurried off to the vessel. This was the last time I saw him. We then turned our attention upon finding a spot most convenient for our comfort, and soon discovered a little roof supported by stakes driven into the sand; it was thatched with leaves of the cocoa-nut tree, considerable part of which was torn or blown off. After spreading the old sail over this roof, we placed our little stock of provisions under it. Soon after came on a heavy shower of rain which penetrated the canvas, and made it nearly as uncomfortable inside, as it would have been out. We were not prepared to catch water, having nothing to put it in. Our next object was to get fire, and after gathering some of the driest fuel to be found, and having a small piece of cotton wick-yarn, with flint and steel, we kindled a fire, which was never afterwards suffered to be extinguished. The night was very dark, but we found a piece of old rope, which when well lighted served for a candle. On examining the ground under the roof, we found perhaps thousands of creeping insects, scorpions, lizards, crickets, c. After scraping them out as well as we could, the most of us having nothing but the damp earth for a bed, laid ourselves down in hopes of some rest; but it being so wet, gave many of us severe colds, and one of the Spaniards was quite sick for several days.

Sunday, 20th.–As soon as day-light came on, we proceeded to take a view of our little island, and found it to measure only one acre, of coarse, white sand; about two feet, and in some spots perhaps three feet above the surface of the ocean. On the highest part were growing some bushes and small mangroves, (the dry part of which was our fuel) and the wild castor oil beans. We were greatly disappointed in not finding the latter suitable food; likewise some of the prickly pear bushes, which gave us only a few pears about the size of our small button pear; the outside has thorns, which if applied to the fingers or lips, will remain there, and cause a severe smarting similar to the nettle; the inside a spungy substance, full of juice and seeds, which are red and a little tartish–had they been there in abundance, we should not have suffered so much for water–but alas! even this substitute was not for us. On the northerly side of the island was a hollow, where the tide penetrated the sand, leaving stagnant water. We presumed, in hurricanes the island was nearly overflowed. According to the best calculations I could make, we were about thirty-five miles from any part of Cuba, one hundred from Trinidad and forty from the usual track of American vessels, or others which might pass that way. No vessel of any considerable size, can safely pass among these Keys (or "Queen's Gardens," as the Spaniards call them) being a large number extending from Cape Cruz to Trinidad, one hundred and fifty miles distance; and many more than the charts have laid down, most of them very low and some covered at high water, which makes it very dangerous for navigators without a skilful pilot. After taking this view of our condition, which was very gloomy, we began to suspect we were left on this desolate island by those merciless plunderers to perish. Of this I am now fully convinced; still we looked anxiously for the pirate's boat to come according to promise with more water and provisions, but looked in vain. We saw them soon after get under way with all sail set and run directly from us until out of our sight, and *we never saw them again*! One may partially imagine our feelings, but they cannot be put into words. Before they were entirely out of sight of us, we raised the white blanket upon a pole, waving it in the air, in hopes, that at two miles distance they would see it and be moved to pity. But pity in such monsters was not to be found. It was not their interest to save us from the lingering death, which we now saw before us. We tried to compose ourselves, trusting to God, who had witnessed our sufferings, would yet make use of some one, as the instrument of his mercy towards us. Our next care, now, was to try for water. We dug several holes in the sand and found it, but quite too salt for use. The tide penetrates probably through the island. We now came on short allowances for water. Having no means of securing what we had by lock and key, some one in the night would slyly drink, and it was soon gone. The next was to bake some bread, which we did by mixing flour with salt water and frying it in lard, allowing ourselves eight quite small pancakes to begin with. The ham was reserved for some more important occasion, and the salt fish was lost for want of fresh water. The remainder of this day was passed in the most serious conversation and reflection. At night, I read prayers from the "Prayer Book," before mentioned, which I most carefully concealed while last on board the pirates. This plan was pursued morning and evening, during our stay there. Then retired for rest and sleep, but realized little of either.

Monday, 21st.–In the morning we walked round the beach, in expectation of finding something useful. On our way picked up a paddle about three feet long, very similar to the Indian canoe paddle, except the handle, which was like that of a shovel, the top part being split off; we laid it by for the present. We likewise found some konchs and roasted them; they were pretty good shell fish, though rather tough. We discovered at low water, a bar or spit of sand extending north-easterly from us, about three miles distant, to a cluster of Keys, which were covered with mangrove trees, perhaps as high as our quince tree. My friend Mr. Bracket and George attempted to wade across, being at that time of tide only up to their armpits; but were pursued by a shark, and returned without success. The tide rises about four feet.

Tuesday, 22d.–We found several pieces of the palmetto or cabbage tree, and some pieces of boards, put them together in the form of a raft, and endeavored to cross, but that proved ineffectual. Being disappointed, we set down to reflect upon other means of relief, intending to do all in our power for safety while our strength continued. While setting here, the sun was so powerful and oppressive, reflecting its rays upon the sea, which was then calm, and the white sand which dazzled the eye, was so painful, that we retired under the awning; there the moschetoes and flies were so numerous, that good rest could not be found. We were, however, a little cheered, when, in scraping out the top of the ground to clear out, I may say, thousands of crickets and bugs, we found a hatchet, which was to us peculiarly serviceable. At night the strong north-easterly wind, which prevails there at all seasons, was so cold as to make it equally uncomfortable with the day. Thus day after day, our sufferings and apprehensions multiplying, we were very generally alarmed.

Thursday, 24th.–This morning, after taking a little coffee, made of the water which we thought least salt, and two or three of the little cakes, we felt somewhat refreshed, and concluded to make another visit to those Keys, in hopes of finding something more, which might make a raft for us to escape the pirates, and avoid perishing by thirst. Accordingly seven of us set off, waded across the bar and searched all the Keys thereabouts. On one we found a number of sugar-box shooks, two lashing plank and some pieces of old spars, which were a part of the Exertion's deck load, that was thrown overboard when she grounded on the bar, spoken of in the first part of the narrative. It seems they had drifted fifteen miles, and had accidentally lodged on these very Keys within our reach. Had the pirates known this, they would undoubtedly have placed us in another direction. They no doubt thought that they could not place us on a worse place. The wind at this time was blowing so strong on shore, as to prevent rafting our stuff round to our island, and we were obliged to haul it upon the beach for the present; then dug for water in the highest place, but found it as salt as ever, and then returned to our habitation. But hunger and thirst began to prey upon us, and our comforts were as few as our hopes.

Friday, 25th.–Again passed over to those Keys to windward in order to raft our stuff to our island, it being most convenient for building. But the surf on the beach was so very rough, that we were again compelled to postpone it. Our courage, however, did not fail where there was the slightest hopes of life. Returning without it, we found on our way an old top timber of some vessel; it had several spikes on it, which we afterwards found very serviceable. In the hollow of an old tree, we found two guarnas of small size, one male, the other female. Only one was caught. After taking off the skin, we judged it weighed a pound and a half. With some flour and lard, (the only things we had except salt water,) it made us a fine little mess. We thought it a rare dish, though a small one for eleven half starved persons. At the same time a small vessel hove in sight; we made a signal to her with the blanket tied to a pole and placed it on the highest tree–some took off their white clothes and waved them in the air, hoping they would come to us; should they be pirates, they could do no more than kill us, and perhaps would give us some water, for which we began to suffer most excessively; but, notwithstanding all our efforts, she took no notice of us.

Saturday, 26th.–This day commenced with moderate weather and smooth sea; at low tide found some cockles; boiled and eat them, but they were very painful to the stomach. David Warren had a fit of strangling, with swelling of the bowels; but soon recovered, and said, "something like salt rose in his throat and choked him." Most of us then set off for the Keys, where the plank and shooks were put together in a raft, which we with pieces of boards paddled over to our island; when we consulted the best plan, either to build a raft large enough for us all to go on, or a boat; but the shooks having three or four nails in each, and having a piece of large reed or bamboo, previously found, of which we made pins, we concluded to make a boat.

Sunday, 27–Commenced our labor, for which I know we need offer no apology. We took the two planks, which were about fourteen feet long, and two and a half wide, and fixed them together for the bottom of the boat; then with moulds made of palmetto bark, cut timber and knees from mangrove trees which spread so much as to make the boat four feet wide at the top, placed them exactly the distance apart of an Havana sugar box.–Her stern was square and the bows tapered to a peak, making her form resemble a flat-iron. We proceeded thus far and returned to rest for the night–but Mr. Bracket was too unwell to get much sleep.

Monday, 28–Went on with the work as fast as possible. Some of the Spaniards had long knives about them, which proved very useful in fitting timbers, and a gimblet of mine, accidentally found on board the pirate, enabled us to use the wooden pins. And now our spirits began to revive, though *water, water*, was continually in our minds. We now feared the pirates might possibly come, find out our plan and put us to death, (although before we had wished to see them, being so much in want of water.) Our labor was extremely burdensome, and the Spaniards considerably peevish–but they would often say to me "never mind captain, by and by, Americana or Spanyola catch them, me go and see 'um hung." We quitted work for the day, cooked some cakes but found it necessary to reduce the quantity again, however small before. We found some herbs on a windward Key, which the Spaniards called Spanish tea.–This when well boiled we found somewhat palatable, although the water was very salt. This herb resembles pennyroyal in look and taste, though not so pungent. In the evening when we were setting round the fire to keep of the moschetoes, I observed David Warren's eyes shone like glass. The mate said to him–"David I think you will die before morning–I think you are struck with death now." I thought so too, and told him, "I thought it most likely we should all die here soon; but as some one of us might survive to carry the tidings to our friends, if you have any thing to say respecting your family, now is the time."–He then said, "I have a mother in Saco where I belong–she is a second time a widow–to-morrow if you can spare a scrap of paper and pencil I will write something." But no tomorrow came to him.–In the course of the night he had another spell of strangling, and soon after expired, without much pain and without a groan. He was about twenty-six years old.–How solemn was this scene to us! Here we beheld the ravages of death commenced upon us. More than one of us considered death a happy release. For myself I thought of my wife and children; and wished to live if God should so order it, though extreme thirst, hunger and exhaustion had well nigh prostrated my fondest hopes.

Tuesday, 29th.–Part of us recommenced labor on the boat, while myself and Mr. Bracket went and selected the highest clear spot of sand on the northern side of the island, where we dug Warren's grave, and boxed it up with shooks, thinking it would be the most suitable spot for the rest of us–whose turn would come next, we knew not. At about ten o'clock, A.M. conveyed the corpse to the grave, followed by us survivers–a scene, whose awful solemnity can never be painted. We stood around the grave, and there I read the funeral prayer from the Rev. Mr. Brooks's Family Prayer Book; and committed the body to the earth; covered it with some pieces of board and sand, and returned to our labor. One of the Spaniards, an old man, named Manuel, who was partial to me, and I to him, made a cross and placed it at the head of the grave saying, "Jesus Christ hath him now." Although I did not believe in any mysterious influence of this cross, yet I was perfectly willing it should stand there. The middle part of the day being very warm, our mouths parched with thirst, and our spirits so depressed, that we made but little progress during the remainder of this day, but in the evening were employed in picking oakum out of the bolt rope taken from the old sail.

Wednesday, 30th.–Returned to labor on the boat with as much vigor as our weak and debilitated state would admit, but it was a day of trial to us all; for the Spaniards and we Americans could not well understand each other's plans, and they being naturally petulant, would not work, nor listen with any patience for Joseph, our English fellow prisoner, to explain our views–they would sometimes undo what they had done, and in a few minutes replace it again; however before night we began to caulk her seams, by means of pieces of hard mangrove, made in form of a caulking-iron, and had the satisfaction of seeing her in a form something like a boat.

Thursday, 31st.–Went on with the work, some at caulking, others at battening the seams with strips of canvas, and pieces of pine nailed over, to keep the oakum in. Having found a suitable pole for a mast, the rest went about making a sail from the one we had used for a covering, also fitting oars of short pieces of boards, in form of a paddle, tied on a pole, we having a piece of fishing line brought by one of the prisoners. Thus, at three P.M. the boat was completed and put afloat.–We had all this time confidently hoped, that she would be sufficiently large and strong to carry us all–we made a trial and were disappointed! This was indeed a severe trial, and the emotions it called up were not easy to be suppressed. She proved leaky, for we had no carpenter's yard, or smith's shop to go to.–And now the question was, "who should go, and how many?" I found it necessary for six; four to row, one to steer and one to bale. Three of the Spaniards and the Frenchman claimed the right, as being best acquainted with the nearest inhabitants; likewise, they had when taken, two boats left at St. Maria, (about forty miles distant,) which they were confident of finding. They promised to return within two or three days for the rest of us–I thought it best to consent–Mr. Bracket it was agreed should go in my stead, because my papers must accompany me as a necessary protection, and my men apprehended danger if they were lost. Joseph Baxter (I think was his name) they wished should go, because he could speak both languages–leaving Manuel, George, Thomas and myself, to wait their return. Having thus made all arrangements, and putting up a keg of the least salt water, with a few pancakes of salt fish, they set off a little before sunset with our best wishes and prayers for their safety and return to our relief.–To launch off into the wide ocean, with strength almost exhausted, and in such a frail boat as this, you will say was very hazardous, and in truth it was; but what else was left to us?–Their intention was to touch at the Key where the Exertion was and if no boat was to be found there, to proceed to St. Maria, and if none there, to go to Trinidad and send us relief.–But alas! it was the last time I ever saw them!–Our suffering this day was most acute.

Tuesday, 5th.–About ten o'clock, A.M. discovered a boat drifting by on the south-eastern side of the island about a mile distant. I deemed it a providential thing to us, and urged Thomas and George trying the raft for her. They reluctantly consented and set off, but it was nearly three P.M. when they came up with her–it was the same boat we had built! Where then was my friend Bracket and those who went with him? Every appearance was unfavorable.–I hoped that a good Providence had yet preserved him.–The two men who went for the boat, found it full of water, without oars, paddle, or sail; being in this condition, and about three miles to the leeward, the men found it impossible to tow her up, so left her, and were until eleven o'clock at night getting back with the raft. They were so exhausted, that had it not been nearly calm, they could never have returned.

Wednesday, 6th.–This morning was indeed the most gloomy I had ever experienced.–There appeared hardly a ray of hope that my friend Bracket could return, seeing the boat was lost. Our provisions nearly gone; our mouths parched extremely with thirst; our strength wasted; our spirits broken, and our hopes imprisoned within the circumference of this desolate island in the midst of an unfrequented ocean; all these things gave to the scene around us the hue of death. In the midst of this dreadful despondence, a sail hove in sight bearing the white flag! Our hopes were raised, of course–but no sooner raised than darkened, by hearing a gun fired. Here then was another gang of pirates. She soon, however, came near enough to anchor, and her boat pushed off towards us with three men in her.–Thinking it now no worse to die by sword than famine, I walked down immediately to meet them. I knew them not.–A moment before the boat touched the ground, a man leaped from her bows and caught me in his arms! *It was Nickola*!–saying, "Do you now believe Nickola is your friend?

yes, said he, *Jamieson* will yet prove himself so."–No words can express my emotions at this moment. This was a friend indeed. The reason of my not recognizing them before, was that they had cut their beards and whiskers. Turning to my fellow-sufferers, Nickola asked–"Are these all that are left of you? where are the others?"–At this moment seeing David's grave–"are they dead then? Ah! I suspected it, I know what you were put here for." As soon as I could recover myself, I gave him an account of Mr. Bracket and the others.–"How unfortunate," he said, "they must be lost, or some pirates have taken them."–"But," he continued, "we have no time to lose; you had better embark immediately with us, and go where you please, we are at your service." The other two in the boat were Frenchmen, one named Lyon, the other Parrikete. They affectionately embraced each of us; then holding to my mouth the nose of a teakettle, filled with wine, said "Drink plenty, no hurt you." I drank as much as I judged prudent. They then gave it to my fellow sufferers–I experienced almost immediate relief, not feeling it in my head; they had also brought in the boat for us, a dish of salt beef and potatoes, of which we took a little. Then sent the boat on board for the other two men, being five in all; who came ashore, and rejoiced enough was I to see among them Thomas Young, one of my crew, who was detained on board the Mexican, but had escaped through Nickola's means; the other a Frenchman, named John Cadedt. I now thought again and again, with troubled emotion, of my dear friend Bracket's fate. I took the last piece of paper I had, and wrote with pencil a few words, informing him (should he come there) that "I and the rest were safe; that I was not mistaken in the friend in whom I had placed so much confidence, that he had accomplished my highest expectations; and that I should go immediately to Trinidad, and requested him to go there also, and apply to Mr. Isaac W. Lord, my consignee, for assistance." I put the paper into a junk bottle, previously found on the beach, put in a stopper, and left it, together with what little flour remained, a keg of water brought from Nickola's vessel, and a few other things which I thought might be of service to him. We then repaired with our friends on board, where we were kindly treated. She was a sloop from Jamaica, of about twelve tons, with a cargo of rum and wine, bound to Trinidad. I asked "which way they intended to go?" They said "to Jamaica if agreeable to me." As I preferred Trinidad, I told them, "if they would give me the Exertion's boat which was along-side (beside their own) some water and provisions, we would take chance in her."–"For perhaps," said I, "you will fare better at Jamaica, than at Trinidad." After a few minutes consultation, they said "you are too much exhausted to row the distance of one hundred miles, therefore we will go and carry you–we consider ourselves at your service." I expressed a wish to take a look at the Exertion, possibly we might hear something of Mr. Bracket. Nickola said "very well," so got under way, and run for her, having a light westerly wind. He then related to me the manner of their desertion from the pirates; as nearly as I can recollect his own words, he said, "A few days since, the pirates took four small vessels, I believe Spaniards; they having but two officers for the two first, the third fell to me as prize master, and having an understanding with the three Frenchmen and Thomas, selected them for my crew, and went on board with orders to follow the Mexican; which I obeyed. The fourth, the pirates took out all but one man and bade him also follow their vessel. Now our schooner leaked so bad, that we left her and in her stead agreed to take this little sloop (which we are now in) together with the one man. The night being very dark we all agreed to desert the pirates–altered our course and touched at St. Maria, where we landed the one man–saw no boats there, could hear nothing from you, and agreed one and all at the risk of our lives to come and liberate you if you were alive; knowing, as we did, that you were put on this Key to perish. On our way we boarded the Exertion, thinking possibly you might have been there. On board her we found a sail and paddle. We took one of the pirate's boats which they had left along-side of her, which proves how we came by two boats. My friend, the circumstance I am now about to relate, will somewhat astonish you. When the pirate's boat with Bolidar was sent to the before mentioned Key, on the 19th of January, it was their intention to leave you prisoners there, where was nothing but salt water and mangroves, and no possibility of escape. This was the plan of Baltizar, their abandoned pilot; but Bolidar's heart failed him, and he objected to it; then, after a conference, Captain Jonnia ordered you to be put on the little island from whence we have now taken you. But after this was done, that night the French and Portuguese part of the Mexican's crew protested against it; so that Captain Jonnia to satisfy them, sent his large boat to take you and your fellow prisoners back again, taking care to select his confidential Spaniards for this errand. And you will believe me they set off from the Mexican, and after spending about as much time as would really have taken them to come to you, they returned, and reported they had been to your island, and landed, and that none of you were there, somebody having taken you off! This, all my companions here know to be true.–I knew it was impossible you could have been liberated, and therefore we determined among ourselves, that should an opportunity occur we would come and save your lives, as we now have." He then expressed, as he hitherto had done (and I believe with sincerity), his disgust with the bad company which he had been in, and looked forward with anxiety to the day when he might return to his native country. I advised him to get on board an American vessel, whenever an opportunity offered, and come to the United States; and on his arrival direct a letter to me; repeating my earnest desire to make some return for the disinterested friendship which he had shown toward me. With the Frenchman I had but little conversation, being unacquainted with the language.

Here ended Nickola's account. "And now" said the Frenchman, "our hearts be easy." Nickola observed he had left all and found us. I gave them my warmest tribute of gratitude, saying I looked upon them under God as the preservers of our lives, and promised them all the assistance which my situation might enable me to afford.–This brings me to,

Thursday evening, 7th, when, at eleven o'clock, we anchored at the creek's mouth, near the Exertion. I was anxious to board her; accordingly took with me Nickola, Thomas, George and two others, well armed, each with a musket and cutlass. I jumped on her deck, saw a fire in the camboose, but no person there: I called aloud Mr. Bracket's name several times, saying "it is Captain Lincoln, don't be afraid, but show yourself," but no answer was given. She had no masts, spars, rigging, furniture, provisions or any think left, except her bowsprit, and a few barrels of salt provisions of her cargo. Her ceiling had holes cut in it, no doubt in their foolish search for money. I left her with peculiar emotions, such as I hope never again to experience; and returned to the little sloop where we remained till–

Friday, 8th–When I had disposition to visit the island on which we were first imprisoned.—-Found nothing there–saw a boat among the mangroves, near the Exertion. Returned, and got under way immediately for Trinidad. In the night while under full sail, run aground on a sunken Key, having rocks above the water, resembling old stumps of trees; we, however, soon got off and anchored. Most of those Keys have similar rocks about them, which navigators must carefully guard against.

Monday, 11th–Got under way–saw a brig at anchor about five miles below the mouth of the harbor; we hoped to avoid her speaking us; but when we opened in sight of her, discovered a boat making towards us, with a number of armed men in her. This alarmed my friends, and as we did not see the brig's ensign hoisted, they declared the boat was a pirate, and looking through the spy-glass, they knew some of them to be the Mexican's men! This state of things was quite alarming. They said, "we will not be taken alive by them." Immediately the boat fired a musket; the ball passed through our mainsail. My friends insisted on beating them off: I endeavored to dissuade them, believing, as I did, that the brig was a Spanish man-of-war, who had sent her boat to ascertain who we were. I thought we had better heave to. Immediately another shot came. Then they insisted on fighting, and said "if I would not help them, I was no friend." I reluctantly acquiesced, and handed up the guns–commenced firing upon them and they upon us. We received several shot through the sails, but no one was hurt on either side. Our boats had been cast adrift to make us go the faster, and we gained upon them–continued firing until they turned from us, and went for our boats, which they took in tow for the brig. Soon after this, it became calm: then I saw that the brig had us in her power.–She manned and armed two more boats for us. We now concluded, since we had scarcely any ammunition, to surrender; and were towed down along-side the brig on board, and were asked by the captain, who could speak English, "what for you fire on the boat?" I told him "we thought her a pirate, and did not like to be taken by them again, having already suffered too much;" showing my papers. He said, "Captain Americana, never mind, go and take some dinner–which are your men?" I pointed them out to him, and he ordered them the liberty of the decks; but my friend Nickola and his three associates were immediately put in irons. They were, however, afterwards taken out of irons and examined; and I understood the Frenchmen agreed to enlist, as they judged it the surest way to better their condition. Whether Nickola enlisted, I do not know, but think that he did, as I understood that offer was made to him: I however endeavored to explain more distinctly to the captain, the benevolent efforts of these four men by whom my life had been saved, and used every argument in my power to procure their discharge. I also applied to the governor, and exerted myself with peculiar interest, dictated as I trust with heartfelt gratitude–and I ardently hope ere this, that Nickola is on his way to this country, where I may have an opportunity of convincing him that such an act of benevolence will not go unrewarded. Previous to my leaving Trinidad, I made all the arrangements in my power with my influential friends, and doubt not, that their laudable efforts will be accomplished.–The sloop's cargo was then taken on board the brig; after which the captain requested a certificate that I was politely treated by him, saying that his name was Captain Candama, of the privateer brig Prudentee of eighteen guns. This request I complied with. His first lieutenant told me he had sailed out of Boston, as commander for T.C. Amory, Esq. during the last war. In the course of the evening my friends were taken out of irons and examined separately, then put back again. The captain invited me to supper in his cabin, and a berth for the night, which was truly acceptable. The next morning after breakfast, I with my people were set on shore with the few things we had, with the promise of the Exertion's small boat in a day or two,–but it was never sent me–the reason, let the reader imagine. On landing at the wharf Casildar, we were immediately taken by soldiers to the guard house, which was a very filthy place; thinking I suppose, and even calling us, pirates. Soon some friends came to see me. Mr. Cotton, who resides there brought us in some soup. Mr. Isaac W. Lord, of Boston, my merchant, came with Captain Tate, who sent immediately to the governor; for I would not show my papers to any one else. He came about sunset, and after examining Manuel my Spanish fellow prisoner, and my papers, said to be, giving me the papers, "Captain, you are at liberty." I was kindly invited by Captain Matthew Rice, of schooner Galaxy, of Boston, to go on board his vessel, and live with him during my stay there. This generous offer I accepted, and was treated by him with the greatest hospitality; for I was hungered and he gave me meat, I was athirst and he gave me drink, I was naked and he clothed me, a stranger and he took me in. He likewise took Manuel and my three men for that night. Next day Mr. Lord rendered me all necessary assistance in making my protest. He had heard nothing from me until my arrival. I was greatly disappointed in not finding Mr. Bracket, and requested Mr. Lord to give him all needful aid if he should come there. To Captain Carnes, of the schooner Hannah, of Boston, I would tender my sincere thanks, for his kindness in giving me a passage to Boston, which I gladly accepted. To those gentlemen of Trinidad, and many captains of American vessels, who gave me sea clothing, c., I offer my cordial gratitude.

I am fully of the opinion that these ferocious pirates are linked in with many inhabitants of Cuba; and the government in many respects appears covertly to encourage them.

It is with heartfelt delight, that, since the above narrative was written, I have learned that Mr. Bracket and his companions are safe; he arrived at Port d'Esprit, about forty leagues east of Trinidad. A letter has been received from him, stating that he should proceed to Trinidad the first opportunity.–It appears that after reaching the wreck, they found a boat from the shore, taking on board some of the Exertion's cargo, in which they proceeded to the above place. Why it was not in his power to come to our relief will no doubt be satisfactorily disclosed when he may be so fortunate as once more to return to his native country and friends.

I felt great anxiety to learn what became of Jamieson, who, my readers will recollect, was detained on board the Spanish brig Prudentee near Trinidad. I heard nothing from him, until I believe eighteen months after I reached home, when I received a letter from him, from Montego Bay, Jamaica, informing me that he was then residing in that island. I immediately wrote to him, and invited him to come on to the United States. He accordingly came on passenger with Captain Wilson of Cohasset, and arrived in Boston, in August, 1824. Our meeting was very affecting. Trying scenes were brought up before us; scenes gone forever, through which we had passed together, where our acquaintance was formed, and since which time, we had never met. I beheld once more the preserver of my life; the instrument, under Providence, of restoring me to my home, my family, and my friends, and I regarded him with no ordinary emotion. My family were delighted to see him, and cordially united in giving him a warm reception. He told me that after we separated in Trinidad, he remained on board the Spanish brig. The commander asked him and his companions if they would enlist; the Frenchmen replied that they would, but he said nothing, being determined to make his escape, the very first opportunity which should present. The Spanish brig afterwards fell in with a Columbian Patriot, an armed brig of eighteen guns. Being of about equal force, they gave battle, and fought between three and four hours. Both parties were very much injured; and, without any considerable advantage on either side, both drew off to make repairs. The Spanish brig Prudentee, put into St. Jago de Cuba. Jamieson was wounded in the action, by a musket ball, through his arm, and was taken on shore, with the other wounded, and placed in the hospital of St. Jago. Here he remained for a considerable time, until he had nearly recovered, when he found an opportunity of escaping, and embarking for Jamaica. He arrived in safety at Kingston, and from there, travelled barefoot over the mountains, until very much exhausted, he reached Montego Bay, where he had friends, and where one of his brothers possessed some property. From this place, he afterwards wrote to me. He told me that before he came to Massachusetts, he saw the villainous pilot of the Mexican, the infamous Baltizar, with several other pirates, brought into Montego Bay, from whence they were to be conveyed to Kingston to be executed. Whether the others were part of the Mexican's crew, or not, I do not know. Baltizar was an old man, and as Jamieson said, it was a melancholy and heart-rending sight, to see him borne to execution with those gray hairs, which might have been venerable in virtuous old age, now a shame and reproach to this hoary villain, for he was full of years, and old in iniquity. When Jamieson received the letter which I wrote him, he immediately embarked with Captain Wilson, and came to Boston, as I have before observed.

According to his own account he was of a very respectable family in Greenock, Scotland. His father when living was a rich cloth merchant, but both his father and mother had been dead many years. He was the youngest of thirteen children, and being, as he said, of a roving disposition, had always followed the seas. He had received a polite education, and was of a very gentlemanly deportment. He spoke several living languages, and was skilled in drawing and painting. He had travelled extensively in different countries, and acquired in consequence an excellent knowledge of their manners and customs. His varied information (for hardly any subject escaped him) rendered him a very entertaining companion. His observations on the character of different nations were very liberal; marking their various traits, their virtues and vices, with playful humorousness, quite free from bigotry, or narrow prejudice.

I was in trade, between Boston and Philadelphia, at the time he came to Massachusetts, and he sailed with me several trips as my mate. He afterwards went to Cuba, and was subsequently engaged in the mackerel fishery, out of the port of Hingham, during the warm season, and in the winter frequently employed himself in teaching navigation to young men, for which he was eminently qualified. He remained with us, until his death, which took place in 1829. At this time he had been out at sea two or three days, when he was taken sick, and was carried into Cape Cod, where he died, on the first day of May, 1829, and there his remains lie buried. Peace be to his ashes! They rest in a strange land, far from his kindred and his native country.

Since his death I have met with Mr. Stewart, of Philadelphia, who was Commercial Agent in Trinidad at the time of my capture. He informed me that the piratical schooner Mexican, was afterwards chased by an English government vessel, from Jamaica, which was cruising in search of it. Being hotly pursued, the pirates deserted their vessel, and fled to the mangrove bushes, on an island similar to that on which they had placed me and my crew to die. The English surrounded them, and thus they were cut off from all hopes of escape. They remained there, I think fourteen days, when being almost entirely subdued by famine, eleven surrendered themselves, and were taken. The others probably perished among the mangroves. The few who were taken were carried by the government vessel into Trinidad. Mr. Stewart said that he saw them himself, and such miserable objects, that had life, he never before beheld. They were in a state of starvation; their beards had grown to a frightful length, their bodies, were covered with filth and vermin, and their countenances were hideous. From Trinidad they were taken to Kingston, Jamaica, and there hung on Friday, the 7th of February, 1823.

About a quarter of an hour before day dawn, the wretched culprits were taken from the jail, under a guard of soldiers from the 50th regiment, and the City Guard. On their arrival at the wherry wharf, the military retired, and the prisoners, with the Town Guard were put on board two wherries, in which they proceeded to Port Royal Point, the usual place of execution in similar cases. They were there met by a strong party of military, consisting of 50 men, under command of an officer. They formed themselves into a square round the place of execution, with the sheriff and his officers with the prisoners in the centre. The gallows was of considerable length, and contrived with a drop so as to prevent the unpleasant circumstances which frequently occur.

The unfortunate men had been in continual prayer from the time they were awakened out of a deep sleep till they arrived at that place, where they were to close their existence.

They all expressed their gratitude for the attention they had met with from the sheriff and the inferior officers. Many pressed the hands of the turnkey to their lips, others to their hearts and on their knees, prayed that God, Jesus Christ, and the Virgin Mary would bless him and the other jailors for their goodness. They all then fervently joined in prayer. To the astonishment of all, no clerical character, of any persuasion, was present. They repeatedly called out "Adonde esta el padre," (Where is the holy father).

The execution of ten pirates.

**The execution of ten pirates.**

Juan Hernandez called on all persons present to hear him–he was innocent; what they had said about his confessing himself guilty was untrue. He had admitted himself guilty, because he hoped for pardon; but that now he was to die, he called God, Jesus Christ, the Holy Ghost, the Virgin Mary, and the Saints, to witness that he spoke the truth–that he was no pirate, no murderer–he had been forced. The Lieutenant of the pirates was a wretch, who did not fear God, and had compelled him to act.

Juan Gutterez and Francisco de Sayas were loud in their protestations of innocence.

Manuel Lima said, for himself, he did not care; he felt for the old man (Miguel Jose). How could he be a pirate who could not help himself? If it were a Christian country, they would have pardoned him for his gray hairs. He was innocent–they had both been forced. Let none of his friends or relations ever venture to sea–he hoped his death would be a warning to them, that the innocent might suffer for the guilty. The language of this young man marked him a superior to the generality of his companions in misfortune. The seamen of the Whim stated that he was very kind to them when prisoners on board the piratical vessel. Just before he was turned off, he addressed the old man–"Adios viejo, para siempre adios."–(Farewell, old man, forever farewell.)

Several of the prisoners cried out for mercy, pardon, pardon.

Domingo Eucalla, the black man, then addressed them. "Do not look for mercy here, but pray to God; we are all brought here to die. This is not built for nothing; here we must end our lives. You know I am innocent, but I must die the same as you all. There is not any body here who can do us any good, so let us think only of God Almighty. We are not children but men, you know that all must die; and in a few years those who kill us must die too. When I was born, God set the way of my death; I do not blame any body. I was taken by the pirates and they made me help them; they would not let me be idle. I could not show that this was the truth, and therefore they have judged me by the people they have found me with. I am put to death unjustly, but I blame nobody. It was my misfortune. Come, let us pray. If we are innocent, so much the less we have to repent. I do not come here to accuse any one. Death must come one day or other; better to the innocent than guilty." He then joined in prayer with the others. He seemed to be much reverenced by his fellow prisoners. He chose those prayers he thought most adapted to the occasion. Hundreds were witnesses to the manly firmness of this negro. Observing a bystander listening attentively to the complaints of one of his fellow wretches, he translated what had been said into English. With a steady pace, and a resolute and resigned countenance, he ascended the fatal scaffold. Observing the executioner unable to untie a knot on the collar of one of the prisoners, he with his teeth untied it. He then prayed most fervently till the drop fell.

Miguel Jose protested his innocence.–"No he robado, no he matado ningune, muero innocente."–(I have robbed no one, I have killed no one, I die innocent. I am an old man, but my family will feel my disgraceful death.)

Francisco Migul prayed devoutly, but inaudibly.–His soul seemed to have quitted the body before he was executed.

Breti Gullimillit called on all to witness his innocence; it was of no use for him to say an untruth, for he was going before the face of God.

Augustus Hernandez repeatedly declared his innocence, requested that no one would say he had made a confession; he had none to make.

Juan Hernandez was rather obstinate when the execution pulled the cap over his eyes. He said, rather passionately–"Quita is de mis ojos."–(Remove it from my eyes.) He then rubbed it up against one of the posts of the gallows.

Miguel Jose made the same complaint, and drew the covering from his eyes by rubbing his head against a fellow sufferer.

Pedro Nondre was loud in his ejaculations for mercy. He wept bitterly. He was covered with marks of deep wounds.

The whole of the ten included in the death warrant, having been placed on the scaffold, and the ropes suspended, the drop was let down. Nondre being an immense heavy man, broke the rope, and fell to the ground alive. Juan Hernandez struggled long. Lima was much convulsed. The old man Gullimillit, and Migul, were apparently dead before the drop fell. Eucalla (the black man) gave one convulsion, and all was over.

When Nondre recovered from the fall and saw his nine lifeless companions stretched in death, he gave an agonizing shriek; he wrung his hands, screamed "Favor, favor, me matan sin causa. O! buenos Christianos, me amparen, ampara me, ampara me, no hay Christiano en asta, tiara?"

(Mercy, mercy, they kill me without cause.–Oh, good Christians, protect me. Oh, protect me. Is there no Christian in this land?)

He then lifted his eyes to Heaven, and prayed long and loud. Upon being again suspended, he was for a long period convulsed. He was an immense powerful man, and died hard.

A piratical station was taken in the Island of Cuba by the U.S. schooners of war, Greyhound and Beagle. They left Thompson's Island June 7, 1823, under the command of Lieuts. Kearney and Newton, and cruised within the Key's on the south side of Cuba, as far as Cape Cruz, touching at all the intermediate ports on the island, to intercept pirates. On the 21st of July, they came to anchor off Cape Cruz, and Lieut. Kearney went in his boat to reconnoitre the shore, when he was fired on by a party of pirates who were concealed among the bushes. A fire was also opened from several pieces of cannon erected on a hill a short distance off. The boat returned, and five or six others were manned from the vessels, and pushed off for the shore, but a very heavy cannonade being kept up by the pirates on the heights, as well as from the boats, were compelled to retreat. The two schooners were then warped in, when they discharged several broadsides, and covered the landing of the boats. After a short time the pirates retreated to a hill that was well fortified. A small hamlet, in which the pirates resided, was set fire to and destroyed. Three guns, one a four pounder, and two large swivels, with several pistols, cutlasses, and eight large boats, were captured. A cave, about 150 feet deep, was discovered, near where the houses were, and after considerable difficulty, a party of seamen got to the bottom, where was found an immense quantity of plunder, consisting of broadcloths, dry goods, female dresses, saddlery, c. Many human bones were also in the cave, supposed to have been unfortunate persons who were taken and put to death. A great many of the articles were brought away, and the rest destroyed. About forty pirates escaped to the heights, but many were supposed to have been killed from the fire of the schooners, as well as from the men who landed. The bushes were so thick that it was impossible to go after them. Several other caves are in the neighborhood, in which it was conjectured they occasionally take shelter.

In 1823, Commodore Porter commanded the United States squadron in these seas; much good was done in preventing new acts of piracy; but these wretches kept aloof and did not venture to sea as formerly, but some were taken.

Almost every day furnished accounts evincing the activity of Commodore Porter, and the officers and men under his command; but for a long time their industry and zeal was rather shown in the *suppression* of piracy than the *punishment* of it. At length, however, an opportunity offered for inflicting the latter, as detailed in the following letter, dated Matanzas, July 10, 1823.

"I have the pleasure of informing you of a brilliant achievement obtained against the pirates on the 5th inst. by two barges attached to Commodore Porter's squadron, the Gallinipper, Lieut. Watson, 18 men, and the Moscheto, Lieut. Inman, 10 men. The barges were returning from a cruise to windward; when they were near Jiguapa Bay, 13 leagues to windward of Matanzas, they entered it–it being a rendezvous for pirates. They immediately discovered a large schooner under way, which they supposed to be a Patriot privateer; and as their stores were nearly exhausted, they hoped to obtain some supplies from her. They therefore made sail in pursuit. When they were within cannon shot distance, she rounded to and fired her long gun, at the same time run up the bloody flag, directing her course towards the shore, and continuing to fire without effect. When she had got within a short distance of the shore, she came to, with springs on her cable, continuing to fire; and when the barges were within 30 yards, they fired their muskets without touching boat or man; our men gave three cheers, and prepared to board; the pirates, discovering their intention, jumped into the water, when the bargemen, calling on the name of 'Allen,' commenced a destructive slaughter, killing them in the water and as they landed. So exasperated were our men, that it was impossible for their officers to restrain them, and many were killed after orders were given to grant quarter. Twenty-seven dead were counted, some sunk, five taken prisoners by the bargemen, and eight taken by a party of Spaniards on shore. The officers calculated that from 30 to 35 were killed. The schooner mounted a long nine pounder on a pivot, and 4 four pounders, with every other necessary armament, and a crew of 50 to 60 men, and ought to have blown the barges to atoms. She was commanded by the notorious Diableto or Little Devil. This statement I have from Lieut. Watson himself, and it is certainly the most decisive operation that has been effected against those murderers, either by the English or American force."

The Pirates fire into Lieut. Kearney's boat, while reconnoitering the shore

**The Pirates fire into Lieut. Kearney's boat, while reconnoitering the shore.**

"This affair occurred on the same spot where the brave Allen fell about one year since. The prize was sent to Thompson's Island."

A British sloop of war, about the same time, captured a pirate schooner off St. Domingo, with a crew of 60 men. She had 200,000 dollars in specie, and other valuable articles on board. The brig Vestal sent another pirate schooner to New-Providence.

## THE ADVENTURES AND EXECUTION OF CAPTAIN JOHN RACKAM.

This John Rackam, as has been reported in the foregoing pages, was quarter-master to Vane's company, till the crew were divided, and Vane turned out of it for refusing to board a French man-of-war, Rackam being voted captain of the division that remained in the brigantine. The 24th of November 1718, was the first day of his command; his first cruise was among the Carribbee Islands, where he took and plundered several vessels.

We have already taken notice, that when Captain Woods Rogers went to the island of Providence with the king's pardon to such of the pirates as should surrender, this brigantine, which Rackam commanded, made its escape through another passage, bidding defiance to the mercy that was offered.

To the windward of Jamaica, a Madeira-man fell into the pirate's way, which they detained two or three days, till they had their market out of her, and then they gave her back to the master, and permitted one Hosea Tidsel, a tavern keeper at Jamaica, who had been picked up in one of their prizes, to depart in her, she being bound for that island.

After this cruise they went into a small island, and cleaned, and spent their Christmas ashore, drinking and carousing as long as they had any liquor left, and then went to sea again for more. They succeeded but too well, though they took no extraordinary prize for above two months, except a ship laden with convicts from Newgate, bound for the plantations, which in a few days was retaken, with all her cargo, by an English man-of-war that was stationed in those seas.

Rackam stood towards the island of Bermuda, and took a ship bound to England from Carolina, and a small pink from New England, both of which he brought to the Bahama Islands, where, with the pitch, tar and stores they cleaned again, and refitted their own vessel; but staying too long in that neighborhood, Captain Rogers, who was Governor of Providence, hearing of these ships being taken, sent out a sloop well manned and armed, which retook both the prizes, though in the mean while the pirate had the good fortune to escape.

From hence they sailed to the back of Cuba, where Rackam kept a little kind of a family, at which place they stayed a considerable time, living ashore with their Delilahs, till their money and provisions were expended, and they concluded it time to look out for more. They repaired their vessel, and were making ready to put to sea, when a guarda de costa came in with a small English sloop, which she had taken as an interloper on the coast. The Spanish guard-ship attacked the pirate, but Rackam being close in behind a little island, she could do but little execution where she lay; the Dons therefore warped into the channel that evening, in order to make sure of her the next morning. Rackam finding his case desperate, and that there was hardly any possibility of escaping, resolved to attempt the following enterprise. The Spanish prize lying for better security close into the land, between the little island and the Main, our desperado took his crew into the boat with their cutlasses, rounded the little island, and fell aboard their prize silently in the dead of the night without being discovered, telling the Spaniards that were aboard her, that if they spoke a word, or made the least noise, they were all dead men; and so they became masters of her. When this was done he slipped her cable, and drove out to sea. The Spanish man-of-war was so intent upon their expected prize, that they minded nothing else, and as soon as day broke, they made a furious fire upon the empty sloop; but it was not long before they were rightly apprised of the matter, when they cursed themselves sufficiently for a company of fools, to be bit out of a good rich prize, as she proved to be, and to have nothing but an old crazy hull in the room of her.

Rackam and his crew had no occasion to be displeased at the exchange, as it enabled them to continue some time longer in a way of life that suited their depraved minds.

In August 1720, we find him at sea again, scouring the harbours and inlets of the north and west parts of Jamaica, where he took several small crafts, which proved no great booty to the rovers; but they had but few men, and therefore were obliged to run at low game till they could increase their company and their strength.

In the beginning of September, they took seven or eight fishing boats in Harbour Island, stole their nets and other tackle, and then went off to the French part of Hispaniola, where they landed, and took the cattle away, with two or three Frenchmen whom they found near the water-side, hunting wild hogs in the evening. The Frenchmen came on board, whether by consent or compulsion is not certainly known. They afterwards plundered two sloops, and returned to Jamaica, on the north coast of which island, near Porto Maria Bay, they took a schooner, Thomas Spenlow, master, it being then the 19th of October. The next day Rackam seeing a sloop in Dry Harbour Bay, stood in and fired a gun; the men all ran ashore, and he took the sloop and lading; but when those ashore found that they were pirates, they hailed the sloop, and let them know they were all willing to come on board of them.

Rackam's coasting the island in this manner proved fatal to him; for intelligence of his expedition came to the governor by a canoe which he had surprised ashore in Ocho Bay: upon this a sloop was immediately fitted out, and sent round the island in quest of him, commanded by Captain Barnet, and manned with a good number of hands. Rackam, rounding the island, and drawing round the western point, called Point Negril, saw a small pettiaga, which, at the sight of the sloop, ran ashore and landed her men, when one of them hailed her. Answer was made that they were Englishmen, and begged the pettiaga's men to come on board and drink a bowl of punch, which they prevailed upon them to do. Accordingly, the company, in an evil hour, came all aboard of the pirate, consisting of nine persons; they were armed with muskets and cutlasses, but what was their real design in so doing we will not pretend to say. They had no sooner laid down their arms and taken up their pipes, than Barnet's sloop, which was in pursuit of Rackam's, came in sight.

The pirates, finding she stood directly towards them, feared the event, and weighed their anchor, which they had but lately let go, and stood off. Captain Barnet gave them chase, and, having advantage of little breezes of wind which blew off the land, came up with her, and brought her into Port Royal, in Jamaica.

About a fortnight after the prisoners were brought ashore, viz. November 16, 1720, Captain Rackam and eight of his men were condemned and executed. Captain Rackam and two others were hung in chains.

But what was very surprising, was the conviction of the nine men that came aboard the sloop on the same day she was taken. They were tried at an adjournment of the court on the 24th of January, the magistracy waiting all that time, it is supposed, for evidence to prove the piratical intention of going aboard the said sloop; for it seems there was no act or piracy committed by them, as appeared by the witnesses against them, two Frenchmen, taken by Rackam off the island of Hispaniola, who merely deposed that the prisoners came on board without any compulsion.

The court considered the prisoners' cases, and the majority of the commissioners being of opinion that they were all guilty of the piracy and felony they were charged with, viz. the going over with a piratical intent to John Rackam, c. then notorious pirates, and by them known to be so, they all received sentence of death, and were executed on the 17th of February at Gallows Point at Port Royal.

Nor holy bell, nor pastoral bleat,
In former days within the vale.
Flapped in the bay the pirate's sheet,
Curses were on the gale;
Rich goods lay on the sand, and murdered men,
Pirate and wreckers kept their revels there.

THE BUCCANEER.

## THE LIFE AND EXPLOITS OF ANNE BONNEY.

This female pirate was a native of Cork. Her father was an attorney, and, by his activity in business, rose to considerable respectability in that place. Anne was the fruit of an unlawful connexion with his own servant maid, with whom he afterwards eloped to America, leaving his own affectionate and lawful wife. He settled at Carolina, and for some time followed his own profession; but soon commenced merchant, and was so successful as to purchase a considerable plantation. There he lived with his servant in the character of his wife; but she dying, his daughter Anne superintended the domestic affairs of her father.

During her residence with her parent she was supposed to have a considerable fortune, and was accordingly addressed by young men of respectable situations in life. It happened with Anne, however, as with many others of her youth and sex, that her feelings, and not her interest, determined her choice of a husband. She married a young sailor without a shilling. The avaricious father was so enraged, that, deaf to the feelings of a parent, he turned his own child out of doors. Upon this cruel usage, and the disappointment of her fortune, Anne and her husband sailed for the island of Providence, in the hope of gaining employment.

Acting a part very different from that of Mary Read, Anne's affections were soon estranged from her husband by Captain Rackam; and eloping with him, she went to sea in men's clothes. Proving with child, the captain put her on shore, and entrusted her to the care of some friends until her recovery, when she again accompanied him in his expeditions.

Upon the king's proclamation offering a pardon to all pirates, he surrendered, and went into the privateering business, as we have related before: he, however, soon embraced an opportunity to return to his favorite employment. In all his piratical exploits Anne accompanied him; and, as we have already recorded, displayed such courage and intrepidity, that she, along with Mary Read and a seaman, were the last three who remained on board when the vessel was taken.

Anne was known to many of the planters in Jamaica, who remembered to have seen her in her father's house, and they were disposed to intercede in her behalf. Her unprincipled conduct, in leaving her own husband and forming an illicit connexion with Rackam, tended, however, to render her friends less active. By a special favor, Rackam was permitted to visit her the day before he was executed; but, instead of condoling with him on account of his sad fate, she only observed, that she was sorry to see him there, but if he had fought like a man he needed not have been hanged like a dog. Being with child, she remained in prison until her recovery, was reprieved from time to time, and though we cannot communicate to our readers any particulars of her future life, or the manner of her death, yet it is certain that she was not executed.

**THE ADVENTURES AND HEROISM OF MARY READ.**

The attention of our readers is now to be directed to the history of two female pirates,–a history which is chiefly remarkable from the extraordinary circumstance of the softer sex assuming a character peculiarly distinguished for every vice that can disgrace humanity, and at the same time for the exertion of the most daring, though brutal, courage.

Mary Read was a native of England, but at what place she was born is not recorded. Her mother married a sailor when she was very young, who, soon after their marriage, went to sea, and never returned. The fruit of that marriage was a sprightly boy. The husband not returning, she again found herself with child, and to cover her shame, took leave of her husband's relations, and went to live in the country, taking her boy along with her. Her son in a short time died, and she was relieved from the burden of his maintenance and education. The mother had not resided long in the country before Mary Read, the subject of the present narrative, was born.

After the birth of Mary, her mother resided in the country for three or four years, until her money was all spent, and her ingenuity was set at work to contrive how to obtain a supply. She knew that her husband's mother was in good circumstances, and could easily support her child, provided she could make her pass for a boy, and her son's child. But it seemed impossible to impose upon an old experienced mother. She, however, presented Mary in the character of her grandson. The old woman proposed to take the boy to live with her, but the mother would not on any account part with her boy; the grandmother, therefore, allowed a crown per week for his support.

The ingenuity of the mother being successful, she reared the daughter as a boy. But as she grew up, she informed her of the secret of her birth, in order that she might conceal her sex. The grandmother, however, dying, the support from that quarter failed, and she was obliged to hire her out as a footboy to a French lady. The strength and manly disposition of this supposed boy increased with her years, and leaving that servile employment, she engaged on board a man-of-war.

The volatile disposition of the youth did not permit her to remain long in this station, and she next went into Flanders, and joined a regiment of foot as a cadet. Though in every action she conducted herself with the greatest bravery, yet she could not obtain a commission, as they were in general bought and sold. She accordingly quitted that service, and enlisted into a regiment of horse; there she behaved herself so valiantly, that she gained the esteem of all her officers. It, however, happened, that her comrade was a handsome young Fleming, and she fell passionately in love with him. The violence of her feelings rendered her negligent of her duty, and effected such a change in her behaviour as attracted the attention of all. Both her comrade and the rest of the regiment deemed her mad. Love, however, is inventive, and as they slept in the same tent, she found means to discover her sex without any seeming design. He was both surprised and pleased, supposing that he would have a mistress to himself; but he was greatly mistaken, and he found that it was necessary to court her for his wife. A mutual attachment took place, and, as soon as convenient, women's clothes were provided for her, and they were publicly married.

The singularity of two troopers marrying caused a general conversation, and many of the officers honored the ceremony with their presence, and resolved to make presents to the bride, to provide her with necessaries. After marriage they were desirous to quit the service, and their discharge being easily obtained, they set up an ordinary under the sign of the "Three Shoes," and soon acquired a considerable run of business.

But Mary Read's felicity was of short duration; the husband died, and peace being concluded, her business diminished. Under these circumstances she again resumed her man's dress, and going into Holland, enlisted into a regiment of foot quartered in one of the frontier towns. But there being no prospect of preferment in time of peace, she went on board a vessel bound for the West Indies.

During the voyage, the vessel was captured by English pirates, and as Mary was the only English person on board, they detained her, and having plundered the vessel of what they chose, allowed it to depart. Mary continued in that unlawful commerce for some time, but the royal pardon being tendered to all those in the West Indies, who should, before a specified day, surrender, the crew to which she was attached, availed themselves of this, and lived quietly on shore with the fruits of their adventures. But from the want of their usual supplies, their money became exhausted; and being informed that Captain Rogers, in the island of Providence, was fitting out some vessels for privateering, Mary, with some others, repaired to that island to serve on board his privateers. We have already heard, that scarcely had the ships sailed, when some of their crews mutinied, and ran off with the ships, to pursue their former mode of life. Among these was Mary Read. She indeed, frequently declared, that the life of a pirate was what she detested, and that she was constrained to it both on the former and present occasion. It was, however, sufficiently ascertained, that both Mary Read and Anne Bonney were among the bravest and most resolute fighters of the whole crew; that when the vessel was taken, these two heroines, along with another of the pirates, were the last three upon deck; and that Mary, having in vain endeavored to rouse the courage of the crew, who had fled below, discharged a pistol amongst them, killing one and wounding another.

Nor was Mary less modest than brave; for though she had remained many years in the character of a sailor, yet no one had discovered her sex, until she was under the necessity of doing so to Anne Bonney. The reason of this was, that Anne, supposing her to be a handsome fellow, became greatly enamored of her, and discovered her sex and wishes to Mary, who was thus constrained to reveal her secret to Anne. Rackam being the paramour of Bonney, and observing her partiality towards Mary, threatened to shoot her lover; so that to prevent any mischief, Anne also informed the captain of the sex of her companion.

Rackam was enjoined to secrecy, and here he behaved honorably; but love again assailed the conquered Mary. It was usual with the pirates to retain all the artists who were captured in the trading-vessels; among these was a very handsome young man, of engaging manners, who vanquished the heart of Mary. In a short time her love became so violent, that she took every opportunity of enjoying his company and conversation; and, after she had gained his friendship, discovered her sex. Esteem and friendship were speedily converted into the most ardent affection, and a mutual flame burned in the hearts of these two lovers. An occurrence soon happened that put the attachment of Mary to a severe trial. Her lover having quarrelled with one of the crew, they agreed to fight a duel on shore. Mary was all anxiety for the fate of her lover, and she manifested a greater concern for the preservation of his life than that of her own; but she could not entertain the idea that he could refuse to fight, and so be esteemed a coward. Accordingly she quarrelled with the man who challenged her lover, and called him to the field two hours before his appointment with her lover, engaged him with sword and pistol, and laid him dead at her feet.

Though no esteem or love had formerly existed, this action was sufficient to have kindled the most violent flame. But this was not necessary, for the lover's attachment was equal, if not stronger than her own; they pledged their faith, which was esteemed as binding as if the ceremony had been performed by a clergyman.

Captain Rackam one day, before he knew that she was a woman, asked her why she followed a line of life that exposed her to so much danger, and at last to the certainty of being hanged. She replied, that, "As to hanging, she thought it no great hardship, for were it not for that, every cowardly fellow would turn pirate, and so infest the seas; and men of courage would starve. That if it was put to her choice, she would not have the punishment less than death, the fear of which kept some dastardly rogues honest; that many of those who are now cheating the widows and orphans, and oppressing their poor neighbors who have no money to obtain justice, would then rob at sea, and the ocean would be as crowded with rogues as the land: so that no merchants would venture out, and the trade in a little time would not be worth following."

Being with child at the time of her trial, her execution was delayed; and it is probable that she would have found favor, but in the mean time she fell sick and died.

Mary Read was of a strong and robust constitution, capable of enduring much exertion and fatigue. She was vain and bold in her disposition, but susceptible of the tenderest emotions, and of the most melting affections. Her conduct was generally directed by virtuous principles, while at the same time, she was violent in her attachments. Though she was inadvertently drawn into that dishonorable mode of life which has stained her character, and given her a place among the criminals noticed in this work, yet she possessed a rectitude of principle and of conduct, far superior to many who have not been exposed to such temptations to swerve from the path of female virtue and honor.

Mary Read kills her antagonist.

**Mary Read kills her antagonist.**

## THE ALGERINE PIRATES.

*Containing accounts of the cruelties and atrocities of the Barbary Corsairs, with narratives of the expeditions sent against them, and the final capture of Algiers by the French in* 1830.

That former den of pirates, the city of Algiers is situated on the shores of a pretty deep bay, by which the northern coast of Africa, is here indented, and may be said to form an irregular triangular figure, the base line of which abuts on the sea, while the apex is formed by the Cassaubah, or citadel, which answered the double purpose of a fort to defend and awe the city, and a palace for the habitation of the Dey and his court.

The hill on which the city is built, slopes rather rapidly upwards, so that every house is visible from the sea, in consequence of which it was always sure to suffer severely from a bombardment. The top of the hill has an elevation of nearly five hundred feet, and exactly at this point is built the citadel; the whole town lying between it and the sea. The houses of Algiers have no roofs, but are all terminated by terraces, which are constantly whitewashed; and as the exterior walls, the fort, the batteries and the walls are similarly beautified, the whole city, from a distance, looks not unlike a vast chalk quarry opened on the side of a hill.

The fortifications towards the sea are of amasing strength, and with the additions made since Lord Exmouth's attack, may be considered as almost impregnable. They occupy the entire of a small island, which lies a short distance in front of the city, to which it is connected at one end by a magnificent mole of solid masonry, while the other which commands the entrance of the port, is crowned with a battery, bristling with cannon of immense calibre, which would instantly sink any vessel which should now attempt to occupy the station taken by the Queen Charlotte on that memorable occasion.

On the land side, the defences are by no means of equal strength, as they were always considered rather as a shelter against an insurrectionary movement of the natives, than as intended to repulse the regular attacks of a disciplined army. In fact defences on this side would be of little use as the city is completely commanded by different hills, particularly that on which the Emperor's fort is built, and was obliged instantly to capitulate, as soon as this latter had fallen into the hands of the French, in 1830.

There are four gates; one opening on the mole, which is thence called the marine gate, one near the citadel, which is termed the new gate; and the other two, at the north and south sides of the city, with the principal street running between them. All these gates are strongly fortified, and outside the three land gates run the remains of a ditch, which once surrounded the city, but is now filled up except at these points. The streets of Algiers are all crooked, and all narrow. The best are scarcely twelve feet in breadth, and even half of this is occupied by the projections of the shops, or the props placed to support the first stories of the houses, which are generally made to advance beyond the lower, insomuch that in many places a laden mule can scarcely pass. Of public buildings, the most remarkable is the Cassaubah, or citadel, the situation of which we have already mentioned. It is a huge, heavy looking brick building, of a square shape, surrounded by high and massive walls, and defended by fifty pieces of cannon, and some mortars, so placed as equally to awe the city and country. The apartments set apart for the habitation of the Dey and the ladies of his harem, are described as extremely magnificent, and abundantly supplied with marble pillars, fountains, mirrors, carpets, ottomans, cushions, and other articles of oriental luxury; but there are others no less valuable and curious, such as the armory, furnished with weapons of every kind, of the finest manufacture, and in the greatest abundance, the treasury, containing not only a profusion of the precious metals, coined or in ingots, but also diamonds, pearls, rubies, and other precious stones of great value; and lastly, the store rooms of immense extent, in which were piled up the richest silk stuffs, velvets, brocades, together with wool, wax, sugar, iron, lead, sabre-blades, gun barrels, and all the different productions of the Algerine territories; for the Dey was not only the first robber but the first merchant in his own dominions.

Next to the Cassaubah, the mole with the marine forts, presented the handsomest and most imposing pile of buildings. The mole is no less than one thousand three hundred feet in length, forming a beautiful terrace walk, supported by arches, beneath which lay splendid magazines, which the French found filled with spars, hemp, cordage, cables, and all manner of marine stores. At the extremity of the mole, lay the barracks of the Janissaries, entrusted with the defence of the marine forts, and consisting of several small separate chambers, in which they each slept on sheepskin mats, while in the centre was a handsome coffee-room. The Bagnios were the buildings, in which Europeans for a long time felt the most interest, inasmuch as it was in these that the Christian slaves taken by the corsairs were confined. For many years previous to the French invasion, however, the number of prisoners had been so trifling, that many of these terrific buildings had fallen to decay, and presented, when the French army entered Algiers, little more than piles of mouldering ruins. The inmates of the Bagnio when taken by the French were the crews of two French brigs, which a short time before had been wrecked off Cape Bingut, a few French prisoners of war made during their advance, and about twenty Greek, and Genoese sailors, who had been there for two years; in all about one hundred and twenty. They represented their condition as bad, though by no means so deplorable as it would have been in former days. The prison was at first so close, that there was some danger of suffocation, to avoid which the Turks had made holes in the walls; but as they neglected to supply these with windows or shutters of any kind, there was no means of excluding wind or rain, from which consequently they often suffered.

On board an Algerine corsair.

**On board an Algerine corsair.**

We shall only trace these pirates back to about the year 1500, when Selim, king of Algiers, being invaded by the Spaniards, at last entreated the assistance of the famous corsair, Oruj Reis, better known by his European name, Barbarossa, composed of two Italian words, signifying *red beard*. Nothing could be more agreeable than the number and hardihood of his naval exploits, had been such an invitation to this ambitious robber, who elated by for some time considering how he might best establish his power by land. Accordingly, attended by five thousand picked men, he entered Algiers, made himself master of the town, assassinated Selim, and had himself proclaimed king in his stead; and thus was established that nest of pirates, fresh swarms from which never ceased to annoy Christian commerce and enslave Christian mariners, until its late final destruction, by the French expedition in 1830.

In a piratical career of many centuries, the countless thousands who have been taken, enslaved, and perished in bondage by these monsters should long ago have drawn upon them the united vengeance of all Christendom. Many a youth of family and fortune, of delicate constitution has been captured and sold in the slave market. His labor through the long hot days would be to cleanse out the foul bed of some large empty reservoir, where he would be made to strip, and descending into the pond, bring up in his arms the black stinking mud, heaped up and pressed against his bosom; or to labor in drawing huge blocks of stone to build the mole; or in building and repairing the fortifications, with numerous other painful and disgusting tasks. The only food was a scanty supply of black bread, and occasionally a few decayed olives, or sheep which had died from some disorder. At night they were crowded into that most horrid of prisons the Bagnio, to sleep on a little filthy straw, amidst the most noisome stenches. Their limbs in chains, and often receiving the lash. Occasionally an individual would be ransomed; when his story would draw tears of pity from all who heard it. Ladies were frequently taken by these monsters and treated in the most inhuman manner. And sometimes whole families were enslaved. Numerous facts, of the most heart-rending description are on record: but our limits oblige us to be brief.

A Spanish lady, the wife of an officer, with her son, a youth of fourteen, and her daughter, six years old, were taken in a Spanish vessel by the Algerines. The barbarians treated her and both her children with the greatest inhumanity. The eldest they kept in chains; and the defenceless little one they wantonly treated so ill, that the unhappy mother was often nearly deprived of her reason at the blows her infant received from these wretches, who plundered them of every thing. They kept them many days at sea on hard and scanty fare, covered only with a few soiled rags; and in this state brought them to Algiers. They had been long confined in a dreadful dungeon in the Bagnio where the slaves are kept, when a messenger was sent to the Aga, or Captain of the Bagnio, for a female slave. It fortunately fell to the lot of the Spanish lady, but at the instant when she was embracing her son, who was tearing himself from his mother with haggard and disordered looks, to go to his imperious drivers; and while in despair she gazed on her little worn-out infant, she heard herself summoned to attend the guard of the prison to a family that had sent for a female slave. She obtained permission to take her little daughter with her. She dreaded being refused, and sent back to the horrid dungeon she was leaving where no difference was paid to rank, and slaves of all conditions were huddled together. She went therefore prepared to accept of anything short of these sufferings. She was refused, as being in every respect opposite to the description of the person sent for. At length her entreaties and tears prevailed; compassion overruled every obstacle; and she, with her little girl, was accepted. But there remained another difficulty; she had left her son chained in the midst of that dungeon from which she had just been rescued. Her kind patrons soon learned the cause of her distress; but to send for the youth and treat him kindly, or in any way above that of a common slave, must hazard the demand of so large a ransom for him and his mother, as would forever preclude the hope of liberty. He was, however, sent for, and the menial offices they were both engaged to perform were only nominal. With circumspection the whole family were sheltered in this manner for three years; when the war with the Spaniards growing more inveterate, the Algerines demanded the youth back to the Bagnio, to work in common with the other slaves, in repairing the damages done to the fortresses by the Spanish cannon. He was now compelled to go, loaded with heavy stones, through the whole of the town; and at almost every step he received dreadful blows, not being able to hasten his pace from the great weight.

Overcome at last with ill usage, the delicacy of his form and constitution gave way to the excessive labor, and he one morning refused the orders of his master, or driver, to rise from the straw on which he was stretched, declaring they might kill him if they chose, for he would not even try to carry another load of stones. Repeated messages had been sent from the Venetian consul's, where his mother and sister were sheltered, to the Aga, to return him; and when the Algerines found that they had absolutely reduced him so near death, they thought it best to spare his life for the sake of future ransom. They agreed, therefore, to let him return to the Christians. His life was for some time despaired of; but through the kind attention he received, he was rescued from the threatened dissolution. His recovery was concealed, for fear of his being demanded back to work; and a few months after, the Spanish peace of 1784 being concluded, a ransom was accepted by the Algerines for this suffering family, and they were set at liberty.

These pirates in old times extended their depredations into the Atlantic as far as the British Channel. They swarmed in the Mediterranean, not only belonging to Algiers, but Tunis, and other ports on the coast of Barbary. Their corsairs making descents on the coasts of those countries which border on the Mediterranean, pillaging the villages and carrying off the inhabitants into slavery. The corsairs were vessels of different descriptions; some large armed ships, and latterly frigates; others were row gallies and the various craft used by the nations which navigate that sea, and had been taken by them and added to their marine. Upon the slaves being landed at Algiers they were marched to the Dey's or Bashaw's palace, when he selected the number which according to law belonged to him; and the rest were sold in the slave market to the highest bidder. A moiety of the plunder, cargoes and vessels taken also belonged to the Dey. Occasionally, a person by pretending to renounce his religion, and turning Mahometan would have his sufferings mitigated.

The most desperate attempts were sometimes made to effect an escape from these ruthless monsters, which occasionally succeeded.

In 1644 William Oakley and four companions escaped from Algiers, in a most miraculous manner, in a canvas boat. There was at this time an English clergyman, Mr. Sprat, in captivity, and the wretched slaves had the privilege of meeting in a cellar, where he would pray with them. Oakley had got into the good graces of his master, and was allowed his time by giving his master two dollars a month. He traded in tobacco and a few trifling articles, so that a strict watch was not kept on his movements. He conceived the project of making a canvas boat. He says I now first opened my design to my comrades, informing them, that I had contrived the model of a boat, which, being formed in pieces, and afterwards put together, might be the means of our deliverance. They greedily grasped at the prospect; but cooler reflection pointed out difficulties innumerable: some of them started objections which they thought insuperable, and these I endeavored to overrule.

We began our work in the cellar which had served for our devotions, though it was not the sanctity of the place, but its privacy, that induced us to this selection. We first provided a piece of wood, twelve feet long, and, that it might escape observation, it was cut in two, being jointed in the middle. Next we procured the timbers of ribs, which, to avoid the same hazard, were in three pieces each, and jointed in two places. The flat side of one of the two pieces was laid over the other, and two holes bored in every joint to receive nails; so that when united, each joint would make an obtuse angle, and approach towards a semicircular figure, as we required. We had, in the formation of an external covering, to avoid hammering and nailing, which would have made such a noise in the cellar as to attract the notice of the Algerines, who are insufferably suspicious about their wives and slaves. Therefore, we provided as much canvas as would cover the boat twice over, and as much pitch, tar and tallow, as would make it a kind of tarpaulin; as also earthen pots in which to melt our materials. The two carpenters and myself were appointed to this service in the cellar. We stopped up all chinks and crevices, that the fumes of these substances might not betray us. But we had not been long at work, when the smell of the melting materials overcame me, and obligated me to go into the streets gasping for breath, where meeting with the cool air, I swooned away, and broke my face in the fall. My companions, finding me in this plight, carried me back, extremely sick and unserviceable. Before long, I heard one of them complain of sickness, and thus he could proceed no further; therefore, I saw if we abandoned our project this night, it might not be resumed, which made me resolve to set the cellar door wide open, while I stood sentinel to give notice of approaching danger. In this way we finished the whole, and then carried it to my shop, which was about a furlong distant.

Every thing was fitted in the cellar, the timbers to the keel, the canvas to the timbers, and the seats to the whole, and then all were taken to pieces again. It was a matter of difficulty, however, to get the pieces conveyed out of the city; but William Adams carried the keel, and hid it at the bottom of a hedge: the rest was carried away with similar precautions. As I was carrying a piece of canvas, which we had bought for a sail, I looked back, and discovered the same spy, who had formerly given us much trouble, following behind. This gave me no small concern; but, observing an Englishman washing clothes by the sea side, I desired his help in washing the canvas. Just as we were engaged with it, the spy came up, and stood on a rock exactly over our heads, to watch us. Therefore, to delude him, I took the canvas and spread it before his face on the top of the rock to dry; he staid his own time, and then marched off. Still I was jealous of his intentions, which induced me to carry the canvas, when dry, straight back to the city, an incident that greatly discouraged my comrades. We also procured a small quantity of provisions, and two goat skins full of fresh water.

In the mean time, I paid my patron my wonted visits, kept up a fair correspondence, and duly gave him his demands; while I secretly turned all my goods to ready money as fast as I could, and putting it into a trunk with a false bottom, I committed it to the charge of Mr. Sprat who faithfully preserved it for me.

The place which we chose for joining the boat together was a hill about half a mile from the city, thinking by that means the better to descry the approach of danger. When the pieces were united, and the canvas drawn on, four of our number carried the boat down to the sea, where, stripping ourselves naked, and putting our clothes within, we carried it as far as we could wade, lest it might be injured by the stones or rocks near the shore. But we soon discovered that our calculations of lading were erroneous; for no sooner had we embarked, than the water came in over the sides, and she was like to sink; so that some new device became necessary. At last, one whose heart most failed him was willing to be excluded, and wished rather to hazard the uncertain torments of land, than the certainty of being drowned at sea. However the boat was still so deeply laden, that we all concluded that it was impossible to venture to sea. At length another went ashore, and she held her head stoutly, and seemed sufficiently capable of our voyage.

Taking a solemn farewell of our two companions left behind, and wishing them as much happiness as could be hoped for in slavery, and they to us as long life as could be expected by men going to their graves, we launched out on the 30th of June 1644, a night ever to be remembered. Our company consisted of John Anthony, William Adams, John Jephs, John the carpenter and myself. We now put to sea, without helm, tackle, or compass. Four of us continually labored at the oars; the employment of the fifth was baling out the water that leaked through the canvas. We struggled hard the first night to get out of the reach of our old masters; but when the day broke, we were still within sight of their ships in the haven and road-stead. Yet, out boat being small, and lying close and snug upon the sea, either was not discovered at all, or else seemed something that was not worth taking up.

On all occasions we found our want of foresight, for now the bread which had lain soaking in the salt water, was quite spoiled, and the tanned skins imparted a nauseous quality to the fresh water. So long as bread was bread, we made no complaints; with careful economy it lasted three days, but then pale famine, which is the most horrible shape in which death can be painted, began to stare us in the face. The expedients on which we fell to assuage our thirst rather inflamed it, and several things added to our distress. For some time the wind was right against us; our labour was incessant, for, although much rowing did not carry us forward, still, cessation of it drove us back; and the season was raging hot, which rendered our toil insupportable. One small alleviation we had in the man whose province it was to bale the water out of the boat; he threw it on our bodies to cool them. However, what with the scorching of the sun and cooling of the water, our skin was blistered all over. By day we were stark naked; by night we had on shirts or loose coats; for we had left our clothing ashore, on purpose to lighten the boat.

One of our number had a pocket dial, which supplied the place of a compass; and, to say the truth, was not ill befitting such a vessel and such mariners. By its aid we steered our course by day, while the stars served as a guide by night; and, if they were obscured, we guessed our way by the motion of the clouds. In this woful plight we continued four days and nights. On the fifth day we were at the brink of despair, and abandoned all hopes of safety. Thence we ceased our labor, and laid aside our oars; for, either we had no strength left to use them, or were reluctant to waste the little we had to no purpose. Still we kept emptying the boat, loth to drown, loth to die, yet knowing no means to avoid death.

They that act least commonly wish the most; and, when we had forsaken useful labor, we resorted to fruitless wishes–that we might be taken up by some ship, if it were but a ship, no matter of what country.

While we lay hulling up and down, our hopes at so low an ebb, we discovered a tortoise, not far from us, asleep in the sea. Had the great Drake discovered the Spanish plate fleet, he could not have been more rejoiced. Once again we bethought ourselves of our oars, and silently rowing to our prey, took it into the boat in great triumph. Having cut off its head, and let it bleed in a vessel, we drank the blood, ate the liver, and sucked the flesh. Our strength and spirits were wonderfully refreshed, and our work was vigorously renewed. Leaving our fears behind us, we began to gather hope, and, about noon, discovered, or thought that we discovered, land. It is impossible to describe our joy and triumph on this occasion. It was new life to us; it brought fresh blood into our veins, and fresh vigor into our pale cheeks: we looked like persons raised from the dead. After further exertion, becoming more confident, we were at last fully satisfied that it was land. Now, like distracted persons, we all leapt into the sea, and, being good swimmers, cooled our parched bodies, never considering that we might become a ready prey to the sharks. But we presently returned to our boat, and from being wearied with the exertion, and somewhat cooled by the sea, lay down to sleep with as much security as if it had been in our beds. It was fortunately of such short duration that the leaking of the boat occasioned no danger.

Refreshed by sleep, we found new strength for our work, and tugged hard at the oar, in hopes of reaching a more stable element before night. But our progress was very slow. Towards evening an island was discovered, which was Fromentere, having already seen Majorca; at least, some of our company, who had navigated these seas, declared that it was so. We debated long to which of the two our course should be directed; and, because the last discovered was much infested with venomous serpents, we all resolved to make for Majorca. The whole of that night we rowed very hard, and also the next, being the sixth from our putting to sea. The island was in sight all day, and about ten at night we came under the land, but it consisted of rocks so steep and craggy that we could not climb up.

Whilst under these rocks a vessel approached very near. Let the reader conceive our apprehensions, after all our toil and labor, of being seized by some Turkish privateer, such as are never off the seas. Thus we were obliged to lie close; and, when the vessel had passed, we crept gently along the coast, as near as we durst to the shore, until finding a suitable place to receive our weather-beaten boat.

We were not insensible of our deliverance on reaching land; though, like men just awakened from a dream, we could not duly appreciate the greatness of it. Having had no food since we got the tortoise, John Anthony and myself set out in search of fresh water, and three remained with the boat. Before proceeding far, we found ourselves in a wood, which created great embarrassment. My comrade wished to go one way, and I wished to go another. How frail and impotent a being is man! That we, whom common dangers by sea had united, should now fall out about our own inclinations at land. Yet so we did. He gave me reproachful words; and it is well that we did not come to blows, but I went my way, and he, seeing me resolute, followed. The path led to one of those watchtowers which the Spaniards keep on the coast to give timely notice of the approach of privateers. Afraid of being fired on, we called to the sentinel, informing him who we were, and earnestly requesting him to direct us to fresh water, and to give us some bread. He very kindly threw down an old mouldy cake, and directed us to a well close at hand. We drank a little water, and ate a bit of the cake, which we had difficulty in swallowing, and then hastened to return to our companions in the boat, to acquaint them with our success.

Though now necessary to leave the boat, we did not do it without regret; but this was lulled by the importunate cravings of hunger and thirst; therefore, making her fast ashore, we departed. Advancing, or rather crawling towards the well, another quarrel rose amongst us, the remembrance of which is so ungrateful that I shall bury it in silence, the best tomb for controversies. One of our company, William Adams, in attempting to drink, was unable to swallow the water, and sunk to the ground, faintly exclaiming, "I am a dead man!" After much straining and forcing, he, at length, got a little over; and when we were all refreshed with the cake and water, we lay down by the side of the well to wait for morning.

When it was broad day, we once more applied to the sentinel, to point out the way to the nearest house or town, which he did, directing us to a house about two miles distant; but our feet were so raw and blistered by the sun that it was long before we could get this short journey over; and then, the owners of the house, concluding from our garb that we came with a pilfering design, presented a fowling-piece, charging us to stand. The first of our number, who could speak the language of the country, mildly endeavored to undeceive him, saying, we were a company of poor creatures, whom the wonderful providence of God had rescued from the slavery of Algiers, and hoped that he would show mercy to our afflictions. The honest farmer, moved with our relation, sent out bread, water and olives. After refreshing ourselves with these, we lay down and rested three or four hours in the field; and, having given him thanks for his charity, prepared to crawl away. Pleased with our gratitude, he called us into his house, and gave us good warm bean pottage, which to me seemed the best food I had ever ate. Again taking leave, we advanced towards Majorca, which was about ten miles distant.

Next morning we arrived in the suburbs, where the singularity of our attire, being barefoot and bare legged, and having nothing on except loose shirts, drawn over our coats, attracted a crowd of enquirers. We gave a circumstantial account of our deliverance; and, as they were willing to contribute to our relief, they supplied us with food, wine, strong waters, and whatever else might renovate our exhausted spirits. They said, however, that we must remain in the suburbs until the viceroy had notice of our arrival. We were called before him, and when he had heard the account of our escape and dangers, he ordered us to be maintained at his expense until we should obtain a passage to our own country; and, in the meantime, the people collected money to buy clothes and shoes.

From Majorca they proceeded to Cadiz, and from thence to England, which they reached in safety.

Several expeditions at different periods were fitted out by different European nations to chastise the pirates. The Emperor, Charles V., in the plenitude of his power, sailed with a formidable armament in the year 1541, and affected a landing. Without doubt he would have taken the city, if a terrible storm had not risen, which destroyed a great part of his fleet and obliged him to re-embark with his shattered forces in the greatest precipitation. The exultation of the Algerines was unbounded; they now looked on themselves as the special favorites of heaven; the most powerful army which had ever attempted their subjection had returned with the loss of one third their number, and a great part of its ships and transports. Prisoners had been taken in such abundance, that to show their worthlessness, they were publicly sold in the market-place at Algiers, at an onion a head.

For nearly a century after this, little occurs of note in Algerine history except a constant system of piracy. In 1655 the British Admiral Blake gave them a drubbing.

The French were the next to attack these common enemies of Europe. Admiral Duguesne commanded the expedition, and after bombarding the place a short time, the Dey himself soon began to be terrified at the destruction these new engines of naval war made, when an unfavorable wind arising, compelled the fleet to make all sail for Toulon.

Relieved from the terror of immediate destruction, the Algerines returned to their old ways, making descents on the coast of Provence, where they committed the most dreadful ravages, killing, burning and destroying all that came in their way. The Dey also recovered, not only his courage, but his humor; for learning what a large sum the late expedition against his city had cost, he sent to say, "that if Louis would give him half the money, he would undertake to burn the whole city to please him." The French accordingly sent a new expedition under the same officers the next year. Duguesne again sailed, and in front of the city was joined by the Marquis D'Affranville, at the head of five other stout ships. A council of war was held and an immediate attack resolved upon, in consequence of which, the vessels having taken up their stations, a hundred bombs were thrown into the town during that day, and as many more on the following night, when the town was observed to be on fire in several places; the Dey's palace, and other public buildings were in ruins; some of the batteries were dismounted, and several vessels sunk in the fort. This speedy destruction soon determined the Dey and Janissaries to sue for peace; and a message to this effect was sent to Duguesne, who consented to cease firing, but refused to negociate regarding terms, until all the captives taken fighting under the French flag were given up as a preliminary step. This was agreed to, and one hundred and forty-two prisoners immediately sent off. In the mean time the soldiery becoming furious, assassinated the Dey and elected a new one, who ordered the flag to be hoisted on the city walls. Hostilities were now renewed with greater fury than before, and the French admiral threw such volleys of bombs into the city, that in less than three days the greatest part of it was reduced to ashes; and the fire burnt with such vehemence that the bay was illuminated to the distance of two or three leagues. Rendered desperate by the carnage around him, the new Dey ordered all the French captives who had been collected into the city to be cruelly murdered, and binding Father Vacher, the French Resident, hand and foot, had him tied to a mortar and fired off like a bomb against the French fleet. This wanton piece of atrocity so exasperated Duguesne, that, laying his fleet as near land as possible, he continued his cannonade until he had destroyed all their shipping, fortifications, buildings; in short, almost the whole of the lower town, and about two-thirds of the upper; when finding nothing else which a naval force could do, and being unprovided for a land expedition, he stood out leisurely to sea, leaving the Algerines to reflect over the sad consequences of their obstinacy. For several years after this they kept in the old piratical track; and upon the British consuls making a complaint to the Dey, on occasion of one of his corsairs having captured a vessel, he openly replied, "It is all very true, but what would you have? the Algerines are a company of rogues, and I am their captain."

To such people force was the argument; and in 1700 Capt. Beach, falling in with seven of their frigates, attacked them, drove them on shore, and burnt them. Expeditions at various times were sent against them, but without effecting much; and most of the maritime nations paid them tribute. But a new power was destined to spring up, from which these pirates were to receive their first check; that power was the United States of America.

In 1792 his corsairs, in a single cruise, swept off ten American vessels, and sent their crews to the Bagnio, so that there were one hundred and fifteen in slavery.

Negociations were at once set on foot; the Dey's demands had of course risen in proportion to the number of his prisoners, and the Americans had not only to pay ransom at a high rate, with presents, marine stores, and yearly tribute, but to build and present to the Dey, as a propitiatory offering, a thirty-six gun frigate; so that the whole expenses fell little short of a million of dollars, in return for which they obtained liberty for their captives, protection for their merchant vessels, and the right of free trade with Algiers. The treaty was signed September 5th, 1795; and from that time, up to 1812, the Dey continued on tolerable good terms with Congress; indeed, so highly was he pleased with them, in 1800, that he signified to the consul his intention of sending an ambassador to the Porte, with the customary presents, in the Washington, a small American frigate, at that time lying in the harbor of Algiers. In vain the consul and captain remonstrated, and represented that they had no authority to send the vessel on such a mission; they were silenced by the assurance that it was a particular honor conferred on them, which the Dey had declined offering to any of the English vessels then in harbor, as he was rather angry with that nation. The Washington was obliged to be prepared for the service; the corsair flag, bearing the turbaned head of Ali, was run up to her main top, under a salute of seven guns; and in this respectable plight she sailed up the Mediterranean, dropped anchor before the seven towers, where, having landed her cargo, she was permitted to resume her own colors, and was thus the first vessel to hoist the American Union in the Thracian Bosphorus.

Algerines in the act of firing off the French consul from a mortar at the French fleet

**Algerines in the act of firing off the French consul from a mortar at the French fleet.**

In 1812, however, the Dey, finding his funds at a low ebb, and receiving from all quarters reports that a wealthy American commerce was afloat, determined on trying them with a new war. He was peculiarly unfortunate in the time chosen, as the States, having about a month previously declared war with Great Britain, had, in fact, withdrawn most of the merchant ships from the sea, so that the only prize which fell into the hands of the Dey's cruizers was a small brig, with a crew of eleven persons. The time at length came for putting an end to these lawless depredations, and peace having been concluded with England, President Madison, in 1815, despatched an American squadron, under commodores Bainbridge and Decatur, with Mr. Shaler, as envoy, on board, to demand full satisfaction for all injuries done to American subjects, the immediate release of such as were captives, the restitution of their property, with an assurance that no future violence should be offered, and also to negociate the preliminaries of a treaty on terms of perfect equality, no proposal of tribute being at all admissible. The squadron reached its destination early in June, and, having captured an Algerine frigate and brig-of-war, suddenly appeared before Algiers, at a moment when all the cruizers were at sea, and delivered, for the consideration of the Divan, the terms on which they were commissioned to make peace, together with a letter from the President to the Dey. Confounded by the sudden and entirely unexpected appearance of this force, the Algerines agreed, on the 30th of June, to the proposals of a treaty, almost without discussion.

It had long been a reproach to Great Britain, the mistress of the sea, that she had tamely suffered a barbarian power to commit such atrocious ravages on the fleets and shores of the minor states along the Mediterranean. At length a good cause was made for chastising them.

At Bona, a few miles to the east of Algiers, was an establishment for carrying on a coral fishery, under the protection of the British flag, which, at the season, was frequented by a great number of boats from the Corsican, Neapolitan, and other Italian ports. On the 23d of May, the feast of Ascension, as the crews of all the boats were preparing to hear mass, a gun was fired from the castle, and at the same time appeared about two thousand, other accounts say four thousand, infantry and cavalry, consisting of Turks, Levanters, and Moors. A part of these troops proceeded towards the country, whilst another band advanced towards the river, where the fishing boats were lying at different distances from the sea; and opening a fire upon the unfortunate fishermen, who were partly on board and partly on land, massacred almost the whole of them. They then seized the English flags, tore them in pieces, and trampling them under foot, dragged them along the ground in triumph. The men who happened to be in the country saved themselves by flight, and declared that they saw the soldiers pillage the house of the British vice-consul, the magazines containing the provisions, and the coral that had been fished up. A few boats escaped, and brought the news to Genoa, whence it was transmitted by the agent of Lloyd's in a despatch, dated June 6th.

No sooner had the account of this atrocious slaughter reached England, than all ranks seemed inflamed with a desire that a great and signal punishment should be taken on this barbarian prince, who was neither restrained by the feelings of humanity nor bound by treaties. An expedition, therefore, was fitted out with all speed at Portsmouth, and the command intrusted to Lord Exmouth, who, after some delays from contrary winds, finally sailed, July 28th, with a fleet complete in all points, consisting of his own ship, the Queen Charlotte, one hundred and twenty guns; the Impregnable, rear admiral, Sir David Milne; ninety guns; Minden, Superb, Albion, each seventy-four guns; the Leander fifty guns, with four more frigates and brigs, bombs, fire-ships, and several smaller vessels, well supplied, in addition to the ordinary means of warfare, with Congreve rockets, and Shrapnell shells, the destructive powers of which have lately been abundantly proved on the continent. August 9, the fleet anchored at Gibraltar, and was there joined by the Dutch admiral, Van Cappillen, commanding five frigates and a corvette, who had been already at Algiers, endeavoring to deliver slaves: but being refused, and finding his force insufficient, had determined on joining himself with the English squadron, which it was understood was under weigh. Meanwhile, the Prometheus, Captain Dashwood, had been sent forward to Algiers to bring off the British consul and family; but could only succeed in getting his wife and daughter, who were obliged to make their escape, disguised in midshipmen's uniform; for the

Dey, having heard through some French papers of the British expedition, had seized the consul, Mr. Macdonnell, and put him in chains; and, hearing of the escape of his wife, immediately ordered the detention of two boats of the Prometheus, which happened to be on shore, and made slaves of the crews, amounting to eighteen men. This new outrage was reported to Lord Exmouth soon after leaving Gibraltar, and of course added not a little to his eagerness to reach Algiers. He arrived off Algiers on the morning of the 27th of August, and sent in his interpreter, Mr. Salame, with Lieutenant Burgess, under a flag of truce, bearing a letter for the Dey, demanding reparation.

Meantime, a light breeze sprung up, and the fleet advanced into the bay, and lay to, at about a mile off Algiers "It was now," says Mr. Salame, in his entertaining narrative, "half-past two, and no answer coming out, notwithstanding we had staid half an hour longer than our instructions, and the fleet being almost opposite the town, with a fine breeze, we thought proper, after having done our duty, to lose no more time, but to go on board, and inform his lordship of what had happened.

"Mr. Burgess, the flag-lieutenant, having agreed with me, we hoisted the signal, *that no answer had been given*, and began to row away towards the Queen Charlotte. After I had given our report to the admiral, of our meeting the captain of the port, and our waiting there, c., I was quite surprised to see how his lordship was altered from what I left him in the morning; for I knew his manner was in general very mild, and now he seemed to me *all-fightful,* as a fierce lion, which had been chained in its cage, and was set at liberty. With all that, his lordship's answer to me was, '*Never mind, we shall see now*;' and at the same time he turned towards the officers, saying, '*Be ready*,' whereupon I saw every one with the match or the string of the lock in his hand, most anxiously expecting the word '*Fire*'!

"No sooner had Salame returned, than his lordship made the signal to know whether all the ships were ready, which being answered in the affirmative, he directly turned the head of the Queen Charlotte towards shore, and, to the utter amazement of the Algerines, ran across all the batteries without firing or receiving a single shot, until he brought up within eighty yards of the south end of the mole, where he lashed her to the mainmast of an Algerine brig, which he had taken as his direction, and had then the pleasure of seeing all the rest of the fleet, including the Dutch frigates, taking up their assigned stations with the same precision and regularity. The position in which the Queen Charlotte was laid was so admirable that she was only exposed to the fire of three or four flanking guns, while her broadside swept the whole batteries, and completely commanded the mole and marine, every part of which could be seen distinctly from her quarter-deck. Up to this moment not a shot had been fired, and the batteries were all crowded with spectators, gazing in astonishment at the quiet and regularity which prevailed through all the British ships, and the dangerous vicinity in which they placed themselves to such formidable means of defence. Lord Exmouth, therefore, began to conceive hopes that his demands would still be granted; but the delay, it appeared, was caused by the Algerines being completely unprepared for so very sudden an approach, insomuch that their guns were not shotted at the moment when the Queen Charlotte swept past them, and they were distinctly seen loading them as the other ships were coming into line. Anxious, if possible, to spare unnecessary effusion of blood, his lordship, standing on the quarter-deck, repeatedly waved his hat as a warning to the multitudes assembled on the mole to retire, but his signal was unheeded, and at a quarter before three in the afternoon the first gun was fired at the Queen Charlotte from the eastern battery, and two more at the Albion and Superb, which were following. Then Lord Exmouth, having seen only *the smoke of the gun,* before the sound reached him, said, with great alacrity, '*That will do; fire my fine fellows!*' and I am sure that before his lordship had finished these words, our broadside was given with great cheering, which was fired three times within five or six minutes; and at the same time the other ships did the same. This first fire was so terrible, that they say more than five hundred persons were killed and wounded by it. And I believe this, because there was a great crowd of people in every part, many of whom, after the first discharge, I saw running away, under the walls, like dogs, walking upon their feet and hands.

"After the attack took place on both sides in this horrible manner, immediately the sky was darkened by the smoke, the sun completely eclipsed, and the horizon became dreary. Being exhausted by the heat of that powerful sun, to which I was exposed the whole day, and my ears being deafened by the roar of the guns, and finding myself in the dreadful danger of such a terrible engagement, in which I had never been before, I was quite at a loss, and like an astonished or stupid man, and did not know myself where I was. At last his lordship, having perceived my situation, said, 'You have done your duty, now go below.' Upon which I began to descend from the quarter-deck, quite confounded and terrified, and not sure that I should reach the cock-pit alive; for it was most tremendous to hear the crashing of the shot, to see the wounded men brought from one part, and the killed from the other; and especially, at such a time, to be found among the *English seamen*! and to witness their manners, their activity, their courage, and their cheerfulness during the battle!–it is really most overpowering and beyond imagination."

The battle continued to rage furiously, and the havoc on both sides was very great. There were some awful moments, particularly when Algerine vessels so near our line were set on fire. The officers surrounding Lord Exmouth had been anxious for permission to make an attempt upon the outer frigate, distant about a hundred yards. He at length consented, and Major Gossett, of the corps of marines, eagerly entreated and obtained permission to accompany Lieutenant Richards in the ship's barge. The frigate was instantly boarded, and, in ten minutes, in a perfect blaze. A gallant young midshipman, although forbidden, was led by his too ardent spirit to follow in support of the barge, in which attempt he was desperately wounded, his brother officer killed, and nine of the crew. The barge, by rowing more rapidly, escaped better, having but one killed.

About sunset the admiral received a message from rear-admiral Milne, stating his severe loss in killed and wounded, amounting to one hundred and fifty, and requesting that, if possible, a frigate might be sent him to take off some of the enemy's fire. The Glasgow accordingly was ordered to get under weigh, but the wind having been laid by the cannonade, she was obliged again to anchor, having obtained a rather more favorable position. The flotilla of mortar, gun, and rocket boats, under the direction of their respective artillery officers, shared to the full extent of their powers the honors and toils of this glorious day. It was by their fire that all the ships in the port (with the exception of the outer frigate already mentioned) were in flames, which, extending rapidly over the whole arsenal, gun-boats, and storehouses, exhibited a spectacle of awful grandeur and interest which no pen can describe. The sloops of war which had been appropriated to aid and assist the ships of the line, and prepare for their retreat, performed not only that duty well, but embraced every opportunity of firing through the intervals, and were constantly in motion. The shells from the bombs were admirably well thrown by the royal marine artillery, and, though directed over and across our own men-of-war, did not produce a single accident. To complete the confusion of the enemy, the admiral now ordered the explosion ship, which had been charged for the occasion, to be brought within the mole; but upon the representation of Sir David Milne that it would do him essential service, if made to act on the battery in his front, it was towed to that spot, and blown up with tremendous effect.

This was almost the final blow;–the enemy's fire had for some time been very slack, and now almost wholly ceased, except that occasionally a few shots and shells were discharged from the higher citadel, upon which the guns of the fleet could not be brought to bear. The admiral, who from the commencement had been in the hottest of the engagement, and had fired until his guns were so hot that they could, some of them, not be used again; now seeing that he had executed the most important part of his instructions, issued orders for drawing off the fleet. This was commenced in excellent order about ten at night, and the usual breeze having set off from shore favored their manoeuvre, so that, all hands being employed in warping and towing, the vessels were got safely into the bay, and anchored, beyond reach of shot, about two o'clock the next morning.

So signal and well contested a victory could not have been gained without a considerable loss and suffering. It amounted in the English fleet, to one hundred and twenty-eight men killed, and six hundred and ninety wounded; in the Dutch squadron, to thirteen killed, and fifty-two wounded; grand total, eight hundred and eighty-three. But the enemy suffered much more severly; they are computed to have lost, in killed and wounded, not less than between six and seven thousand men. The loss sustained by the Algerines by the destruction in the mole was four large frigates, of forty-four guns. Five large corvettes, from twenty-four to thirty guns. All the gun and mortar-boats, except seven; thirty destroyed. Several merchant brigs and schooners. A great number of small vessels of various descriptions. All the pontoons, lighters, c., Store-houses and arsenal, with all the timber, and various marine articles destroyed in part. A great many gun-carriages, mortar-beds, casks, and ships' stores of all descriptions.

Negociations were immediately opened in form; and on the 30th August the admiral published a notification to the fleet, that all demands had been complied with, the British consul had been indemnified for his losses, and the Dey, in presence of all his officers, had made him a public apology for the insults offered him. On the 1st of September, Lord Exmouth had the pleasure of informing the secretary of the Admiralty, that all the slaves in the city of Algiers, and its immediate vicinity were embarked; as also 357,000 dollars for Naples, and 25,000 dollars for Sardinia.

The number of slaves thus released amounted to one thousand and eighty-three, of whom four hundred and seventy-one were Neapolitans, two hundred and thirty-six Sicilians, one hundred and seventy-three Romans, six Tuscans, one hundred and sixty-one Spaniards, one Portuguese, seven Greeks, twenty-eight Dutch, and not *one Englishman.* Were there an action more than another on which an Englishman would willingly risk the fame and honor of his nation, it would be this attack on Algiers, which, undertaken solely at her own risk, and earned solely by the expenditure of her own blood and her own resources, rescued not a single subject of her own from the tyrant's grasp, while it freed more than a thousand belonging to other European powers.

In August, 1816, the strength of Algiers seemed annihilated; her walls were in ruins, her haughty flag was humbled to the dust; her gates lay open to a hostile power, and terms were dictated in the palace of her princes. A year passed, the hostile squadron had left her ports, the clang of the workman's hammer, the hum of busy men resounded through her streets, fresh walls had risen, new and more formidable batteries had been added; again she resumed her attitude as of yore, bid defiance to her foes, and declared war on civilization:–again her blood-stained corsairs swept the seas, eager for plunder, ready for combat;–Christian commerce once more became shackled by her enterprise, and Christian captives once more sent up their cry for deliverance. In 1819, her piracies had become so numerous that the Congress of Aix-la-Chapelle caused it to be notified to the Dey, that their cessation was required, and would be enforced, by a combined French and English squadron. His reply was brief and arrogant, and the admirals were obliged to leave without obtaining the least satisfaction. By menaces, however, accompanied by the presence of some cruisers, England, France, and the United States caused their flags to be respected.

Ali, the successor of Amar, had died in 1818, and was succeeded by Hassein Pasha, who, from the commencement of his reign, evinced the strongest antipathy to the French power. In 1824, he imposed an arbitrary tax through all his provinces on French goods and manufactures; the consul's house was frequently entered and searched in a vexatious manner, contrary to the express stipulations of treaties; and, finally, April, 1827, the consul himself, having gone at the feast of Bayram to pay his respects, was, upon a slight difference of opinion arising during their conversation, struck across the mouth with a fly-flap which the Dey held in his hand, and in consequence soon after left Algiers, while the Dey ordered the destruction of all the French establishments along the coast towards Bona, and oppressed in every manner the French residents within his dominions. A blockade was instantly commenced by the French, and maintained for nearly three years, until it was found that they suffered much more by it than the Dey, the expense having reached nearly 800,000*l* sterling, while he appeared no way inconvenienced by their efforts, and even treated them with such contempt as to order his forts to fire on the vessel of Admiral Le da Bretonnière, who, in 1829, had gone there under a flag of truce to make a final proposal of terms of accommodation. So signal a violation of the laws of nations could not be overlooked, even by the imbecile administrations of Charles X. All France was in an uproar; the national flag had been dishonored, and her ambassador insulted; the cry for war became loud and universal; conferences on the subject were held; the oldest and most experienced mariners were invited by the minister at war to assist in his deliberations; and an expedition was finally determined on in the month of

February, 1830, to consist of about thirty-seven thousand men, a number which it was calculated would not only be sufficient to overcome all opposition which might be encountered, but to enable the French to reduce the kingdom to a province, and retain it in subjection for any length of time that might be considered advisable. No sooner was this decision promulgated, than all the necessary preparations were commenced with the utmost diligence. It was now February, and the expedition was to embark by the end of April, so that no time could be lost. The arsenals, the naval and military workships, were all in full employment. Field and breaching batteries were mounted on a new principle lately adopted; gabions, earth-bags, *chevaux-de-frise,* and projectiles were made in the greatest abundance maps, notes, and all the information that could be procured respecting Barbary were transmitted to the war office, where their contents were compared and digested, and a plan of operations was drawn out. The commissariat were busied in collecting provisions, waggons, and fitting out an efficient hospital train; a deputy-commissary was despatched to reconnoitre the coasts of Spain and the Balearic Islands, to ascertain what resources could be drawn from them, and negociate with the king for leave to establish military hospitals at Port Mahon. Eighteen regiments of the line, three squadrons of cavalry, and different corps of artillery and engineers were ordered to hold themselves in readiness; four hundred transports were assembled, and chartered by government in the port of Marseilles, while the vessels of war, which were to form the convoy, were appointed their rendezvous in the neighborhood of Toulon. After some hesitation as to who should command this important expedition, the Count de Bourmont, then minister at war, thought fit to appoint himself; and his etat-major was soon complete, Desprez acting as chief, and Tholozé as second in command. Maubert de Neuilly was chosen provost-marshal, De Bartillat (who afterwards wrote an entertaining account of the expedition) quarter-master general, and De Carne commissary-general to the forces. In addition to these, there were about twenty aid-de-camps, orderlies, and young men of rank attached to the staff, together with a Spanish general, an English colonel, a Russian colonel and lieutenant, and two Saxon officers, deputed by their respective governments. There were also a section of engineer-geographers, whose business was to survey and map the country as it was conquered, "and," says M. Roget, who was himself employed in the service we have just mentioned, and to whose excellent work, written in that capacity, we are so much indebted, "twenty-four interpreters, the half of whom knew neither French nor Arabic, were attached-to the different corps of the army, in order to facilitate their intercourse with the inhabitants." As the minister had determined on risking his own reputation on the expedition, the supplies were all, of course, of the completest kind, and in the greatest abundance. Provisions for three months were ordered; an equal quantity was to be forwarded as soon as the army had landed in Africa; and, amongst the other materials furnished we observe, in looking over the returns, thirty wooden legs, and two hundred crutches, for the relief of the unfortunate heroes, a boring apparatus to sink pumps, if water should run short, and a balloon, with two aeronauts, to reconnoitre the enemy's position, in case, as was represented to be their wont, they should entrench themselves under the shelter of hedges and brushwood.

The French effected a landing at Sidy-el-Ferruch, a small promontory, about five leagues to the west of Algiers, and half a league to the east of the river Massaflran, where it discharges itself into the bay. On the 14th of June they all landed without opposition.

After a continued series of engagements and skirmishes the army got within cannon shot of Algiers, where they broke ground and began entrenching, and the French works being completed, the heavy breaching cannon were all mounted; and at day-break on the 4th of July, General Lahitte, having assured himself by personal inspection that all was ready, ordered the signal rocket to be thrown, and at the same moment the whole French batteries opened their fire within point blank distance, and with a report which shook the whole of Algiers, and brought the garrison, who were little expecting so speedy an attack, running to their posts. The artillery was admirably served, and from one battery which enfiladed the fort, the balls were seen to sweep away at once an entire row of Algerine cannoneers from their guns. The Turks displayed the most undaunted courage; they answered shot for shot, supplied with fresh men the places of such as were slain, stopped up with woolsacks the breaches made by the balls, replaced the cannon which the French fire had dismounted, and never relaxed their exertions for a moment. But the nature of their works was ill-calculated to withstand the scientific accuracy with which the besiegers made their attack. Every ball now told–the tower in the centre was completely riddled by shots and shells; the bursting of these latter had disabled great numbers of the garrison. By seven o'clock the besieged had begun to retire from the most damaged part of their works; by half-past eight the whole outer line of defence was abandoned, and by nine the fire of the fort was extinct. The Turkish general, finding opposition hopeless, had sent to the Dey for commands; and in reply was ordered to retreat with his whole remaining force to the Cassaubah, and leave three negroes to blow up the fort. The tranquillity with which they performed this fatal task deserves record. The French, finding the enemy's fire to fail, directed all theirs towards effecting a practicable breach. The fort seemed to be abandoned;–two red flags floated still on its outside line of defence, and a third on the angle towards the city. Three negroes were seen calmly walking on the ramparts, and from time to time looking over, as if to examine what progress the breach was making. One of them, struck by a cannon-ball, fell, and the others, as if to revenge his death, ran to a cannon, pointed it, and fired three shots. At the third, the gun turned over, and they were unable to replace it. They tried another, and as they were in the act of raising it, a shot swept the legs from under one of them. The remaining negro gazed for a moment on his comrade, drew him a little back, left him, and once more examined the breach. He then snatched one of the flags, and retired to the interior of the tower; in a few minutes he re-appeared, took a second and descended. The French continued to cannonade, and the breach appeared almost practicable, when suddenly they were astounded by a terrific explosion, which shook the whole ground as with an earthquake; an immense column of smoke, mixed with streaks of flame, burst from the centre of the fortress, masses of solid masonry were hurled into the air to an amazing height, while cannon, stones, timbers, projectiles, and dead bodies, were scattered in every direction–the negro had done his duty–the fort was blown up.

In half an hour the French sappers and miners were at work repairing the smoking ruins, their advanced guards had effected a reconnoissance along the side of the hill towards the fort Bab-azoona, and their engineers had broken ground for new works within seven hundred yards of the Cassaubah. But these preparations were unnecessary; the Dey had resigned all further intention of resistance, and at two o'clock a flag of truce was announced, which proved to be Sidy Mustapha, the Dey's private secretary, charged with offers of paying the whole expense of the campaign, relinquishing all his demands on France, and making any further reparation that the French general might require, on condition that the troops should not enter Algiers. These proposals met with an instant negative:–Bourmont felt that Algiers was in his power, and declared that he would grant no other terms than an assurance of life to the Dey and inhabitants, adding that if the gates were not opened he should recommence his fire. Scarcely had Mustapha gone, than two other deputies appeared, sent by the townsmen to plead in their behalf. They were a Turk called Omar, and a Moor named Bouderba, who having lived for some time at Marseilles, spoke French perfectly. They received nearly the same answer as Mustapha; but they proved themselves better diplomatists, for they spoke so much to the general of the danger, there would be in refusing the Janissaries all terms, and the probability that if thus driven to despair they might make a murderous resistance, and afterwards destroy all the wealth and blow up all the forts before surrendering, that Bourmont, yielding to their representations, became less stern in his demands; and Mustapha having returned about the same time with the English vice-consul, as a mediator, the following terms were finally committed to paper, and sent to the Dey by an interpreter.

"1. The fort of the Cassaubah, with all the other forts dependent on Algiers, and the harbor, shall be placed in the hands of the French troops the 5th of July, at 10 o'clock, A.M.

"2. The general-in-chief of the French army ensures the Dey of Algiers personal liberty, and all his private property.

"3. The Dey shall be free to retire with his family and wealth wherever he pleases. While he remains at Algiers he and his family shall be under the protection of the commander-in-chief. A guard shall insure his safety, and that of his family.

"4. The same advantages, and same protection are assured to all the soldiers of the militia.

"5. The exercise of the Mohammedan religion shall remain free; the liberty of the inhabitants of all classes, their religion, property, commerce, and industry shall receive no injury; their women shall be respected: the general takes this on his own responsibility.

"6. The ratification of this convention to be made before 10 A.M., on the 5th of July, and the French troops immediately after to take possession of the Cassaubah, and other forts."

These terms were so much more favorable than the Dey could have expected, that, of course, not a moment was lost in signifying his acceptance: he only begged to be allowed two hours more to get himself and his goods out of the Cassaubah, and these were readily granted. It may, indeed, be wondered at that he and his Janissaries should be allowed to retain all their ill-gotten booty, under the name of private property; but

Count de Bourmont, though not without talent, was essentially a weak man, and was in this instance overreached by the wily Moor. The whole of next morning an immense number of persons were seen flying from Algiers, previous to the entry of the French army, and carrying with them all their goods, valuables, and money. They fled by the fort Bab-azoona, on the roads towards Constantina and Bleeda; and about a hundred mounted Arabs were seen caracolling on the beach, as if to cover their retreat. No opposition to it, however, was made by the French troops, or by their navy, which had now again come in sight.

At twelve o'clock the general, with his staff, artillery, and a strong guard, entered the Cassaubah, and at the same moment all the other forts were taken possession of by French troops. No one appeared to make a formal surrender, nor did any one present himself on the part of the inhabitants, to inquire as to what protection they were to receive, yet, on the whole, we believe the troops conducted themselves, at least on this occasion, with signal forbearance; and that of the robberies which took place, the greater number were perpetrated by Moors and Jews. One was rather ingenious. The minister of finance had given up the public treasures to commissioners regularly appointed for the purpose. Amongst others, the mint was visited, a receipt given of its containing bullion to the amount of 25,000 or 30,000 francs, the door sealed, and a sentry placed. Next morning the seal was perfect, the sentry at his post, but the bullion was gone through a small hole made in the back wall.

The amount of public property found in Algiers, and appropriated by the French, was very considerable, and much more than repaid the expenses of the expedition. The blockade of the last three years had, by interrupting their commerce, caused an accumulation of the commodities in which the Algerines generally paid their tribute, so that the storehouses at the Cassaubah were abundantly filled with wool, hides, leather, wax, lead and copper. Quantities of grain, silks, muslins, and gold and silver tissues were also found, as well as salt, of which the Dey had reserved to himself a monopoly, and, by buying it very cheap at the Balearic Isles, used to sell it at an extravagant rate to his subjects. The treasure alone amounted to nearly fifty million of francs, and the cannon, projectiles, powder magazines, and military stores, together with the public buildings, foundries, dock-yards, and vessels in the harbor, were estimated at a still larger amount; while the entire expense of the expedition, including land and sea service, together with the maintenance of an army of occupation up to January, 1831, was computed not to exceed 48,500,000 francs; so that France must have realized, by her first connection with Algiers, a sum not far short of $3,000,000 sterling–a larger amount, we will venture to say, than is likely to accrue to her again, even after many years of colonization.

In a few days the Dey had embarked for Naples, which he chose as his future place of residence; the Janissaries were sent in French vessels to Constantinople; the Bey of Tippery made his submissions, and swore allegiance to the French King; orders were issued, and laws enacted in his name; the Arabs and Kalyles came into market as usual with their fowl and game; a French soldier was tolerably safe, as long as he avoided going to any distance beyond the outposts; and, on the whole, Algiers the warlike, had assumed all the appearance of a French colony.

**THE ADVENTURES, TRIAL AND EXECUTION OF CAPTAIN GOW.** Captain Gow sailed from Amsterdam, in July, 1724, on board the George, galley, for Santa Cruz, where they took in bees'-wax. Scarcely had they sailed from that place, when Gow and several others, who had formed a conspiracy, seized the vessel. One of the conspirators cried, "There is a man overboard." The captain instantly ran to the side of the vessel, when he was seized by two men, who attempted to throw him over; he however so struggled, that he escaped from their hands. One Winter, with a knife, attempted to cut him in the throat, but missing his aim, the captain was yet saved. But Gow coming aft shot him through the body and throwing him over the rail he caught hold of the main sheet; but Gow taking up an axe, with two blows so disabled him that he fell into the sea and was drowned. The conspirators proceeded to murder all who were not in their horrid plot, which being done, James Williams came upon deck, and striking one of the guns with his cutlass, saluted Gow in the following words: "Captain Gow, you are welcome, welcome to your command." Williams was declared lieutenant, and the other officers being appointed, the captain addressed them, saying: "If, hereafter, I see any of you whispering together, or if any of you refuse to obey my orders, let every such man depend upon it, that he shall certainly go the same way as those that are just gone before."

Their first prize was the Sarah Snow, of Bristol. After they had rifled the vessel and received one man from it, they allowed her to prosecute her voyage. The Delight, of Poole, was the next vessel that fell into their hands; but they not long after captured two others, from one of which they received a quantity of fish, and from the other bread, beef, and pork. They also forced two men from the latter ship. A French ship, not long after, furnished them with wine, oil, figs, oranges, and lemons, to the value of 500*l*. In a short time after, they captured their last prize, and, as she made no resistance, they plundered and dismissed her.

They next sailed for the Orkney Isles to clean, but were apprehended by a gentleman of that country, brought up to London, and tried before a Court of Admiralty, in May, 1725. When the first indictment was read, Gow obstinately refused to plead, for which the Court ordered his thumbs to be tied together with whipcord. The punishment was several times repeated by the executioner and another officer, they drawing the cord every time till it broke. But he still being stubborn, refusing to submit to the court, the sentence was pronounced against him, which the law appoints in such cases; that is, "That he should be taken back to prison, and there pressed to death." The gaoler was then ordered to conduct him back, and see that the sentence was executed the next morning; meanwhile the trials of the prisoners, his companions, went forward.

But the next morning, when the press was prepared, pursuant to the order of the Court the day before, he was so terrified with the apprehension of dying in that manner, that he sent his humble petition to the Court, praying that he might be admitted to plead. This request being granted, he was brought again to the bar, and arraigned upon the first indictment, to which he pleaded Not guilty. Then the depositions that had been given against the other prisoners were repeated, upon which he was convicted, and received the sentence of death accordingly, which he suffered in company with Captain Weaver and William Ingham.

Gow killing the Captain

**Gow killing the Captain.**

The stories of these two men are so interwoven with others, that it will be impossible to distinguish many of their particular actions. They were, however, proved to have been concerned, if not the principal actors, in the following piracies: first, the seizing a Dutch ship in August, 1722, and taking from thence a hundred pieces of Holland, value 800*l*.; a thousand pieces of eight, value 250*l*. Secondly, the entering and pillaging the Dolphin of London, William Haddock, out of which they got three hundred pieces of eight, value 75*l*.; forty gallons of rum, and other things, on the twentieth of November in the same year. Thirdly, the stealing out of a ship called the Don Carlos, Lot Neekins, master, four hundred ounces of silver, value 100*l*. fifty gallons of rum, value 30*s*. a thousand pieces of eight, a hundred pistoles, and other valuable goods. And fourthly, the taking from a ship called the England, ten pipes of wine, value 250*l*. The two last charges both in the year 1721. Weaver returned home, and came to Mr. Thomas Smith, at Bristol, in a very ragged condition; and pretending that he had been robbed by pirates, Smith, who had been acquainted with him eight or nine years before, provided him with necessaries, and he walked about unmolested for some time. But Captain Joseph Smith, who knew him when a pirate, one day met him, and asked him to go and take a bottle with him; when they were in the tavern he told him that he had been a considerable sufferer by his boarding his vessel "therefore," said he, "as I understand that you are in good circumstances, I expect that you will make me some restitution; which if you do, I will never hurt a hair of your head, because you were very civil to me when I was in your hands." But as this recompense was never given. Weaver was apprehended and executed.

**PIRATE'S SONG.**

To the mast nail our flag it is dark as the grave,
Or the death which it bears while it sweeps o'er the wave;
Let our deck clear for action, our guns be prepared;
Be the boarding-axe sharpened, the scimetar bared:
Set the canisters ready, and then bring to me,
For the last of my duties, the powder-room key.
It shall never be lowered, the black flag we bear;
If the sea be denied us, we sweep through the air.
Unshared have we left our last victory's prey;
It is mine to divide it, and yours to obey:
There are shawls that might suit a sultana's white neck,
And pearls that are fair as the arms they will deck;
There are flasks which, unseal them, the air will disclose
Diametta's fair summers, the home of the rose.
I claim not a portion: I ask but as mine–
'Tis to drink to our victory–one cup of red wine.
Some fight, 'tis for riches–some fight, 'tis for fame:
The first I despise, and the last is a name.
I fight, 'tis for vengeance! I love to see flow,
At the stroke of my sabre, the life of my foe.

Lightning Source UK Ltd.
Milton Keynes UK
10 November 2010

162662UK00001B/249/P